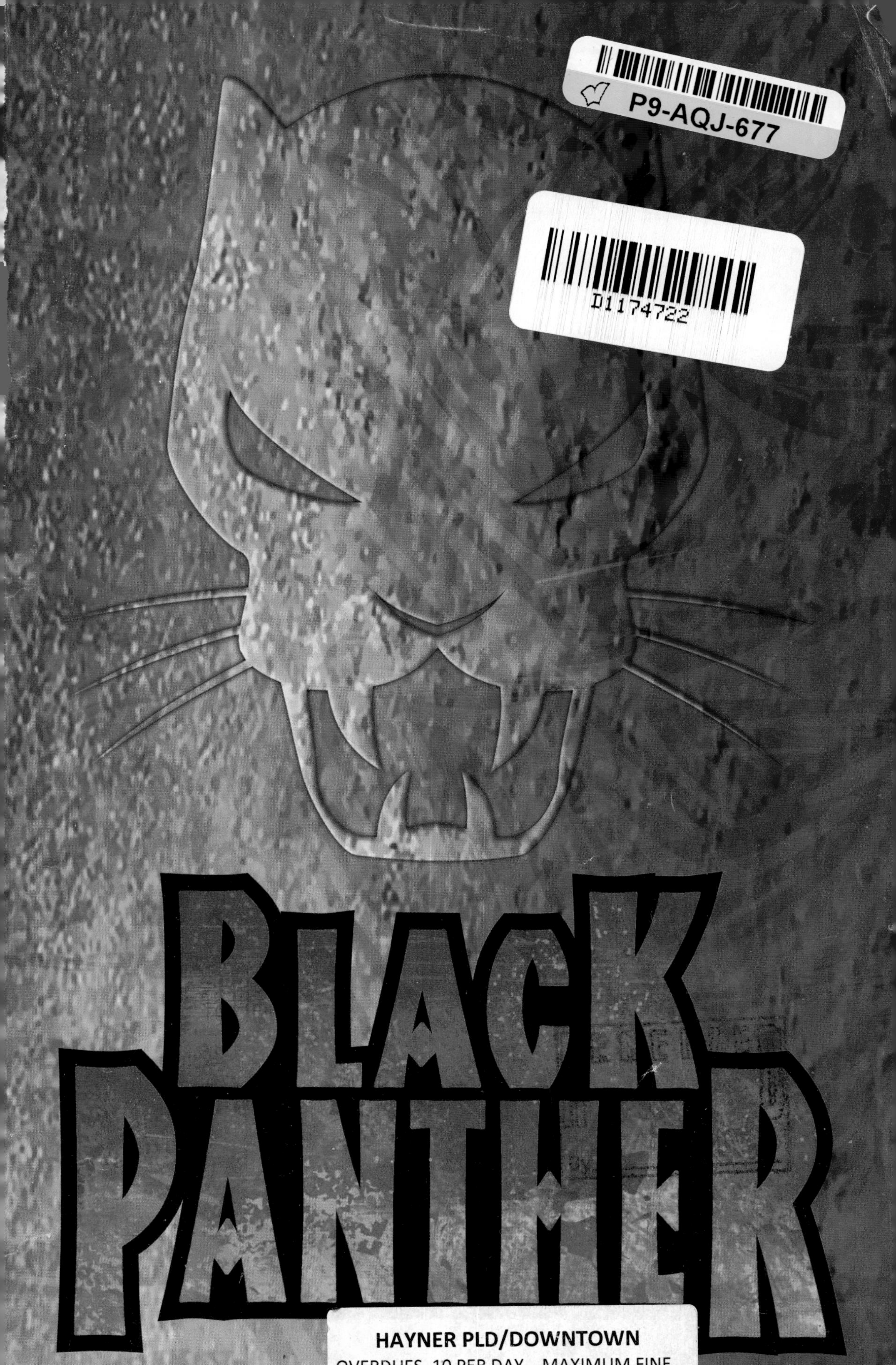
BLACK
PANTHER

WRITER: **Reginald Hudlin**

PENCILER: **John Romita Jr.**

INKER: **Klaus Janson**

COLORIST: **Dean White**

LETTERERS: **VC's Randy Gentile & Chris Eliopoulos**

COVER ARTISTS: **John Romita Jr., Esad Ribic, Frank Cho, John Cassaday, Terry Dodson & Kaare Andrews**

ASSISTANT EDITOR: **Cory Sedlmeier**

EDITOR: **Axel Alonso**

Black Panther created by **Stan Lee and Jack Kirby**

COLLECTION EDITOR: **Jennifer Grünwald**

ASSOCIATE EDITOR: **Sarah Brunstad**

ASSOCIATE MANAGING EDITOR: **Alex Starbuck**

EDITOR, SPECIAL PROJECTS: **Mark D. Beazley**

VP, PRODUCTION & SPECIAL PROJECTS: **Jeff Youngquist**

SVP PRINT, SALES & MARKETING: **David Gabriel**

Special thanks to **Jeof Vita**

EDITOR IN CHIEF: **Axel Alonso**

CHIEF CREATIVE OFFICER: **Joe Quesada**

PUBLISHER: **Dan Buckley**

EXECUTIVE PRODUCER: **Alan Fine**

# WHO IS THE BLACK PANTHER

**BLACK PANTHER: WHO IS THE BLACK PANTHER.** Contains material originally published in magazine form as BLACK PANTHER #1-6 and FANTASTIC FOUR #52-53. Third edition. Second printing 2016. ISBN# 978-0-7851-9799-7. Published by MARVEL WORLDWIDE, INC., a subsidiary of MARVEL ENTERTAINMENT, LLC. OFFICE OF PUBLICATION: 135 West 50th Street, New York, NY 10020. Copyright © 2015 MARVEL. No similarity between any of the names, characters, persons, and/or institutions in this magazine with those of any living or dead person or institution is intended, and any such similarity which may exist is purely coincidental. **Printed in the U.S.A.** ALAN FINE, President, Marvel Entertainment; DAN BUCKLEY, President, TV, Publishing & Brand Management; JOE QUESADA, Chief Creative Officer; TOM BREVOORT, SVP of Publishing; DAVID BOGART, SVP of Business Affairs & Operations, Publishing & Partnership; C.B. CEBULSKI, VP of Brand Management & Development, Asia; DAVID GABRIEL, SVP of Sales & Marketing, Publishing; JEFF YOUNGQUIST, VP of Production & Special Projects; DAN CARR, Executive Director of Publishing Technology; ALEX MORALES, Director of Publishing Operations; SUSAN CRESPI, Production Manager; STAN LEE, Chairman Emeritus. For information regarding advertising in Marvel Comics or on Marvel.com, please contact Vit DeBellis, Integrated Sales Manager, at vdebellis@marvel.com. For Marvel subscription inquiries, please call 888-511-5480. **Manufactured between 4/27/2016 and 5/23/2016 by R.R. DONNELLEY, INC., OWENSVILLE, MO, USA.**

10 9 8 7 6 5 4 3 2

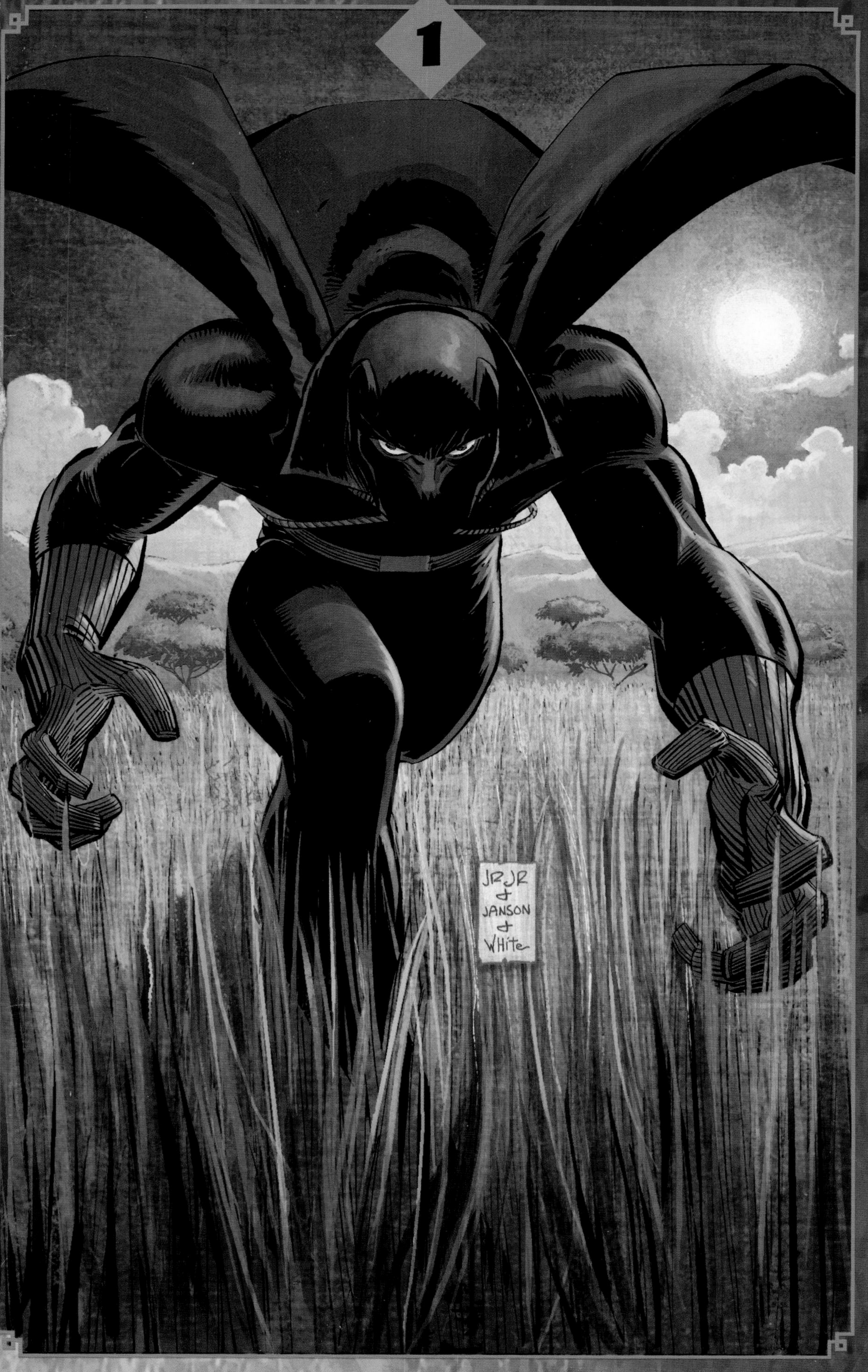
1
JRJR
&
JANSON
&
WHITE

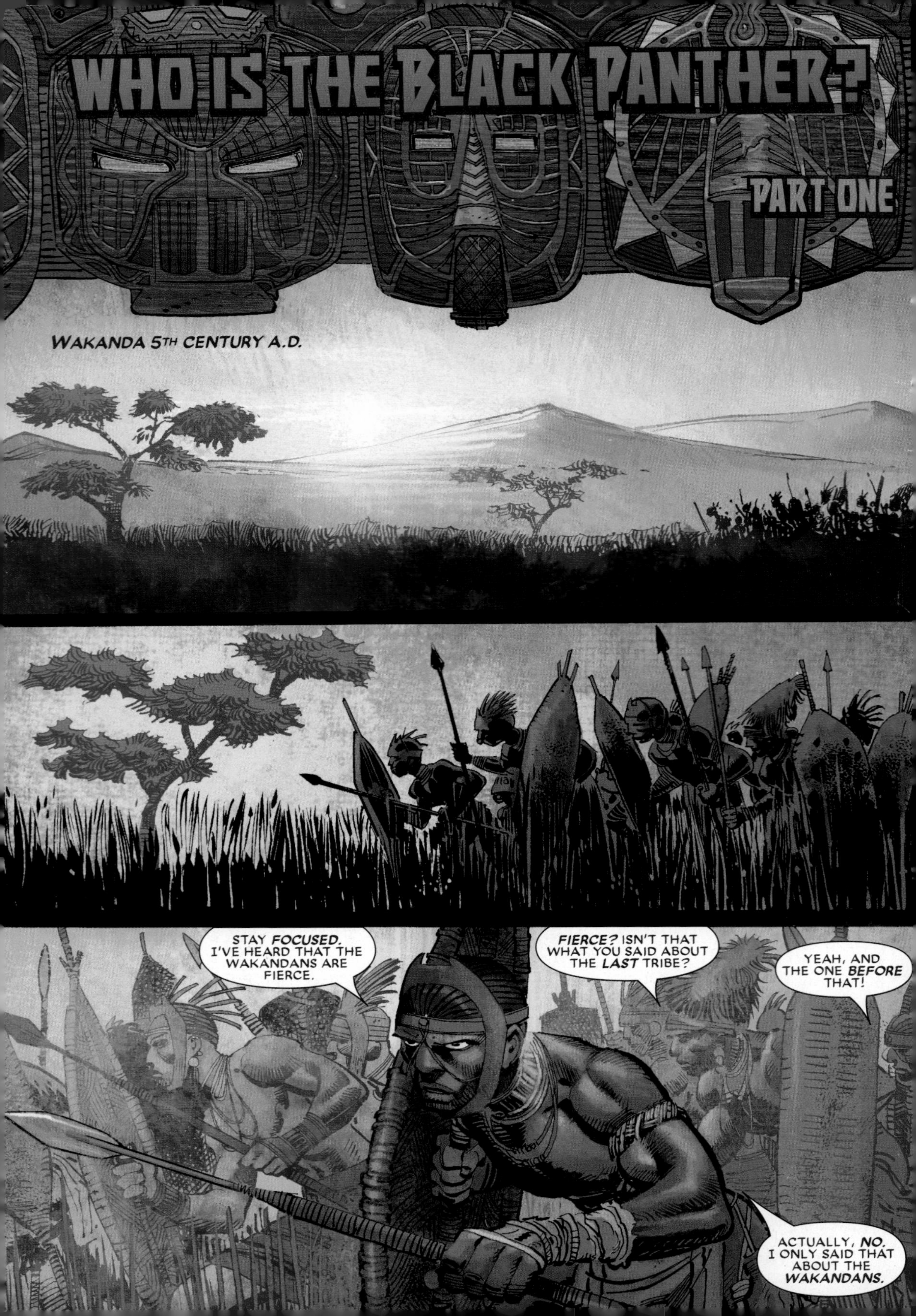
WHO IS THE BLACK PANTHER?
PART ONE
WAKANDA 5TH CENTURY A.D.
STAY FOCUSED. I'VE HEARD THAT THE WAKANDANS ARE FIERCE.
FIERCE? ISN'T THAT WHAT YOU SAID ABOUT THE LAST TRIBE?
YEAH, AND THE ONE BEFORE THAT!
ACTUALLY, NO. I ONLY SAID THAT ABOUT THE WAKANDANS.

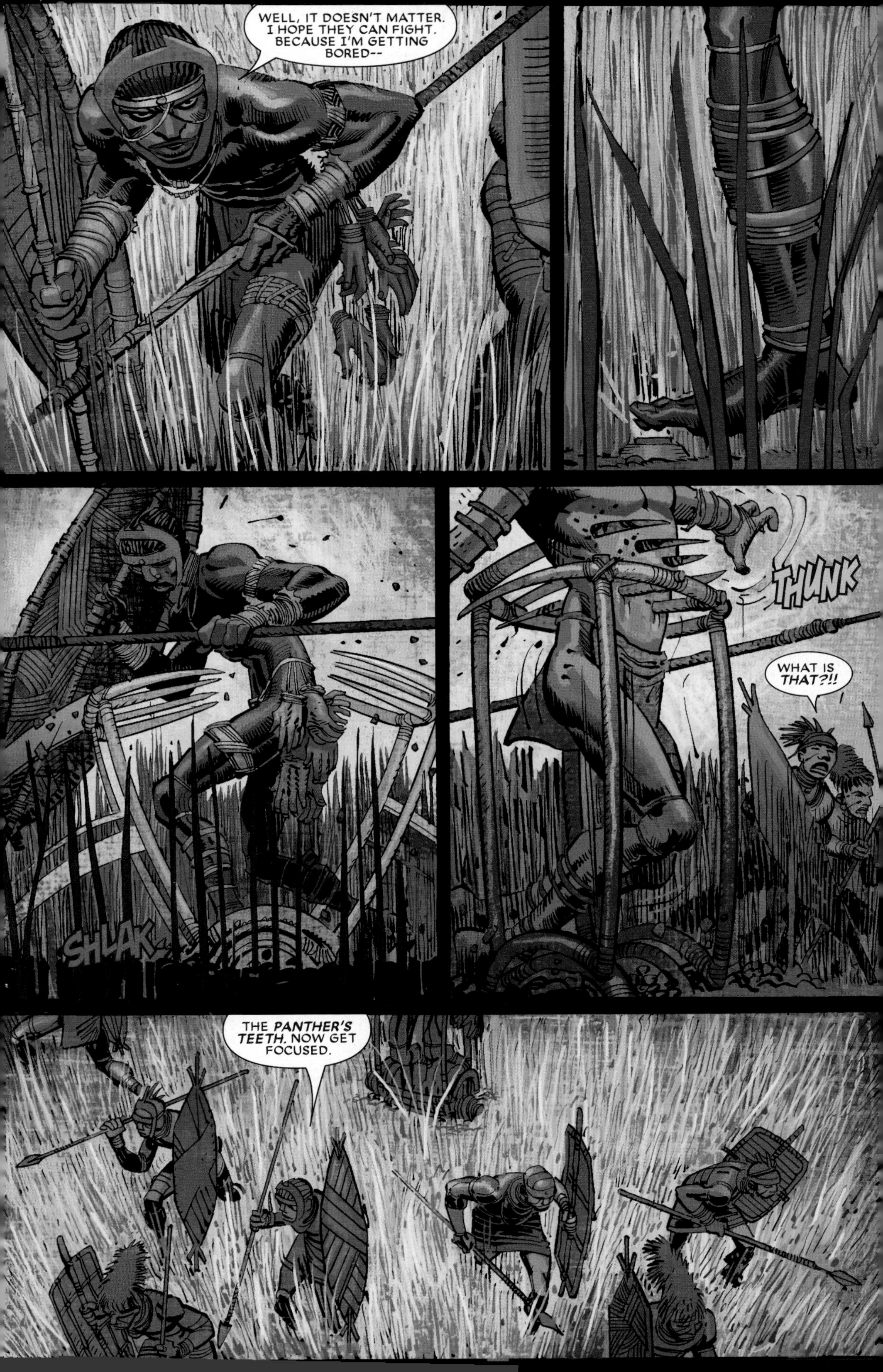
WELL, IT DOESN'T MATTER. I HOPE THEY CAN FIGHT. BECAUSE I'M GETTING BORED--
SHLAK
THUNK
WHAT IS THAT?!!
THE PANTHER'S TEETH. NOW GET FOCUSED.

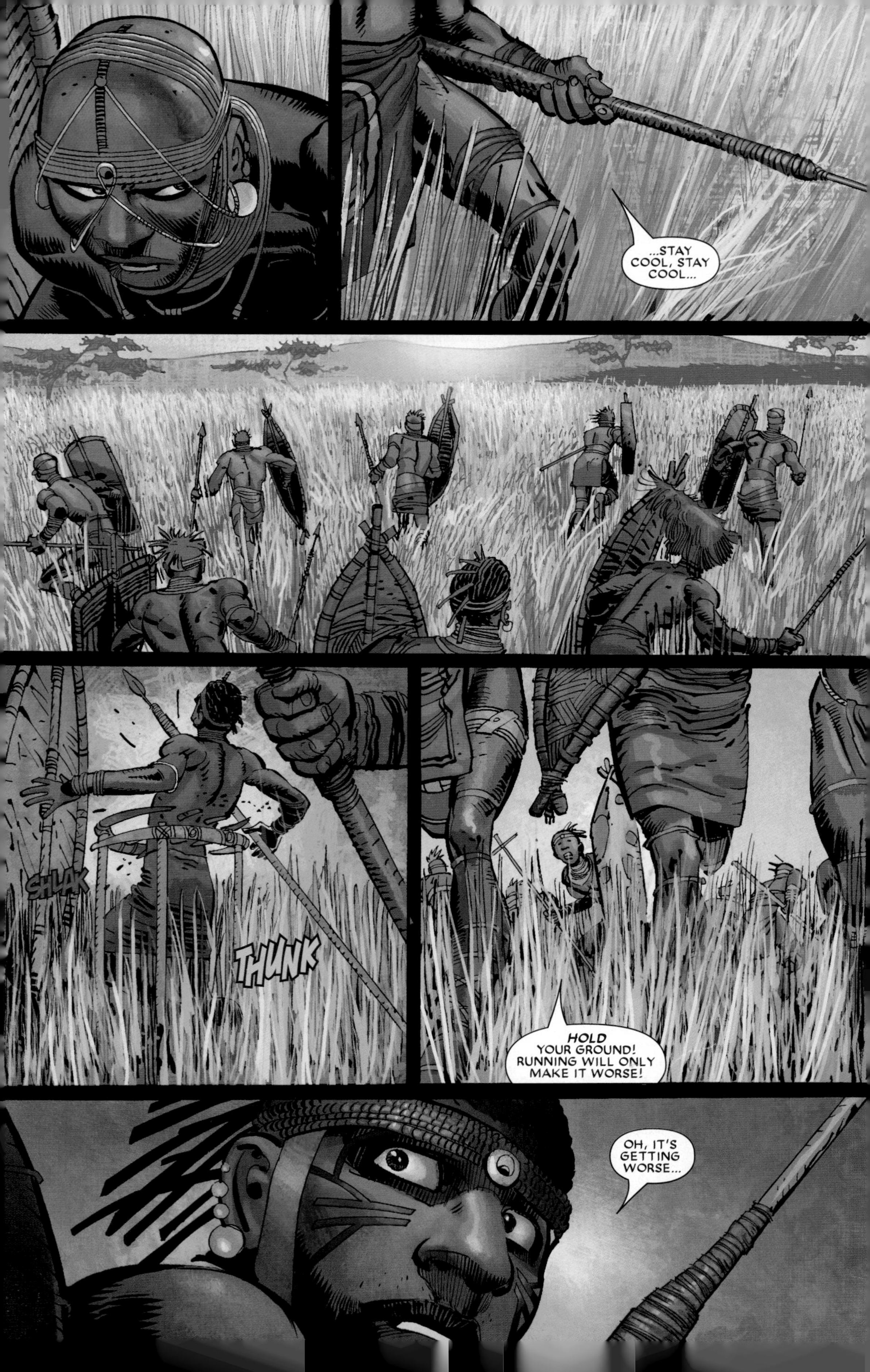
...STAY COOL, STAY COOL...
SHLAK
THUNK
HOLD YOUR GROUND! RUNNING WILL ONLY MAKE IT WORSE!
OH, IT'S GETTING WORSE...

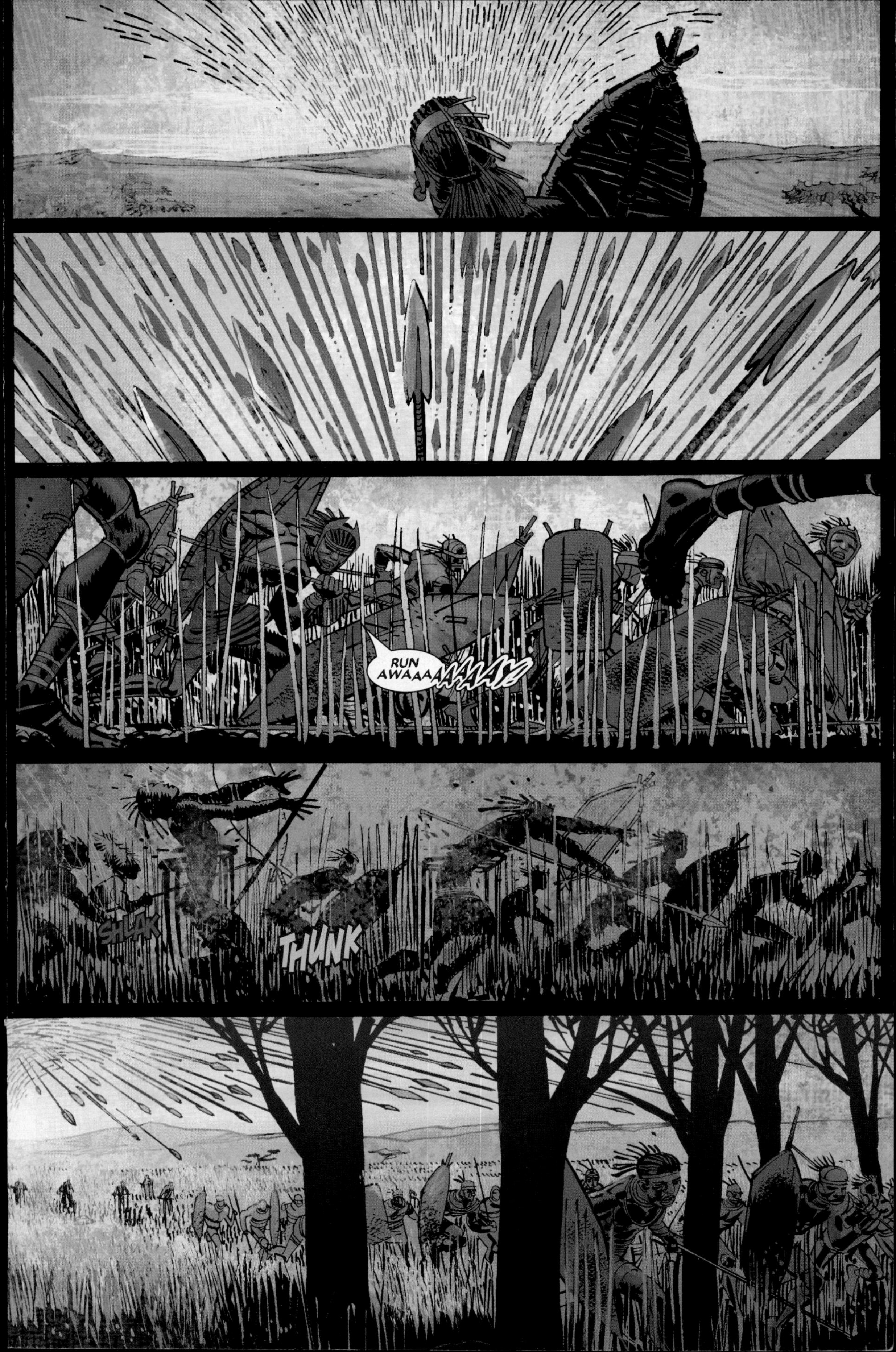
RUN AWAAAAAAAAAAY!
SHLAK
THUNK

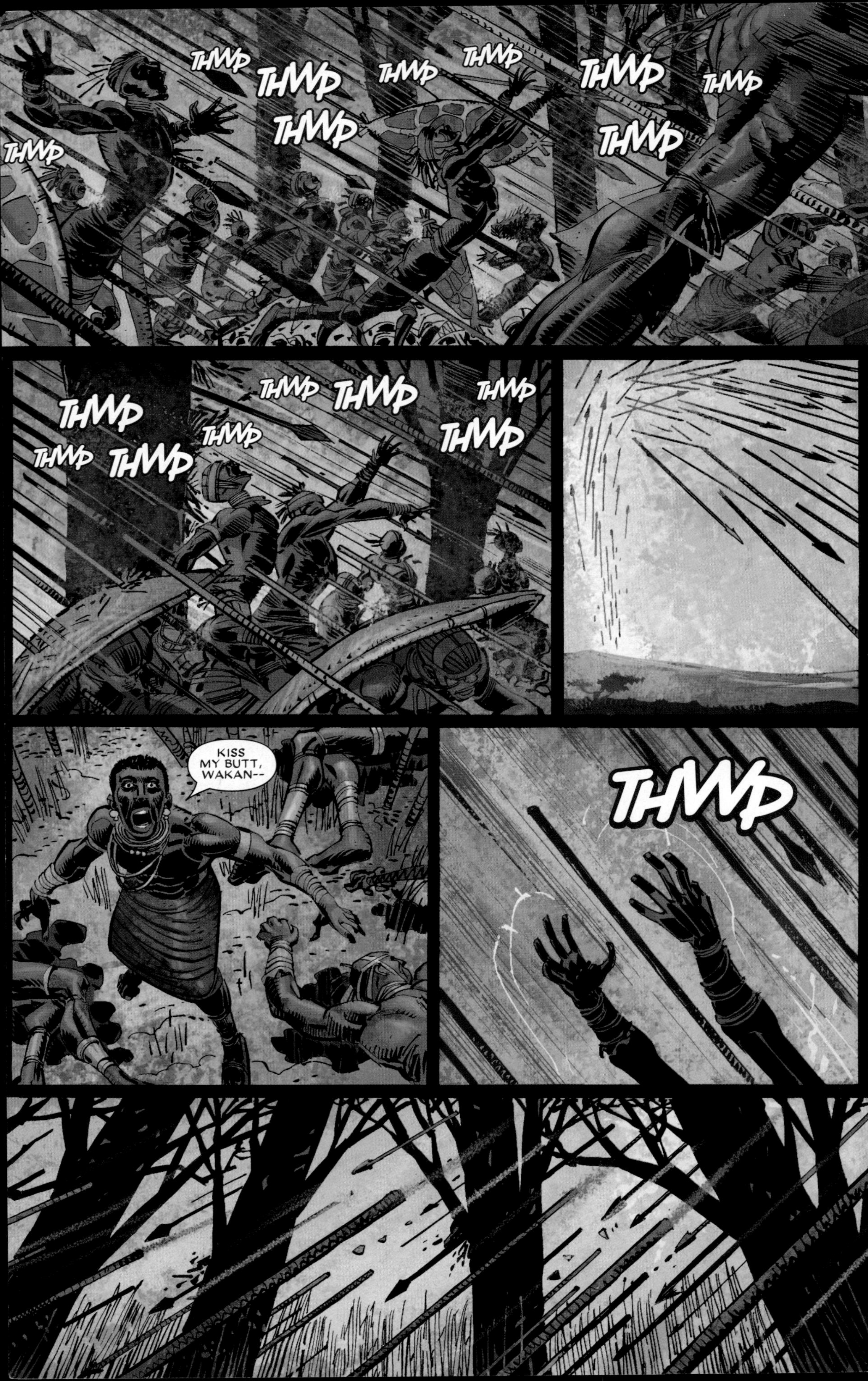
THWP
THWP
THWP
THWP
THWP
THWP
THWP
THWP
THWP
THWP
THWP
THWP
THWP
THWP
THWP
THWP
THWP
KISS MY BUTT, WAKAN--
THWP

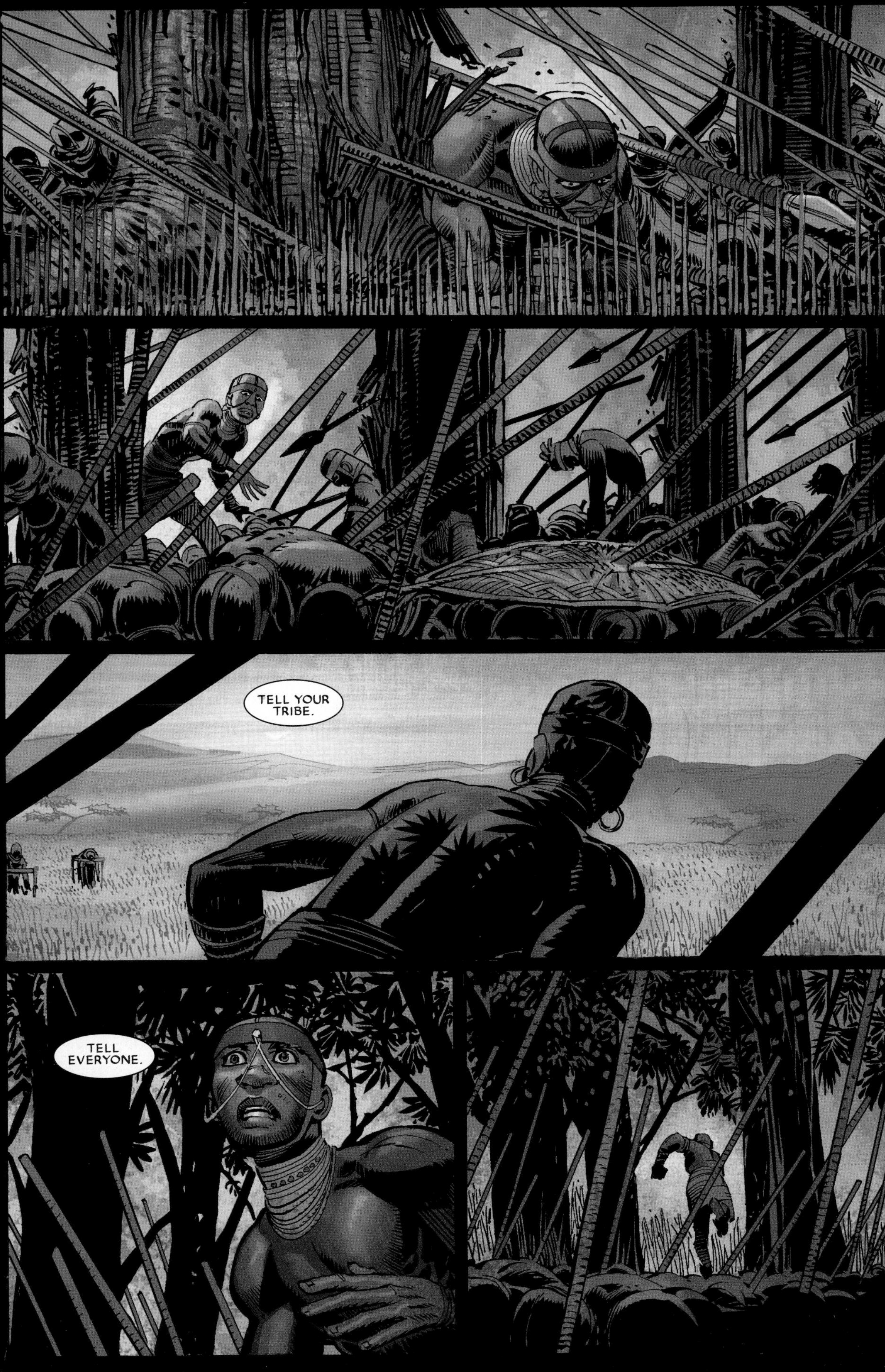
TELL YOUR TRIBE.
TELL EVERYONE.

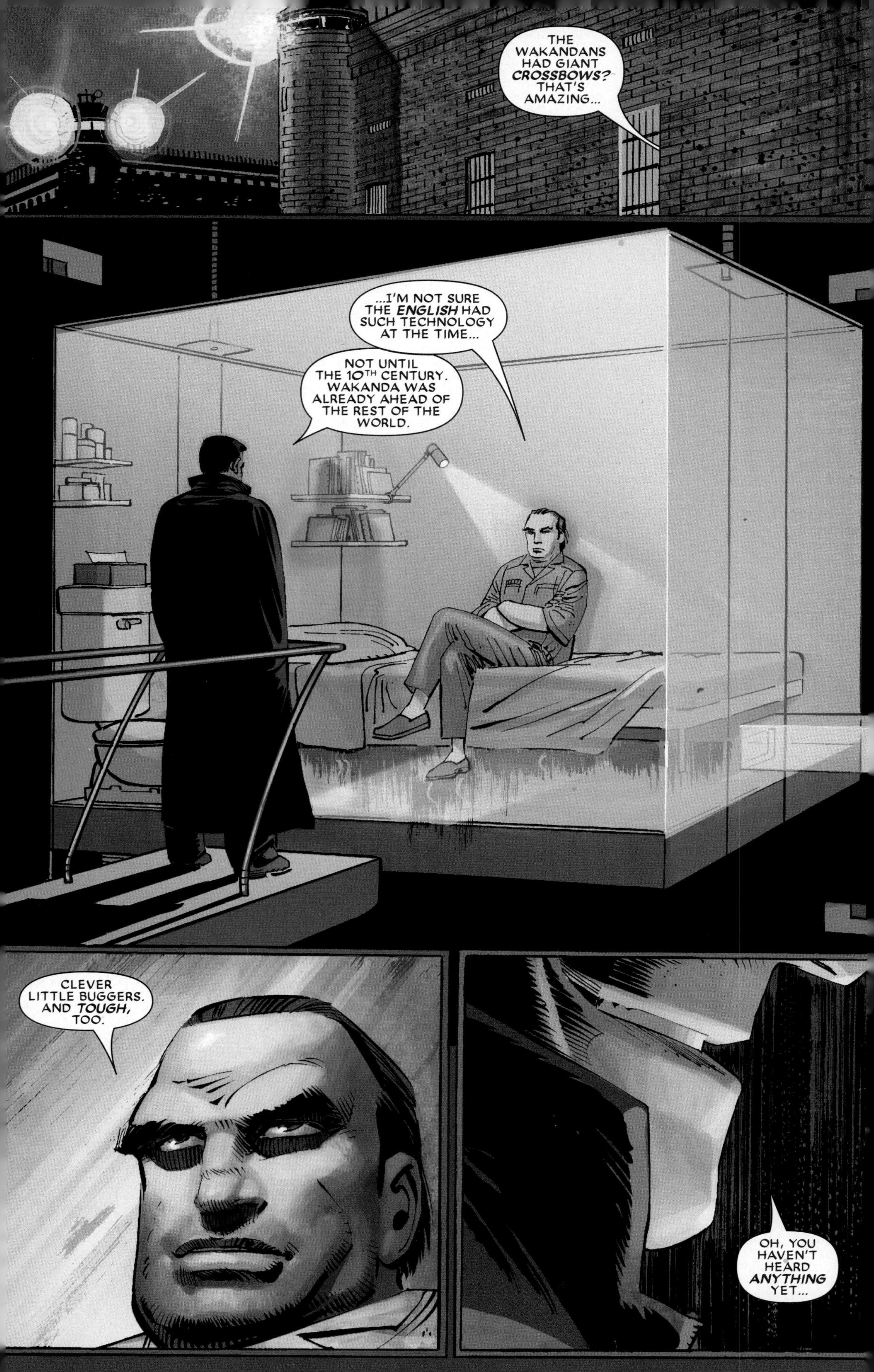
THE WAKANDANS HAD GIANT CROSSBOWS? THAT'S AMAZING...
...I'M NOT SURE THE ENGLISH HAD SUCH TECHNOLOGY AT THE TIME...
NOT UNTIL THE 10TH CENTURY. WAKANDA WAS ALREADY AHEAD OF THE REST OF THE WORLD.
CLEVER LITTLE BUGGERS. AND TOUGH, TOO.
OH, YOU HAVEN'T HEARD ANYTHING YET...

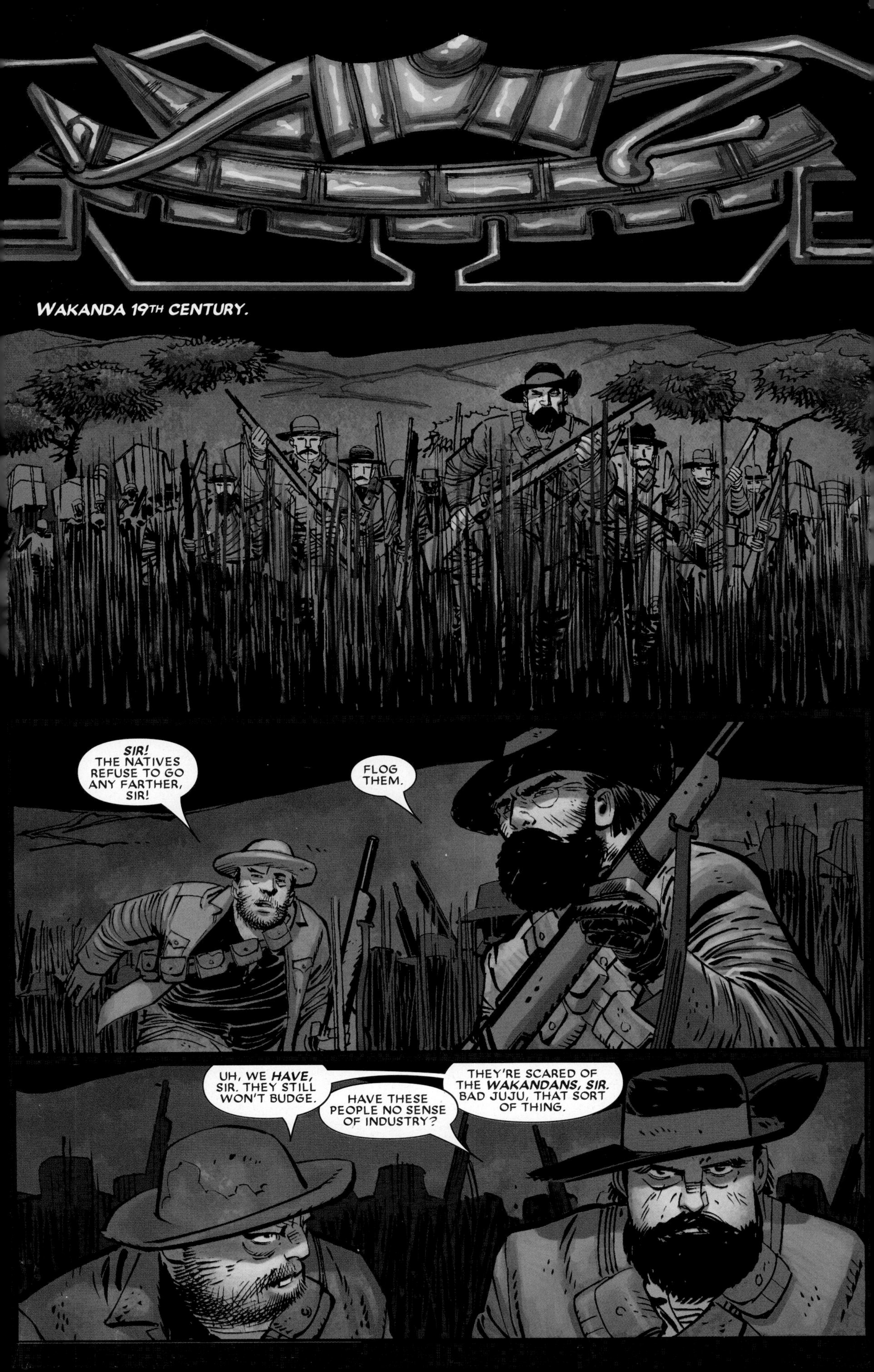
WAKANDA 19TH CENTURY.
SIR! THE NATIVES REFUSE TO GO ANY FARTHER, SIR!
FLOG THEM.
UH, WE HAVE, SIR. THEY STILL WON'T BUDGE.
THEY'RE SCARED OF THE WAKANDANS, SIR. BAD JUJU, THAT SORT OF THING.
HAVE THESE PEOPLE NO SENSE OF INDUSTRY?

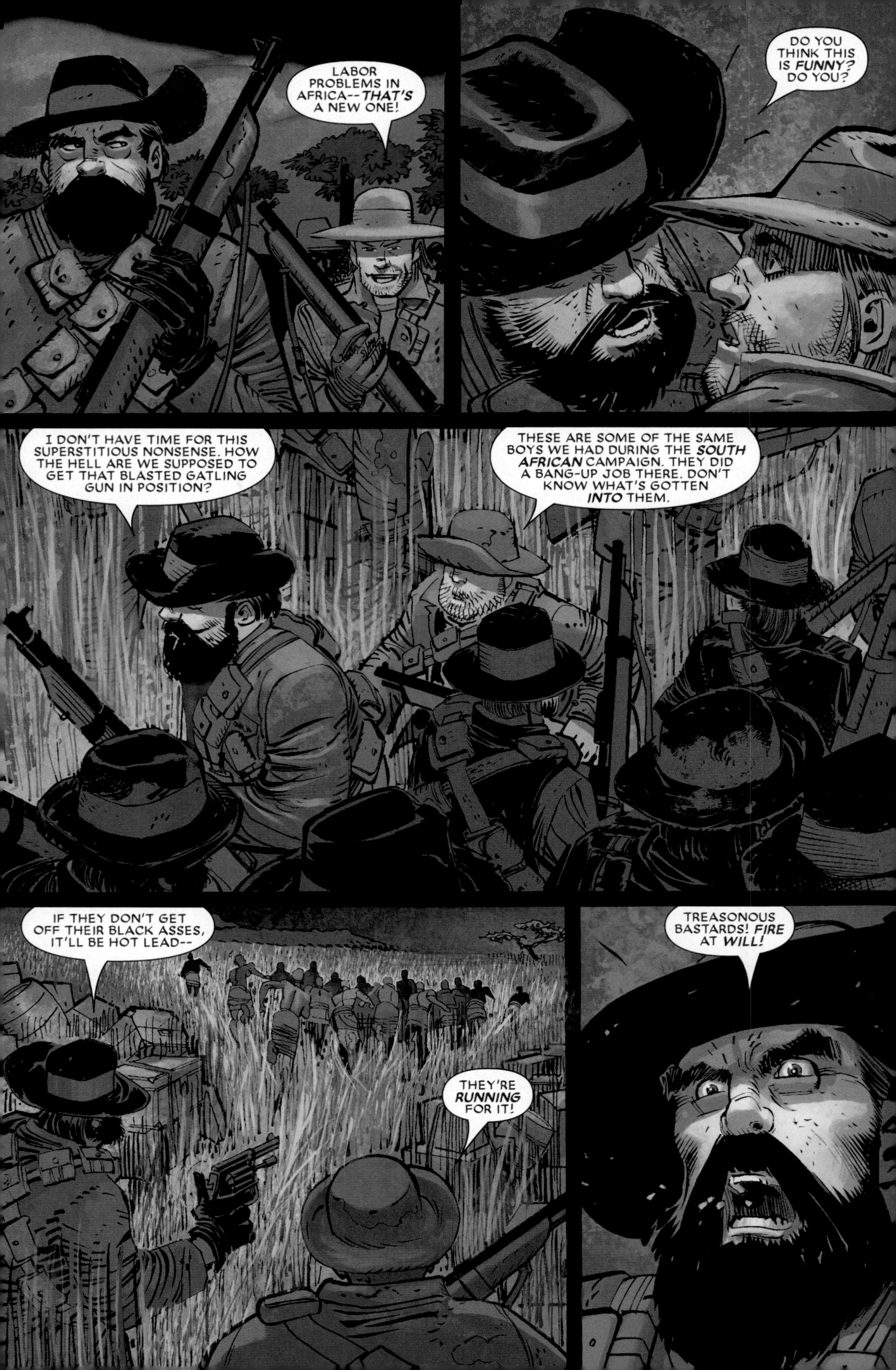
LABOR PROBLEMS IN AFRICA--THAT'S A NEW ONE!
DO YOU THINK THIS IS FUNNY? DO YOU?
I DON'T HAVE TIME FOR THIS SUPERSTITIOUS NONSENSE. HOW THE HELL ARE WE SUPPOSED TO GET THAT BLASTED GATLING GUN IN POSITION?
THESE ARE SOME OF THE SAME BOYS WE HAD DURING THE SOUTH AFRICAN CAMPAIGN. THEY DID A BANG-UP JOB THERE. DON'T KNOW WHAT'S GOTTEN INTO THEM.
IF THEY DON'T GET OFF THEIR BLACK ASSES, IT'LL BE HOT LEAD--
THEY'RE RUNNING FOR IT!
TREASONOUS BASTARDS! FIRE AT WILL!

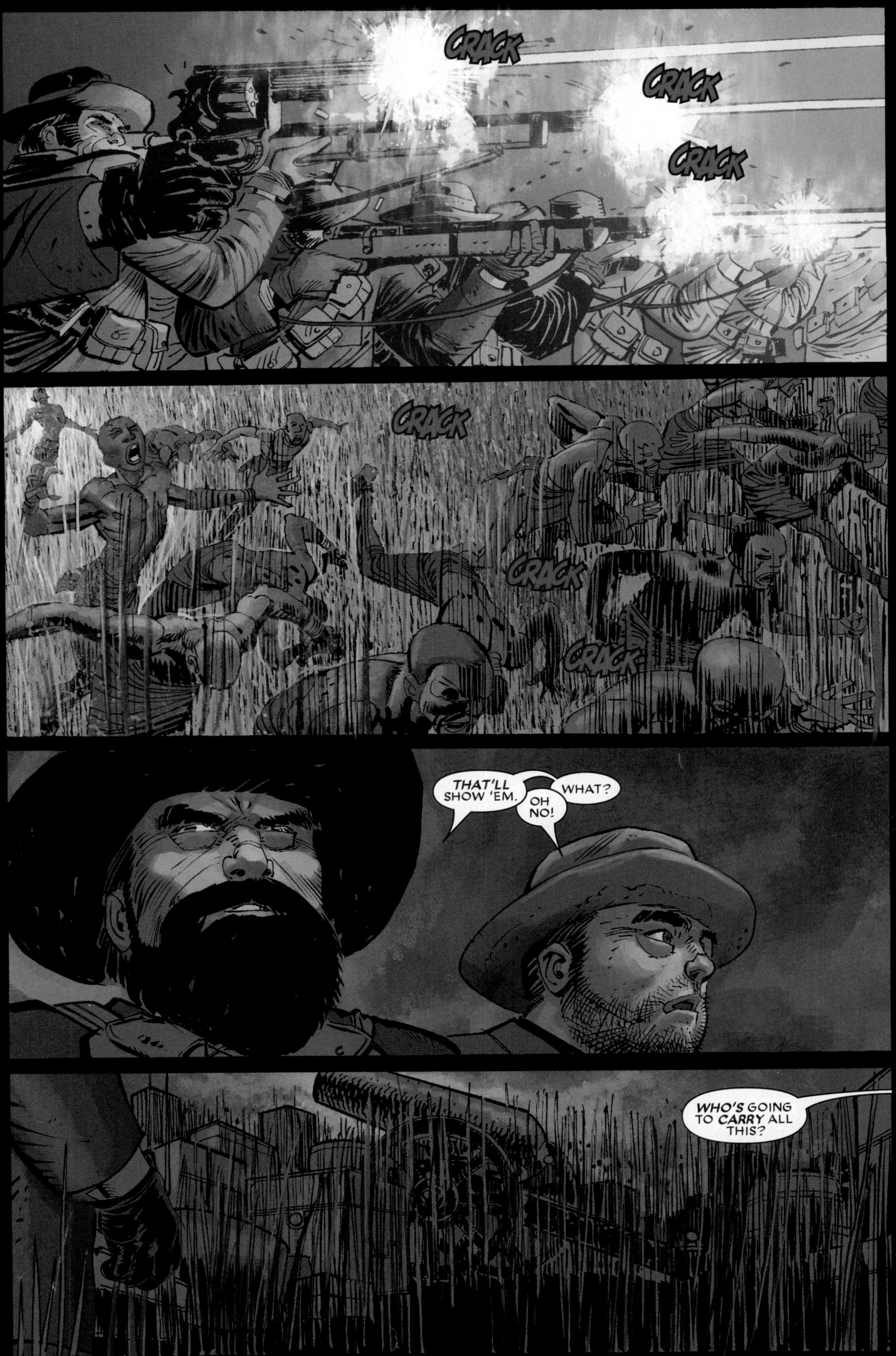
CRACK
CRACK
CRACK
CRACK
CRACK
CRACK
THAT'LL SHOW 'EM.
WHAT?
OH NO!
WHO'S GOING TO CARRY ALL THIS?

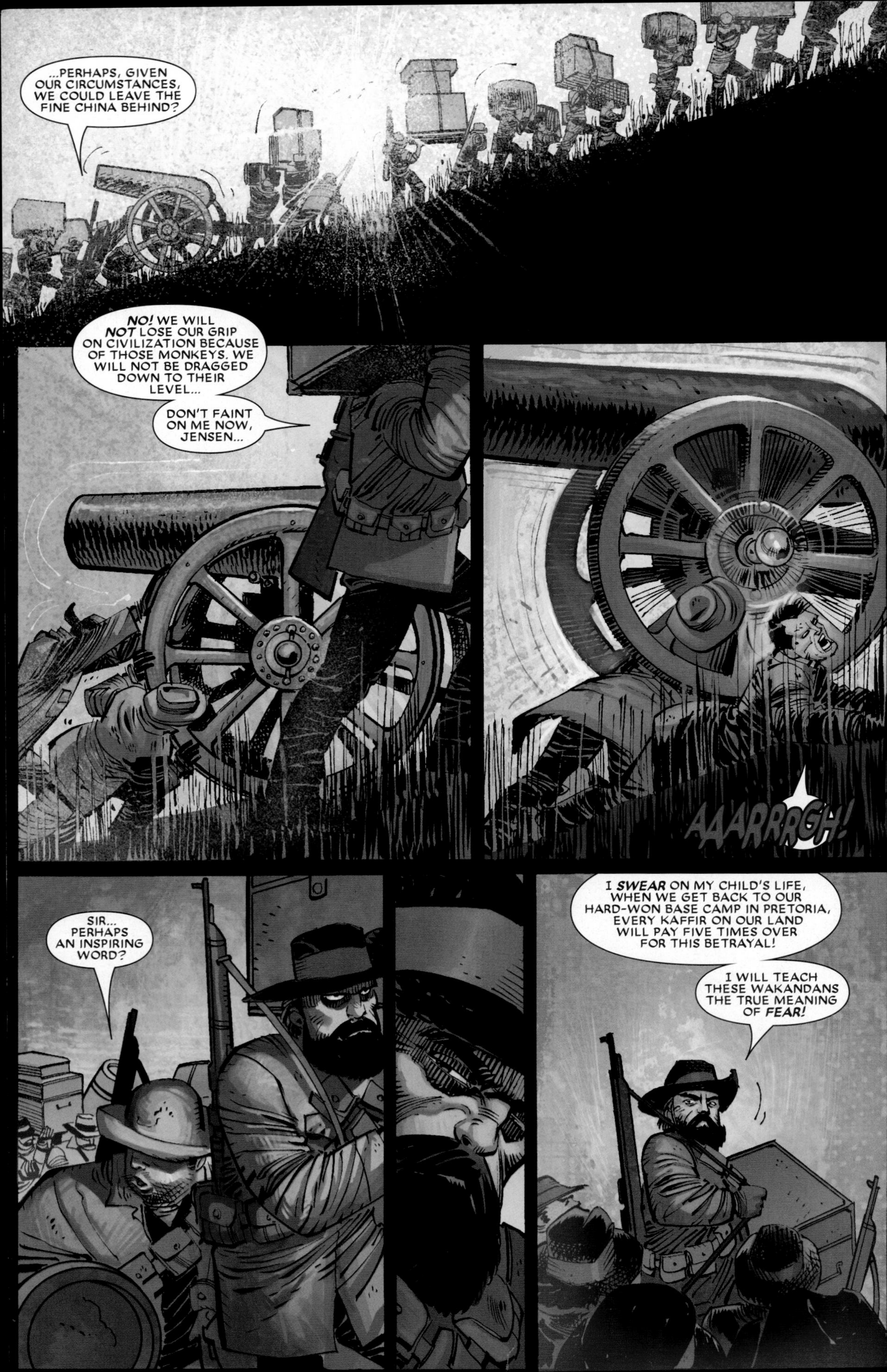
...PERHAPS, GIVEN OUR CIRCUMSTANCES, WE COULD LEAVE THE FINE CHINA BEHIND?
NO! WE WILL NOT LOSE OUR GRIP ON CIVILIZATION BECAUSE OF THOSE MONKEYS. WE WILL NOT BE DRAGGED DOWN TO THEIR LEVEL...
DON'T FAINT ON ME NOW, JENSEN...
AAARRRGH!
SIR... PERHAPS AN INSPIRING WORD?
I SWEAR ON MY CHILD'S LIFE, WHEN WE GET BACK TO OUR HARD-WON BASE CAMP IN PRETORIA, EVERY KAFFIR ON OUR LAND WILL PAY FIVE TIMES OVER FOR THIS BETRAYAL!
I WILL TEACH THESE WAKANDANS THE TRUE MEANING OF FEAR!

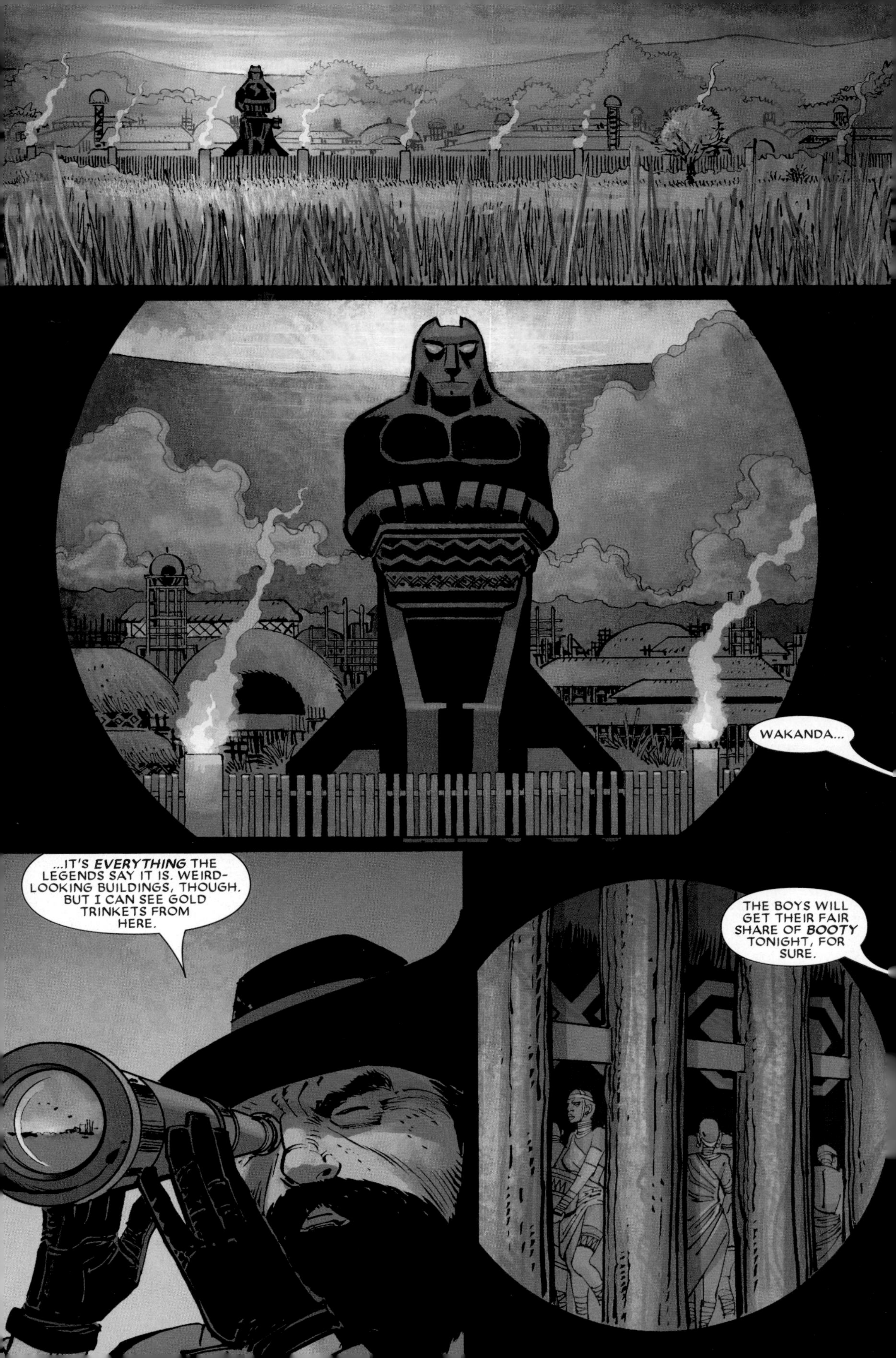
WAKANDA...
...IT'S EVERYTHING THE LEGENDS SAY IT IS. WEIRD-LOOKING BUILDINGS, THOUGH. BUT I CAN SEE GOLD TRINKETS FROM HERE.
THE BOYS WILL GET THEIR FAIR SHARE OF BOOTY TONIGHT, FOR SURE.

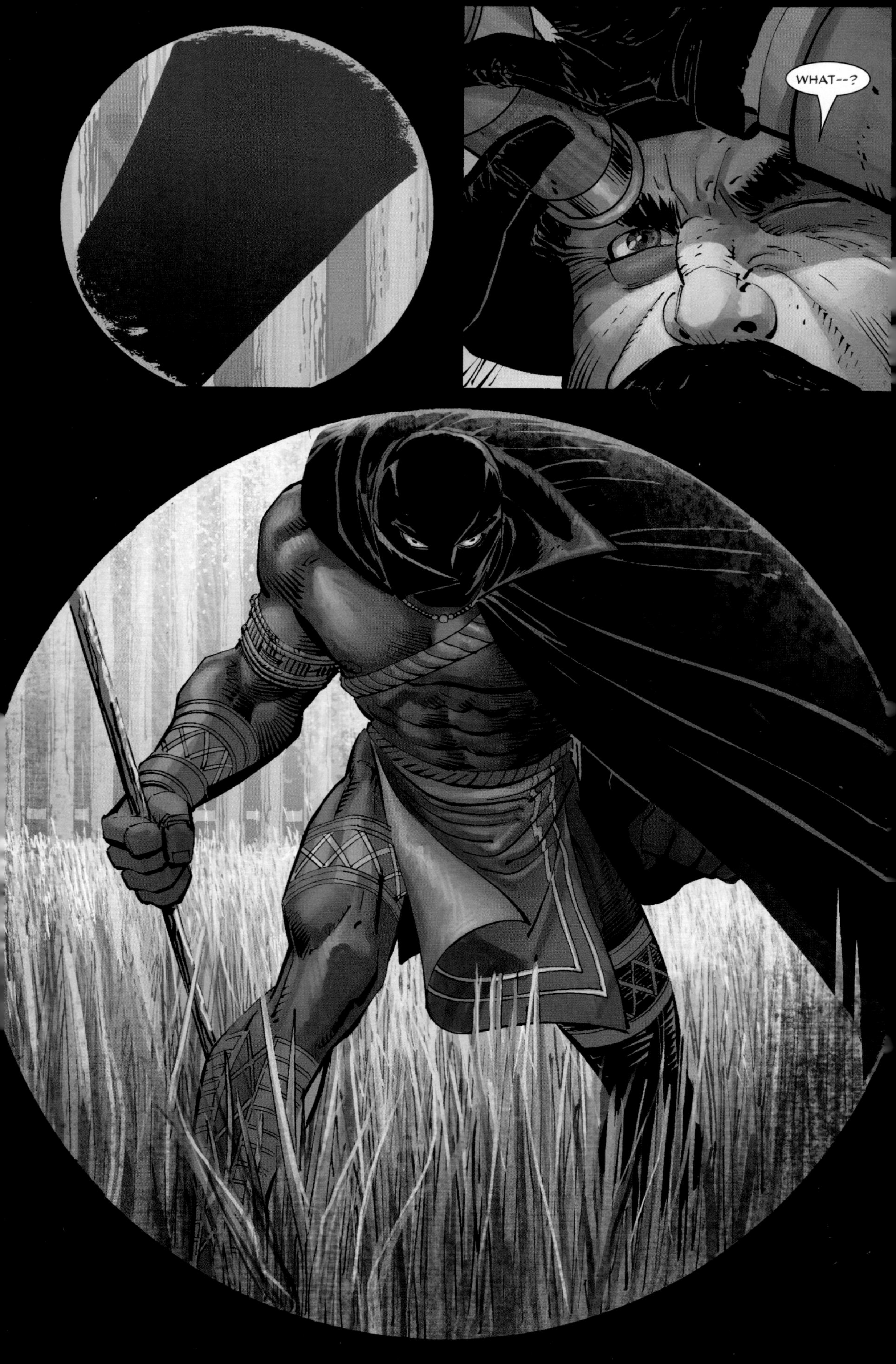
WHAT--?

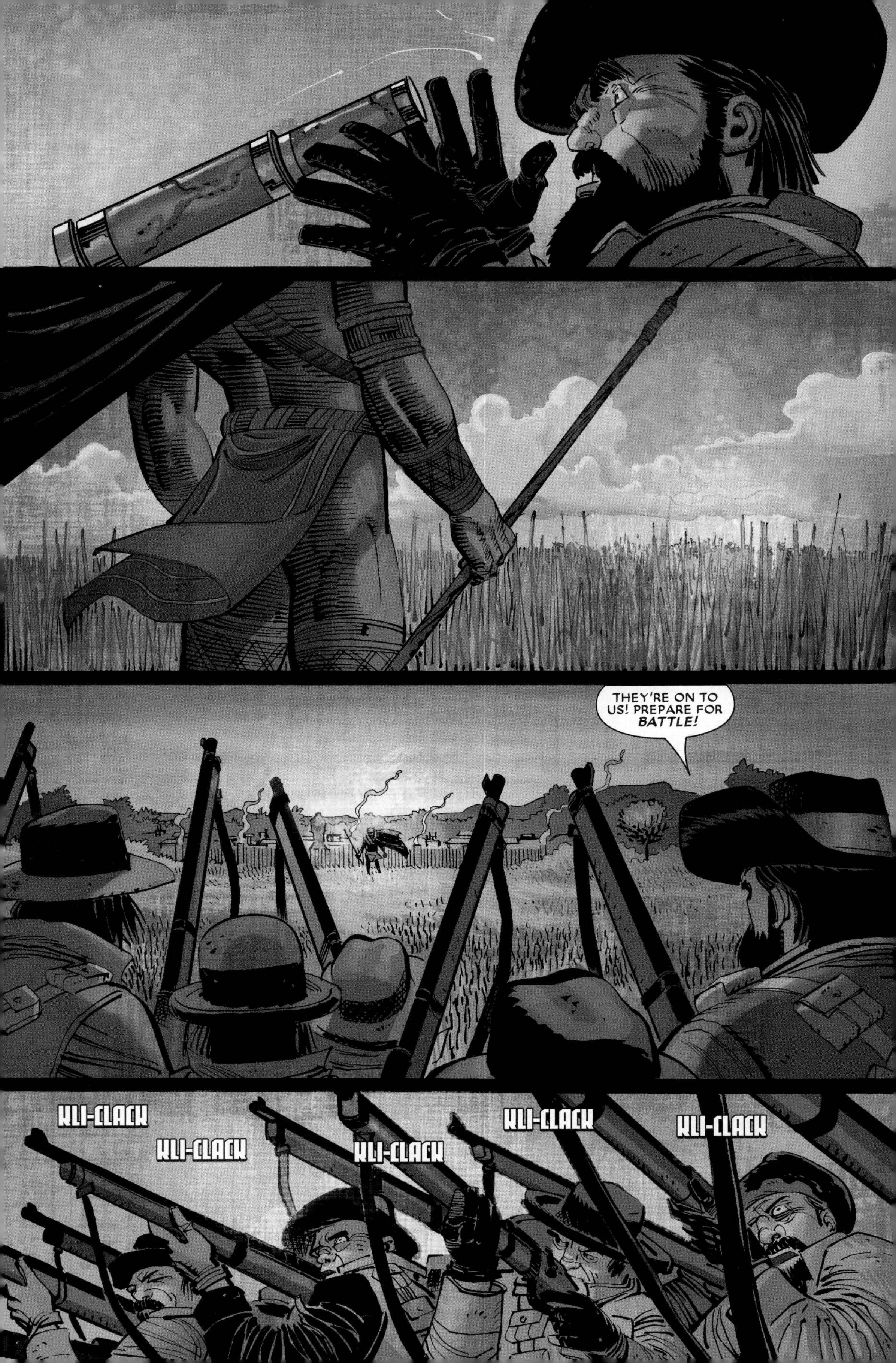
THEY'RE ON TO US! PREPARE FOR *BATTLE!*
KLI-CLACK
KLI-CLACK
KLI-CLACK
KLI-CLACK
KLI-CLACK

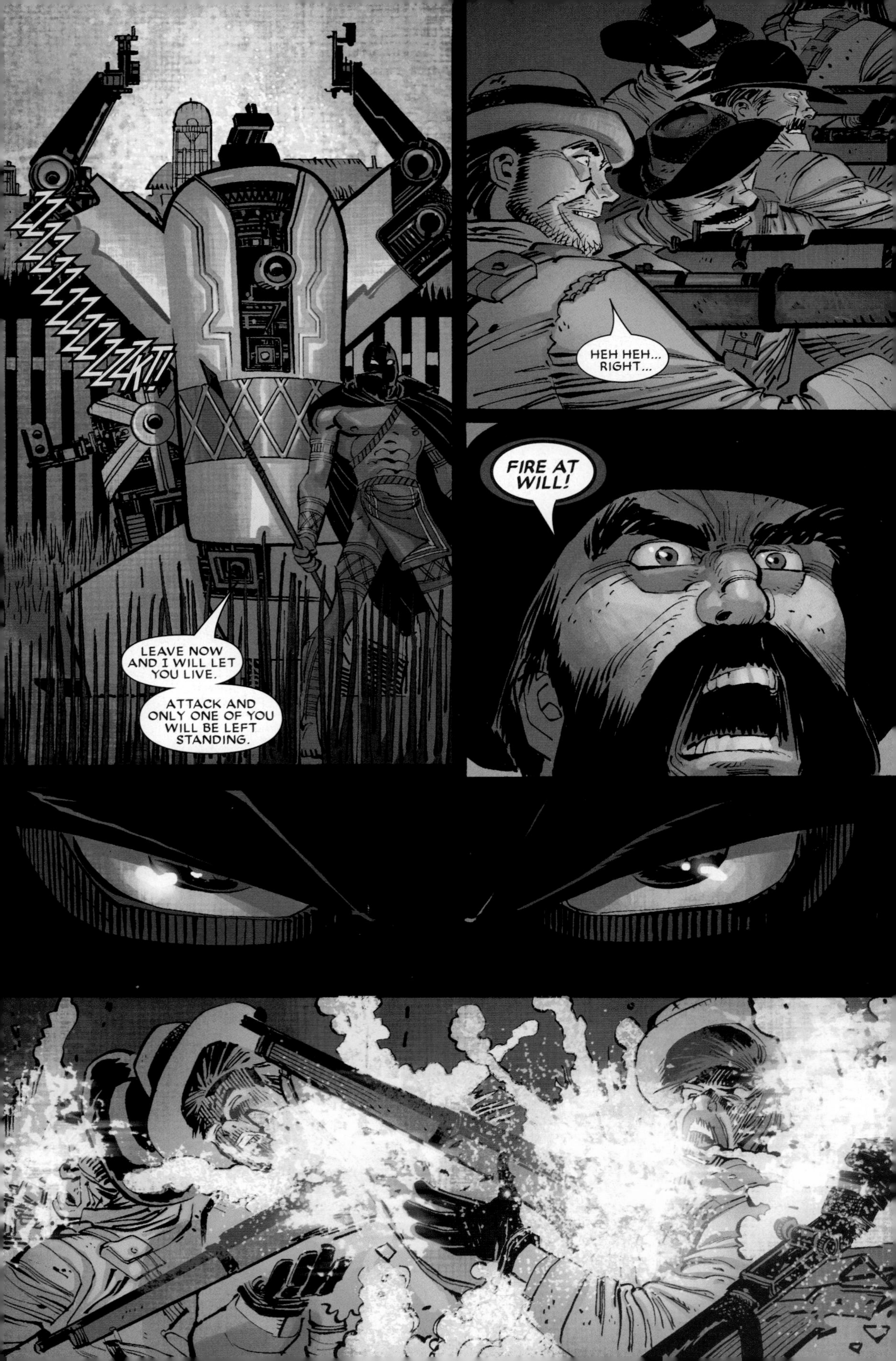

ZZZZZZZZZZKT!
LEAVE NOW AND I WILL LET YOU LIVE.
ATTACK AND ONLY ONE OF YOU WILL BE LEFT STANDING.
HEH HEH... RIGHT...
FIRE AT WILL!

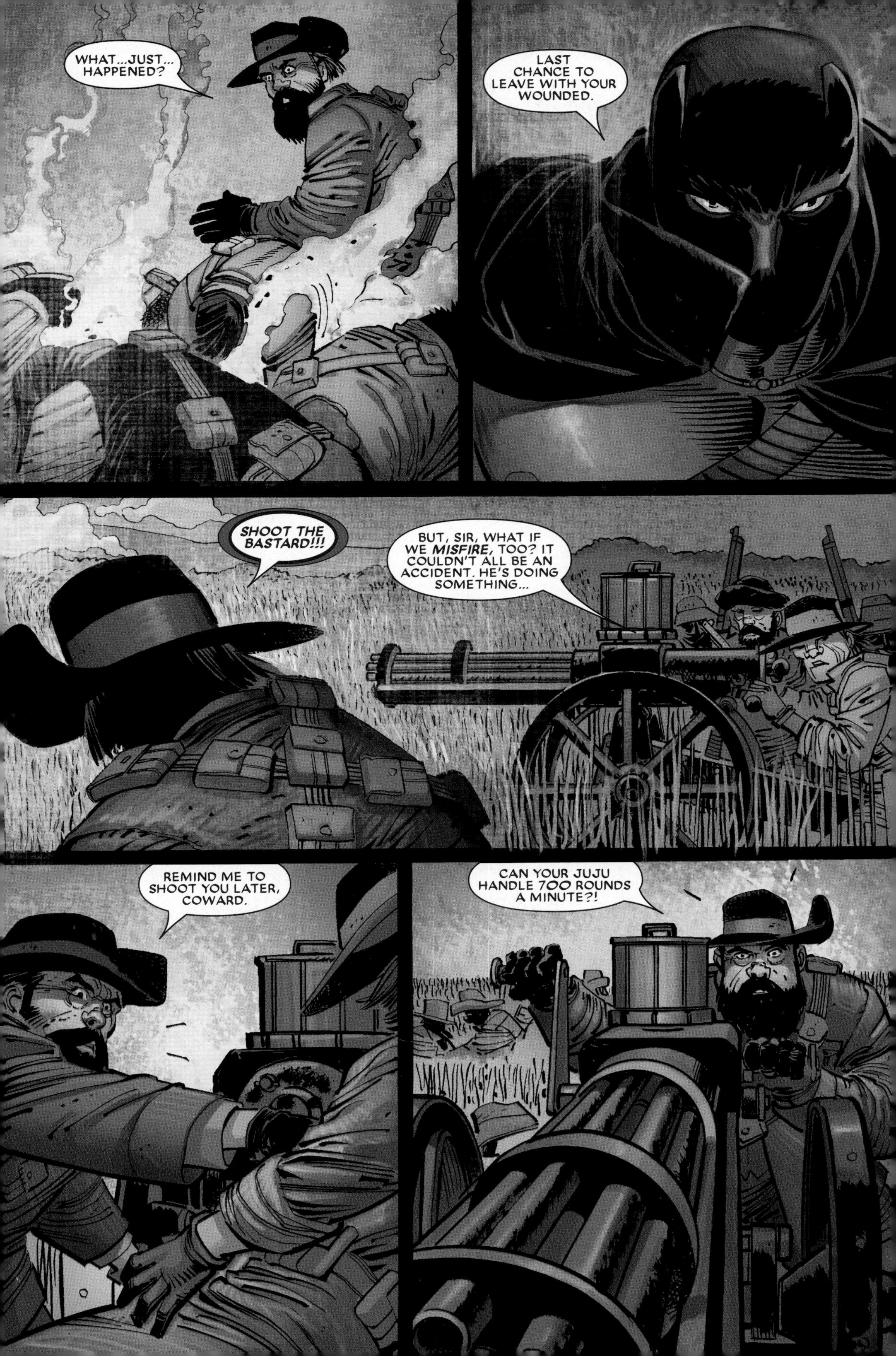
WHAT...JUST... HAPPENED?
LAST CHANCE TO LEAVE WITH YOUR WOUNDED.
SHOOT THE BASTARD!!!
BUT, SIR, WHAT IF WE MISFIRE, TOO? IT COULDN'T ALL BE AN ACCIDENT. HE'S DOING SOMETHING...
REMIND ME TO SHOOT YOU LATER, COWARD.
CAN YOUR JUJU HANDLE 700 ROUNDS A MINUTE?!

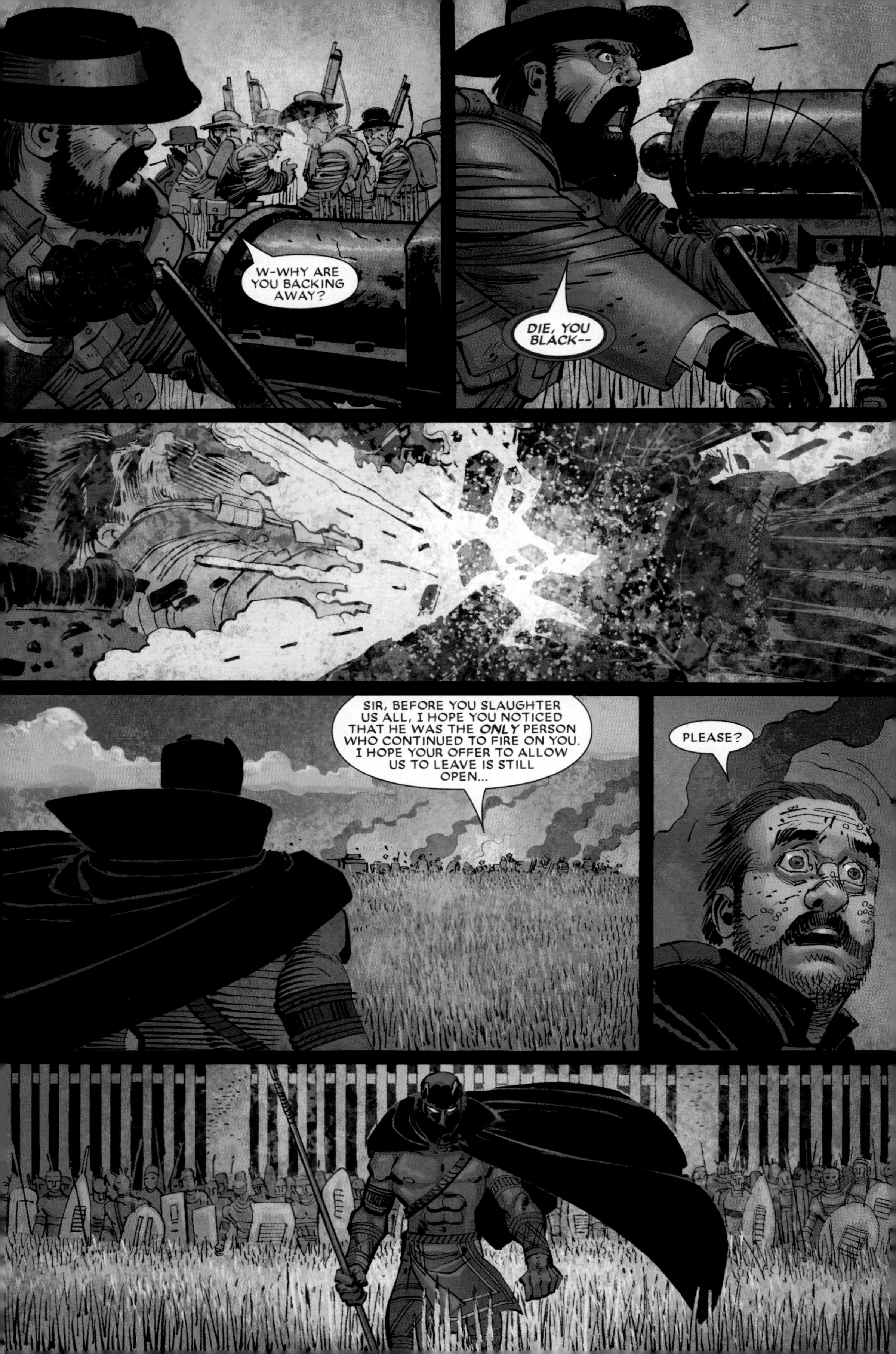
W-WHY ARE YOU BACKING AWAY?
DIE, YOU BLACK--
SIR, BEFORE YOU SLAUGHTER US ALL, I HOPE YOU NOTICED THAT HE WAS THE *ONLY* PERSON WHO CONTINUED TO FIRE ON YOU. I HOPE YOUR OFFER TO ALLOW US TO LEAVE IS STILL OPEN...
PLEASE?

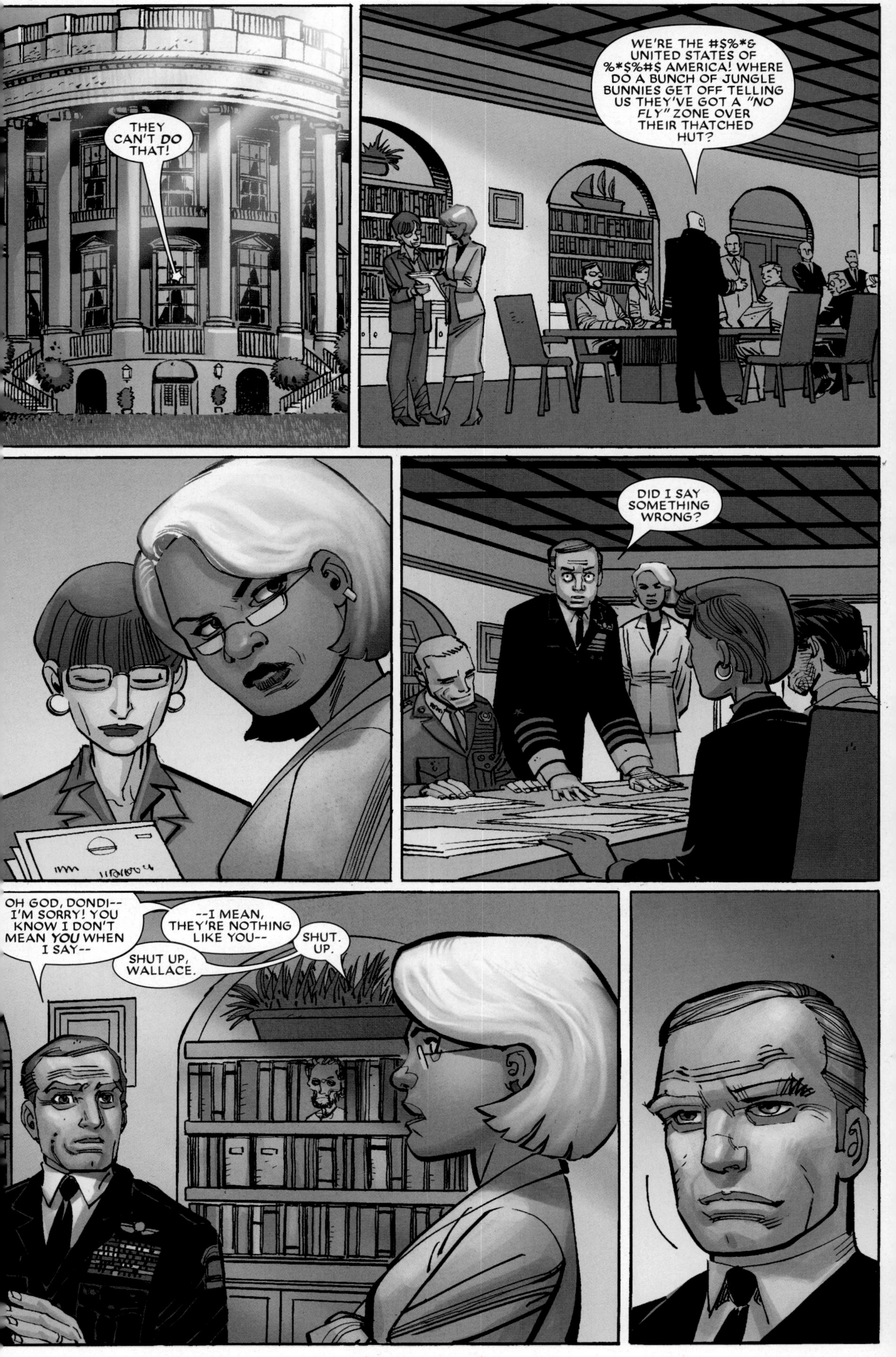
THEY CAN'T *DO* THAT!
WE'RE THE #$%*& UNITED STATES OF %*$%#$ AMERICA! WHERE DO A BUNCH OF JUNGLE BUNNIES GET OFF TELLING US THEY'VE GOT A *"NO FLY"* ZONE OVER THEIR THATCHED HUT?
DID I SAY SOMETHING WRONG?
OH GOD, DONDI-- I'M SORRY! YOU KNOW I DON'T MEAN *YOU* WHEN I SAY--
SHUT UP, WALLACE.
--I MEAN, THEY'RE NOTHING LIKE YOU--
SHUT. UP.

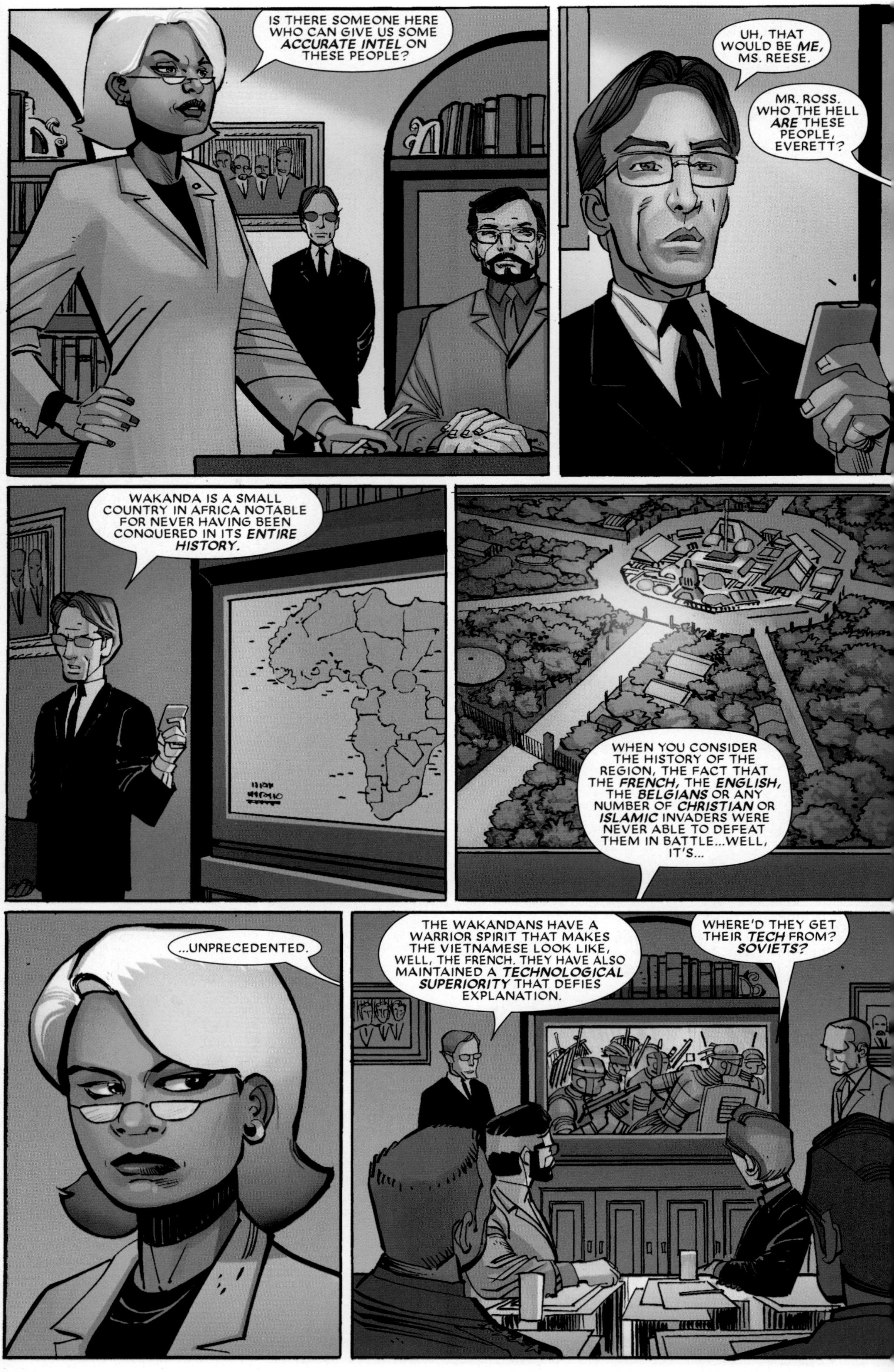
IS THERE SOMEONE HERE WHO CAN GIVE US SOME ACCURATE INTEL ON THESE PEOPLE?
UH, THAT WOULD BE ME, MS. REESE.
MR. ROSS. WHO THE HELL ARE THESE PEOPLE, EVERETT?
WAKANDA IS A SMALL COUNTRY IN AFRICA NOTABLE FOR NEVER HAVING BEEN CONQUERED IN ITS ENTIRE HISTORY.
WHEN YOU CONSIDER THE HISTORY OF THE REGION, THE FACT THAT THE FRENCH, THE ENGLISH, THE BELGIANS OR ANY NUMBER OF CHRISTIAN OR ISLAMIC INVADERS WERE NEVER ABLE TO DEFEAT THEM IN BATTLE...WELL, IT'S...
...UNPRECEDENTED.
THE WAKANDANS HAVE A WARRIOR SPIRIT THAT MAKES THE VIETNAMESE LOOK LIKE, WELL, THE FRENCH. THEY HAVE ALSO MAINTAINED A TECHNOLOGICAL SUPERIORITY THAT DEFIES EXPLANATION.
WHERE'D THEY GET THEIR TECH FROM? SOVIETS?

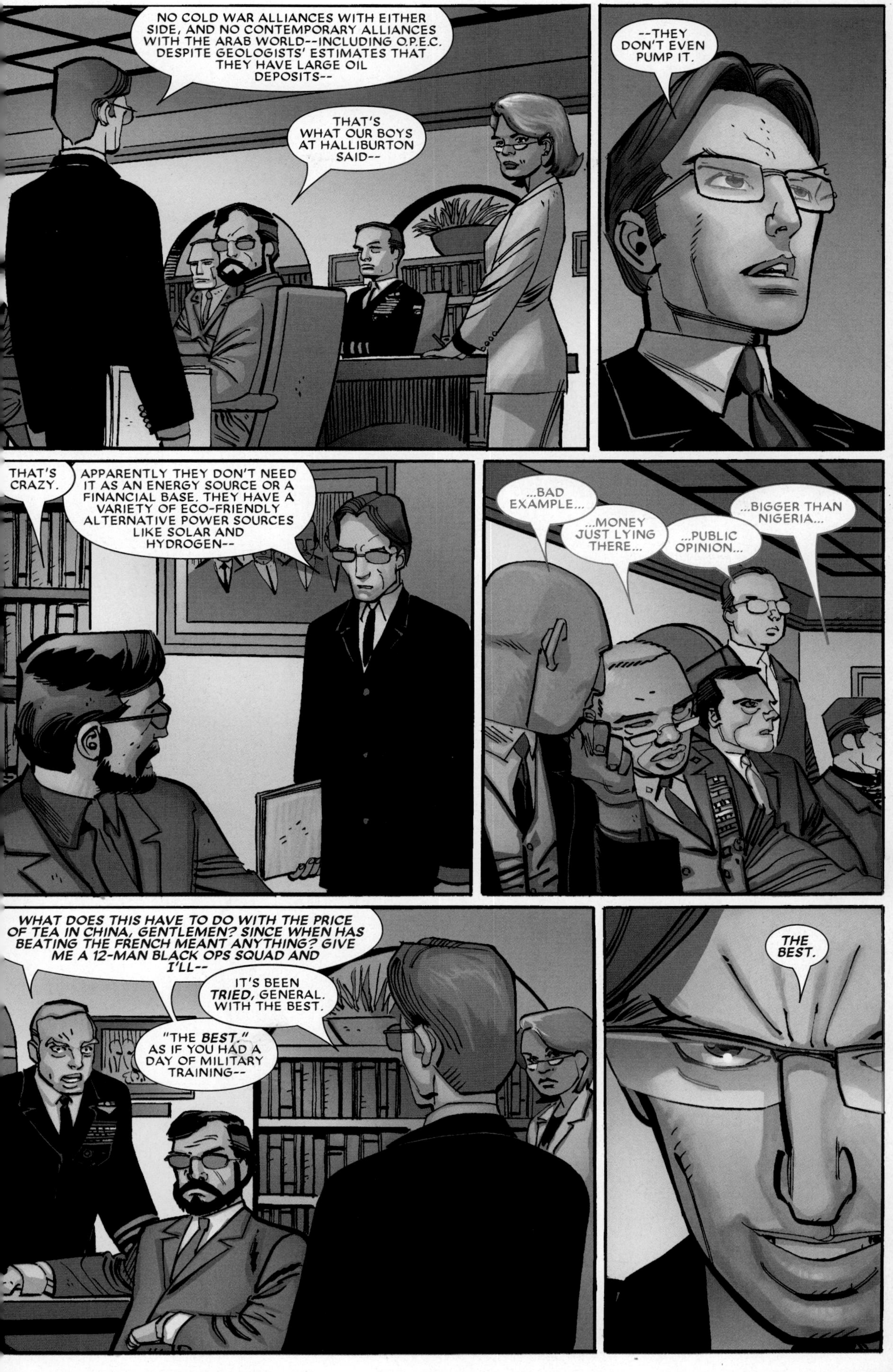
NO COLD WAR ALLIANCES WITH EITHER SIDE, AND NO CONTEMPORARY ALLIANCES WITH THE ARAB WORLD--INCLUDING O.P.E.C. DESPITE GEOLOGISTS' ESTIMATES THAT THEY HAVE LARGE OIL DEPOSITS--
THAT'S WHAT OUR BOYS AT HALLIBURTON SAID--
--THEY DON'T EVEN PUMP IT.
THAT'S CRAZY.
APPARENTLY THEY DON'T NEED IT AS AN ENERGY SOURCE OR A FINANCIAL BASE. THEY HAVE A VARIETY OF ECO-FRIENDLY ALTERNATIVE POWER SOURCES LIKE SOLAR AND HYDROGEN--
...BAD EXAMPLE...
...MONEY JUST LYING THERE...
...PUBLIC OPINION...
...BIGGER THAN NIGERIA...
WHAT DOES THIS HAVE TO DO WITH THE PRICE OF TEA IN CHINA, GENTLEMEN? SINCE WHEN HAS BEATING THE FRENCH MEANT ANYTHING? GIVE ME A 12-MAN BLACK OPS SQUAD AND I'LL--
IT'S BEEN TRIED, GENERAL. WITH THE BEST.
"THE BEST." AS IF YOU HAD A DAY OF MILITARY TRAINING--
THE BEST.

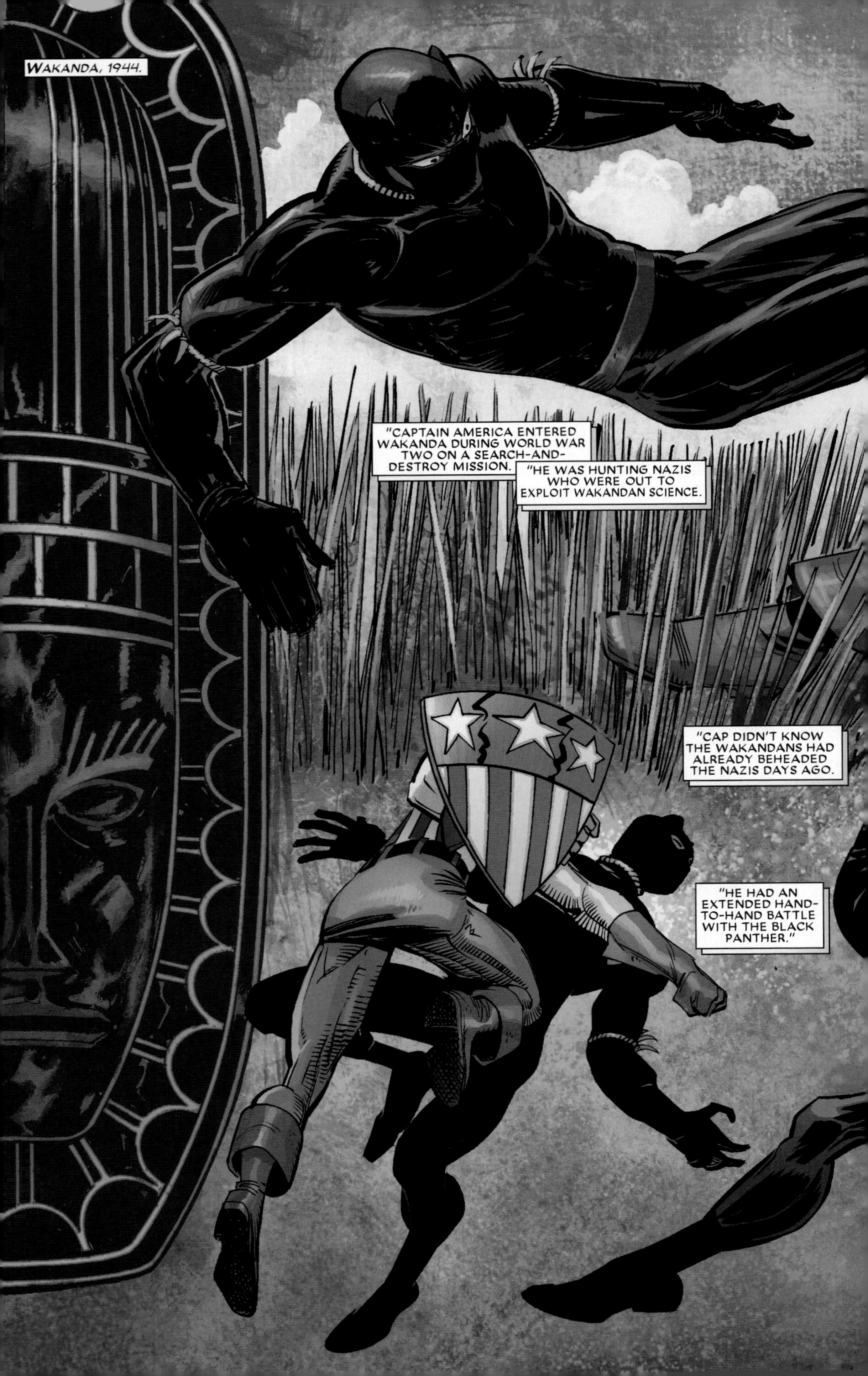
WAKANDA, 1944.
"CAPTAIN AMERICA ENTERED WAKANDA DURING WORLD WAR TWO ON A SEARCH-AND-DESTROY MISSION.
"HE WAS HUNTING NAZIS WHO WERE OUT TO EXPLOIT WAKANDAN SCIENCE.
"CAP DIDN'T KNOW THE WAKANDANS HAD ALREADY BEHEADED THE NAZIS DAYS AGO.
"HE HAD AN EXTENDED HAND-TO-HAND BATTLE WITH THE BLACK PANTHER."

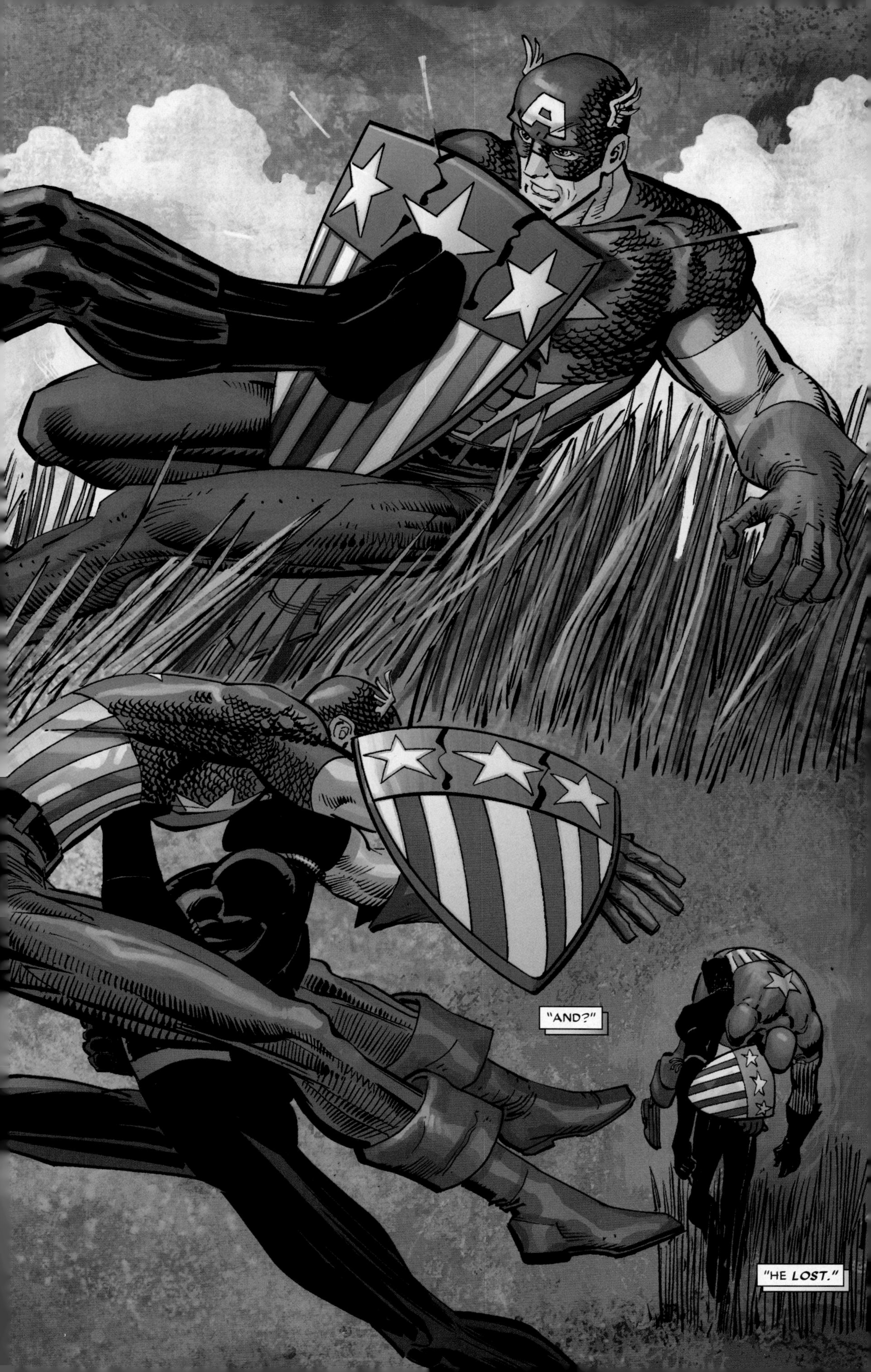
"AND?"
"HE LOST."

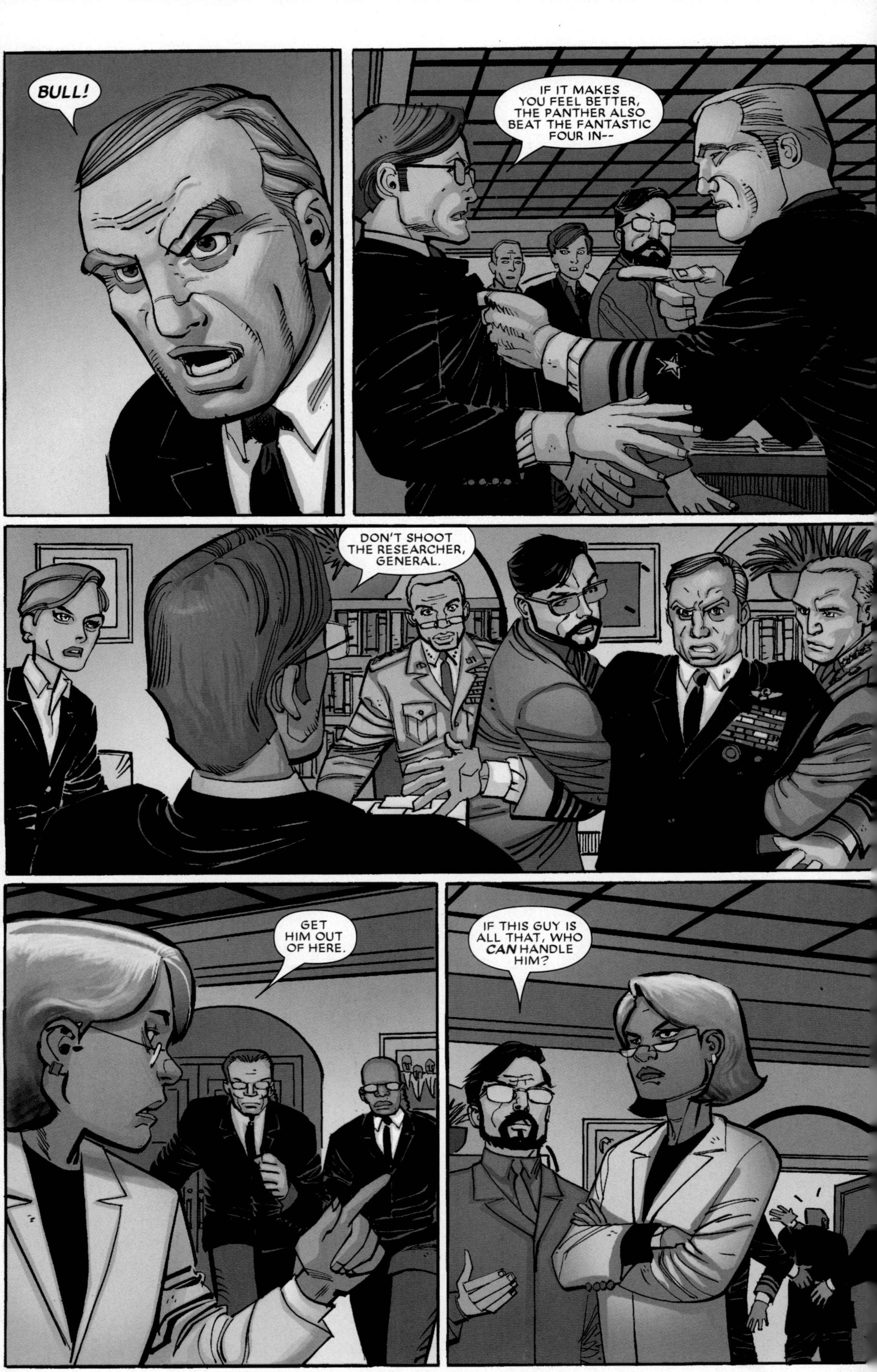
BULL!
IF IT MAKES YOU FEEL BETTER, THE PANTHER ALSO BEAT THE FANTASTIC FOUR IN--
DON'T SHOOT THE RESEARCHER, GENERAL.
GET HIM OUT OF HERE.
IF THIS GUY IS ALL THAT, WHO CAN HANDLE HIM?

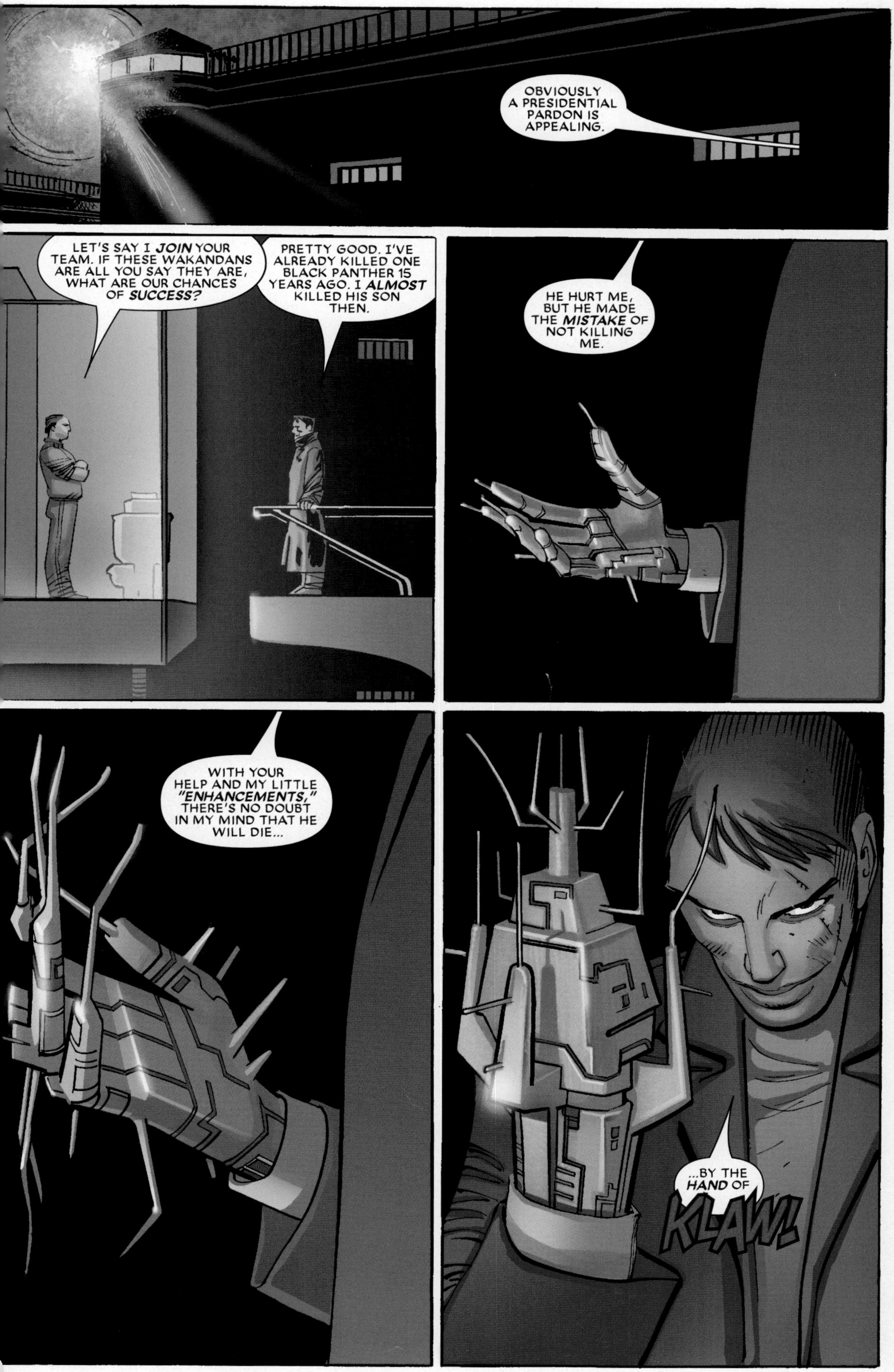
OBVIOUSLY A PRESIDENTIAL PARDON IS APPEALING.
LET'S SAY I JOIN YOUR TEAM. IF THESE WAKANDANS ARE ALL YOU SAY THEY ARE, WHAT ARE OUR CHANCES OF SUCCESS?
PRETTY GOOD. I'VE ALREADY KILLED ONE BLACK PANTHER 15 YEARS AGO. I ALMOST KILLED HIS SON THEN.
HE HURT ME, BUT HE MADE THE MISTAKE OF NOT KILLING ME.
WITH YOUR HELP AND MY LITTLE "ENHANCEMENTS," THERE'S NO DOUBT IN MY MIND THAT HE WILL DIE...
...BY THE HAND OF
KLAW!

# 2

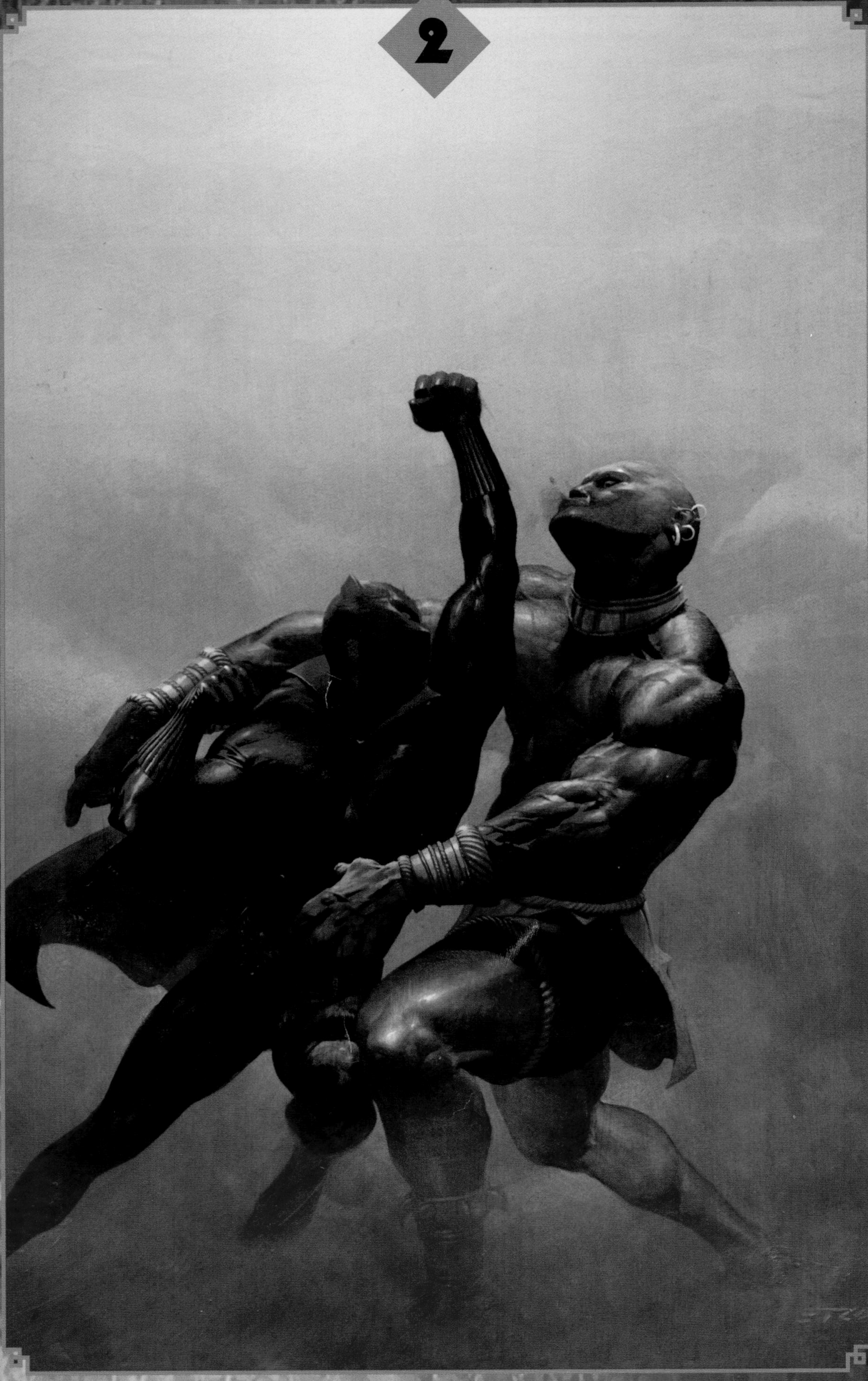

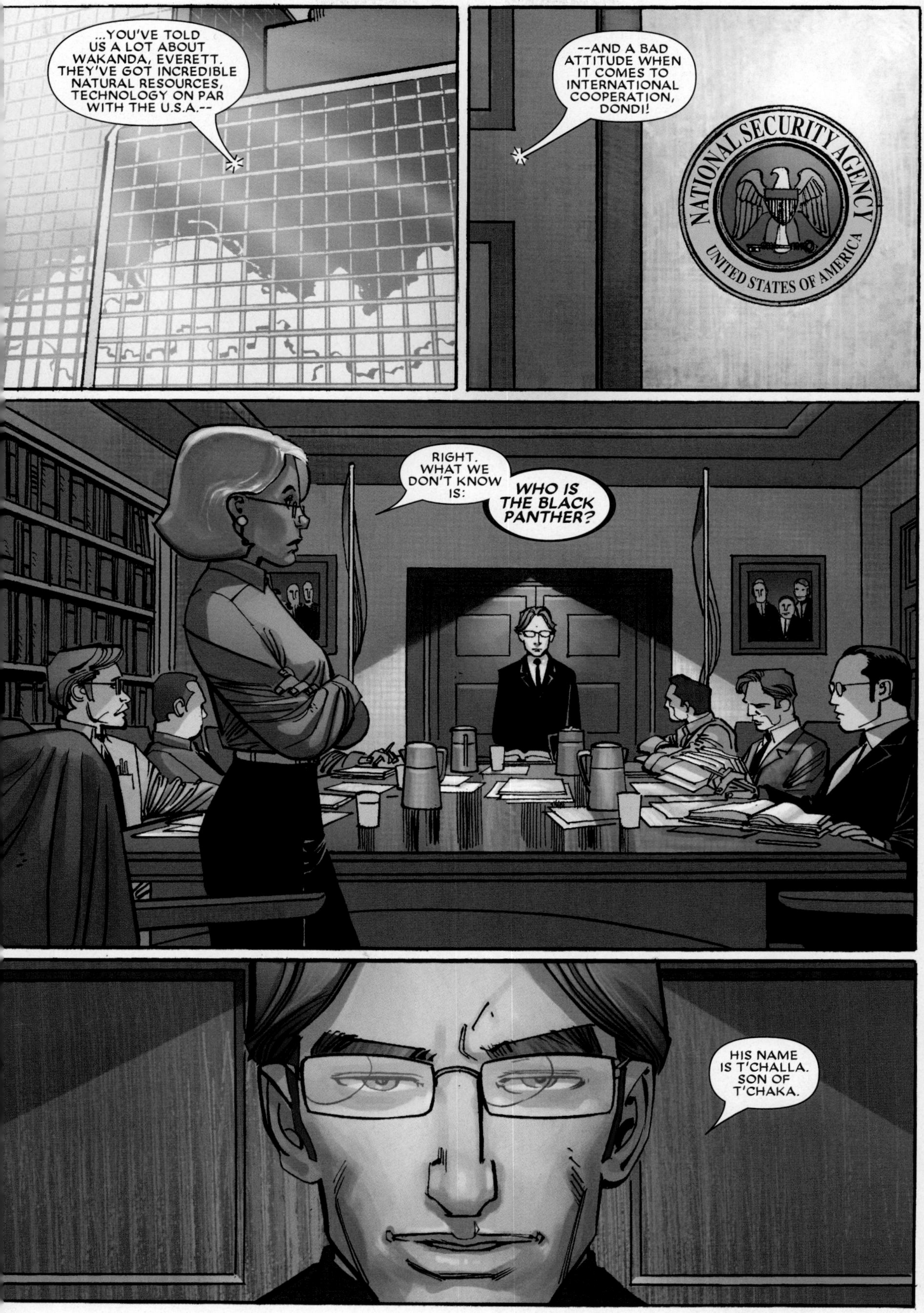
...YOU'VE TOLD US A LOT ABOUT WAKANDA, EVERETT. THEY'VE GOT INCREDIBLE NATURAL RESOURCES, TECHNOLOGY ON PAR WITH THE U.S.A.--
--AND A BAD ATTITUDE WHEN IT COMES TO INTERNATIONAL COOPERATION, DONDI!
NATIONAL SECURITY AGENCY
UNITED STATES OF AMERICA
RIGHT. WHAT WE DON'T KNOW IS:
WHO IS THE BLACK PANTHER?
HIS NAME IS T'CHALLA. SON OF T'CHAKA.

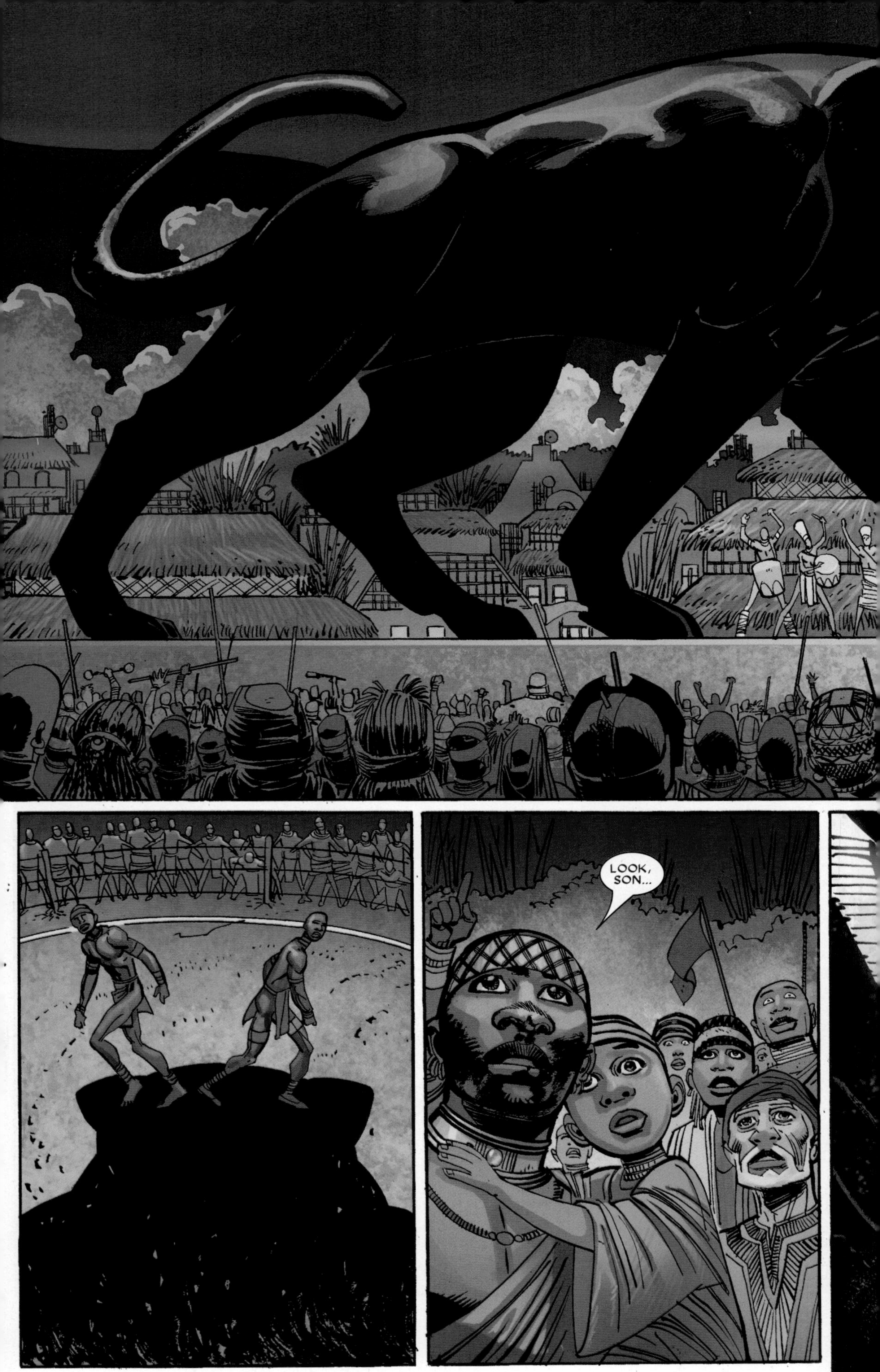
LOOK, SON...

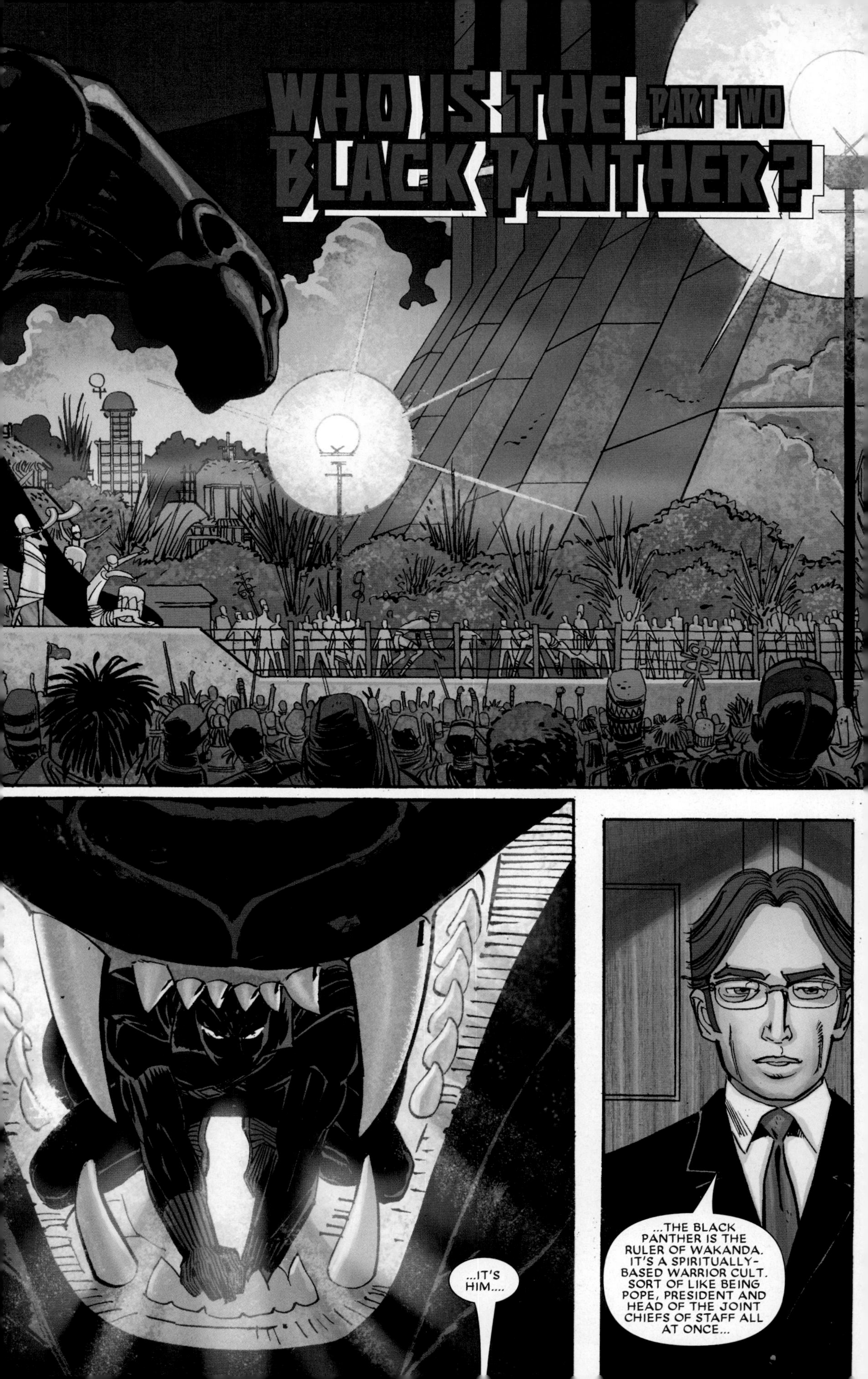
WHO IS THE BLACK PANTHER?
PART TWO
...IT'S HIM....
...THE BLACK PANTHER IS THE RULER OF WAKANDA. IT'S A SPIRITUALLY-BASED WARRIOR CULT. SORT OF LIKE BEING POPE, PRESIDENT AND HEAD OF THE JOINT CHIEFS OF STAFF ALL AT ONCE...

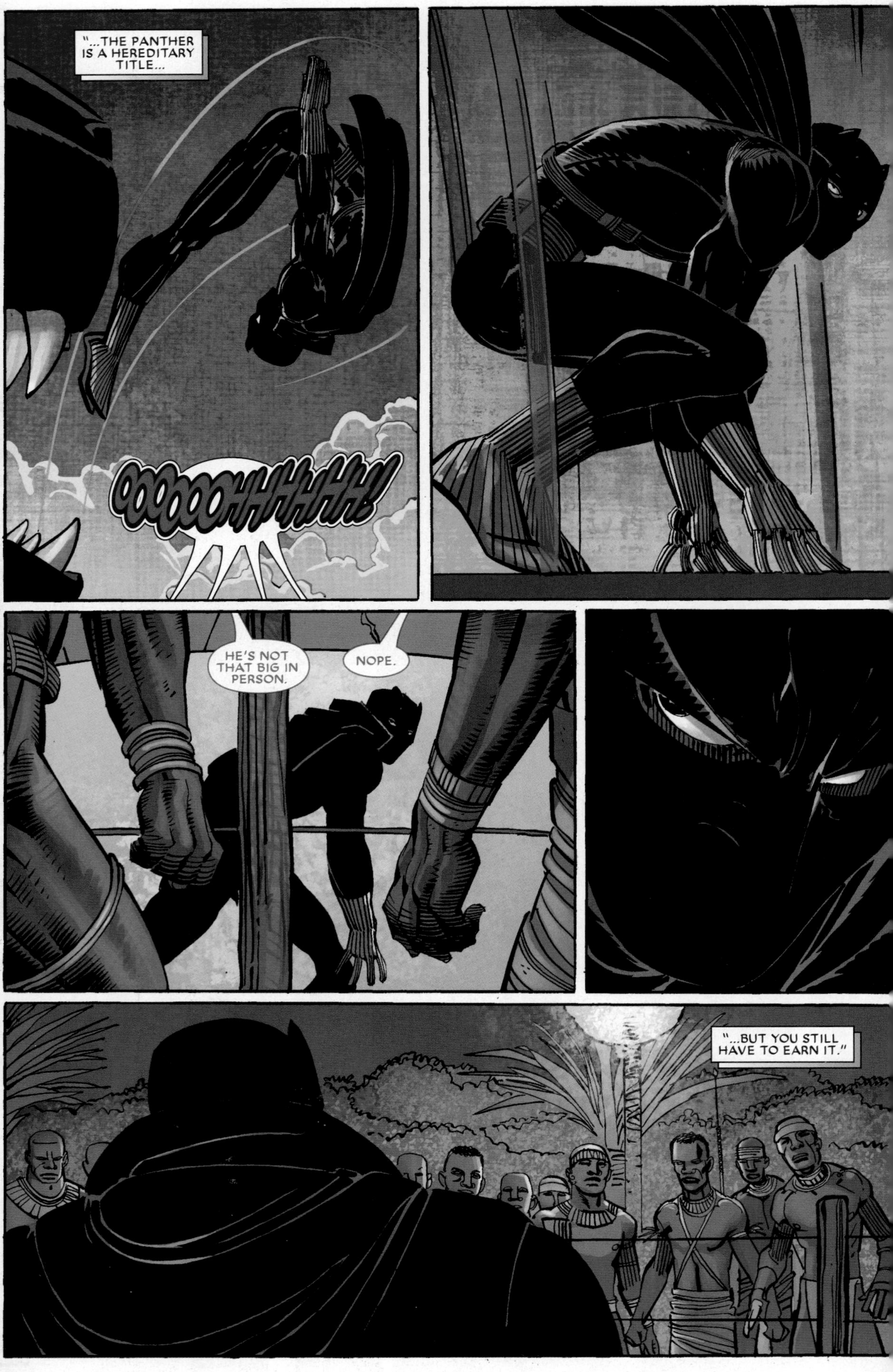
"...THE PANTHER IS A HEREDITARY TITLE...
OOOOOOOHHHHHHH!!
HE'S NOT THAT BIG IN PERSON.
NOPE.
"...BUT YOU STILL HAVE TO EARN IT."

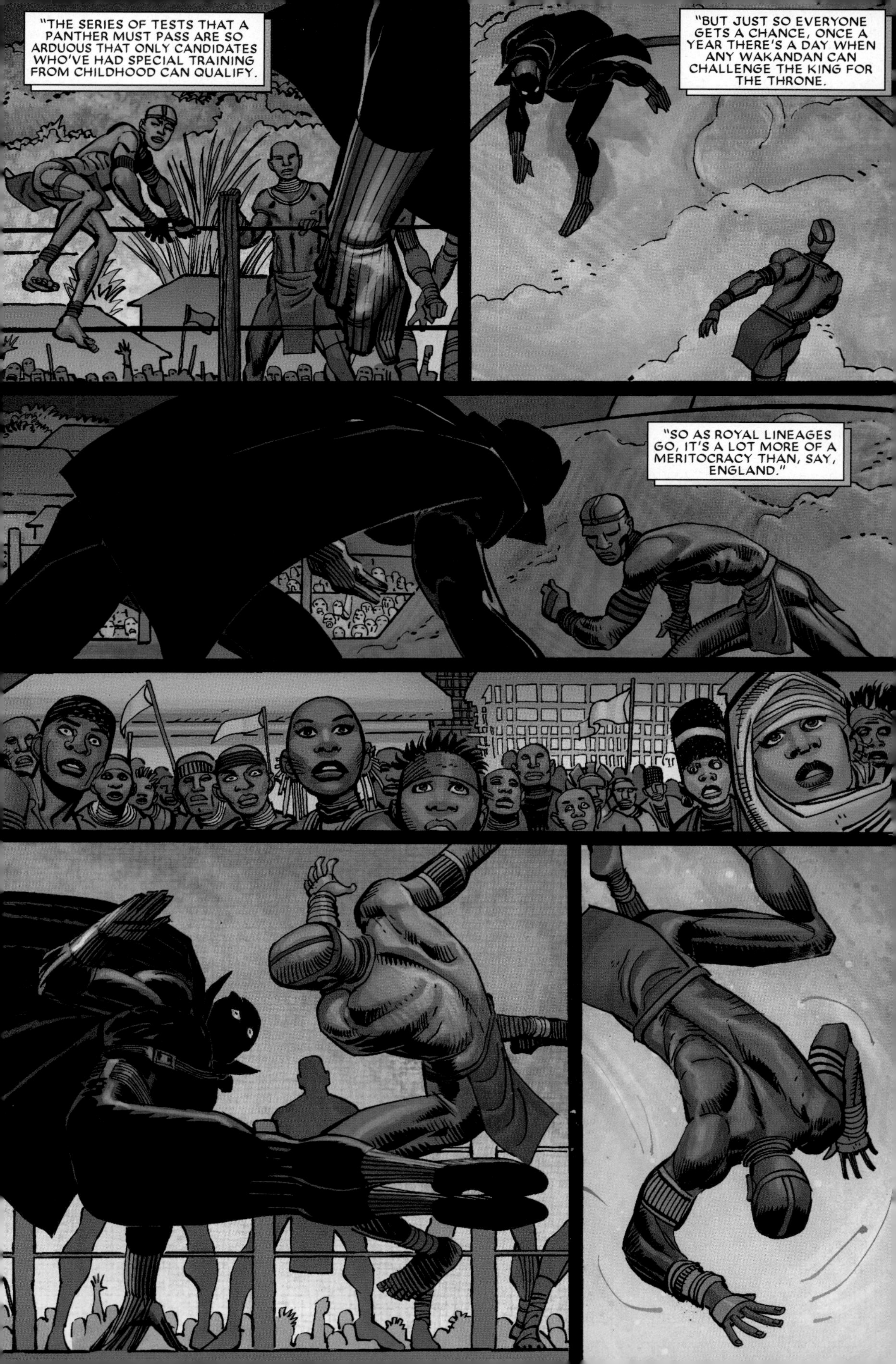
"THE SERIES OF TESTS THAT A PANTHER MUST PASS ARE SO ARDUOUS THAT ONLY CANDIDATES WHO'VE HAD SPECIAL TRAINING FROM CHILDHOOD CAN QUALIFY.
"BUT JUST SO EVERYONE GETS A CHANCE, ONCE A YEAR THERE'S A DAY WHEN ANY WAKANDAN CAN CHALLENGE THE KING FOR THE THRONE.
"SO AS ROYAL LINEAGES GO, IT'S A LOT MORE OF A MERITOCRACY THAN, SAY, ENGLAND."

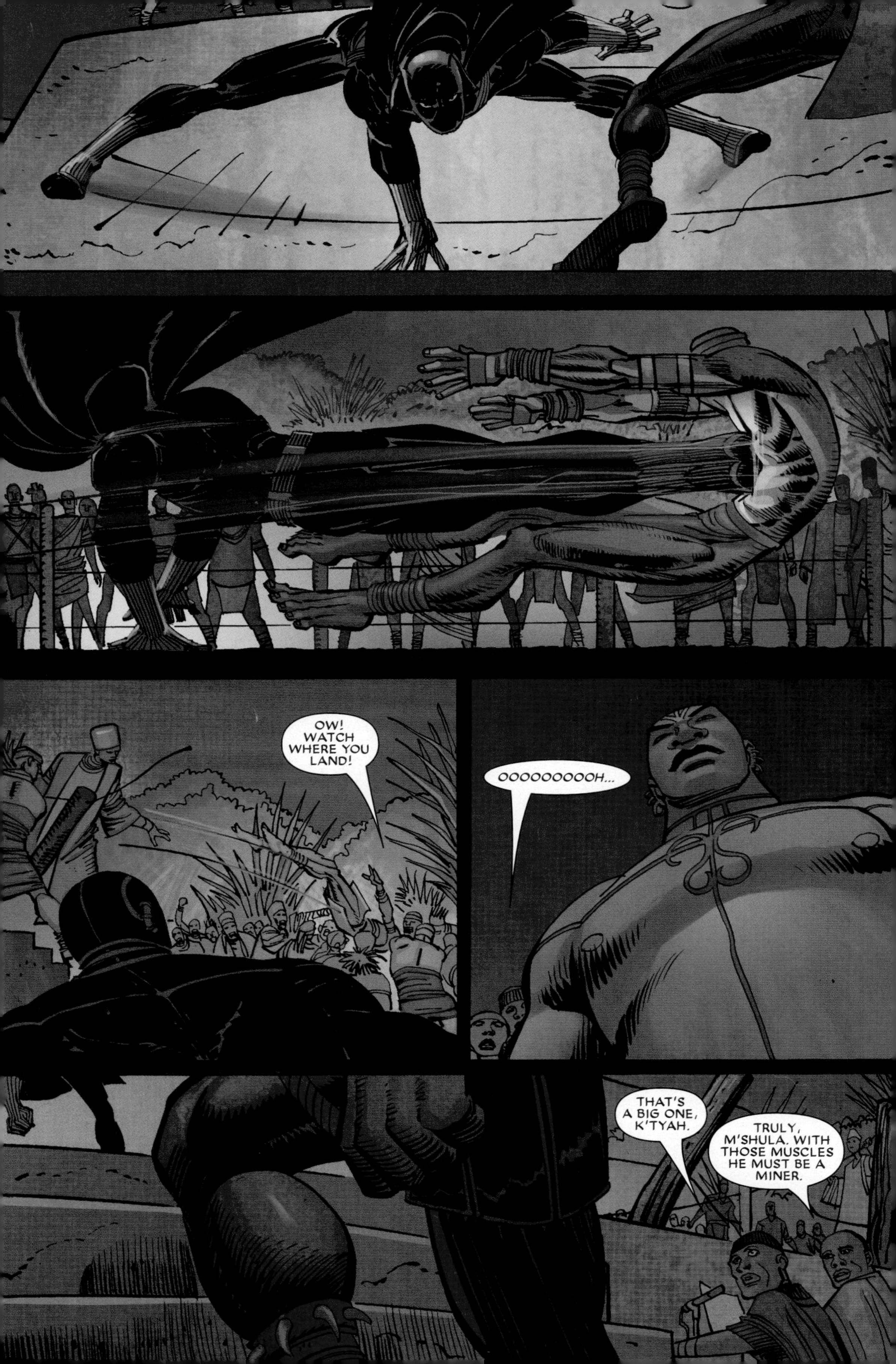
OW! WATCH WHERE YOU LAND!
OOOOOOOOOH...
THAT'S A BIG ONE, K'TYAH.
TRULY, M'SHULA. WITH THOSE MUSCLES HE MUST BE A MINER.

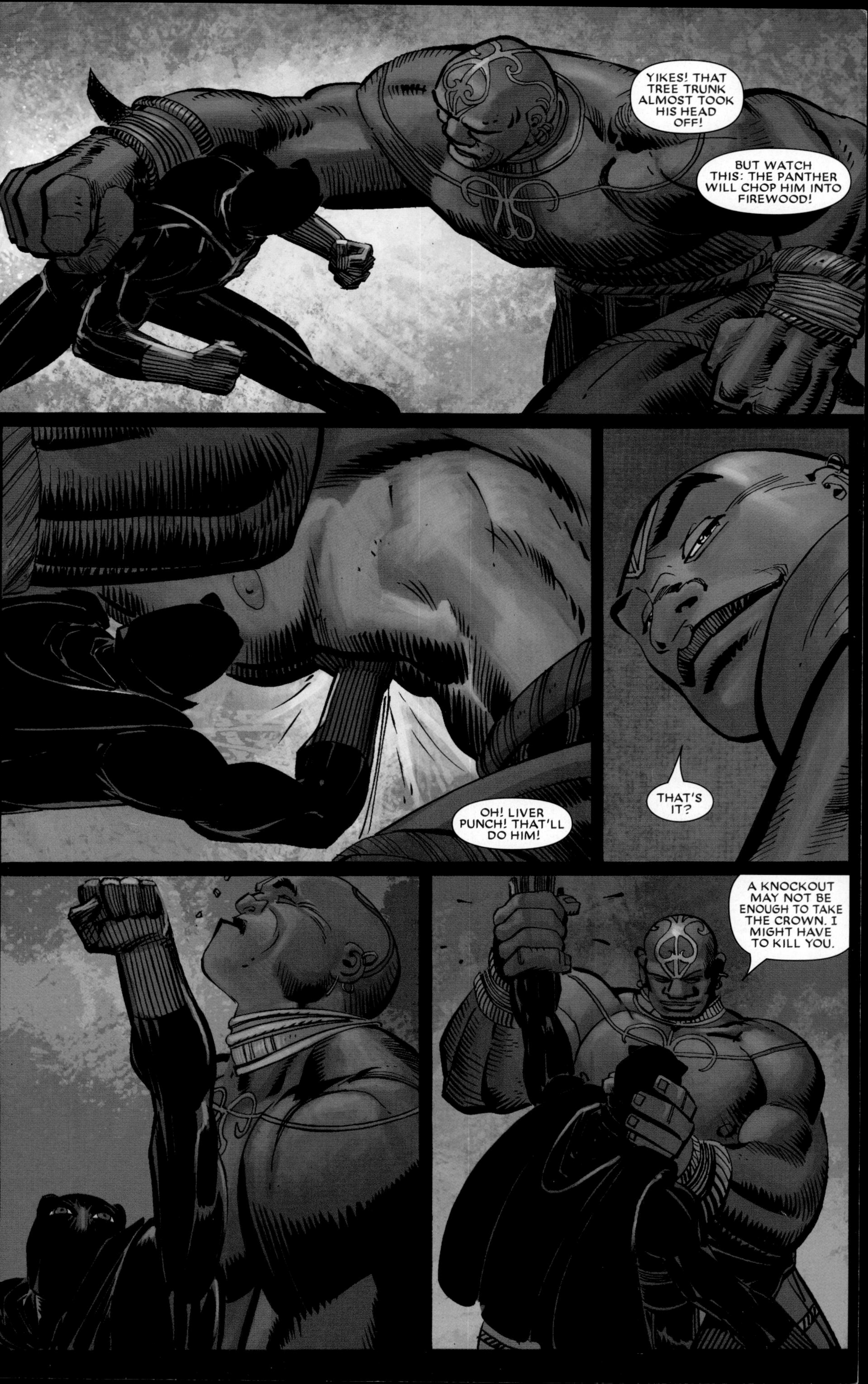
YIKES! THAT TREE TRUNK ALMOST TOOK HIS HEAD OFF!
BUT WATCH THIS: THE PANTHER WILL CHOP HIM INTO FIREWOOD!
OH! LIVER PUNCH! THAT'LL DO HIM!
THAT'S IT?
A KNOCKOUT MAY NOT BE ENOUGH TO TAKE THE CROWN. I MIGHT HAVE TO KILL YOU.

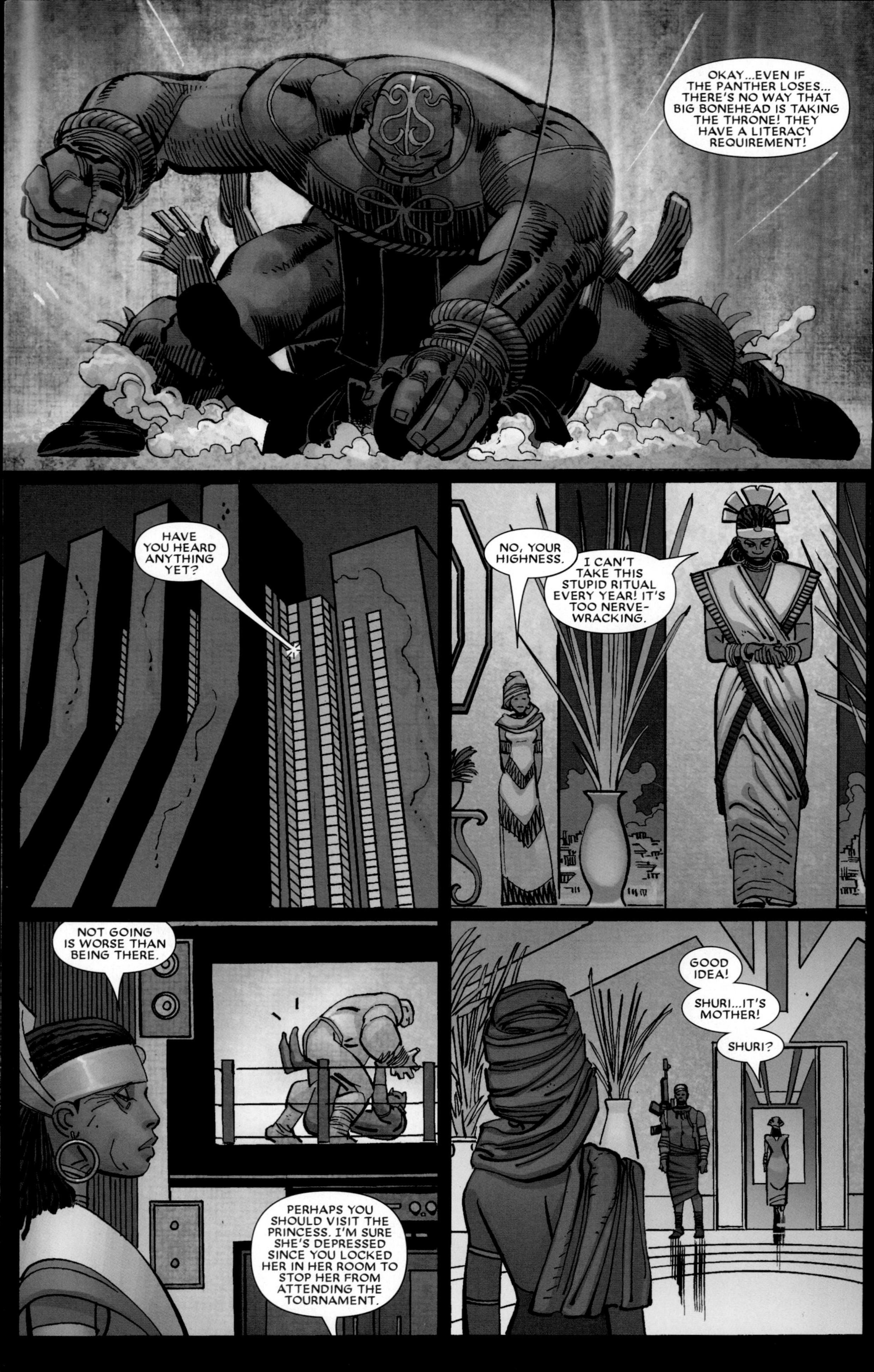
OKAY...EVEN IF THE PANTHER LOSES... THERE'S NO WAY THAT BIG BONEHEAD IS TAKING THE THRONE! THEY HAVE A LITERACY REQUIREMENT!
HAVE YOU HEARD ANYTHING YET?
NO, YOUR HIGHNESS.
I CAN'T TAKE THIS STUPID RITUAL EVERY YEAR! IT'S TOO NERVE-WRACKING.
NOT GOING IS WORSE THAN BEING THERE.
PERHAPS YOU SHOULD VISIT THE PRINCESS. I'M SURE SHE'S DEPRESSED SINCE YOU LOCKED HER IN HER ROOM TO STOP HER FROM ATTENDING THE TOURNAMENT.
GOOD IDEA!
SHURI...IT'S MOTHER!
SHURI?

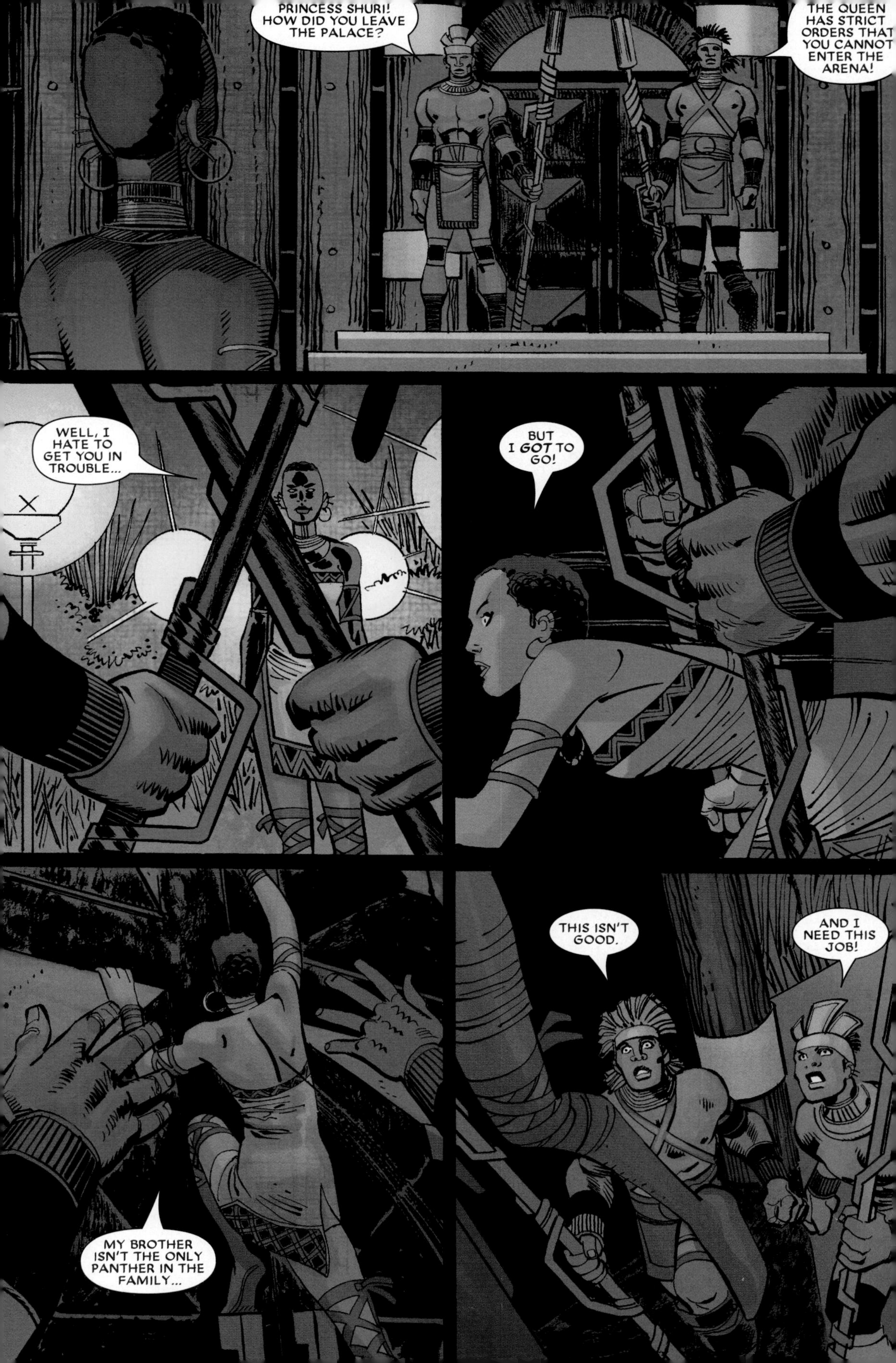
PRINCESS SHURI! HOW DID YOU LEAVE THE PALACE?
THE QUEEN HAS STRICT ORDERS THAT YOU CANNOT ENTER THE ARENA!
WELL, I HATE TO GET YOU IN TROUBLE...
BUT I GOT TO GO!
MY BROTHER ISN'T THE ONLY PANTHER IN THE FAMILY...
THIS ISN'T GOOD.
AND I NEED THIS JOB!

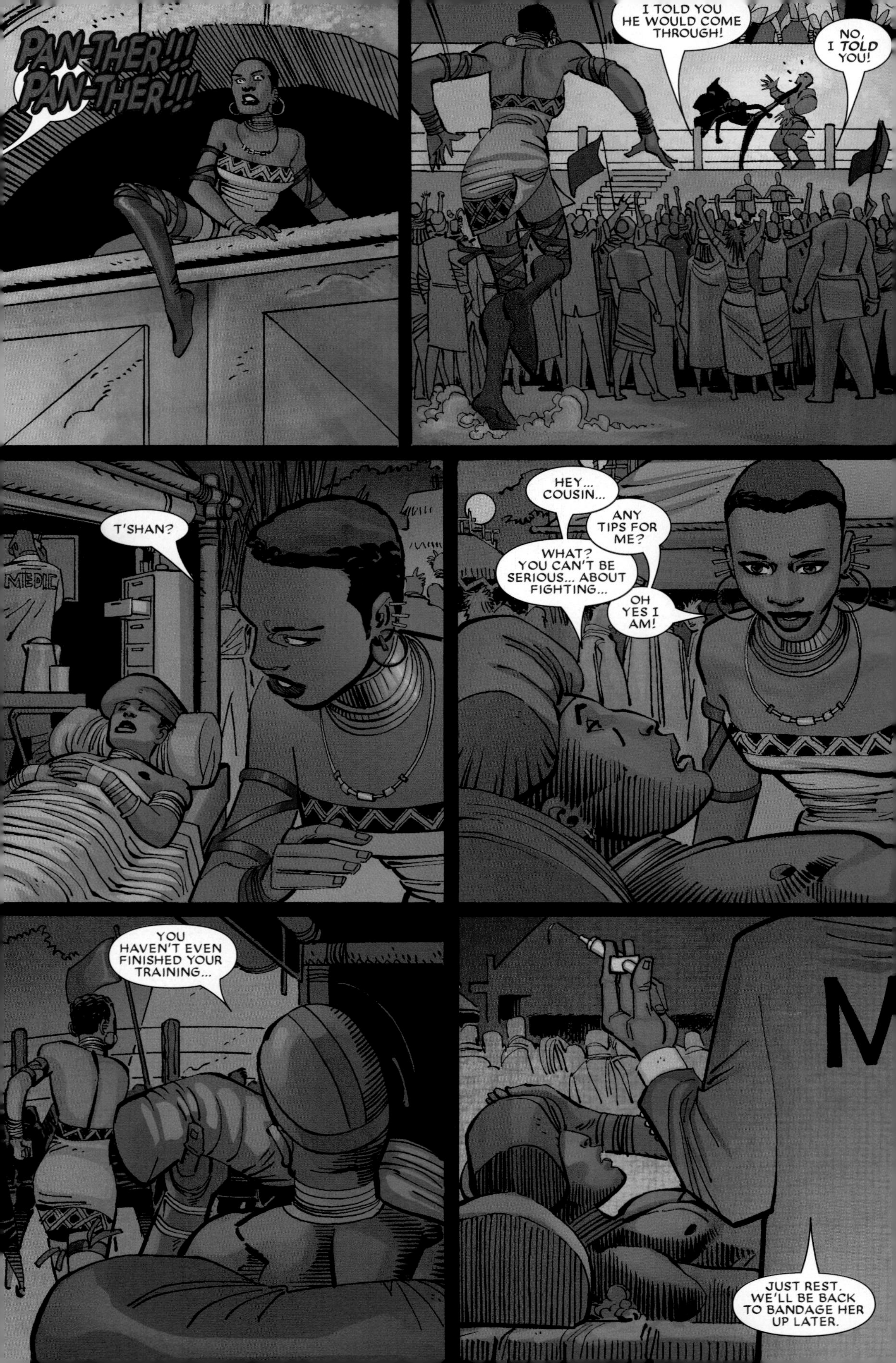
PAN-THER!!! PAN-THER!!!
I TOLD YOU HE WOULD COME THROUGH!
NO, I *TOLD* YOU!
T'SHAN?
MEDIC
HEY... COUSIN...
ANY TIPS FOR ME?
WHAT? YOU CAN'T BE SERIOUS... ABOUT FIGHTING...
OH YES I AM!
YOU HAVEN'T EVEN FINISHED YOUR TRAINING...
JUST REST. WE'LL BE BACK TO BANDAGE HER UP LATER.

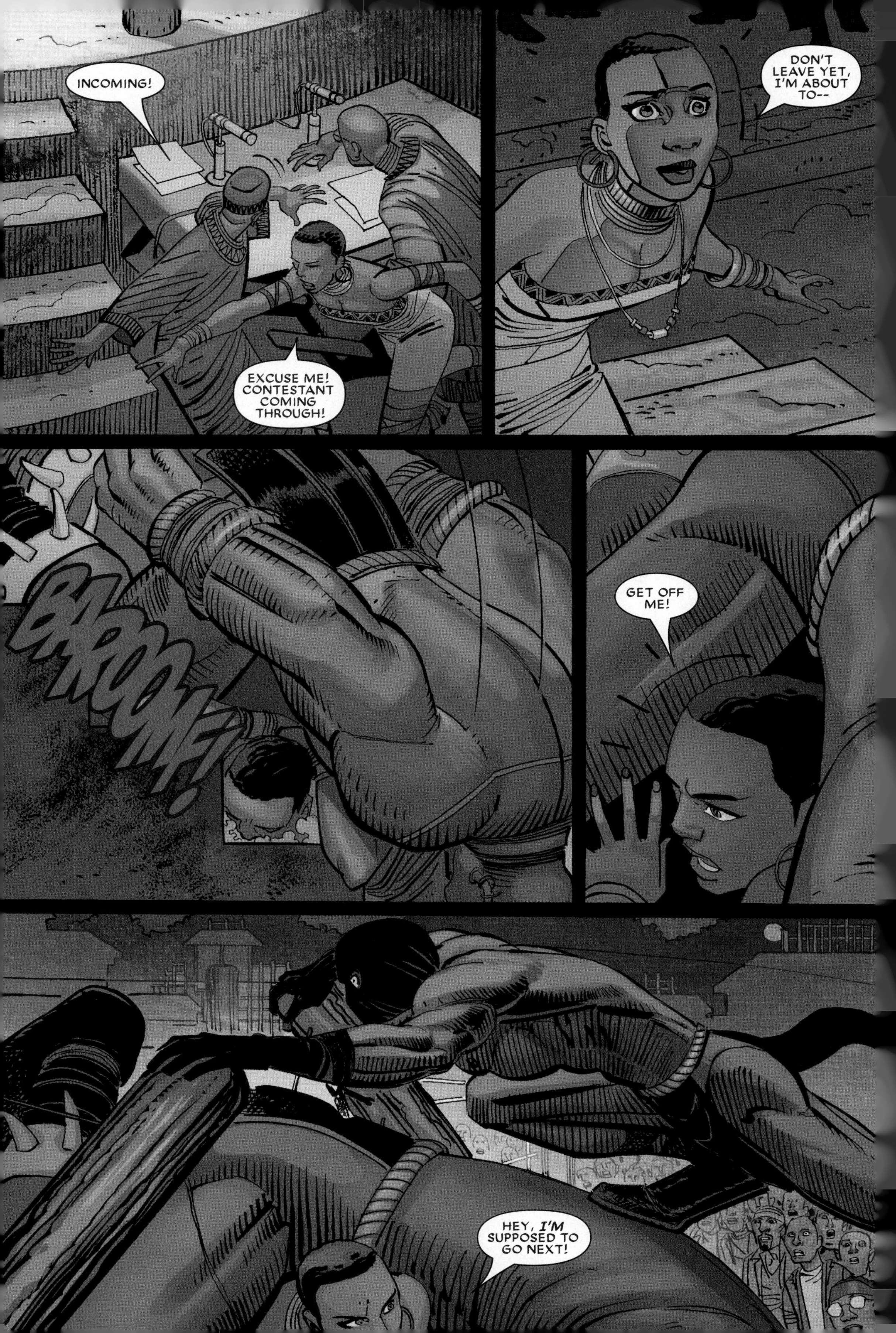
INCOMING!
EXCUSE ME! CONTESTANT COMING THROUGH!
DON'T LEAVE YET, I'M ABOUT TO--
BROOM!
GET OFF ME!
HEY, *I'M* SUPPOSED TO GO NEXT!

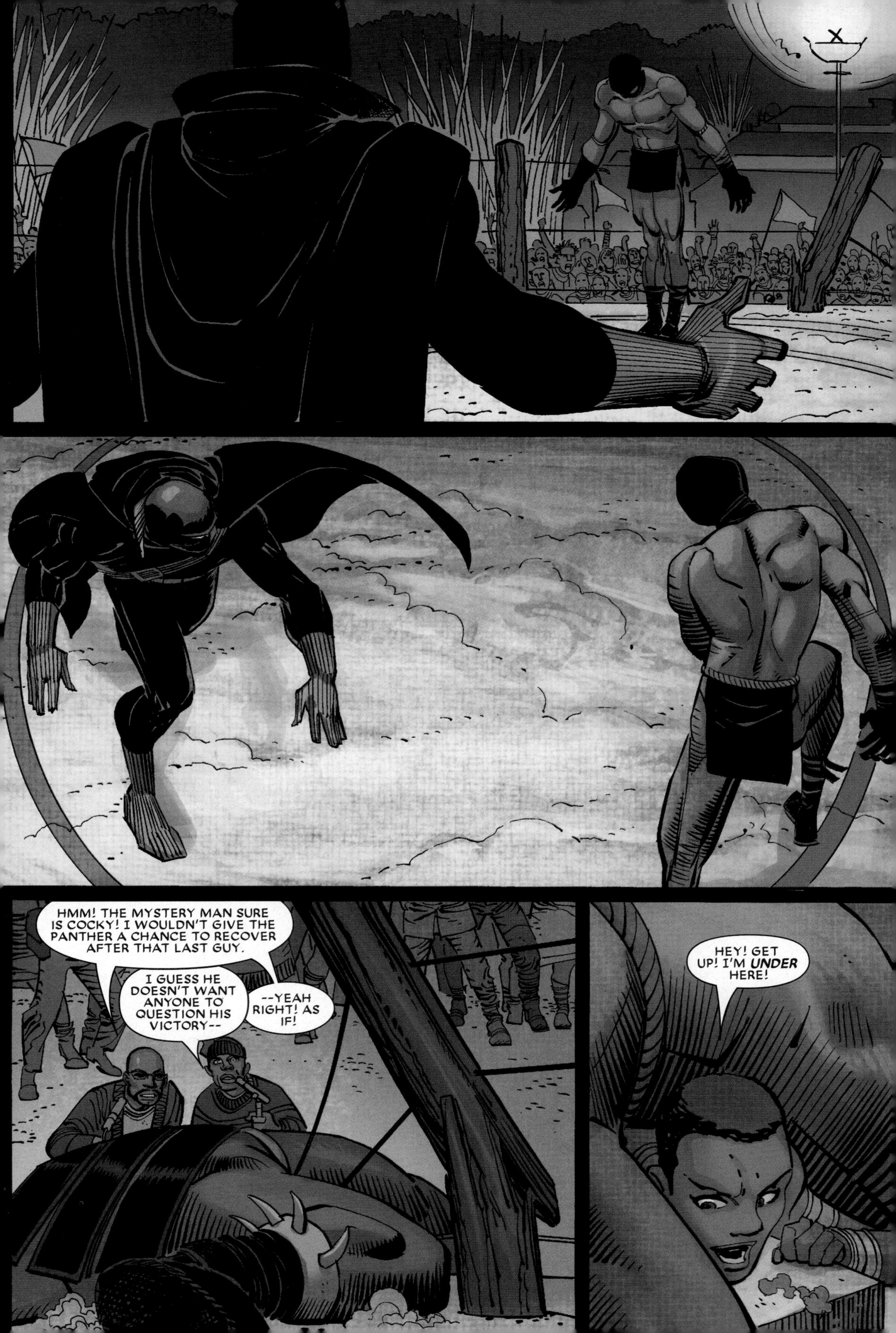
HMM! THE MYSTERY MAN SURE IS COCKY! I WOULDN'T GIVE THE PANTHER A CHANCE TO RECOVER AFTER THAT LAST GUY.
I GUESS HE DOESN'T WANT ANYONE TO QUESTION HIS VICTORY--
--YEAH RIGHT! AS IF!
HEY! GET UP! I'M UNDER HERE!

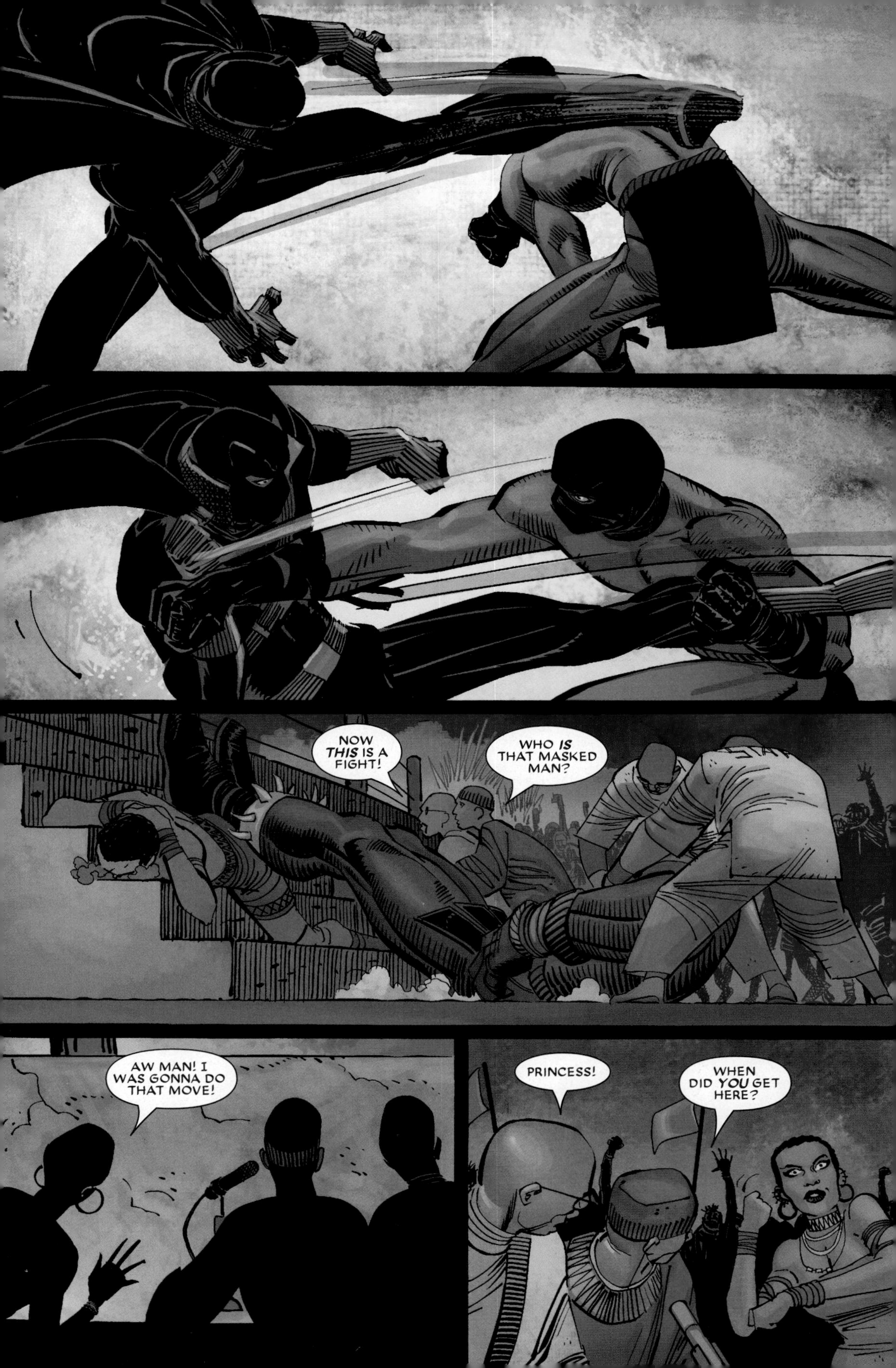
NOW THIS IS A FIGHT!
WHO IS THAT MASKED MAN?
AW MAN! I WAS GONNA DO THAT MOVE!
PRINCESS!
WHEN DID YOU GET HERE?

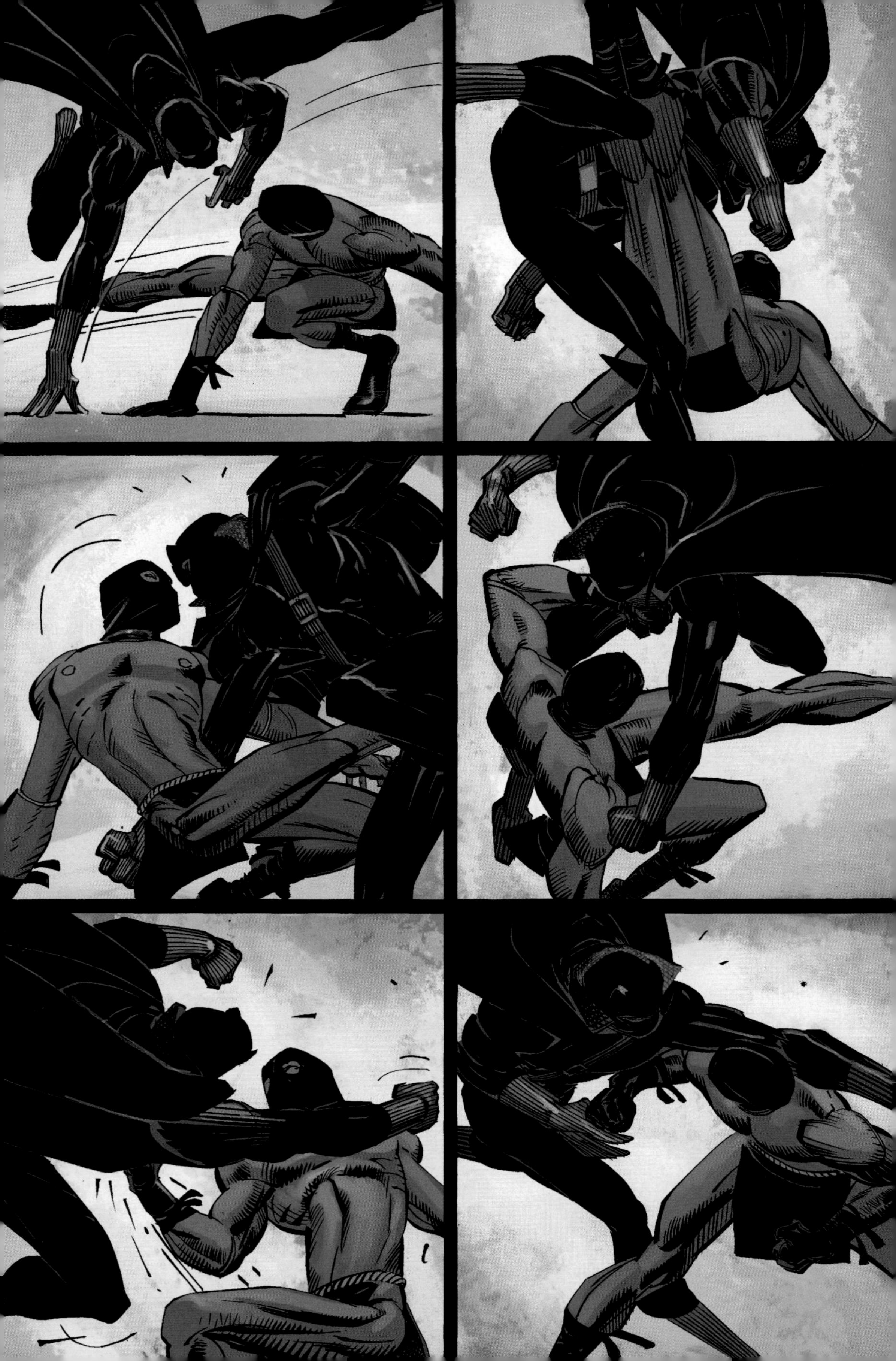

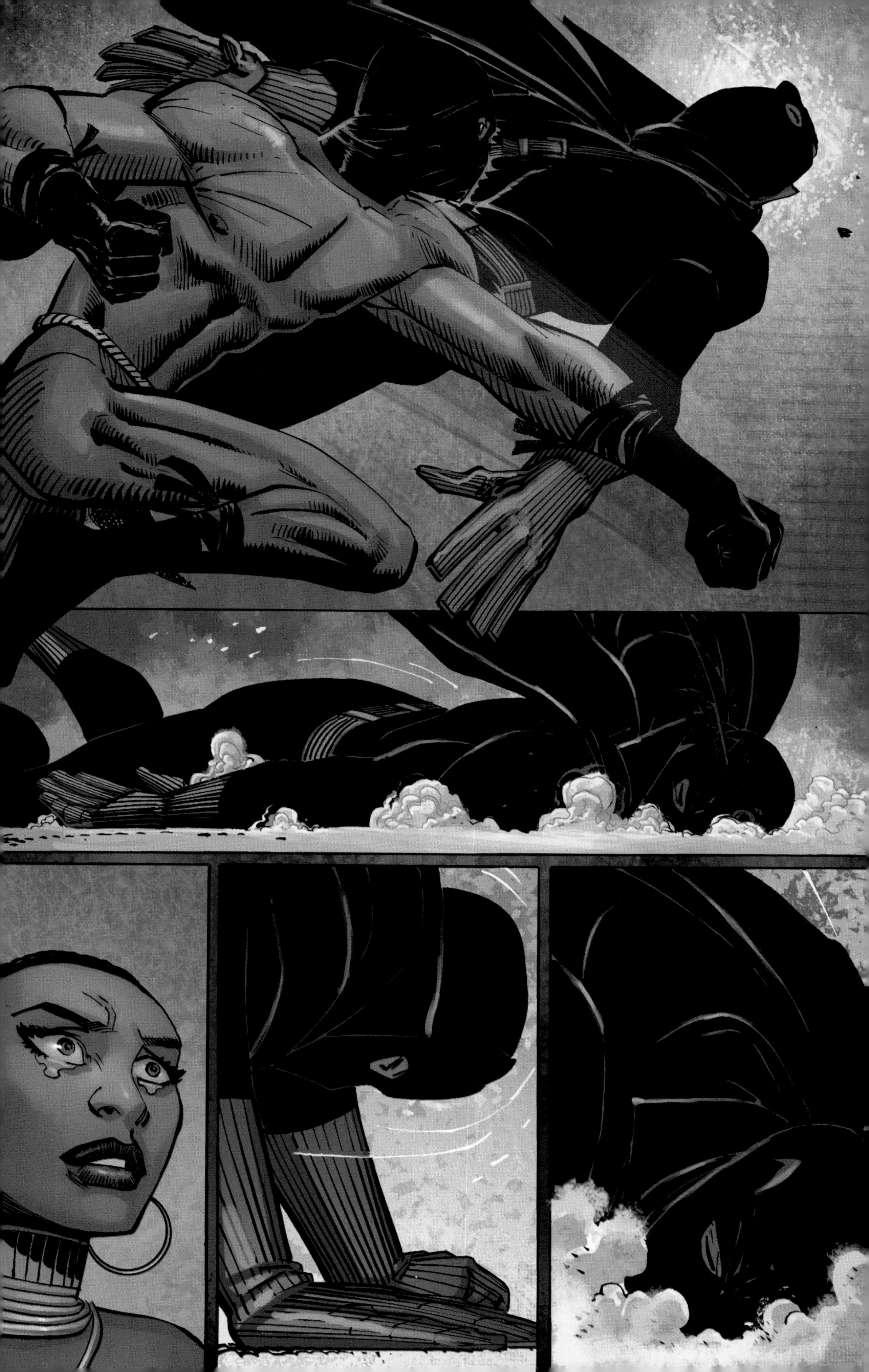

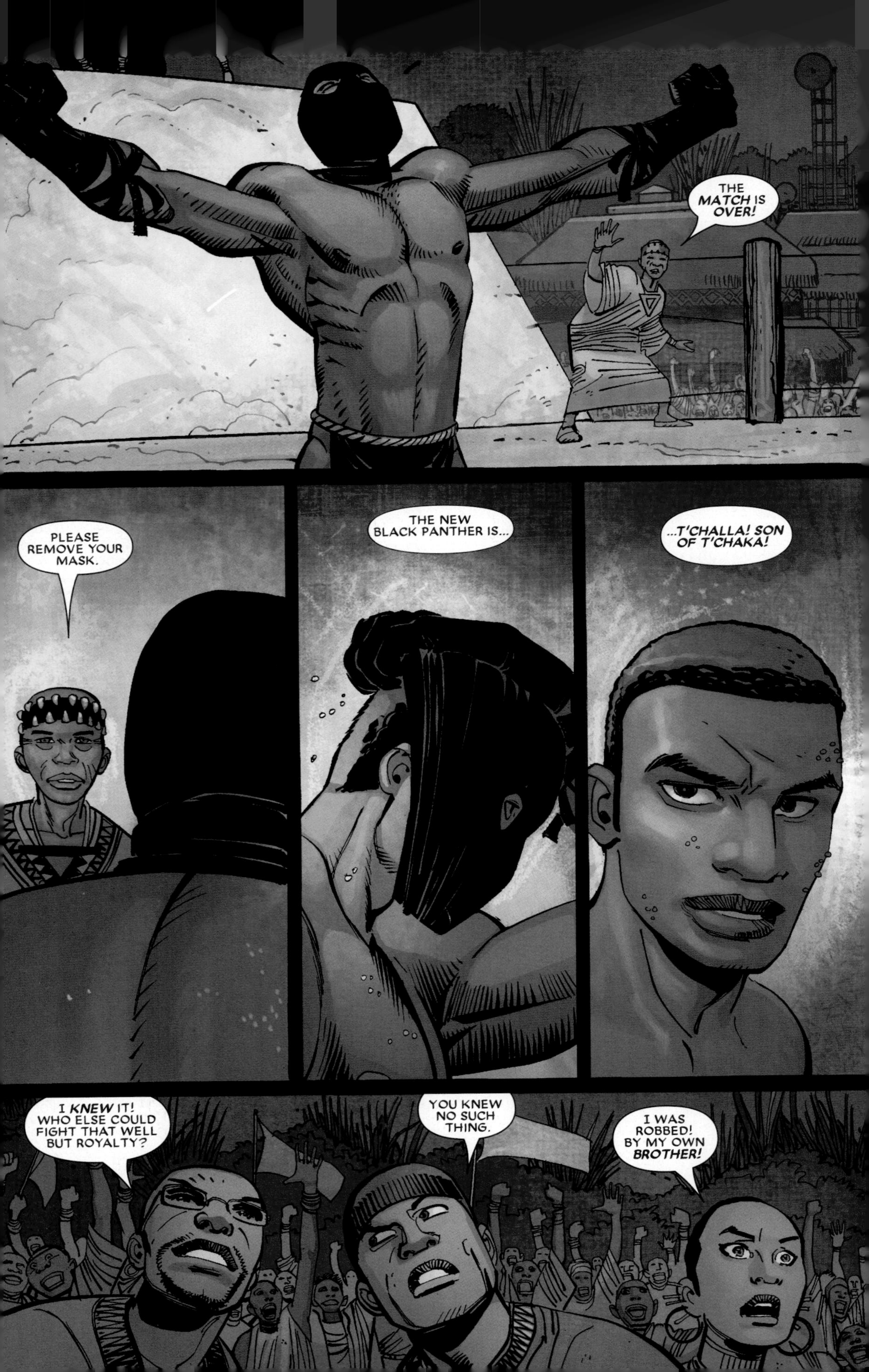

THE MATCH IS OVER!
PLEASE REMOVE YOUR MASK.
THE NEW BLACK PANTHER IS...
...T'CHALLA! SON OF T'CHAKA!
I KNEW IT! WHO ELSE COULD FIGHT THAT WELL BUT ROYALTY?
YOU KNEW NO SUCH THING.
I WAS ROBBED! BY MY OWN BROTHER!

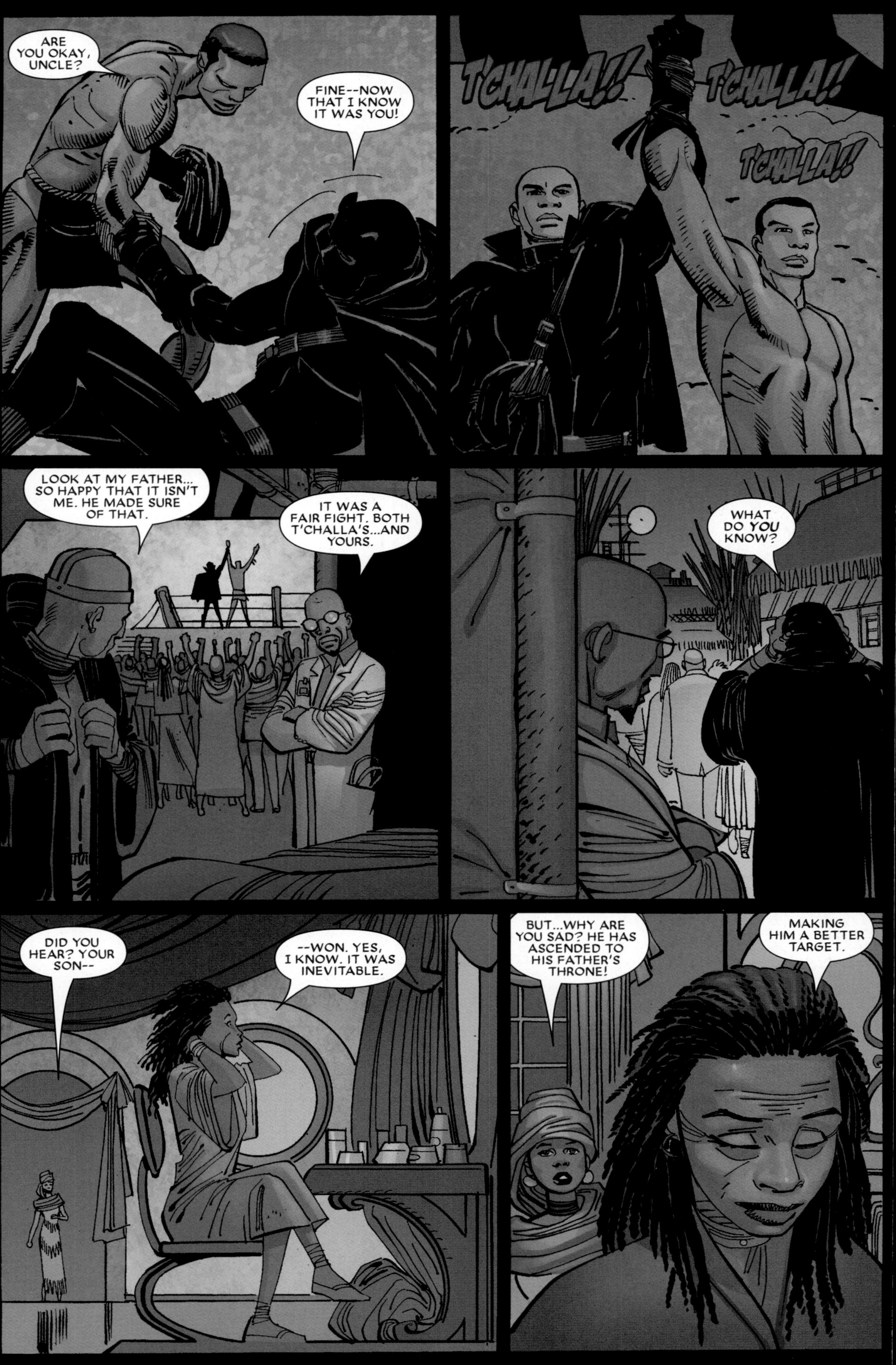
ARE YOU OKAY, UNCLE?
FINE--NOW THAT I KNOW IT WAS YOU!
T'CHALLA!!
T'CHALLA!!
T'CHALLA!!
LOOK AT MY FATHER... SO HAPPY THAT IT ISN'T ME. HE MADE SURE OF THAT.
IT WAS A FAIR FIGHT. BOTH T'CHALLA'S...AND YOURS.
WHAT DO *YOU* KNOW?
DID YOU HEAR? YOUR SON--
--WON. YES, I KNOW. IT WAS INEVITABLE.
BUT...WHY ARE YOU SAD? HE HAS ASCENDED TO HIS FATHER'S THRONE!
MAKING HIM A BETTER TARGET.

...SO WHAT WE'VE GOT HERE IS A HIGHLY MILITARISTIC CULTURE WITH NO TIES TO THE UNITED STATES....

THEY'RE A ROGUE STATE!

BEFORE YOU GO ADDING THEM TO THE "AXIS OF EVIL," I SHOULD POINT OUT THAT THEY HAVE NEVER INVADED *ANYONE*. THE ONLY TIME THEY'VE TAKEN HOSTILE ACTION IS DEFENDING THEIR OWN BORDERS.

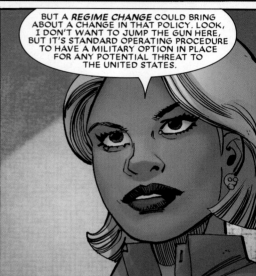

BUT A *REGIME CHANGE* COULD BRING ABOUT A CHANGE IN THAT POLICY. LOOK, I DON'T WANT TO JUMP THE GUN HERE, BUT IT'S STANDARD OPERATING PROCEDURE TO HAVE A MILITARY OPTION IN PLACE FOR ANY POTENTIAL THREAT TO THE UNITED STATES.

I CERTAINLY DON'T WANT TO SPEAK IN THE PLACE OF THE RECENTLY DEPARTED GENERAL, BUT WITH OUR MILITARY FORCES STRETCHED ALL OVER THE MIDDLE EAST, DO WE EVEN HAVE THE RESOURCES--?

YOU'RE RIGHT, MR. ROSS, THAT IS *NOT* YOUR AREA OF EXPERTISE. YOU JUST KEEP PROVIDING ACCURATE INFORMATION.

BESIDES, THIS CONFLICT WOULD NOT BE APPROPRIATE FOR CONVENTIONAL FORCES. THIS IS A JOB FOR SPECIAL FORCES.

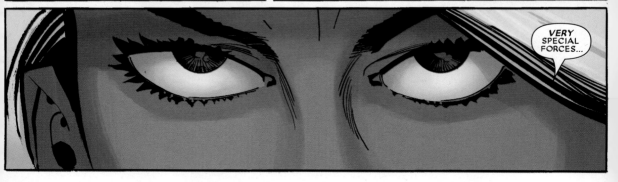

*VERY* SPECIAL FORCES...

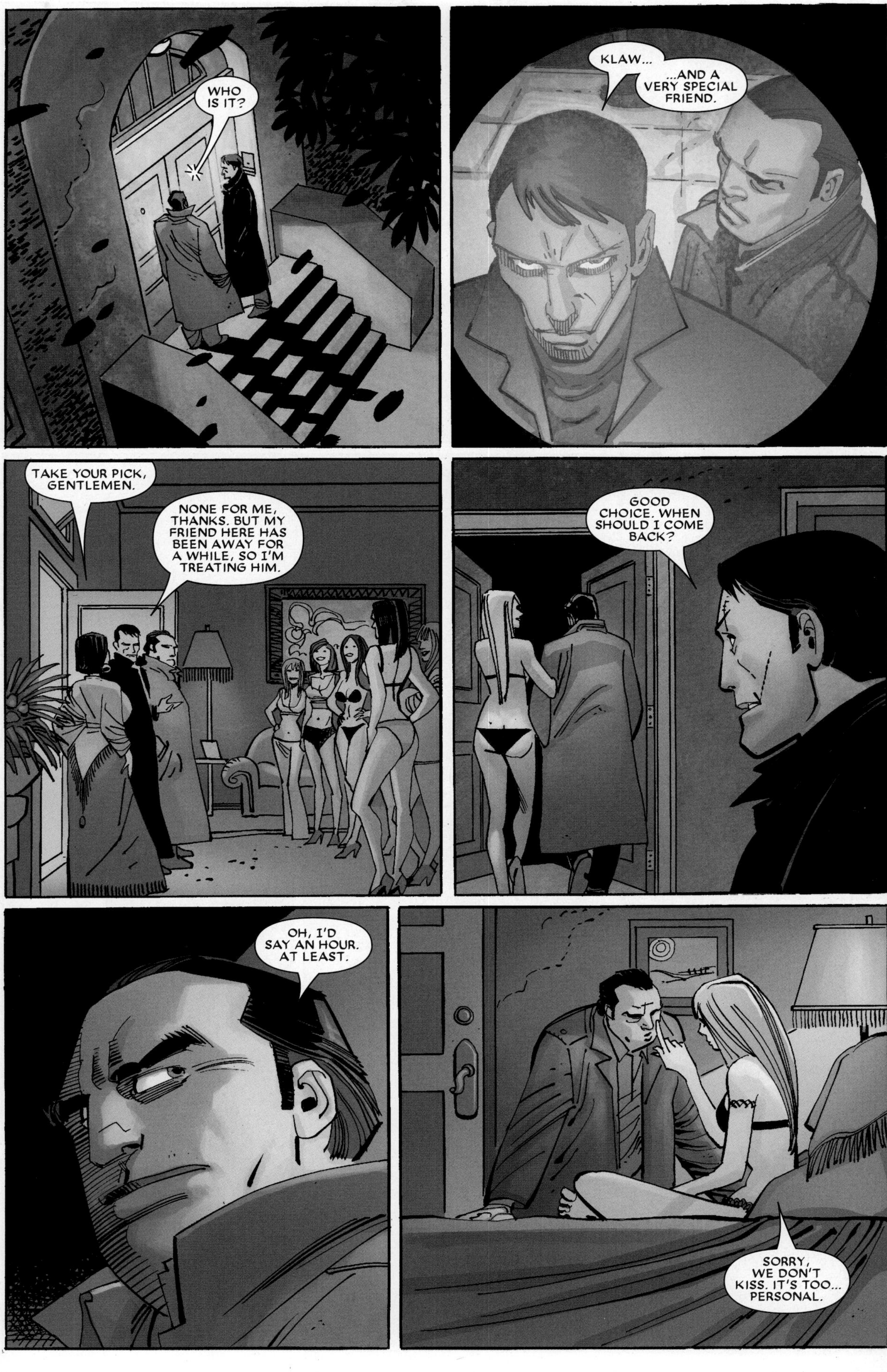
WHO IS IT?
KLAW...
...AND A VERY SPECIAL FRIEND.
TAKE YOUR PICK, GENTLEMEN.
NONE FOR ME, THANKS. BUT MY FRIEND HERE HAS BEEN AWAY FOR A WHILE, SO I'M TREATING HIM.
GOOD CHOICE. WHEN SHOULD I COME BACK?
OH, I'D SAY AN HOUR. AT LEAST.
SORRY, WE DON'T KISS. IT'S TOO... PERSONAL.

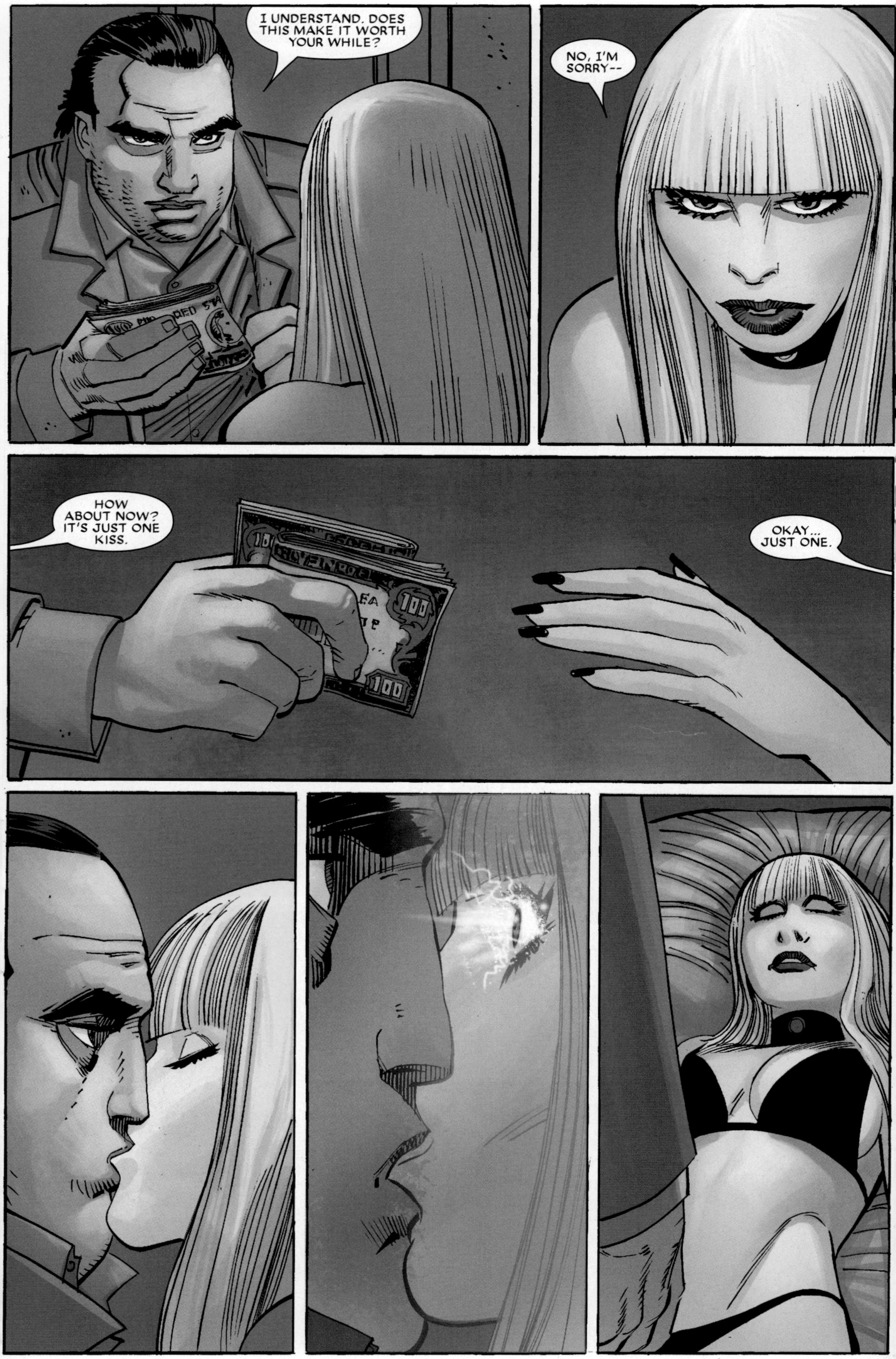
I UNDERSTAND. DOES THIS MAKE IT WORTH YOUR WHILE?
NO, I'M SORRY--
HOW ABOUT NOW? IT'S JUST ONE KISS.
OKAY... JUST ONE.

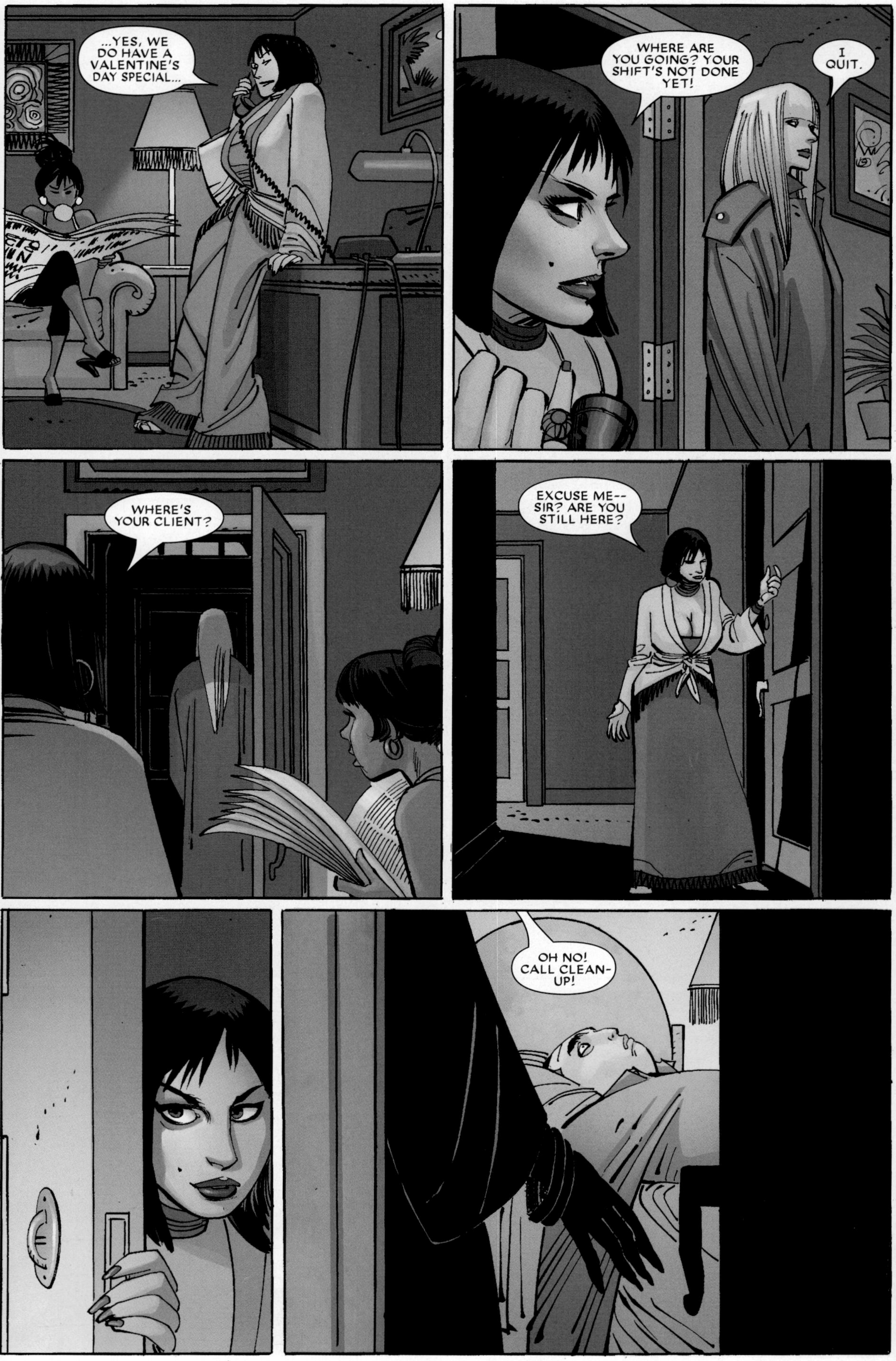
...YES, WE DO HAVE A VALENTINE'S DAY SPECIAL...
WHERE ARE YOU GOING? YOUR SHIFT'S NOT DONE YET!
I QUIT.
WHERE'S YOUR CLIENT?
EXCUSE ME-- SIR? ARE YOU STILL HERE?
OH NO! CALL CLEAN-UP!

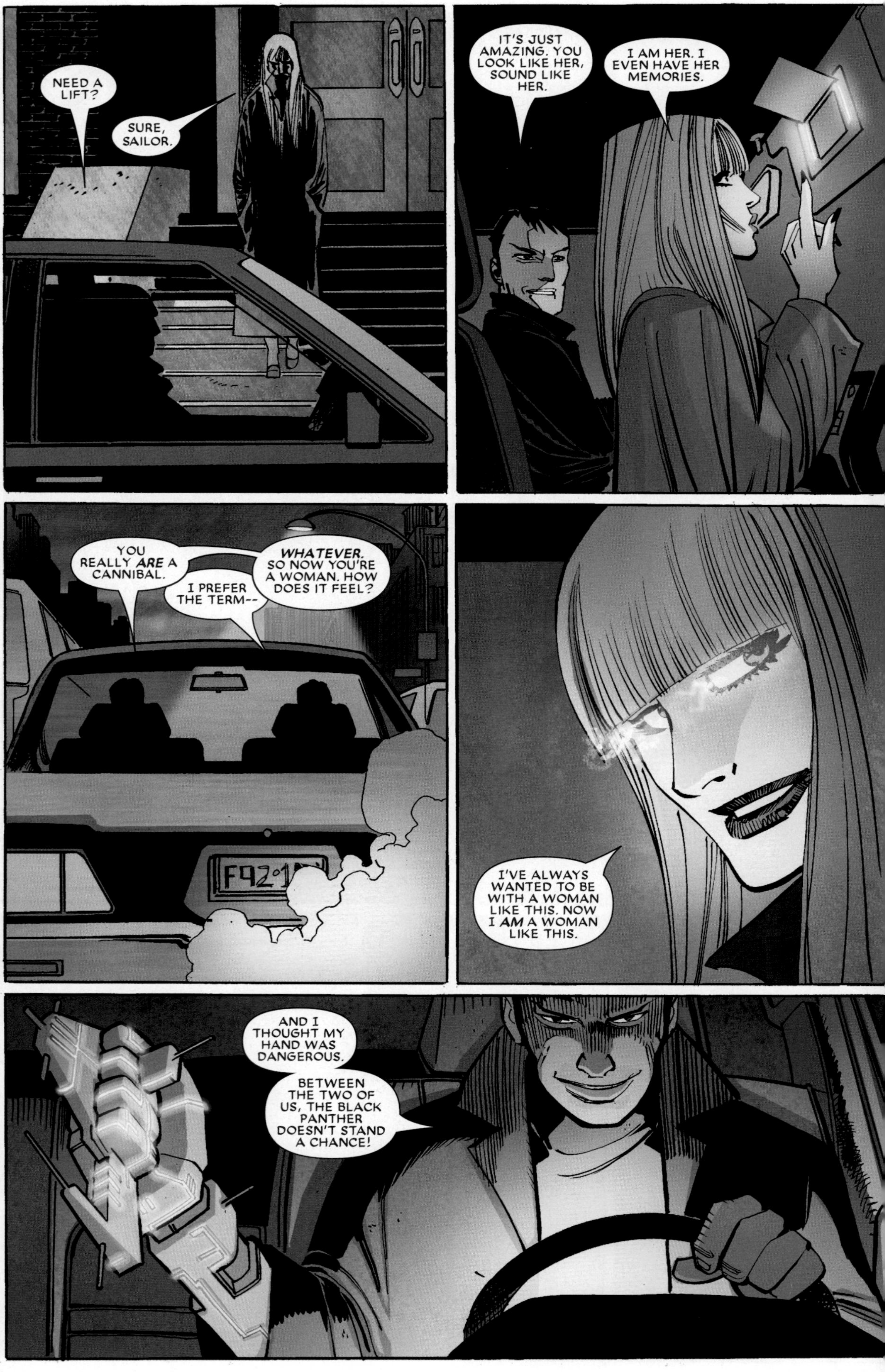
NEED A LIFT?
SURE, SAILOR.
IT'S JUST AMAZING. YOU LOOK LIKE HER, SOUND LIKE HER.
I AM HER. I EVEN HAVE HER MEMORIES.
YOU REALLY ARE A CANNIBAL.
I PREFER THE TERM--
WHATEVER. SO NOW YOU'RE A WOMAN. HOW DOES IT FEEL?
I'VE ALWAYS WANTED TO BE WITH A WOMAN LIKE THIS. NOW I AM A WOMAN LIKE THIS.
AND I THOUGHT MY HAND WAS DANGEROUS.
BETWEEN THE TWO OF US, THE BLACK PANTHER DOESN'T STAND A CHANCE!

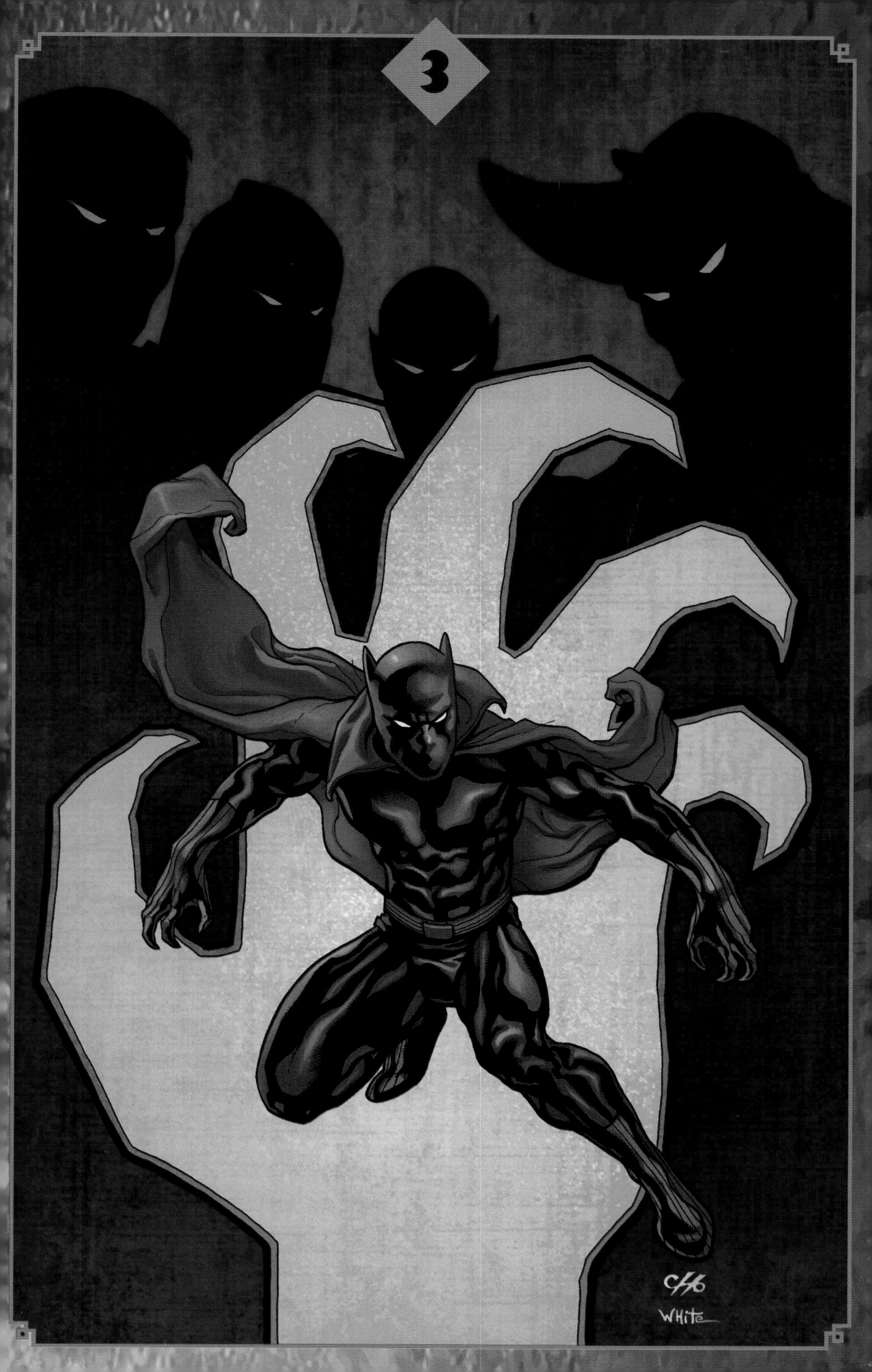
3
WHITE

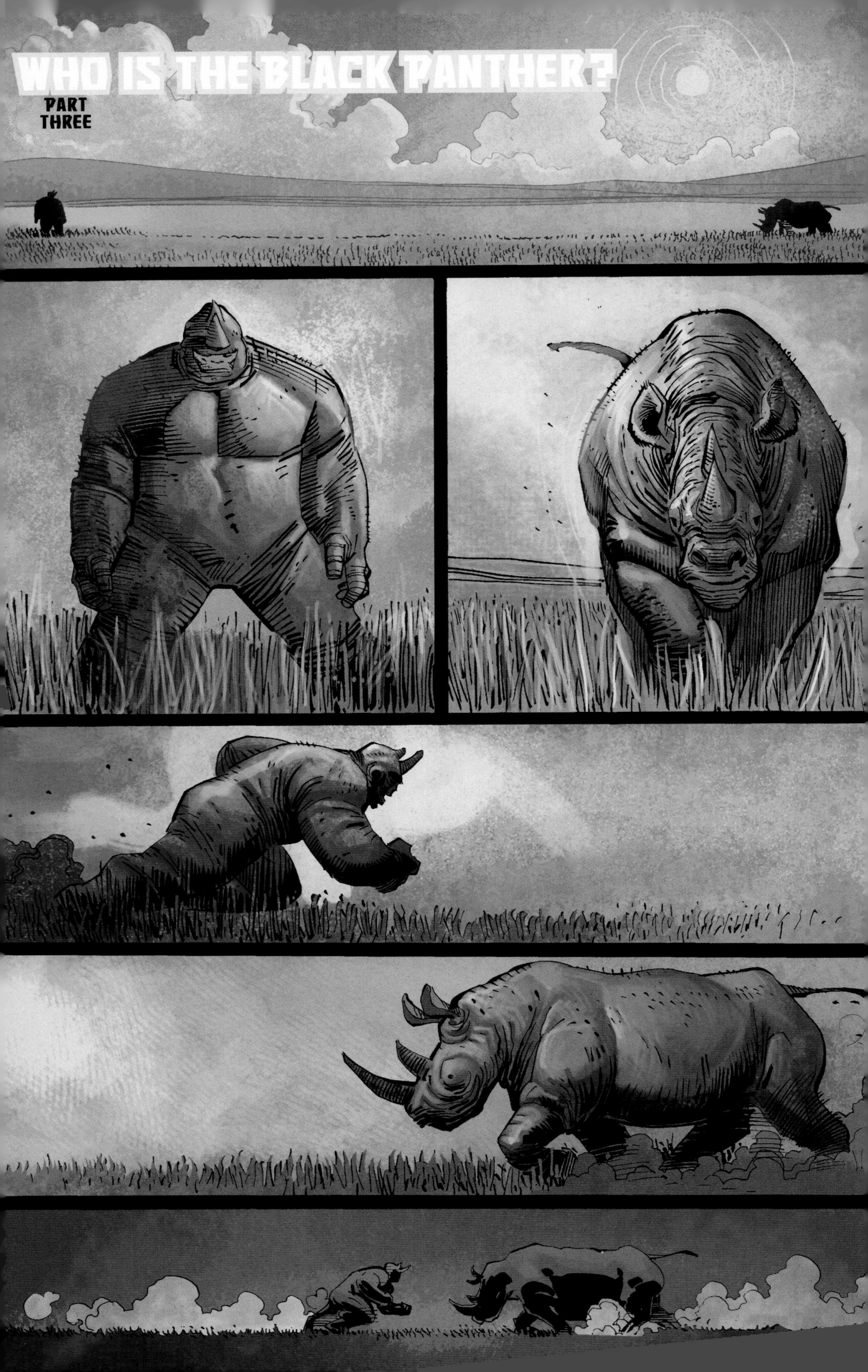
WHO IS THE BLACK PANTHER?
PART THREE

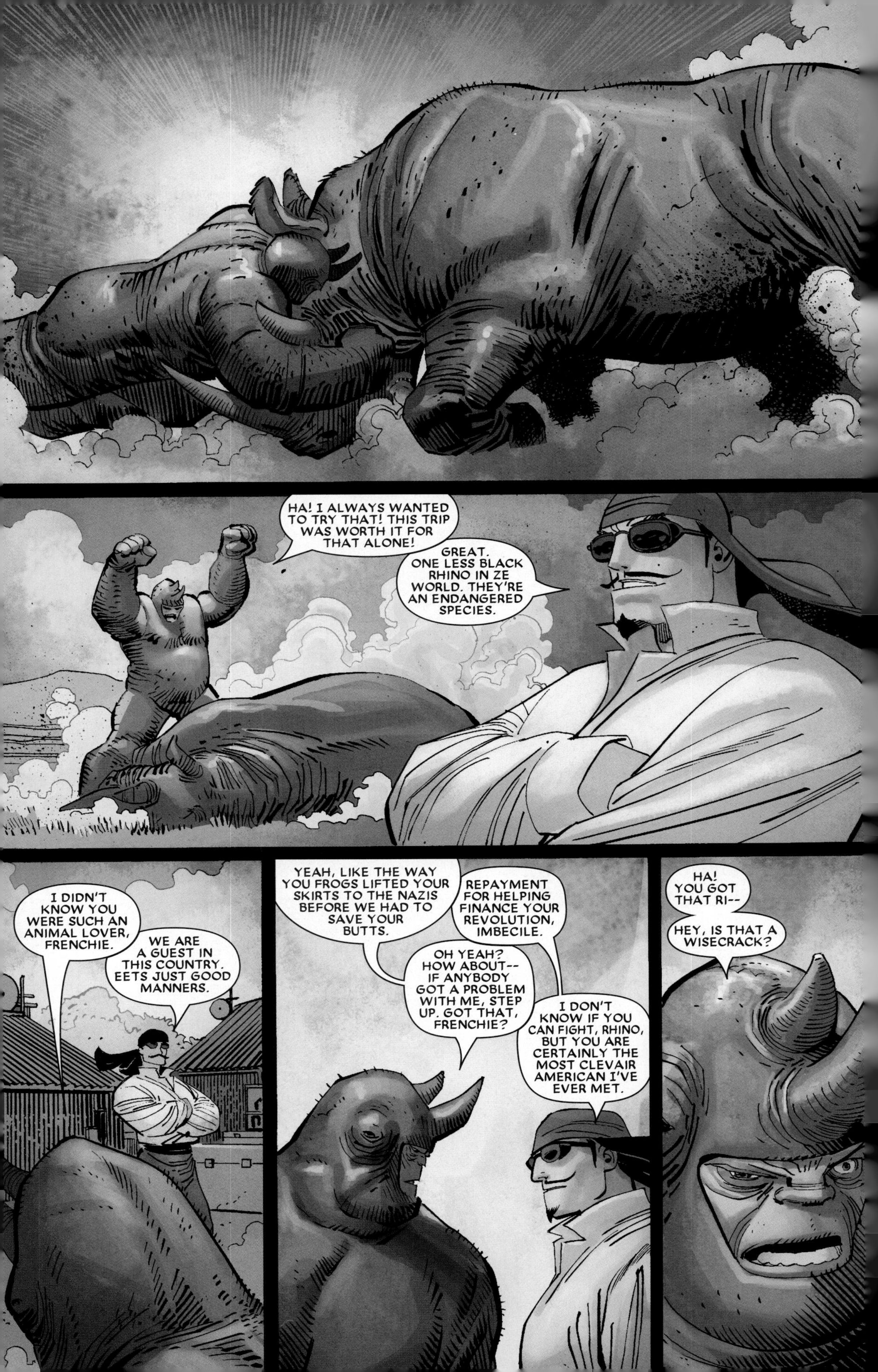
HA! I ALWAYS WANTED TO TRY THAT! THIS TRIP WAS WORTH IT FOR THAT ALONE!
GREAT. ONE LESS BLACK RHINO IN ZE WORLD. THEY'RE AN ENDANGERED SPECIES.
I DIDN'T KNOW YOU WERE SUCH AN ANIMAL LOVER, FRENCHIE.
WE ARE A GUEST IN THIS COUNTRY. EETS JUST GOOD MANNERS.
YEAH, LIKE THE WAY YOU FROGS LIFTED YOUR SKIRTS TO THE NAZIS BEFORE WE HAD TO SAVE YOUR BUTTS.
REPAYMENT FOR HELPING FINANCE YOUR REVOLUTION, IMBECILE.
OH YEAH? HOW ABOUT-- IF ANYBODY GOT A PROBLEM WITH ME, STEP UP. GOT THAT, FRENCHIE?
I DON'T KNOW IF YOU CAN FIGHT, RHINO, BUT YOU ARE CERTAINLY THE MOST CLEVAIR AMERICAN I'VE EVER MET.
HA! YOU GOT THAT RI--
HEY, IS THAT A WISECRACK?

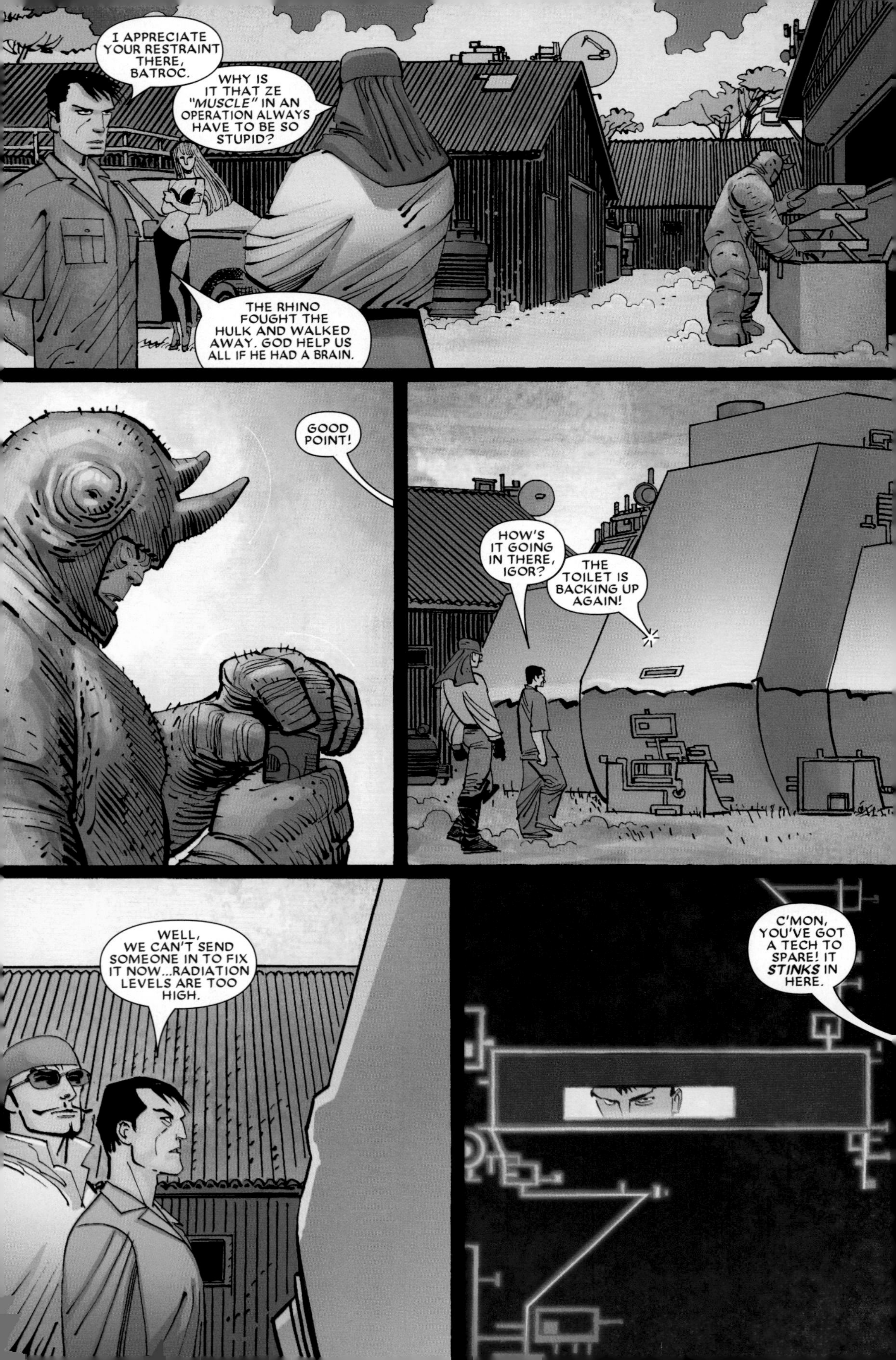
I APPRECIATE YOUR RESTRAINT THERE, BATROC.
WHY IS IT THAT ZE "MUSCLE" IN AN OPERATION ALWAYS HAVE TO BE SO STUPID?
THE RHINO FOUGHT THE HULK AND WALKED AWAY. GOD HELP US ALL IF HE HAD A BRAIN.
GOOD POINT!
HOW'S IT GOING IN THERE, IGOR?
THE TOILET IS BACKING UP AGAIN!
WELL, WE CAN'T SEND SOMEONE IN TO FIX IT NOW...RADIATION LEVELS ARE TOO HIGH.
C'MON, YOU'VE GOT A TECH TO SPARE! IT STINKS IN HERE.

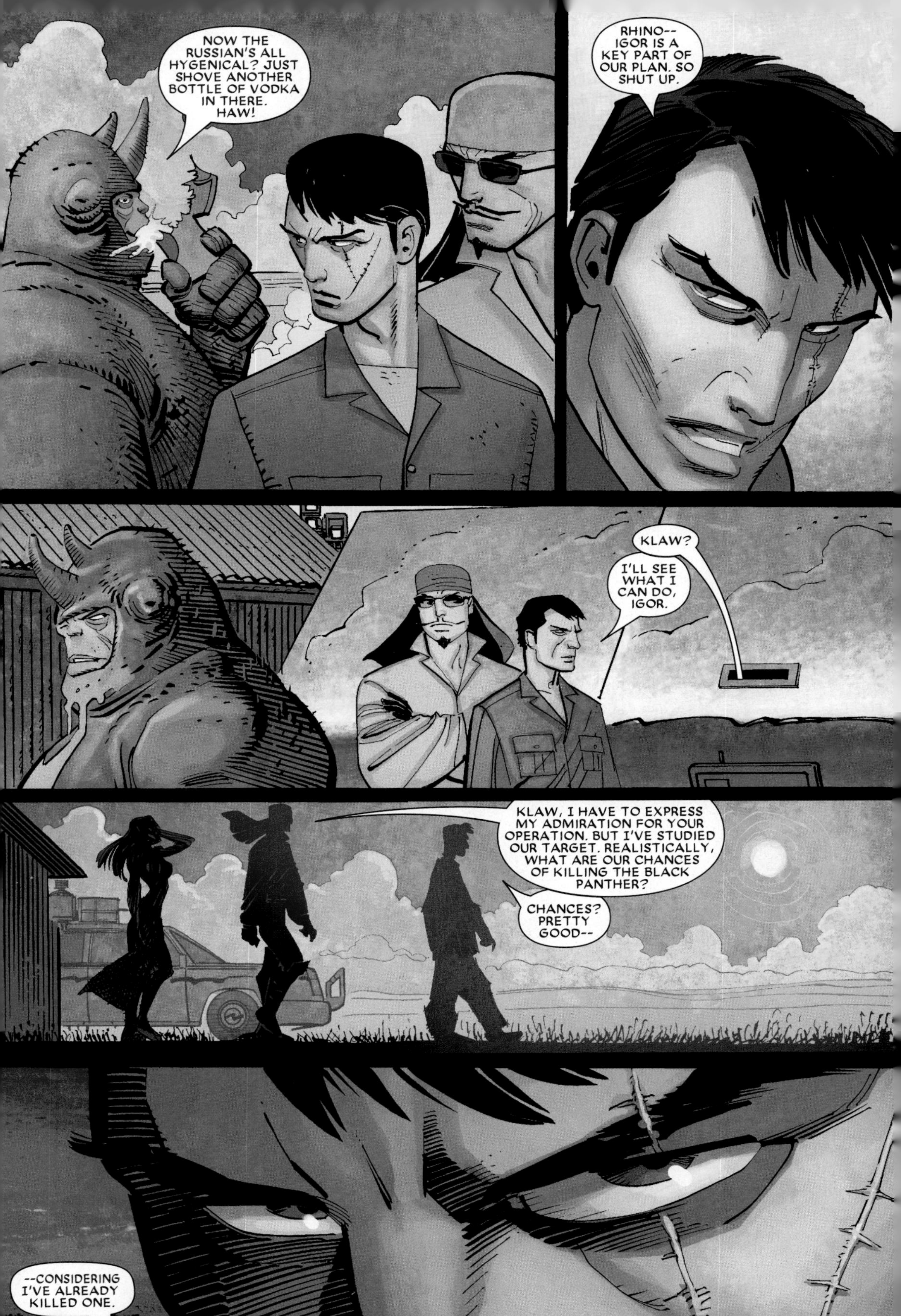
NOW THE RUSSIAN'S ALL HYGENICAL? JUST SHOVE ANOTHER BOTTLE OF VODKA IN THERE. HAW!
RHINO-- IGOR IS A KEY PART OF OUR PLAN. SO SHUT UP.
KLAW?
I'LL SEE WHAT I CAN DO, IGOR.
KLAW, I HAVE TO EXPRESS MY ADMIRATION FOR YOUR OPERATION. BUT I'VE STUDIED OUR TARGET. REALISTICALLY, WHAT ARE OUR CHANCES OF KILLING THE BLACK PANTHER?
CHANCES? PRETTY GOOD--
--CONSIDERING I'VE ALREADY KILLED ONE.

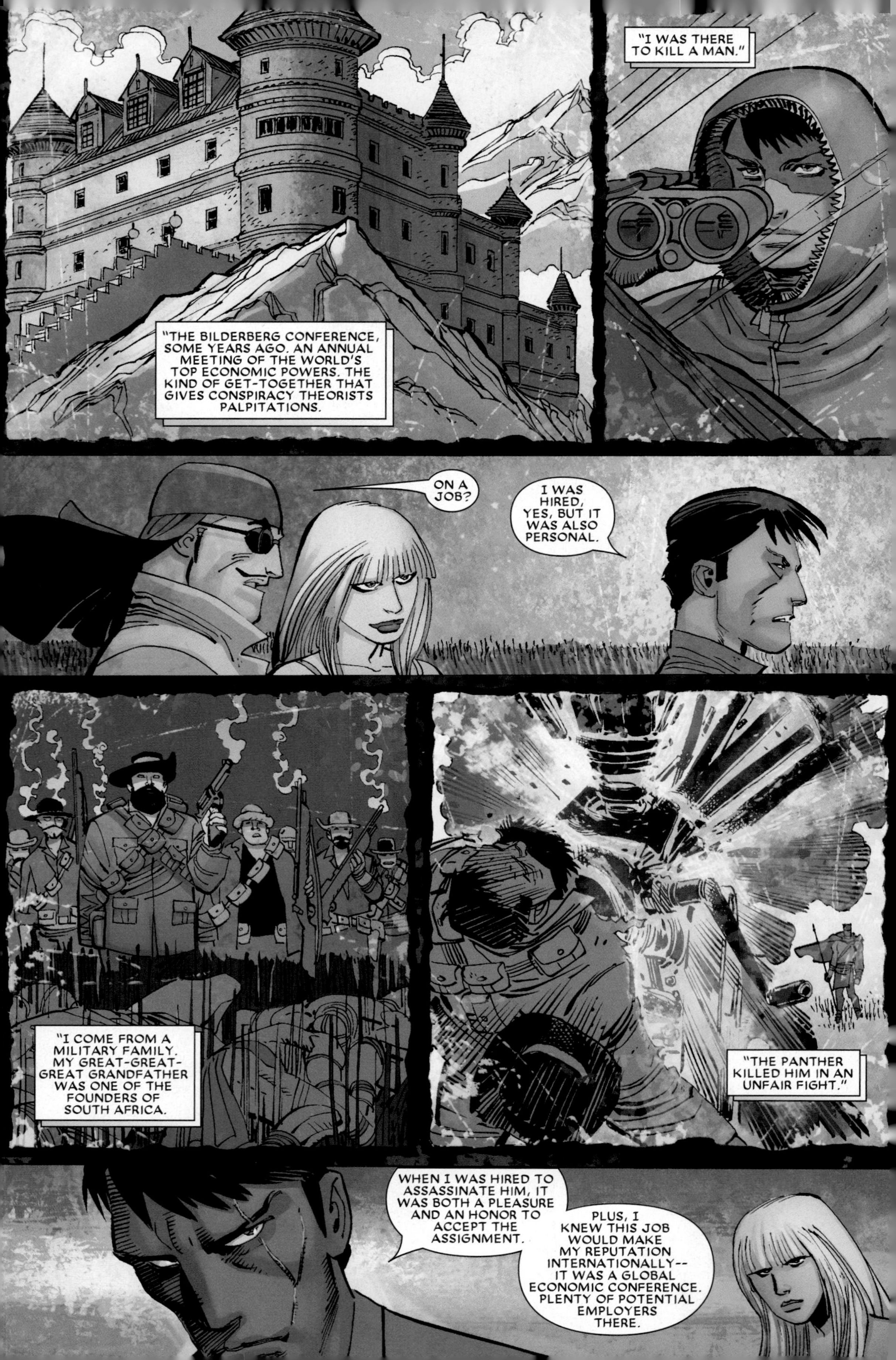
"THE BILDERBERG CONFERENCE, SOME YEARS AGO. AN ANNUAL MEETING OF THE WORLD'S TOP ECONOMIC POWERS. THE KIND OF GET-TOGETHER THAT GIVES CONSPIRACY THEORISTS PALPITATIONS.
"I WAS THERE TO KILL A MAN."
ON A JOB?
I WAS HIRED, YES, BUT IT WAS ALSO PERSONAL.
"I COME FROM A MILITARY FAMILY. MY GREAT-GREAT-GREAT GRANDFATHER WAS ONE OF THE FOUNDERS OF SOUTH AFRICA.
"THE PANTHER KILLED HIM IN AN UNFAIR FIGHT."
WHEN I WAS HIRED TO ASSASSINATE HIM, IT WAS BOTH A PLEASURE AND AN HONOR TO ACCEPT THE ASSIGNMENT.
PLUS, I KNEW THIS JOB WOULD MAKE MY REPUTATION INTERNATIONALLY-- IT WAS A GLOBAL ECONOMIC CONFERENCE. PLENTY OF POTENTIAL EMPLOYERS THERE.

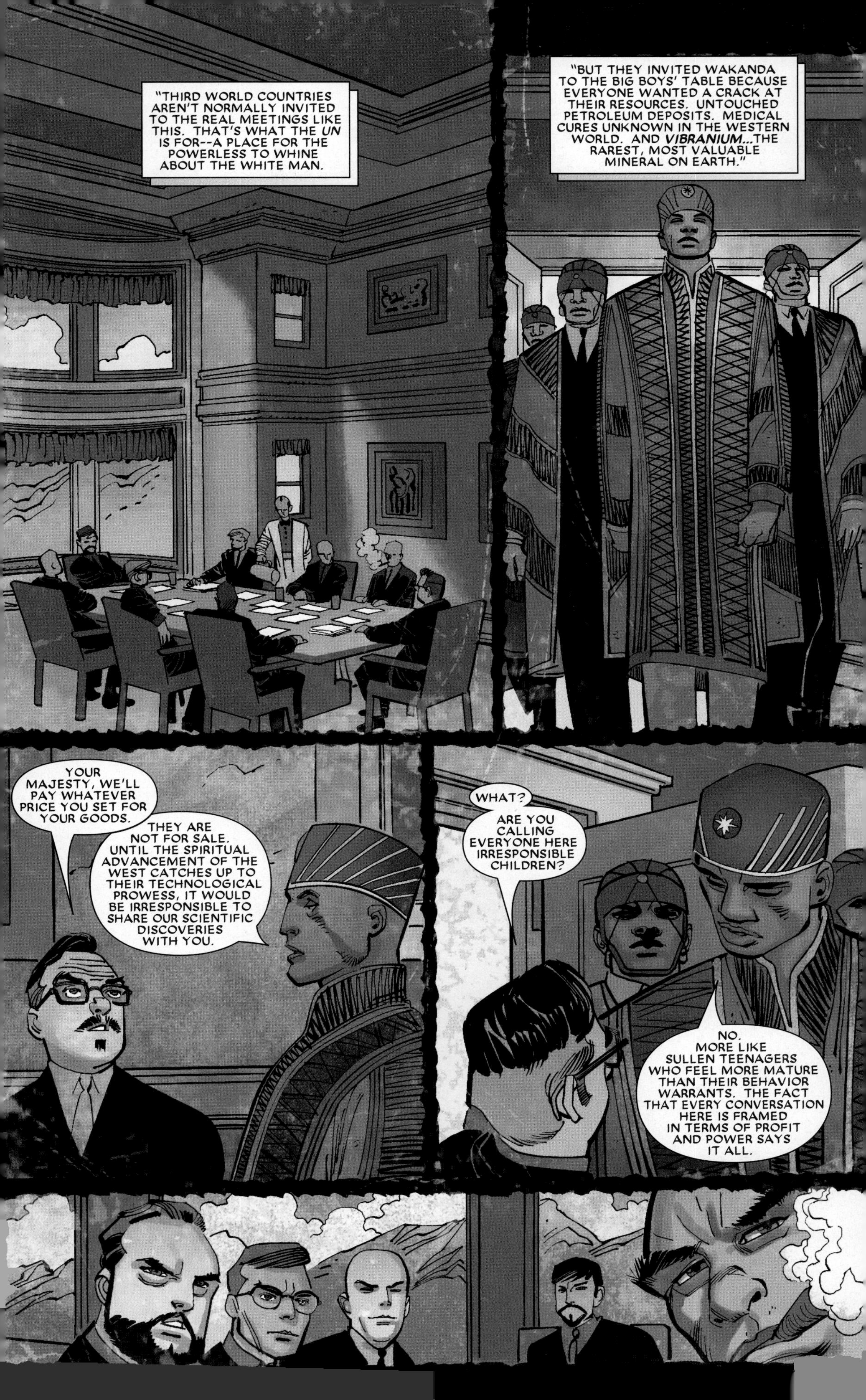
"THIRD WORLD COUNTRIES AREN'T NORMALLY INVITED TO THE REAL MEETINGS LIKE THIS. THAT'S WHAT THE *UN* IS FOR--A PLACE FOR THE POWERLESS TO WHINE ABOUT THE WHITE MAN.
"BUT THEY INVITED WAKANDA TO THE BIG BOYS' TABLE BECAUSE EVERYONE WANTED A CRACK AT THEIR RESOURCES. UNTOUCHED PETROLEUM DEPOSITS. MEDICAL CURES UNKNOWN IN THE WESTERN WORLD. AND ***VIBRANIUM...*** THE RAREST, MOST VALUABLE MINERAL ON EARTH."
YOUR MAJESTY, WE'LL PAY WHATEVER PRICE YOU SET FOR YOUR GOODS.
THEY ARE NOT FOR SALE. UNTIL THE SPIRITUAL ADVANCEMENT OF THE WEST CATCHES UP TO THEIR TECHNOLOGICAL PROWESS, IT WOULD BE IRRESPONSIBLE TO SHARE OUR SCIENTIFIC DISCOVERIES WITH YOU.
WHAT?
ARE YOU CALLING EVERYONE HERE IRRESPONSIBLE CHILDREN?
NO. MORE LIKE SULLEN TEENAGERS WHO FEEL MORE MATURE THAN THEIR BEHAVIOR WARRANTS. THE FACT THAT EVERY CONVERSATION HERE IS FRAMED IN TERMS OF PROFIT AND POWER SAYS IT ALL.

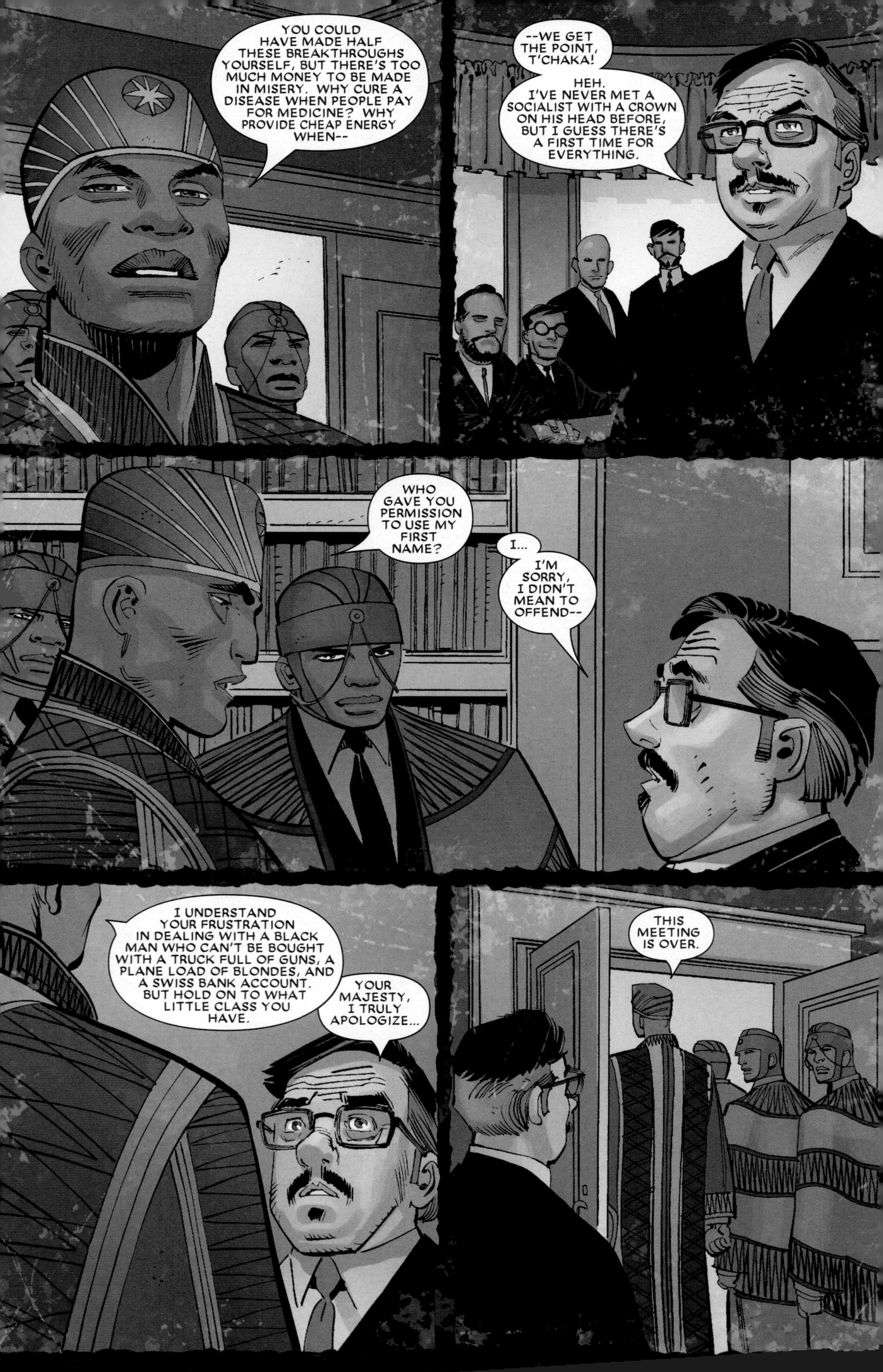
YOU COULD HAVE MADE HALF THESE BREAKTHROUGHS YOURSELF, BUT THERE'S TOO MUCH MONEY TO BE MADE IN MISERY. WHY CURE A DISEASE WHEN PEOPLE PAY FOR MEDICINE? WHY PROVIDE CHEAP ENERGY WHEN--
--WE GET THE POINT, T'CHAKA!
HEH. I'VE NEVER MET A SOCIALIST WITH A CROWN ON HIS HEAD BEFORE, BUT I GUESS THERE'S A FIRST TIME FOR EVERYTHING.
WHO GAVE YOU PERMISSION TO USE MY FIRST NAME?
I...
I'M SORRY, I DIDN'T MEAN TO OFFEND--
I UNDERSTAND YOUR FRUSTRATION IN DEALING WITH A BLACK MAN WHO CAN'T BE BOUGHT WITH A TRUCK FULL OF GUNS, A PLANE LOAD OF BLONDES, AND A SWISS BANK ACCOUNT. BUT HOLD ON TO WHAT LITTLE CLASS YOU HAVE.
YOUR MAJESTY, I TRULY APOLOGIZE...
THIS MEETING IS OVER.

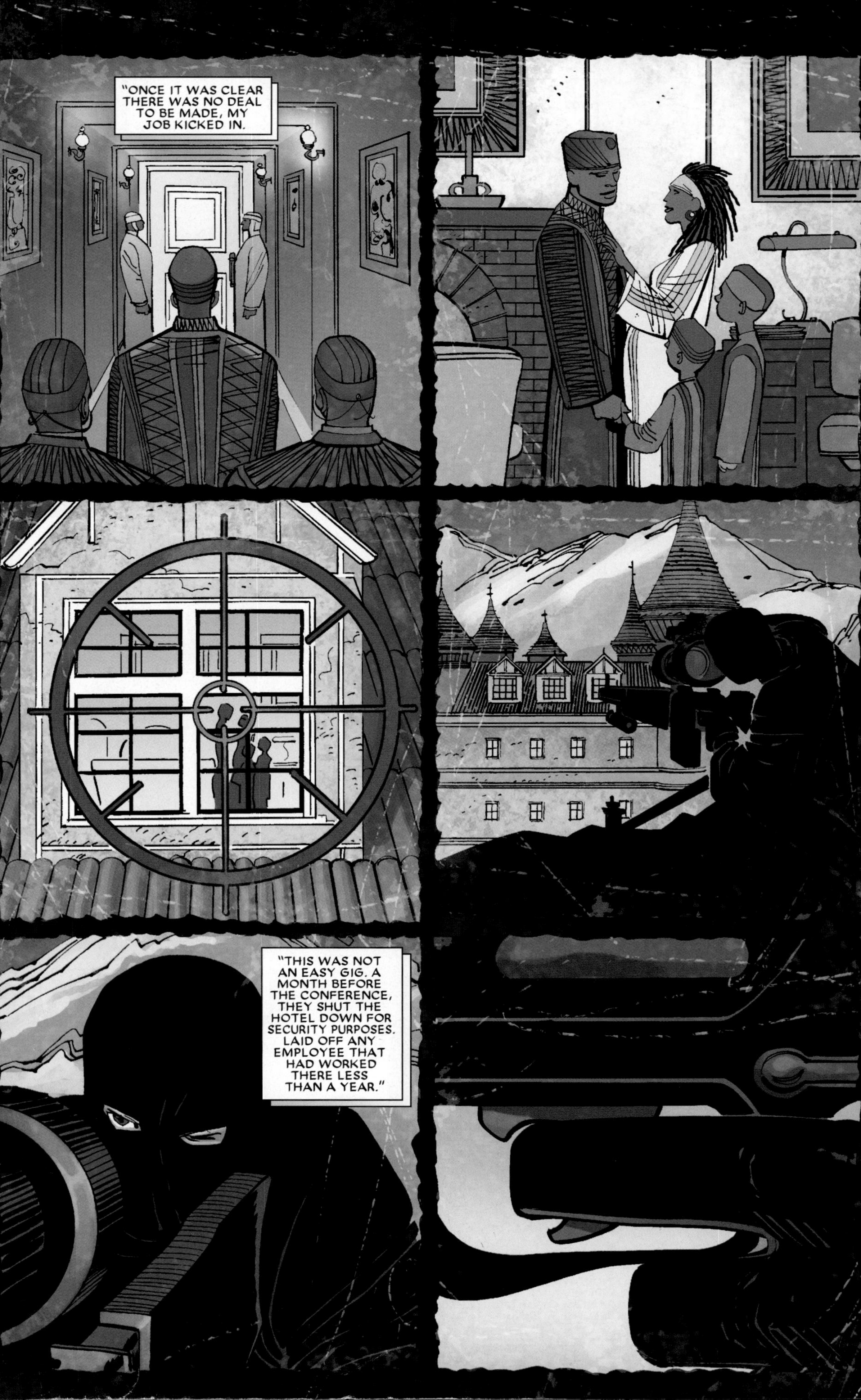
"ONCE IT WAS CLEAR THERE WAS NO DEAL TO BE MADE, MY JOB KICKED IN.
"THIS WAS NOT AN EASY GIG. A MONTH BEFORE THE CONFERENCE, THEY SHUT THE HOTEL DOWN FOR SECURITY PURPOSES. LAID OFF ANY EMPLOYEE THAT HAD WORKED THERE LESS THAN A YEAR."

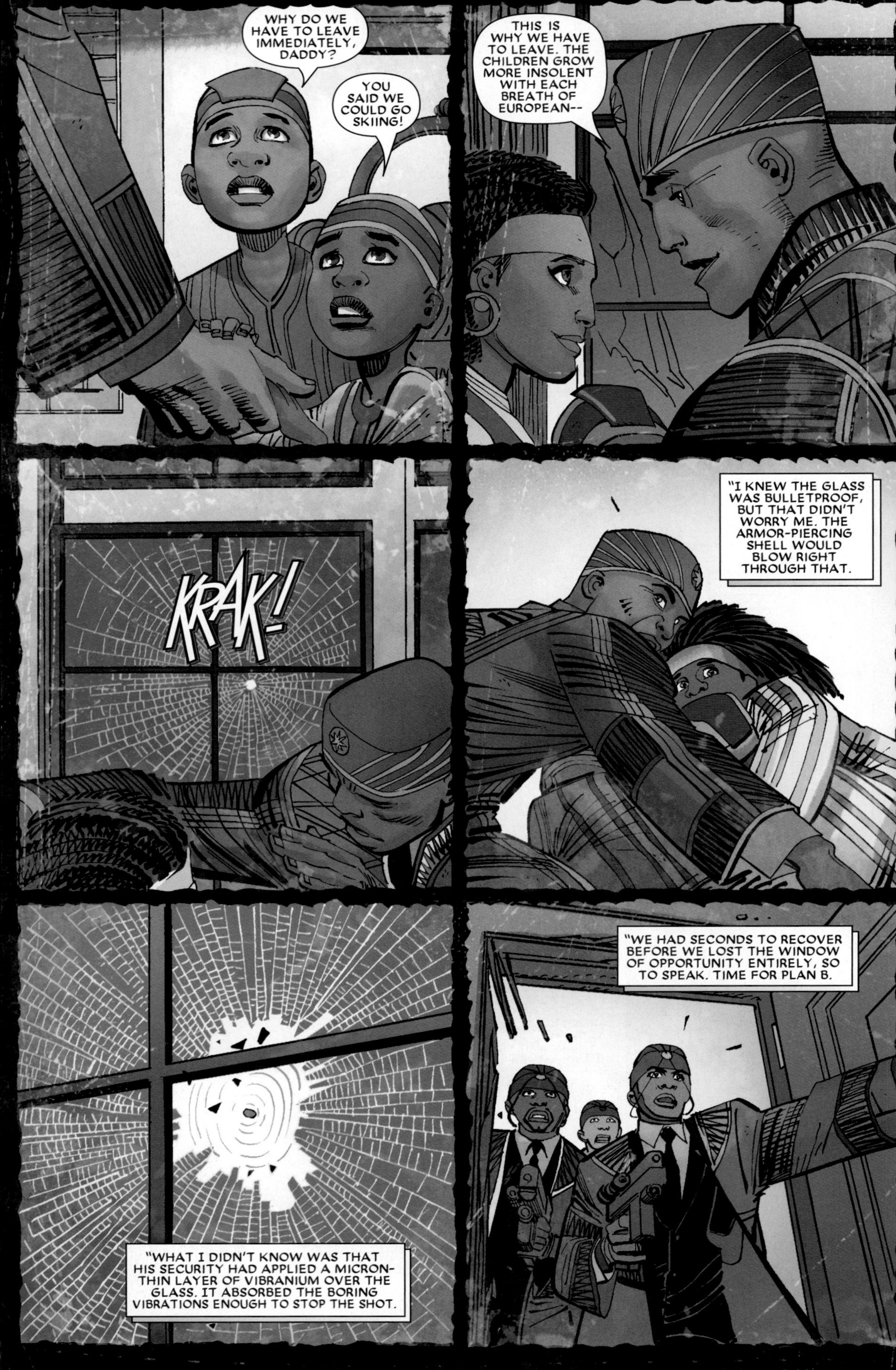
WHY DO WE HAVE TO LEAVE IMMEDIATELY, DADDY?
YOU SAID WE COULD GO SKIING!
THIS IS WHY WE HAVE TO LEAVE. THE CHILDREN GROW MORE INSOLENT WITH EACH BREATH OF EUROPEAN--
KRAK!
"I KNEW THE GLASS WAS BULLETPROOF, BUT THAT DIDN'T WORRY ME. THE ARMOR-PIERCING SHELL WOULD BLOW RIGHT THROUGH THAT.
"WHAT I DIDN'T KNOW WAS THAT HIS SECURITY HAD APPLIED A MICRON-THIN LAYER OF VIBRANIUM OVER THE GLASS. IT ABSORBED THE BORING VIBRATIONS ENOUGH TO STOP THE SHOT.
"WE HAD SECONDS TO RECOVER BEFORE WE LOST THE WINDOW OF OPPORTUNITY ENTIRELY, SO TO SPEAK. TIME FOR PLAN B.

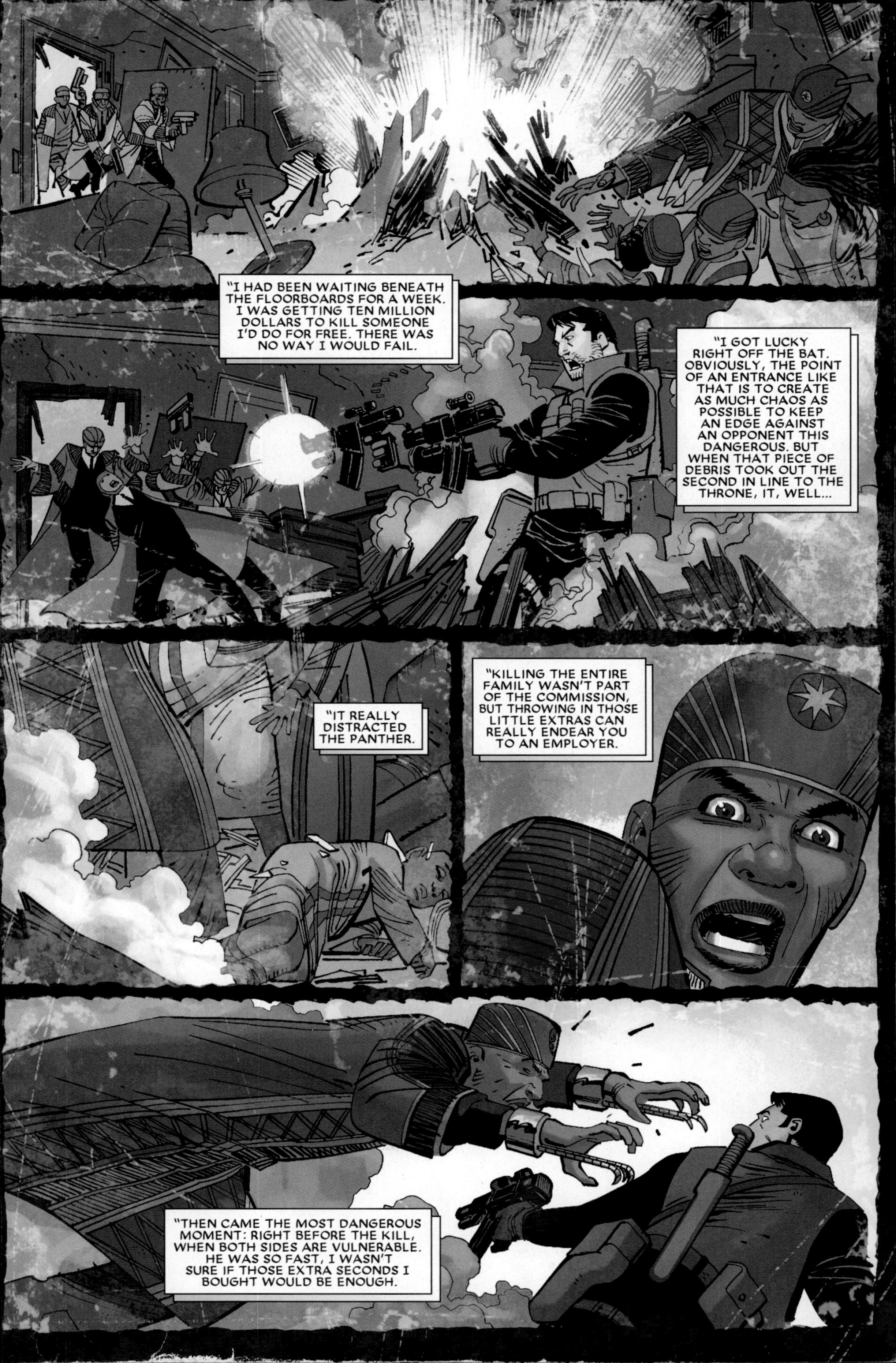
"I HAD BEEN WAITING BENEATH THE FLOORBOARDS FOR A WEEK. I WAS GETTING TEN MILLION DOLLARS TO KILL SOMEONE I'D DO FOR FREE. THERE WAS NO WAY I WOULD FAIL.
"I GOT LUCKY RIGHT OFF THE BAT. OBVIOUSLY, THE POINT OF AN ENTRANCE LIKE THAT IS TO CREATE AS MUCH CHAOS AS POSSIBLE TO KEEP AN EDGE AGAINST AN OPPONENT THIS DANGEROUS. BUT WHEN THAT PIECE OF DEBRIS TOOK OUT THE SECOND IN LINE TO THE THRONE, IT, WELL...
"IT REALLY DISTRACTED THE PANTHER.
"KILLING THE ENTIRE FAMILY WASN'T PART OF THE COMMISSION, BUT THROWING IN THOSE LITTLE EXTRAS CAN REALLY ENDEAR YOU TO AN EMPLOYER.
"THEN CAME THE MOST DANGEROUS MOMENT: RIGHT BEFORE THE KILL, WHEN BOTH SIDES ARE VULNERABLE. HE WAS SO FAST, I WASN'T SURE IF THOSE EXTRA SECONDS I BOUGHT WOULD BE ENOUGH.

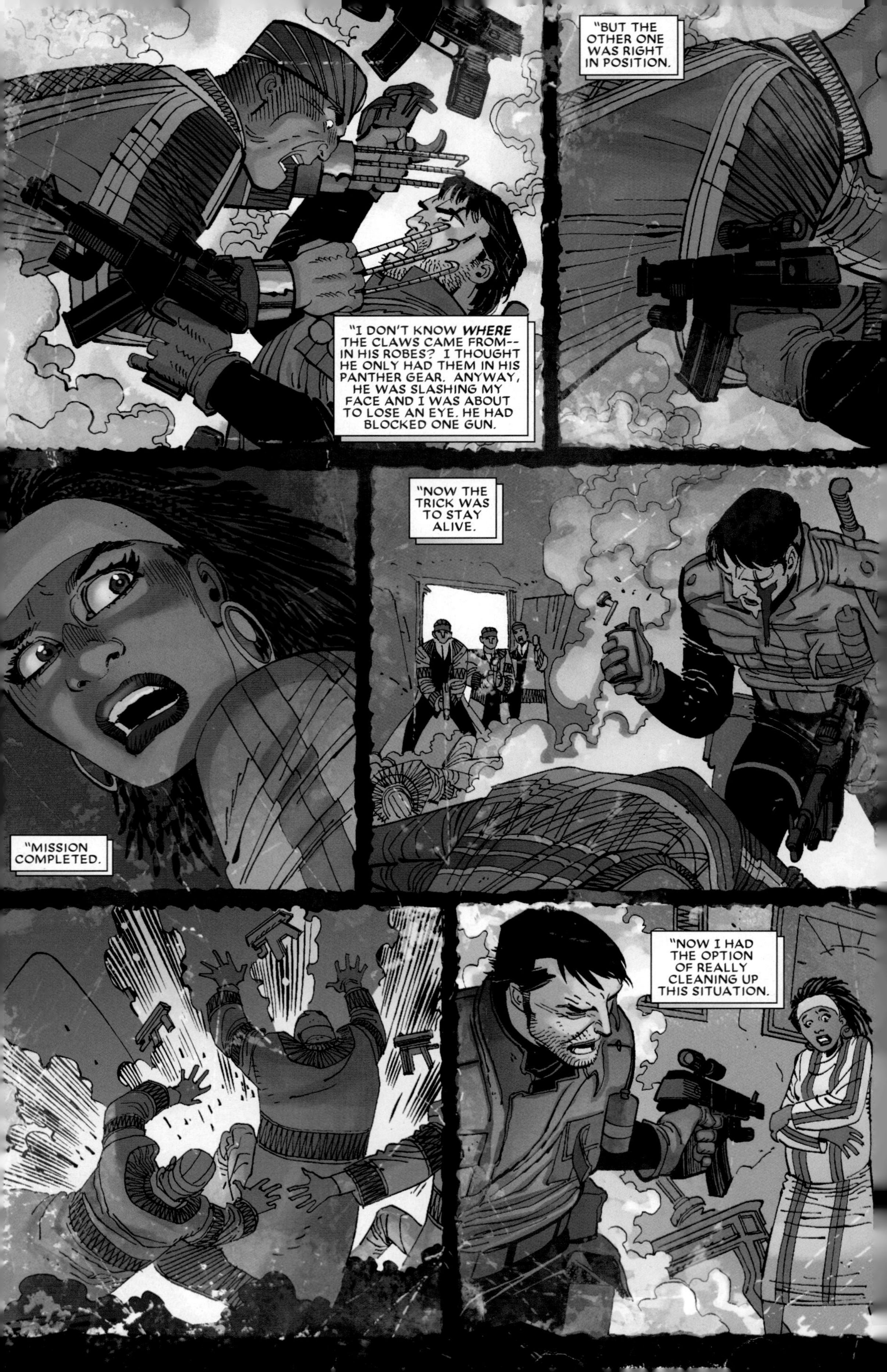
"I DON'T KNOW *WHERE* THE CLAWS CAME FROM-- IN HIS ROBES? I THOUGHT HE ONLY HAD THEM IN HIS PANTHER GEAR. ANYWAY, HE WAS SLASHING MY FACE AND I WAS ABOUT TO LOSE AN EYE. HE HAD BLOCKED ONE GUN.
"BUT THE OTHER ONE WAS RIGHT IN POSITION.
"MISSION COMPLETED.
"NOW THE TRICK WAS TO STAY ALIVE.
"NOW I HAD THE OPTION OF REALLY CLEANING UP THIS SITUATION.

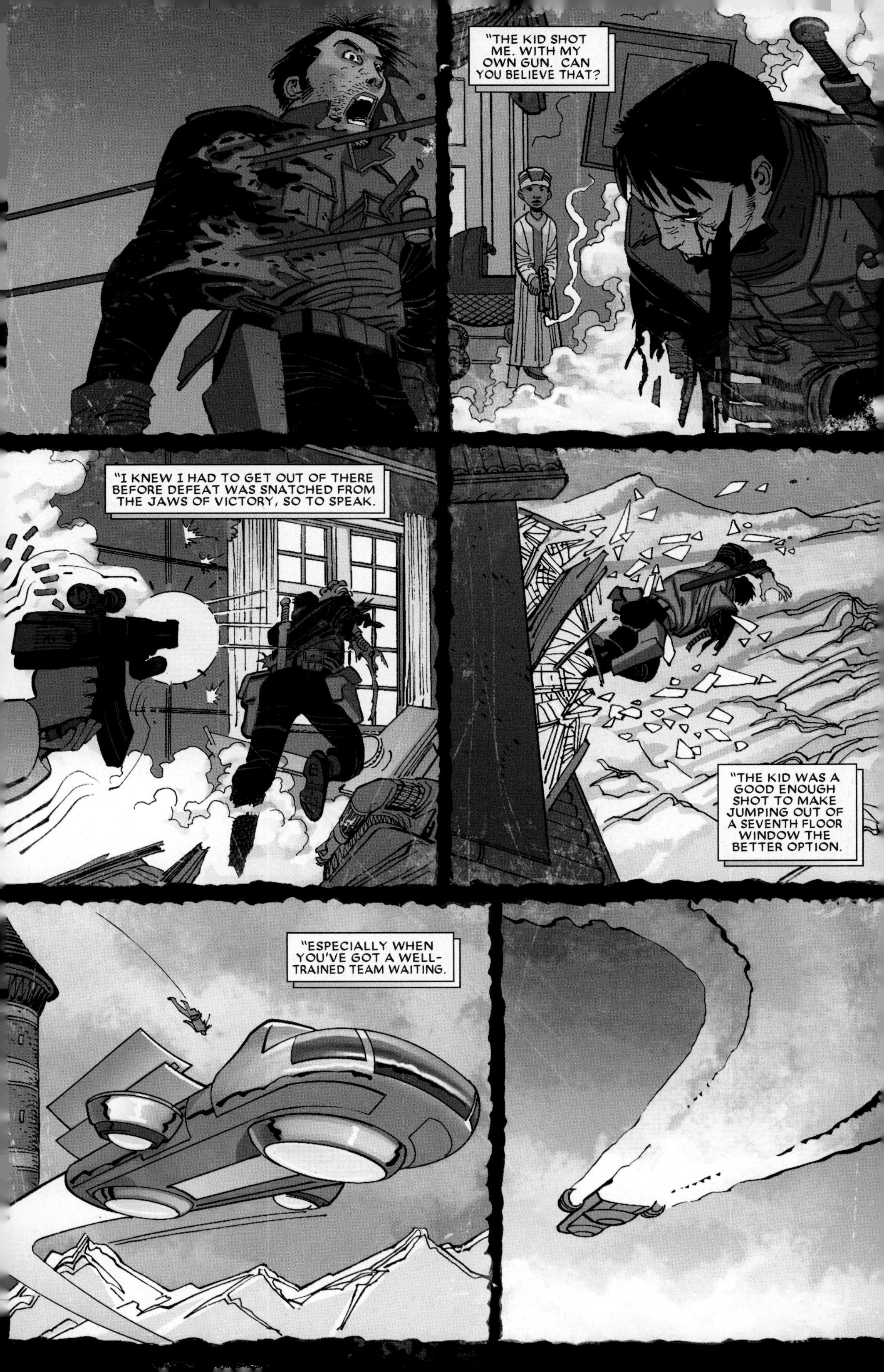
"THE KID SHOT ME. WITH MY OWN GUN. CAN YOU BELIEVE THAT?
"I KNEW I HAD TO GET OUT OF THERE BEFORE DEFEAT WAS SNATCHED FROM THE JAWS OF VICTORY, SO TO SPEAK.
"THE KID WAS A GOOD ENOUGH SHOT TO MAKE JUMPING OUT OF A SEVENTH FLOOR WINDOW THE BETTER OPTION.
"ESPECIALLY WHEN YOU'VE GOT A WELL-TRAINED TEAM WAITING.

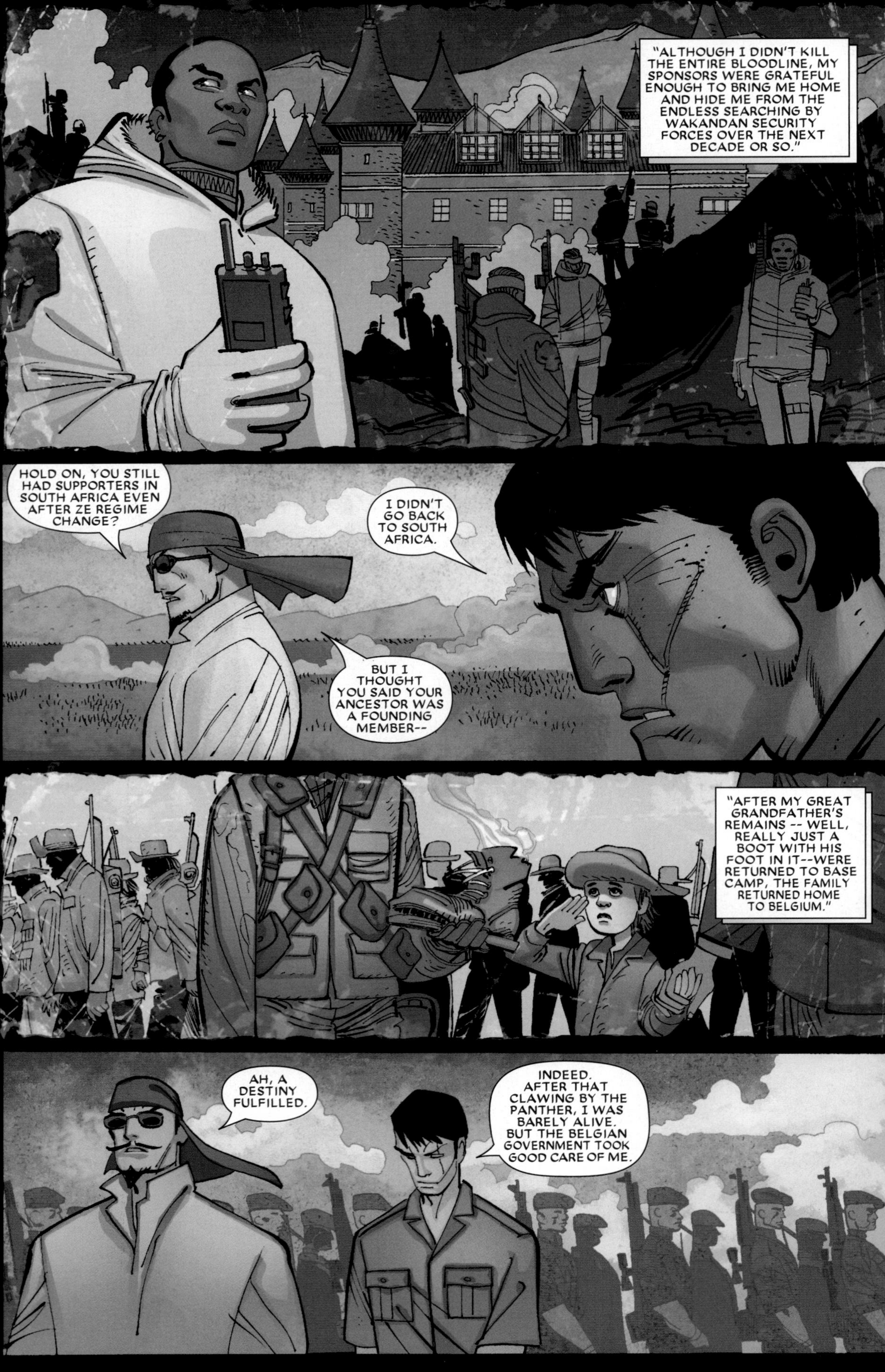
"ALTHOUGH I DIDN'T KILL THE ENTIRE BLOODLINE, MY SPONSORS WERE GRATEFUL ENOUGH TO BRING ME HOME AND HIDE ME FROM THE ENDLESS SEARCHING BY WAKANDAN SECURITY FORCES OVER THE NEXT DECADE OR SO."
HOLD ON, YOU STILL HAD SUPPORTERS IN SOUTH AFRICA EVEN AFTER ZE REGIME CHANGE?
I DIDN'T GO BACK TO SOUTH AFRICA.
BUT I THOUGHT YOU SAID YOUR ANCESTOR WAS A FOUNDING MEMBER--
"AFTER MY GREAT GRANDFATHER'S REMAINS -- WELL, REALLY JUST A BOOT WITH HIS FOOT IN IT--WERE RETURNED TO BASE CAMP, THE FAMILY RETURNED HOME TO BELGIUM."
AH, A DESTINY FULFILLED.
INDEED. AFTER THAT CLAWING BY THE PANTHER, I WAS BARELY ALIVE. BUT THE BELGIAN GOVERNMENT TOOK GOOD CARE OF ME.

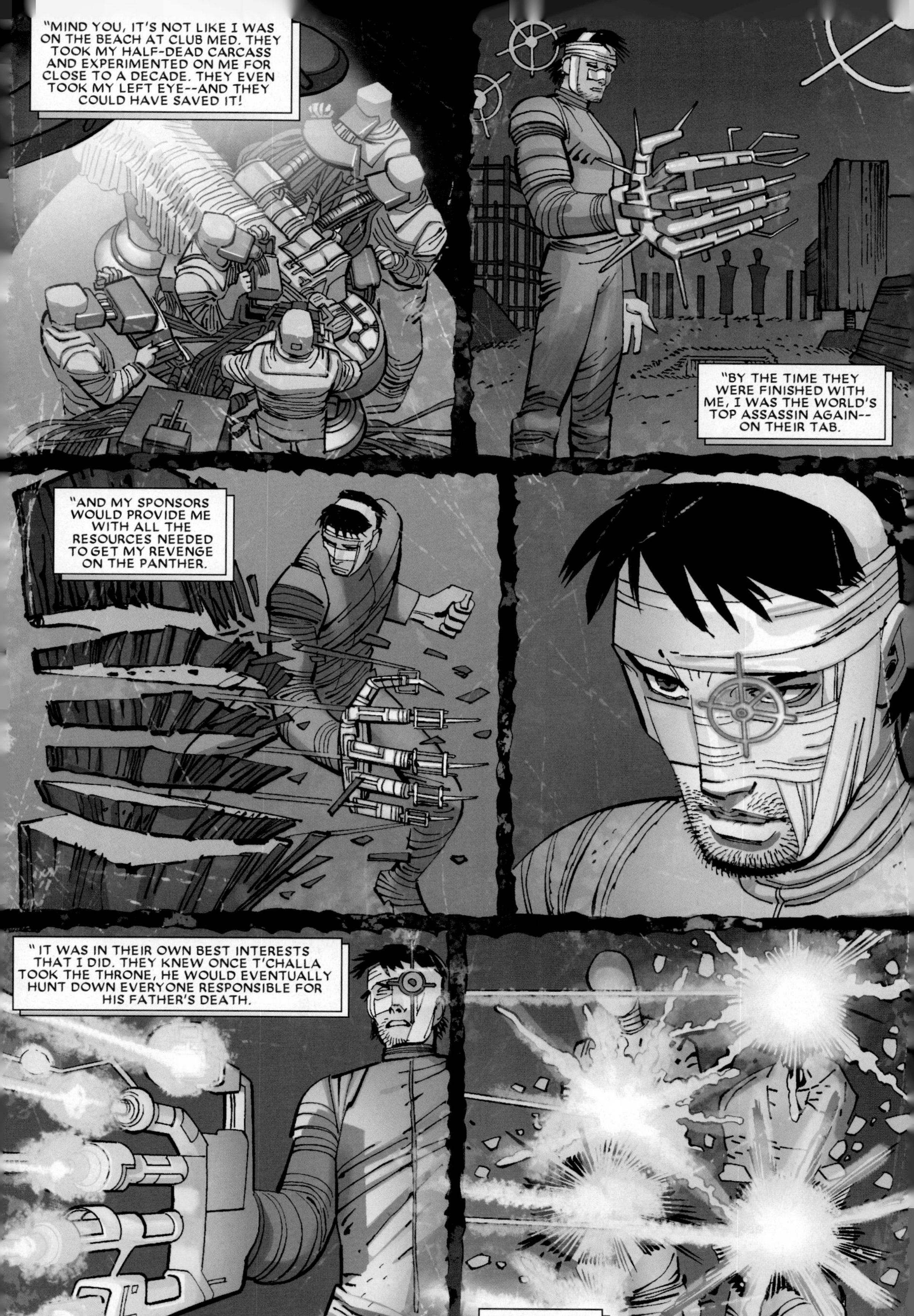
"MIND YOU, IT'S NOT LIKE I WAS ON THE BEACH AT CLUB MED. THEY TOOK MY HALF-DEAD CARCASS AND EXPERIMENTED ON ME FOR CLOSE TO A DECADE. THEY EVEN TOOK MY LEFT EYE--AND THEY COULD HAVE SAVED IT!
"BY THE TIME THEY WERE FINISHED WITH ME, I WAS THE WORLD'S TOP ASSASSIN AGAIN--ON THEIR TAB.
"AND MY SPONSORS WOULD PROVIDE ME WITH ALL THE RESOURCES NEEDED TO GET MY REVENGE ON THE PANTHER.
"IT WAS IN THEIR OWN BEST INTERESTS THAT I DID. THEY KNEW ONCE T'CHALLA TOOK THE THRONE, HE WOULD EVENTUALLY HUNT DOWN EVERYONE RESPONSIBLE FOR HIS FATHER'S DEATH.
"THEY NEEDED A PRE-EMPTIVE STRIKE."

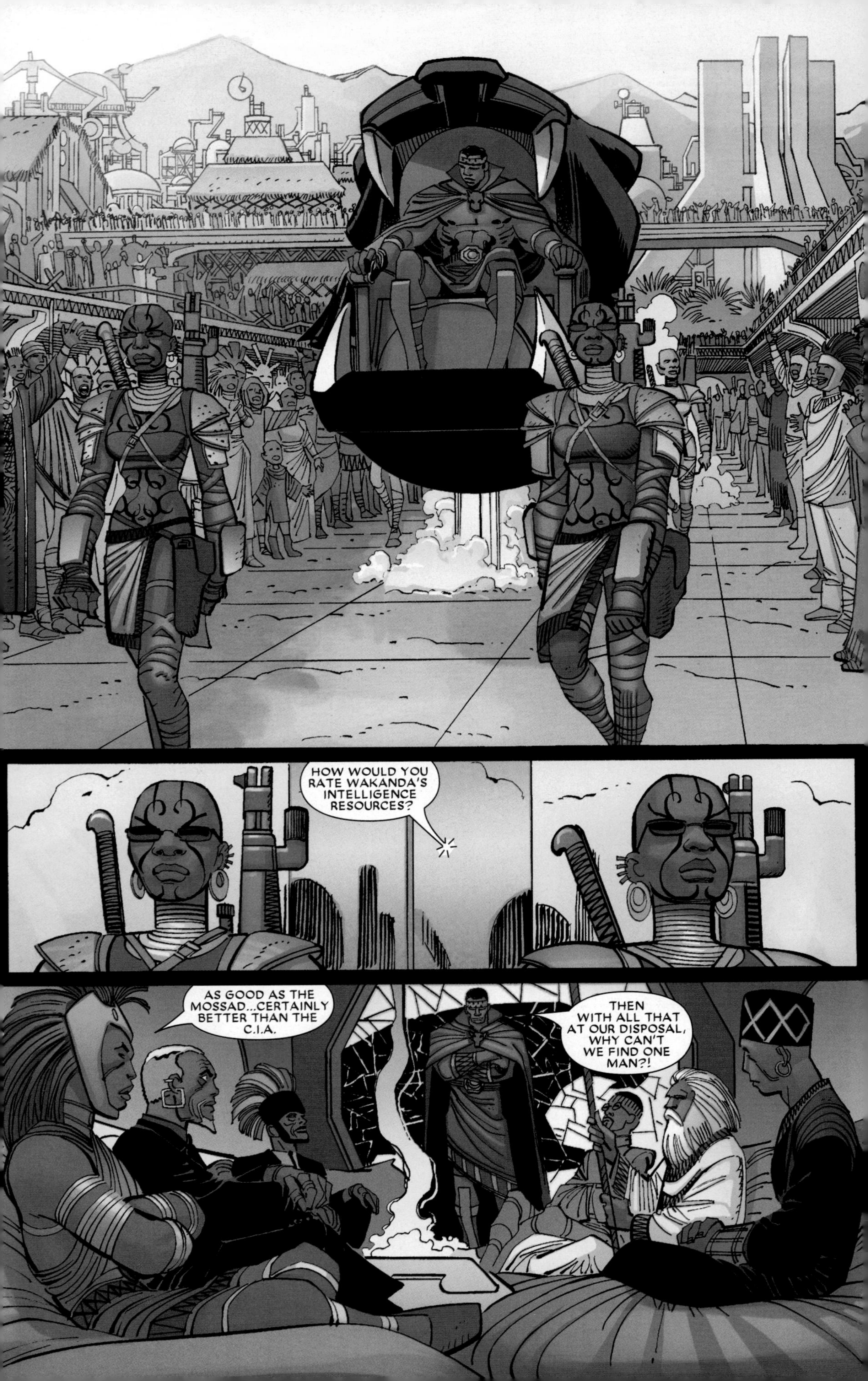
HOW WOULD YOU RATE WAKANDA'S INTELLIGENCE RESOURCES?
AS GOOD AS THE MOSSAD...CERTAINLY BETTER THAN THE C.I.A.
THEN WITH ALL THAT AT OUR DISPOSAL, WHY CAN'T WE FIND ONE MAN?!

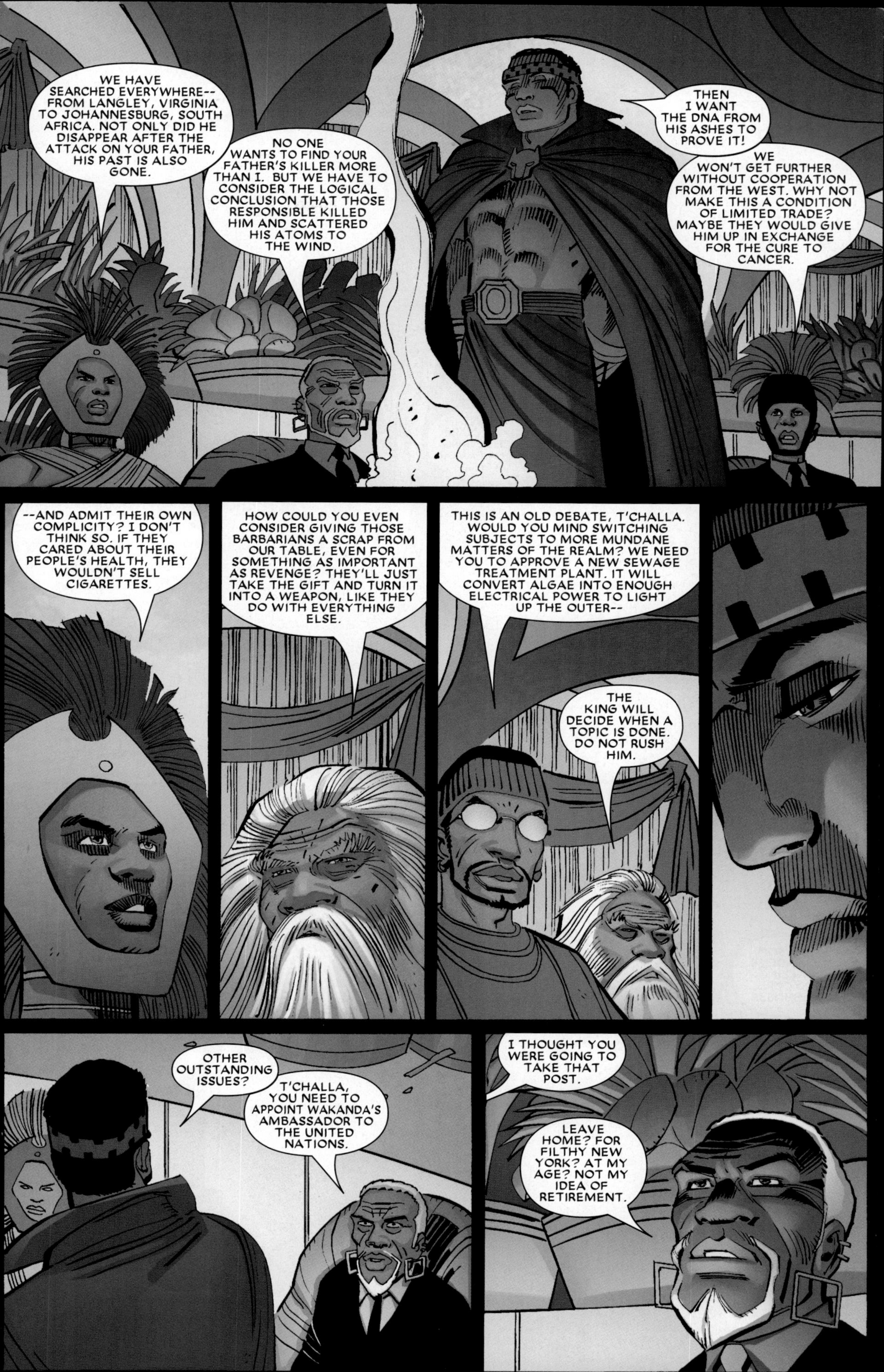
WE HAVE SEARCHED EVERYWHERE-- FROM LANGLEY, VIRGINIA TO JOHANNESBURG, SOUTH AFRICA. NOT ONLY DID HE DISAPPEAR AFTER THE ATTACK ON YOUR FATHER, HIS PAST IS ALSO GONE.
NO ONE WANTS TO FIND YOUR FATHER'S KILLER MORE THAN I. BUT WE HAVE TO CONSIDER THE LOGICAL CONCLUSION THAT THOSE RESPONSIBLE KILLED HIM AND SCATTERED HIS ATOMS TO THE WIND.
THEN I WANT THE DNA FROM HIS ASHES TO PROVE IT!
WE WON'T GET FURTHER WITHOUT COOPERATION FROM THE WEST. WHY NOT MAKE THIS A CONDITION OF LIMITED TRADE? MAYBE THEY WOULD GIVE HIM UP IN EXCHANGE FOR THE CURE TO CANCER.
--AND ADMIT THEIR OWN COMPLICITY? I DON'T THINK SO. IF THEY CARED ABOUT THEIR PEOPLE'S HEALTH, THEY WOULDN'T SELL CIGARETTES.
HOW COULD YOU EVEN CONSIDER GIVING THOSE BARBARIANS A SCRAP FROM OUR TABLE, EVEN FOR SOMETHING AS IMPORTANT AS REVENGE? THEY'LL JUST TAKE THE GIFT AND TURN IT INTO A WEAPON, LIKE THEY DO WITH EVERYTHING ELSE.
THIS IS AN OLD DEBATE, T'CHALLA. WOULD YOU MIND SWITCHING SUBJECTS TO MORE MUNDANE MATTERS OF THE REALM? WE NEED YOU TO APPROVE A NEW SEWAGE TREATMENT PLANT. IT WILL CONVERT ALGAE INTO ENOUGH ELECTRICAL POWER TO LIGHT UP THE OUTER--
THE KING WILL DECIDE WHEN A TOPIC IS DONE. DO NOT RUSH HIM.
OTHER OUTSTANDING ISSUES?
T'CHALLA, YOU NEED TO APPOINT WAKANDA'S AMBASSADOR TO THE UNITED NATIONS.
I THOUGHT YOU WERE GOING TO TAKE THAT POST.
LEAVE HOME? FOR FILTHY NEW YORK? AT MY AGE? NOT MY IDEA OF RETIREMENT.

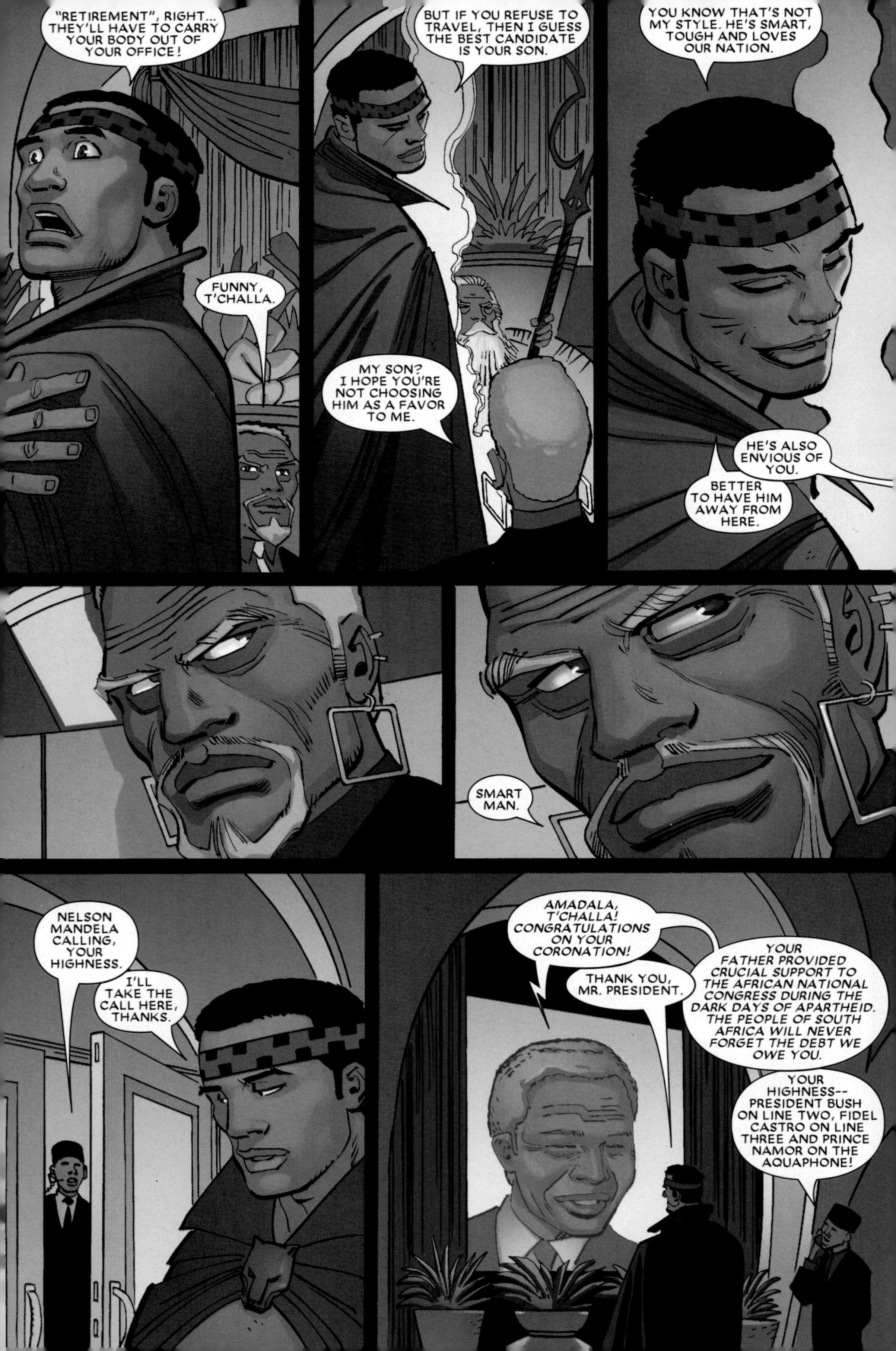

"RETIREMENT", RIGHT... THEY'LL HAVE TO CARRY YOUR BODY OUT OF YOUR OFFICE!
FUNNY, T'CHALLA.
BUT IF YOU REFUSE TO TRAVEL, THEN I GUESS THE BEST CANDIDATE IS YOUR SON.
MY SON? I HOPE YOU'RE NOT CHOOSING HIM AS A FAVOR TO ME.
YOU KNOW THAT'S NOT MY STYLE. HE'S SMART, TOUGH AND LOVES OUR NATION.
HE'S ALSO ENVIOUS OF YOU.
BETTER TO HAVE HIM AWAY FROM HERE.
SMART MAN.
NELSON MANDELA CALLING, YOUR HIGHNESS.
I'LL TAKE THE CALL HERE, THANKS.
AMADALA, T'CHALLA! CONGRATULATIONS ON YOUR CORONATION!
THANK YOU, MR. PRESIDENT.
YOUR FATHER PROVIDED CRUCIAL SUPPORT TO THE AFRICAN NATIONAL CONGRESS DURING THE DARK DAYS OF APARTHEID. THE PEOPLE OF SOUTH AFRICA WILL NEVER FORGET THE DEBT WE OWE YOU.
YOUR HIGHNESS-- PRESIDENT BUSH ON LINE TWO, FIDEL CASTRO ON LINE THREE AND PRINCE NAMOR ON THE AQUAPHONE!

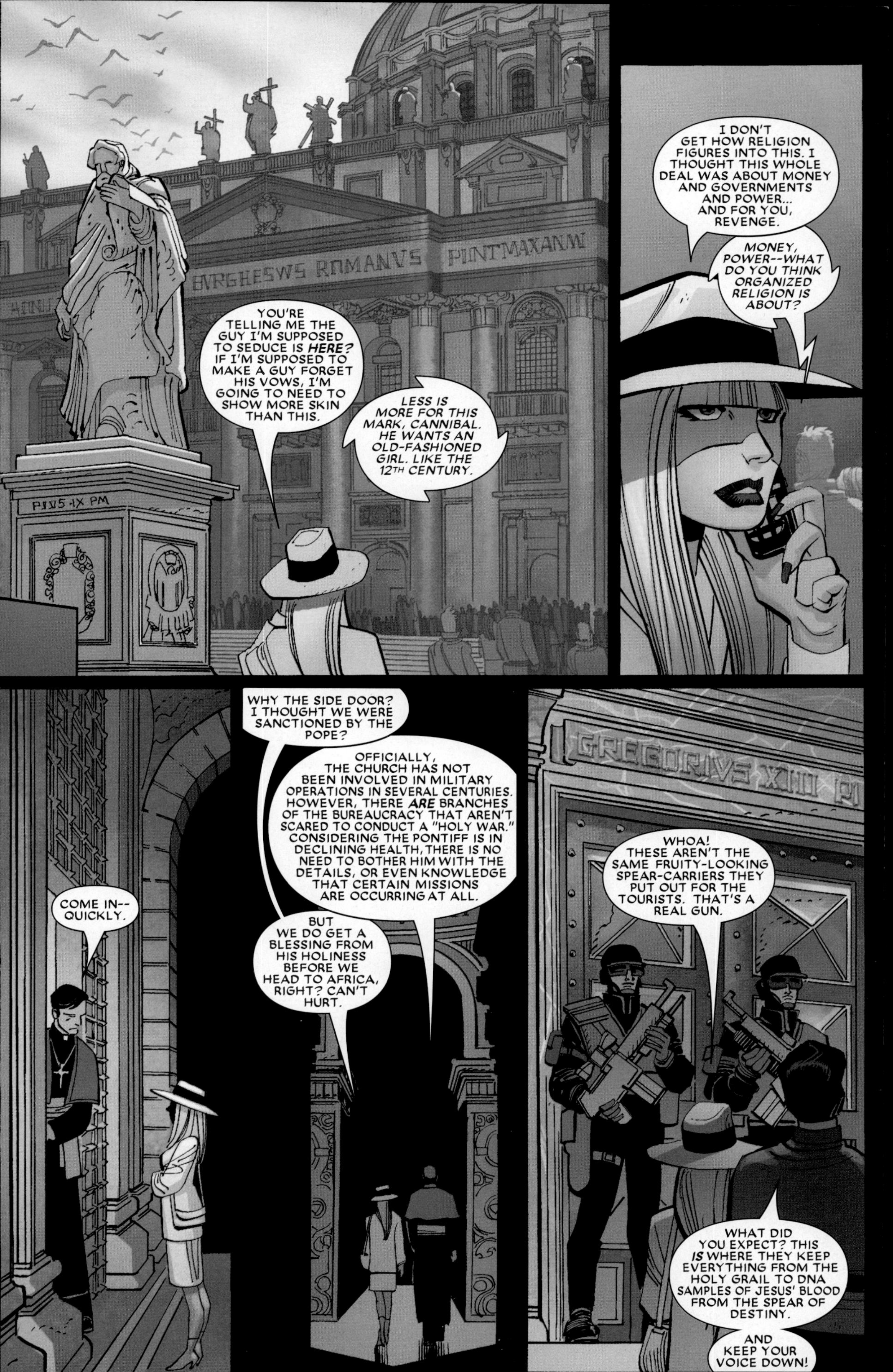
BVRGHESWS ROMANVS PINTMAXANM
PIVS IX PM
YOU'RE TELLING ME THE GUY I'M SUPPOSED TO SEDUCE IS HERE? IF I'M SUPPOSED TO MAKE A GUY FORGET HIS VOWS, I'M GOING TO NEED TO SHOW MORE SKIN THAN THIS.
LESS IS MORE FOR THIS MARK, CANNIBAL. HE WANTS AN OLD-FASHIONED GIRL. LIKE THE 12TH CENTURY.
I DON'T GET HOW RELIGION FIGURES INTO THIS. I THOUGHT THIS WHOLE DEAL WAS ABOUT MONEY AND GOVERNMENTS AND POWER... AND FOR YOU, REVENGE.
MONEY, POWER--WHAT DO YOU THINK ORGANIZED RELIGION IS ABOUT?
COME IN-- QUICKLY.
WHY THE SIDE DOOR? I THOUGHT WE WERE SANCTIONED BY THE POPE?
OFFICIALLY, THE CHURCH HAS NOT BEEN INVOLVED IN MILITARY OPERATIONS IN SEVERAL CENTURIES. HOWEVER, THERE ARE BRANCHES OF THE BUREAUCRACY THAT AREN'T SCARED TO CONDUCT A "HOLY WAR." CONSIDERING THE PONTIFF IS IN DECLINING HEALTH, THERE IS NO NEED TO BOTHER HIM WITH THE DETAILS, OR EVEN KNOWLEDGE THAT CERTAIN MISSIONS ARE OCCURRING AT ALL.
BUT WE DO GET A BLESSING FROM HIS HOLINESS BEFORE WE HEAD TO AFRICA, RIGHT? CAN'T HURT.
GREGORIVS XIII P
WHOA! THESE AREN'T THE SAME FRUITY-LOOKING SPEAR-CARRIERS THEY PUT OUT FOR THE TOURISTS. THAT'S A REAL GUN.
WHAT DID YOU EXPECT? THIS IS WHERE THEY KEEP EVERYTHING FROM THE HOLY GRAIL TO DNA SAMPLES OF JESUS' BLOOD FROM THE SPEAR OF DESTINY.
AND KEEP YOUR VOICE DOWN!

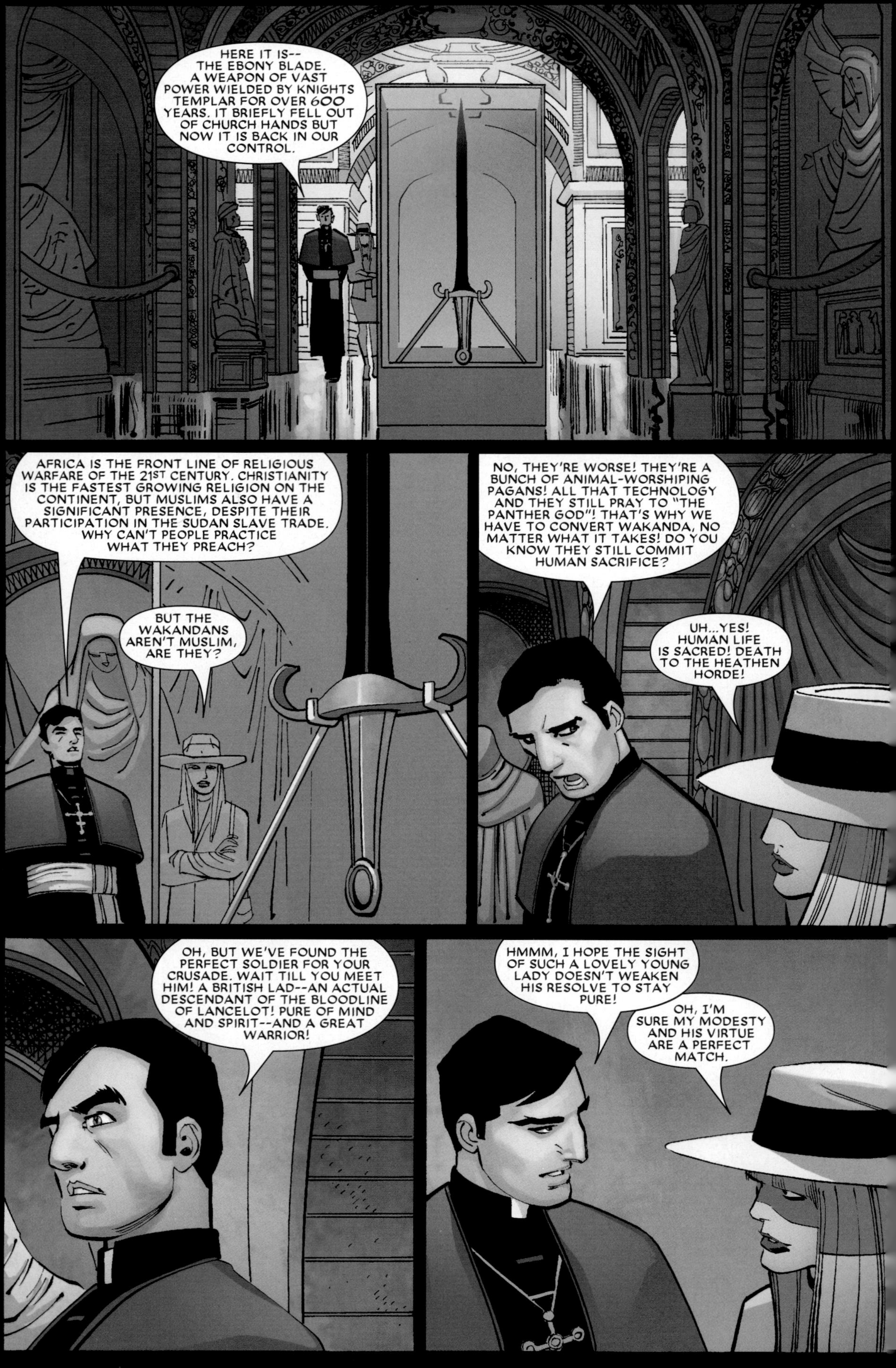
HERE IT IS-- THE EBONY BLADE. A WEAPON OF VAST POWER WIELDED BY KNIGHTS TEMPLAR FOR OVER 600 YEARS. IT BRIEFLY FELL OUT OF CHURCH HANDS BUT NOW IT IS BACK IN OUR CONTROL.
AFRICA IS THE FRONT LINE OF RELIGIOUS WARFARE OF THE 21ST CENTURY. CHRISTIANITY IS THE FASTEST GROWING RELIGION ON THE CONTINENT, BUT MUSLIMS ALSO HAVE A SIGNIFICANT PRESENCE, DESPITE THEIR PARTICIPATION IN THE SUDAN SLAVE TRADE. WHY CAN'T PEOPLE PRACTICE WHAT THEY PREACH?
BUT THE WAKANDANS AREN'T MUSLIM, ARE THEY?
NO, THEY'RE WORSE! THEY'RE A BUNCH OF ANIMAL-WORSHIPING PAGANS! ALL THAT TECHNOLOGY AND THEY STILL PRAY TO "THE PANTHER GOD"! THAT'S WHY WE HAVE TO CONVERT WAKANDA, NO MATTER WHAT IT TAKES! DO YOU KNOW THEY STILL COMMIT HUMAN SACRIFICE?
UH...YES! HUMAN LIFE IS SACRED! DEATH TO THE HEATHEN HORDE!
OH, BUT WE'VE FOUND THE PERFECT SOLDIER FOR YOUR CRUSADE. WAIT TILL YOU MEET HIM! A BRITISH LAD--AN ACTUAL DESCENDANT OF THE BLOODLINE OF LANCELOT! PURE OF MIND AND SPIRIT--AND A GREAT WARRIOR!
HMMM, I HOPE THE SIGHT OF SUCH A LOVELY YOUNG LADY DOESN'T WEAKEN HIS RESOLVE TO STAY PURE!
OH, I'M SURE MY MODESTY AND HIS VIRTUE ARE A PERFECT MATCH.

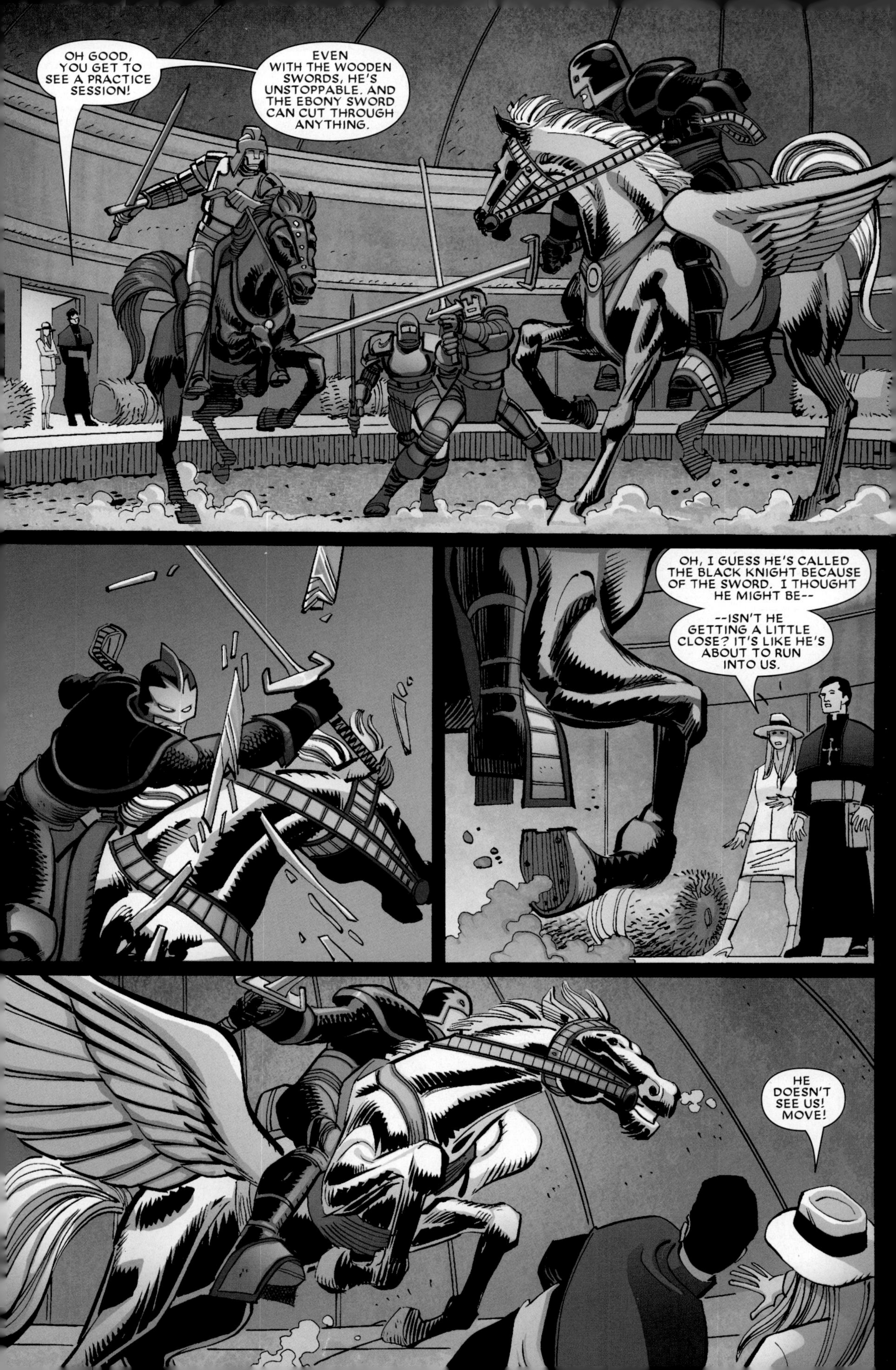
OH GOOD, YOU GET TO SEE A PRACTICE SESSION!
EVEN WITH THE WOODEN SWORDS, HE'S UNSTOPPABLE. AND THE EBONY SWORD CAN CUT THROUGH ANYTHING.
OH, I GUESS HE'S CALLED THE BLACK KNIGHT BECAUSE OF THE SWORD. I THOUGHT HE MIGHT BE--
--ISN'T HE GETTING A LITTLE CLOSE? IT'S LIKE HE'S ABOUT TO RUN INTO US.
HE DOESN'T SEE US! MOVE!

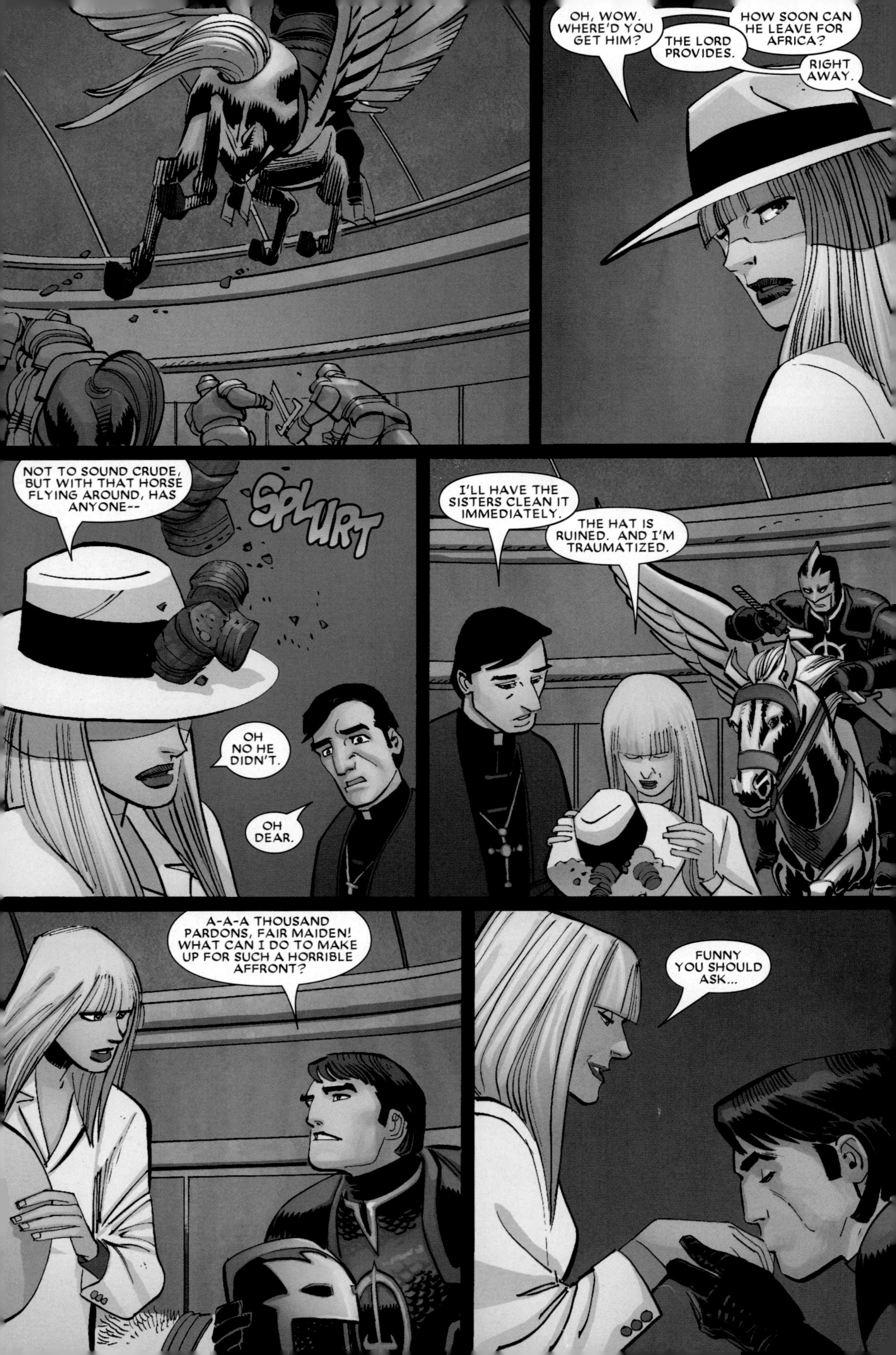
OH, WOW. WHERE'D YOU GET HIM?
THE LORD PROVIDES.
HOW SOON CAN HE LEAVE FOR AFRICA?
RIGHT AWAY.
NOT TO SOUND CRUDE, BUT WITH THAT HORSE FLYING AROUND, HAS ANYONE--
SPLURT
OH NO HE DIDN'T.
OH DEAR.
I'LL HAVE THE SISTERS CLEAN IT IMMEDIATELY.
THE HAT IS RUINED. AND I'M TRAUMATIZED.
A-A-A THOUSAND PARDONS, FAIR MAIDEN! WHAT CAN I DO TO MAKE UP FOR SUCH A HORRIBLE AFFRONT?
FUNNY YOU SHOULD ASK...

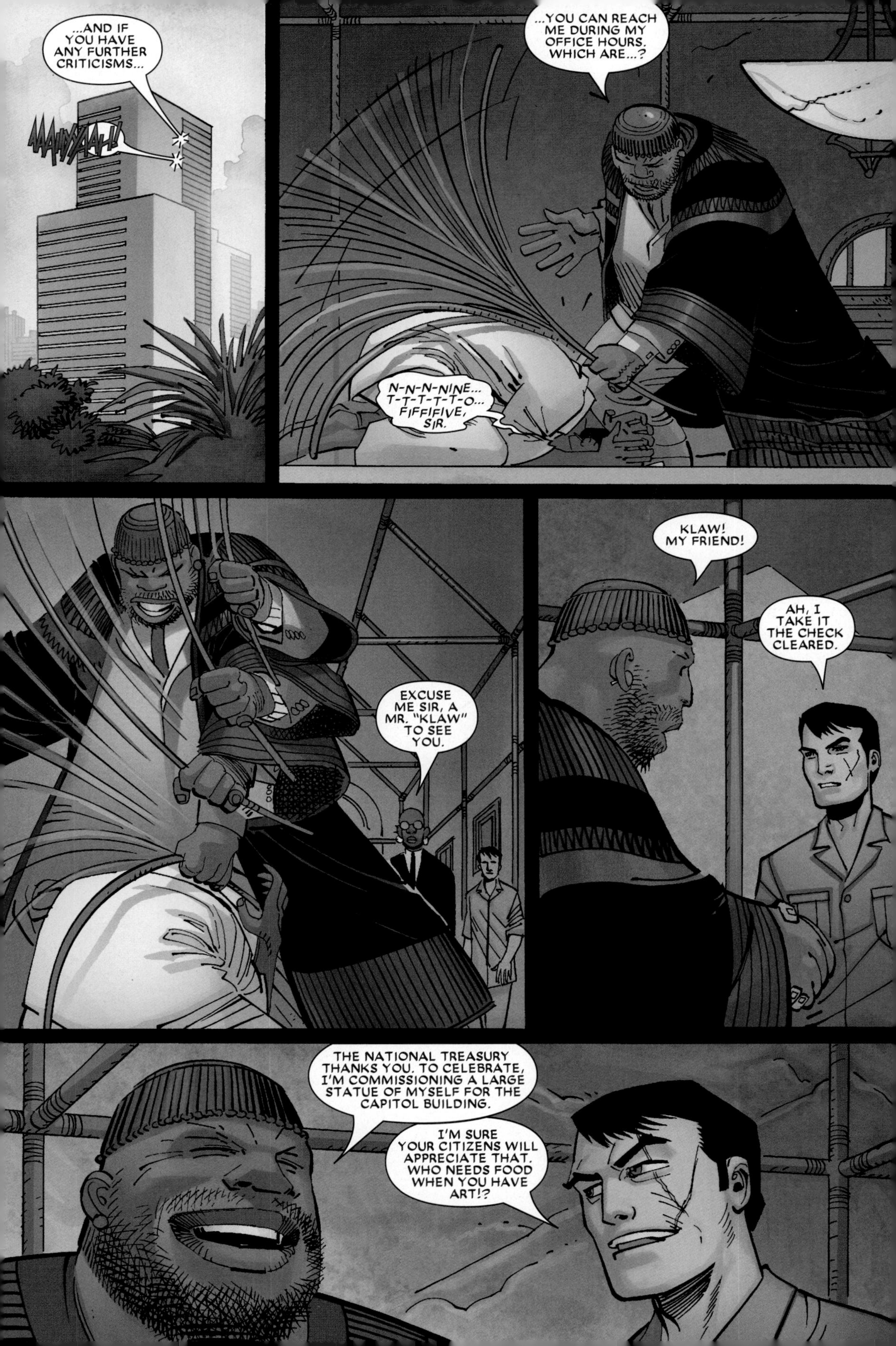
...AND IF YOU HAVE ANY FURTHER CRITICISMS...
AAAHYAAH!
...YOU CAN REACH ME DURING MY OFFICE HOURS. WHICH ARE...?
N-N-N-NINE... T-T-T-T-T-O... FIFFIFIVE, SIR.
EXCUSE ME SIR, A MR. "KLAW" TO SEE YOU.
KLAW! MY FRIEND!
AH, I TAKE IT THE CHECK CLEARED.
THE NATIONAL TREASURY THANKS YOU. TO CELEBRATE, I'M COMMISSIONING A LARGE STATUE OF MYSELF FOR THE CAPITOL BUILDING.
I'M SURE YOUR CITIZENS WILL APPRECIATE THAT. WHO NEEDS FOOD WHEN YOU HAVE ART!?

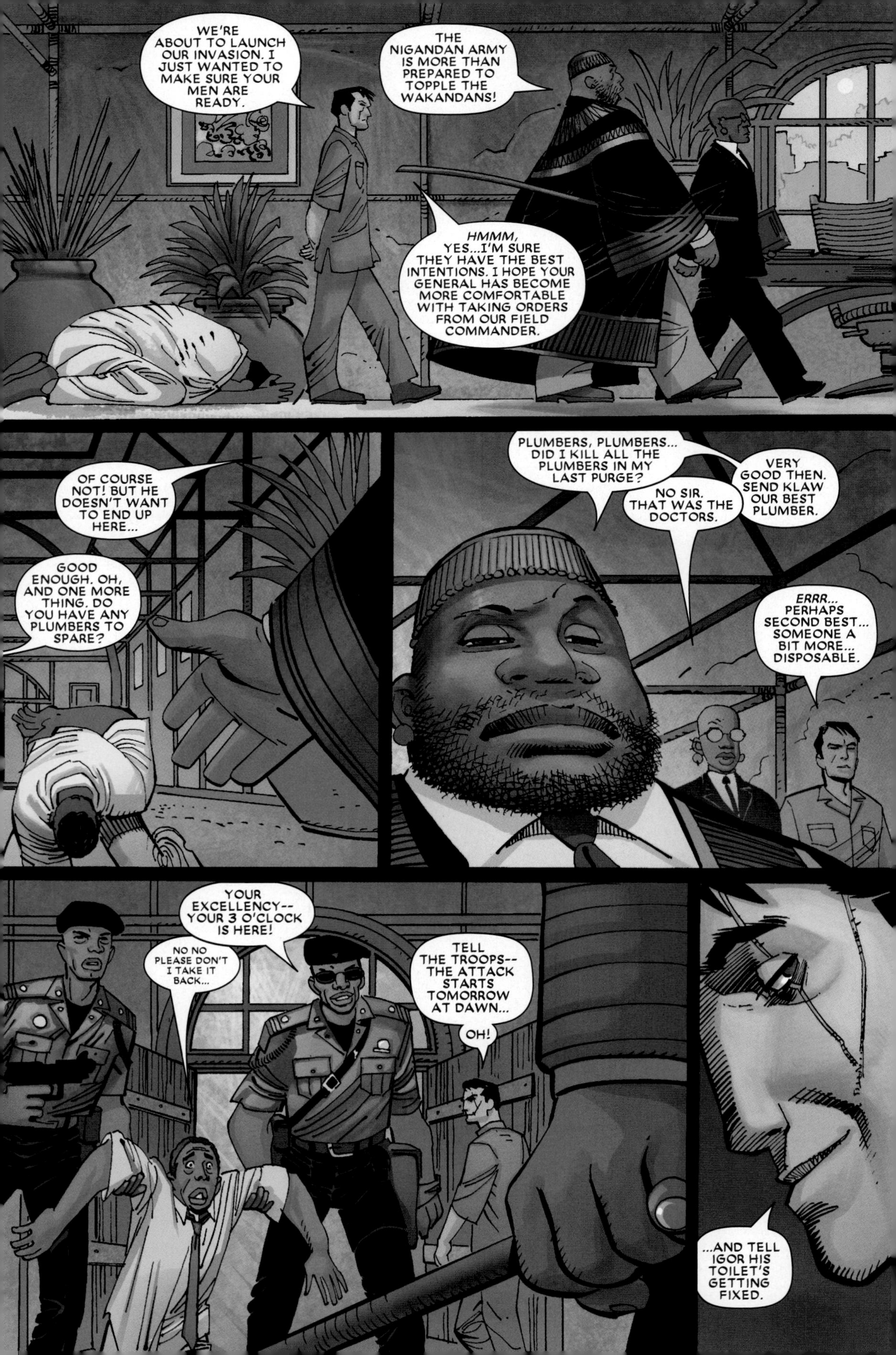
WE'RE ABOUT TO LAUNCH OUR INVASION. I JUST WANTED TO MAKE SURE YOUR MEN ARE READY.
THE NIGANDAN ARMY IS MORE THAN PREPARED TO TOPPLE THE WAKANDANS!
*HMMM,* YES...I'M SURE THEY HAVE THE BEST INTENTIONS. I HOPE YOUR GENERAL HAS BECOME MORE COMFORTABLE WITH TAKING ORDERS FROM OUR FIELD COMMANDER.
OF COURSE NOT! BUT HE DOESN'T WANT TO END UP HERE...
GOOD ENOUGH. OH, AND ONE MORE THING. DO YOU HAVE ANY PLUMBERS TO SPARE?
PLUMBERS, PLUMBERS... DID I KILL ALL THE PLUMBERS IN MY LAST PURGE?
NO SIR. THAT WAS THE DOCTORS.
VERY GOOD THEN. SEND KLAW OUR BEST PLUMBER.
*ERRR...* PERHAPS SECOND BEST... SOMEONE A BIT MORE... DISPOSABLE.
YOUR EXCELLENCY-- YOUR 3 O'CLOCK IS HERE!
NO NO PLEASE DON'T I TAKE IT BACK...
TELL THE TROOPS-- THE ATTACK STARTS TOMORROW AT DAWN...
OH!
...AND TELL IGOR HIS TOILET'S GETTING FIXED.

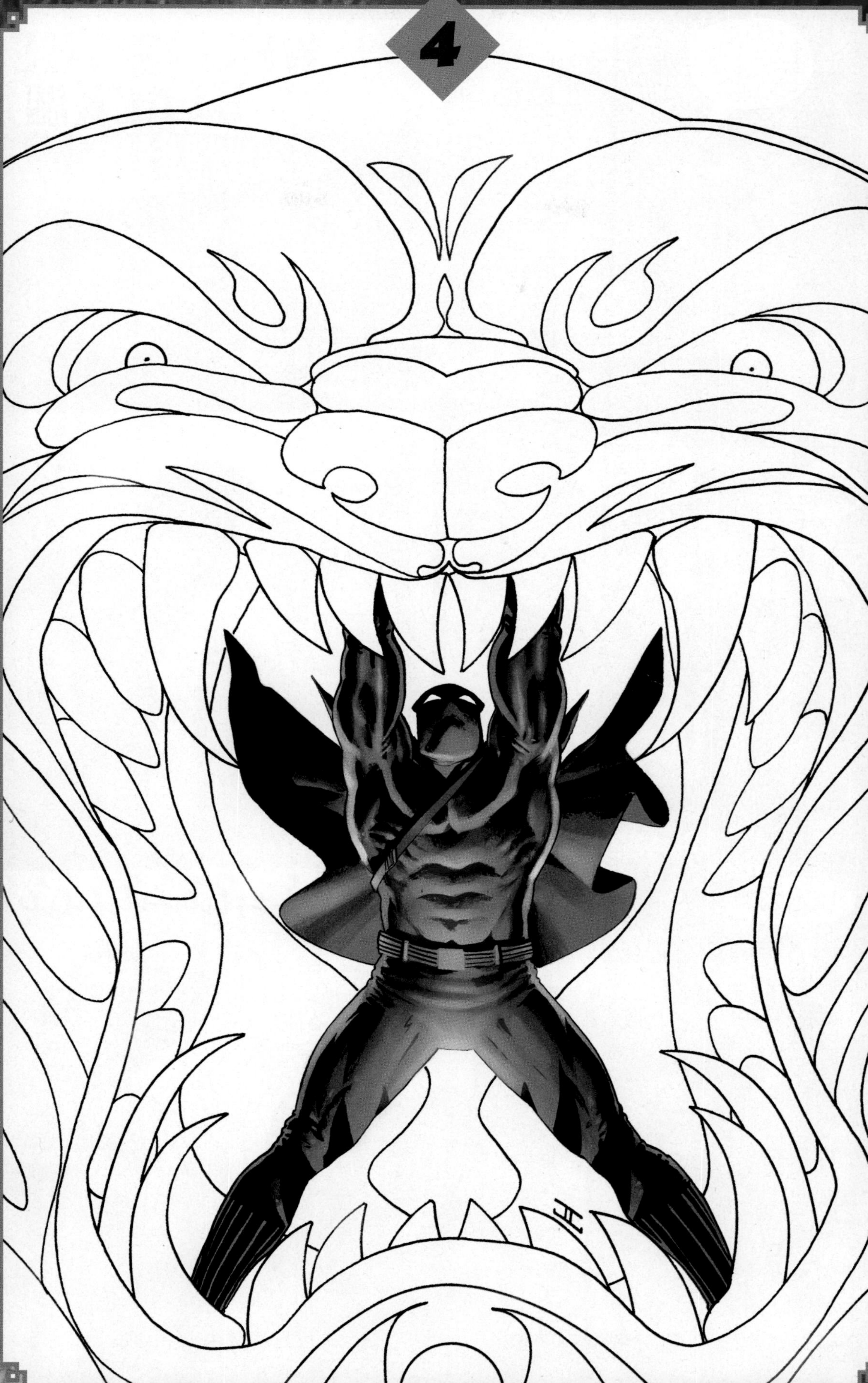
4

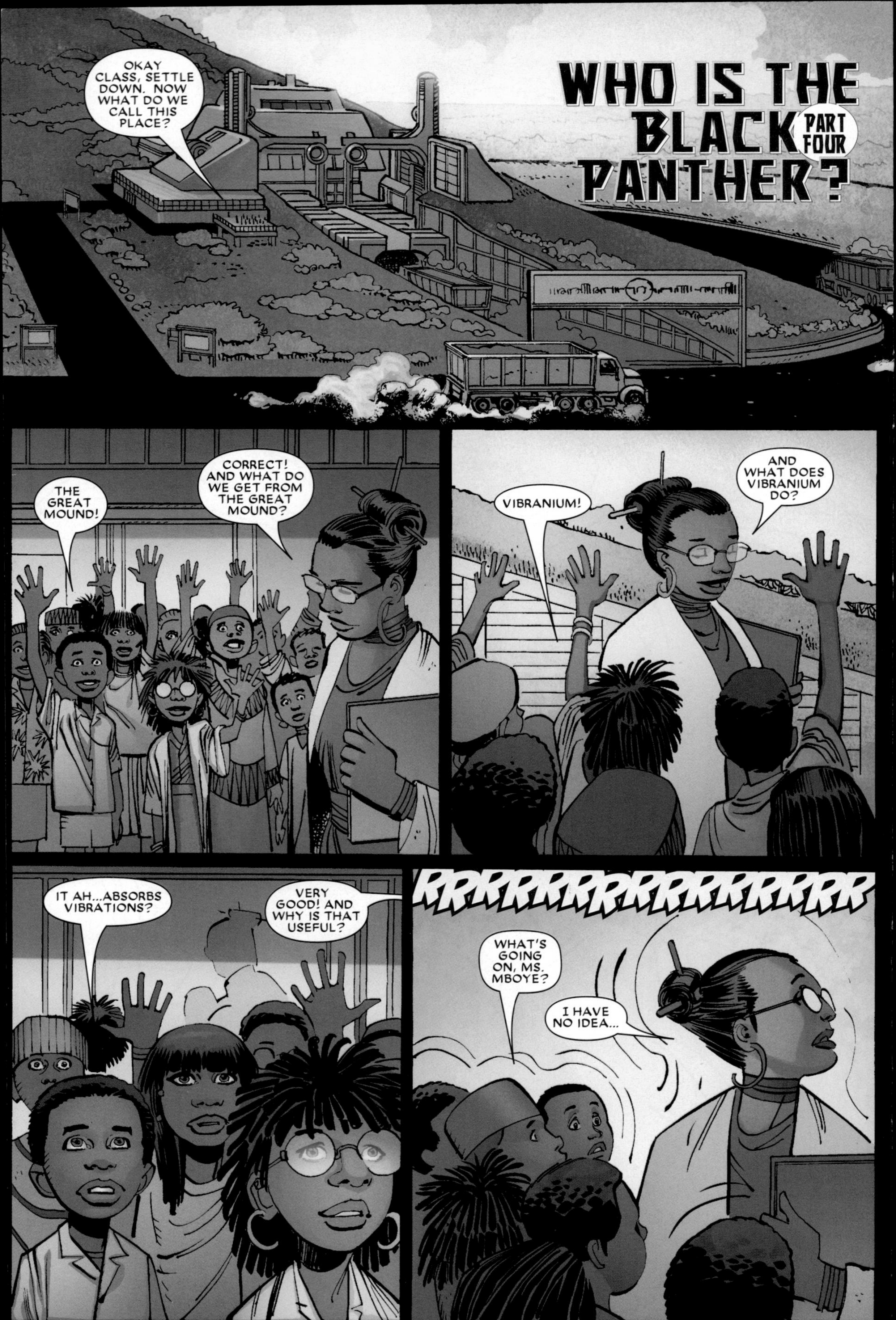

OKAY CLASS, SETTLE DOWN. NOW WHAT DO WE CALL THIS PLACE?
WHO IS THE BLACK PANTHER? PART FOUR
THE GREAT MOUND!
CORRECT! AND WHAT DO WE GET FROM THE GREAT MOUND?
VIBRANIUM!
AND WHAT DOES VIBRANIUM DO?
IT AH...ABSORBS VIBRATIONS?
VERY GOOD! AND WHY IS THAT USEFUL?
RRRRRRRRRRRRRRRRRRR
WHAT'S GOING ON, MS. MBOYE?
I HAVE NO IDEA...

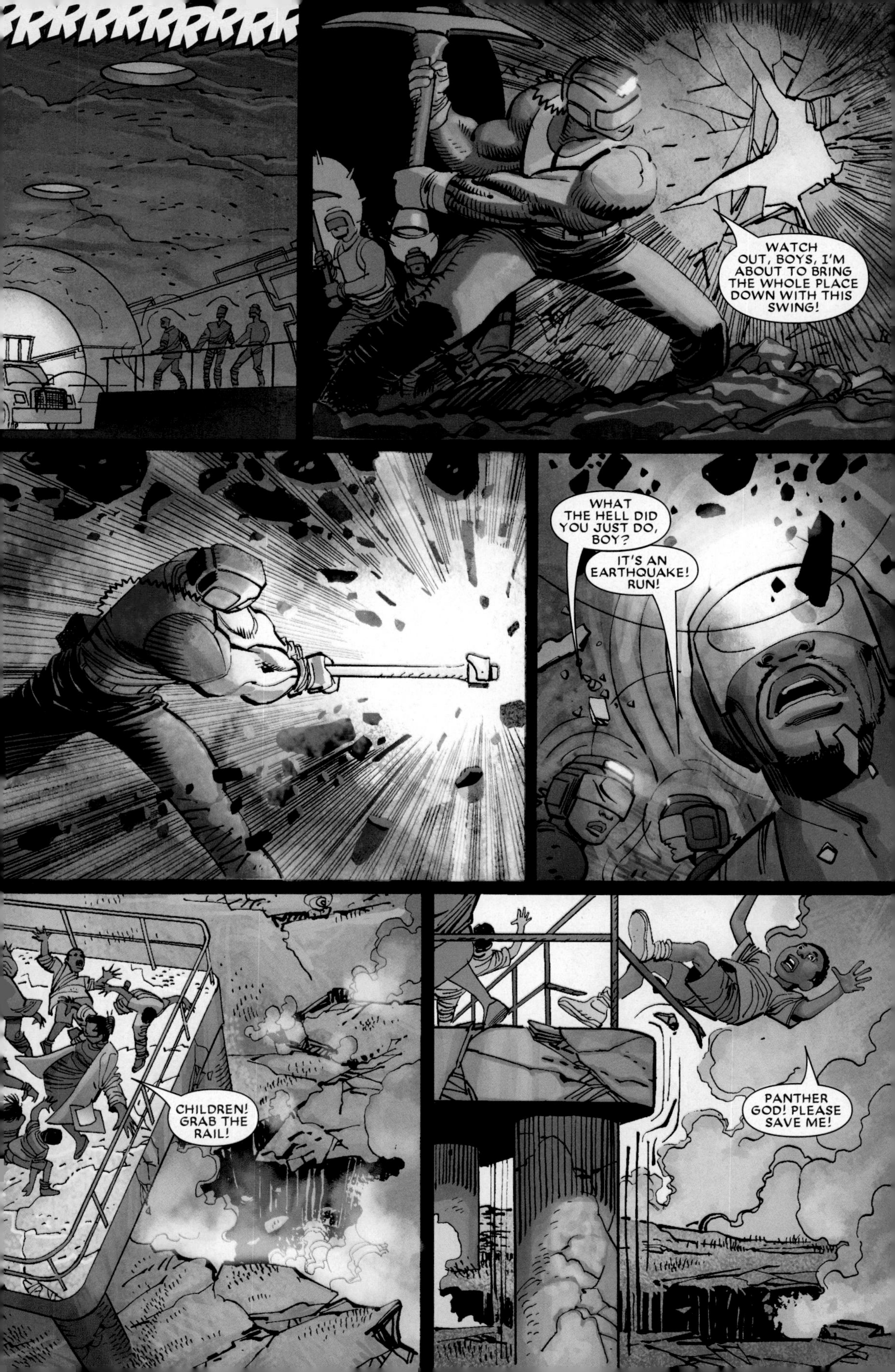
RRRRRRRRRRRR
WATCH OUT, BOYS, I'M ABOUT TO BRING THE WHOLE PLACE DOWN WITH THIS SWING!
WHAT THE HELL DID YOU JUST DO, BOY?
IT'S AN EARTHQUAKE! RUN!
CHILDREN! GRAB THE RAIL!
PANTHER GOD! PLEASE SAVE ME!

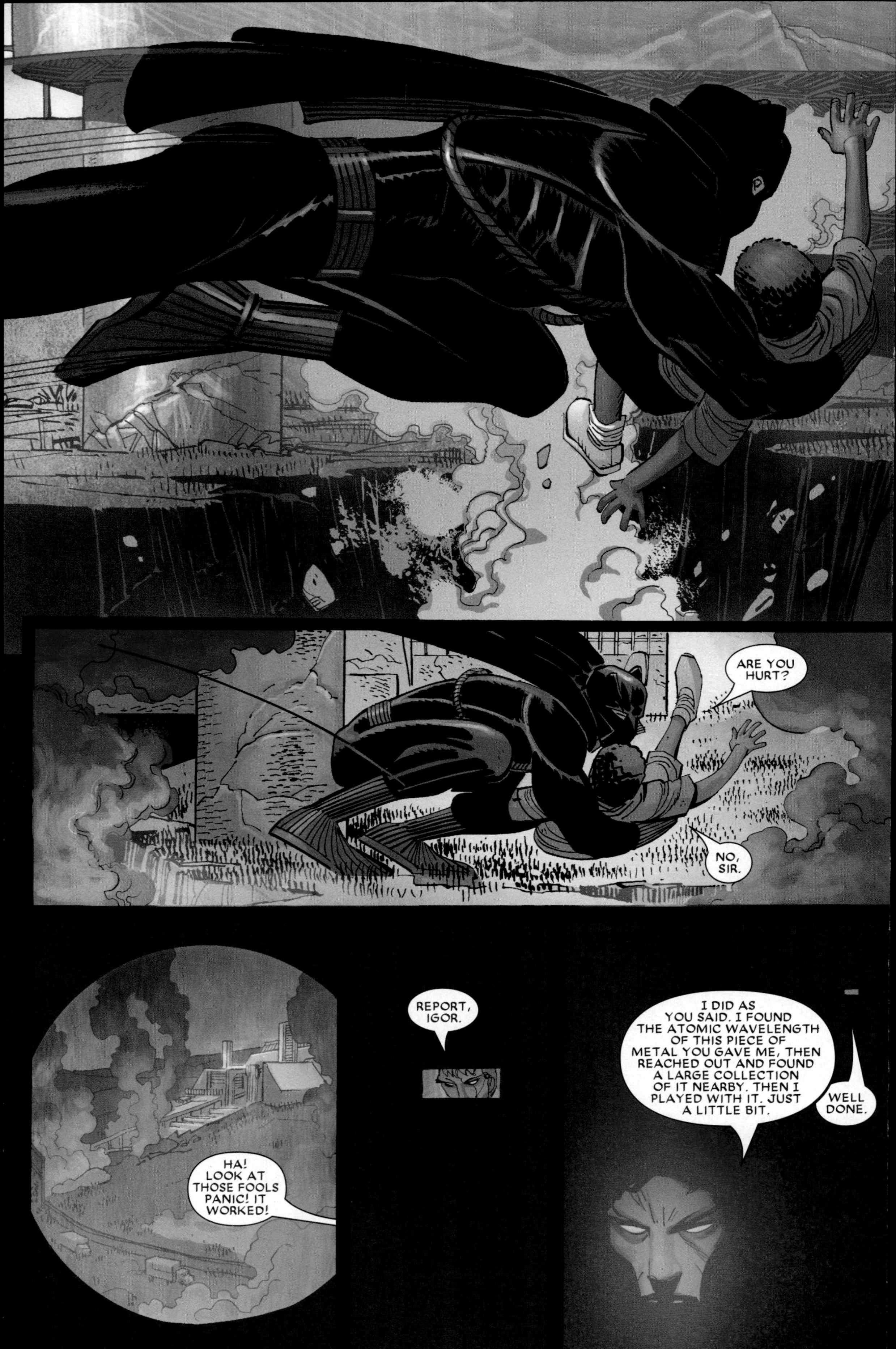
ARE YOU HURT?
NO, SIR.
REPORT, IGOR.
HA! LOOK AT THOSE FOOLS PANIC! IT WORKED!
I DID AS YOU SAID. I FOUND THE ATOMIC WAVELENGTH OF THIS PIECE OF METAL YOU GAVE ME, THEN REACHED OUT AND FOUND A LARGE COLLECTION OF IT NEARBY. THEN I PLAYED WITH IT. JUST A LITTLE BIT.
WELL DONE.

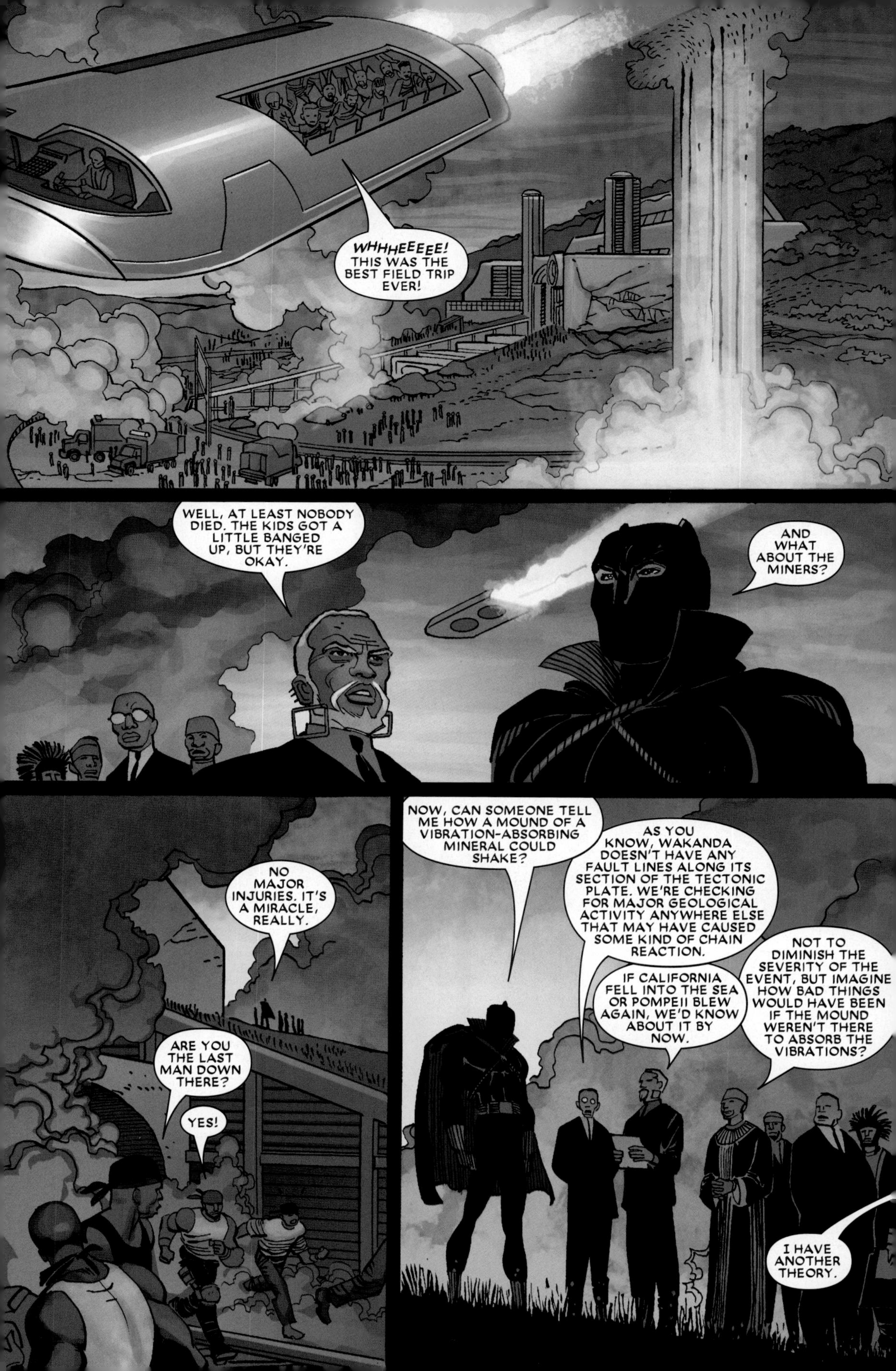
WHHHEEEEE! THIS WAS THE BEST FIELD TRIP EVER!
WELL, AT LEAST NOBODY DIED. THE KIDS GOT A LITTLE BANGED UP, BUT THEY'RE OKAY.
AND WHAT ABOUT THE MINERS?
NO MAJOR INJURIES. IT'S A MIRACLE, REALLY.
ARE YOU THE LAST MAN DOWN THERE?
YES!
NOW, CAN SOMEONE TELL ME HOW A MOUND OF A VIBRATION-ABSORBING MINERAL COULD SHAKE?
AS YOU KNOW, WAKANDA DOESN'T HAVE ANY FAULT LINES ALONG ITS SECTION OF THE TECTONIC PLATE. WE'RE CHECKING FOR MAJOR GEOLOGICAL ACTIVITY ANYWHERE ELSE THAT MAY HAVE CAUSED SOME KIND OF CHAIN REACTION.
IF CALIFORNIA FELL INTO THE SEA OR POMPEII BLEW AGAIN, WE'D KNOW ABOUT IT BY NOW.
NOT TO DIMINISH THE SEVERITY OF THE EVENT, BUT IMAGINE HOW BAD THINGS WOULD HAVE BEEN IF THE MOUND WEREN'T THERE TO ABSORB THE VIBRATIONS?
I HAVE ANOTHER THEORY.

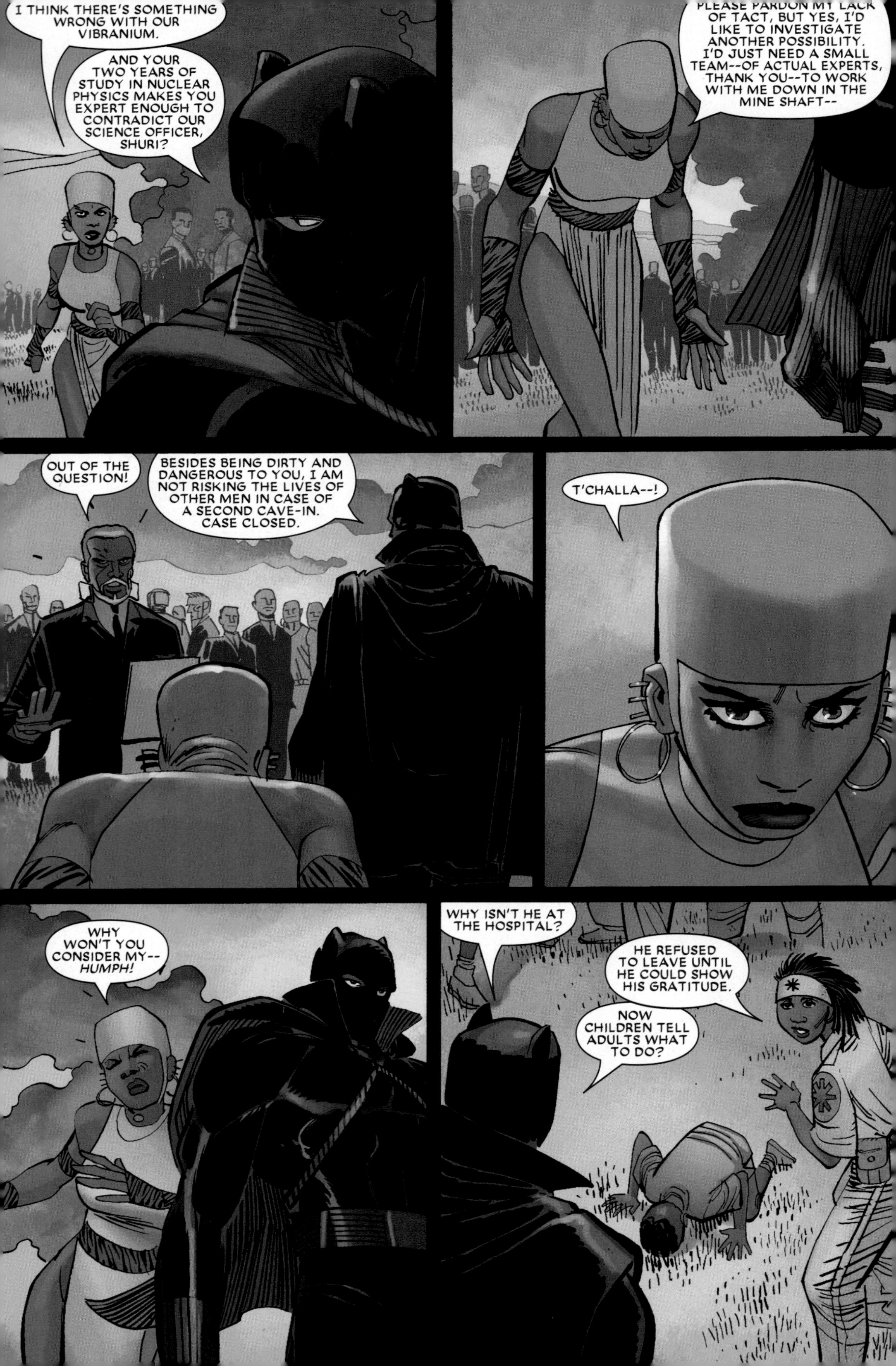
I THINK THERE'S SOMETHING WRONG WITH OUR VIBRANIUM.
AND YOUR TWO YEARS OF STUDY IN NUCLEAR PHYSICS MAKES YOU EXPERT ENOUGH TO CONTRADICT OUR SCIENCE OFFICER, SHURI?
PLEASE PARDON MY LACK OF TACT, BUT YES, I'D LIKE TO INVESTIGATE ANOTHER POSSIBILITY. I'D JUST NEED A SMALL TEAM--OF ACTUAL EXPERTS, THANK YOU--TO WORK WITH ME DOWN IN THE MINE SHAFT--
OUT OF THE QUESTION!
BESIDES BEING DIRTY AND DANGEROUS TO YOU, I AM NOT RISKING THE LIVES OF OTHER MEN IN CASE OF A SECOND CAVE-IN. CASE CLOSED.
T'CHALLA--!
WHY WON'T YOU CONSIDER MY-- *HUMPH!*
WHY ISN'T HE AT THE HOSPITAL?
HE REFUSED TO LEAVE UNTIL HE COULD SHOW HIS GRATITUDE.
NOW CHILDREN TELL ADULTS WHAT TO DO?

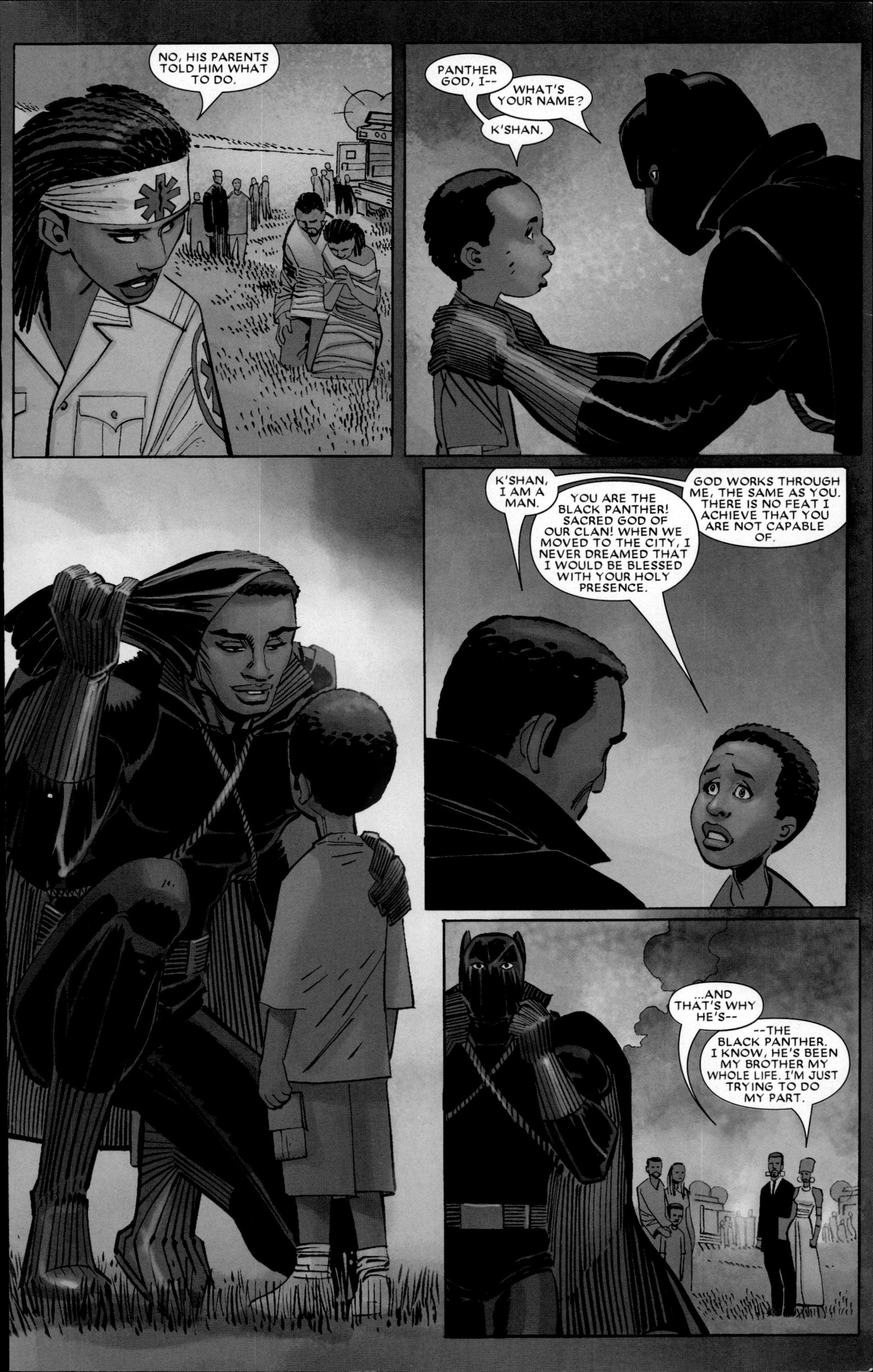
NO, HIS PARENTS TOLD HIM WHAT TO DO.
PANTHER GOD, I--
WHAT'S YOUR NAME?
K'SHAN.
K'SHAN, I AM A MAN.
YOU ARE THE BLACK PANTHER! SACRED GOD OF OUR CLAN! WHEN WE MOVED TO THE CITY, I NEVER DREAMED THAT I WOULD BE BLESSED WITH YOUR HOLY PRESENCE.
GOD WORKS THROUGH ME, THE SAME AS YOU. THERE IS NO FEAT I ACHIEVE THAT YOU ARE NOT CAPABLE OF.
...AND THAT'S WHY HE'S--
--THE BLACK PANTHER. I KNOW, HE'S BEEN MY BROTHER MY WHOLE LIFE. I'M JUST TRYING TO DO MY PART.

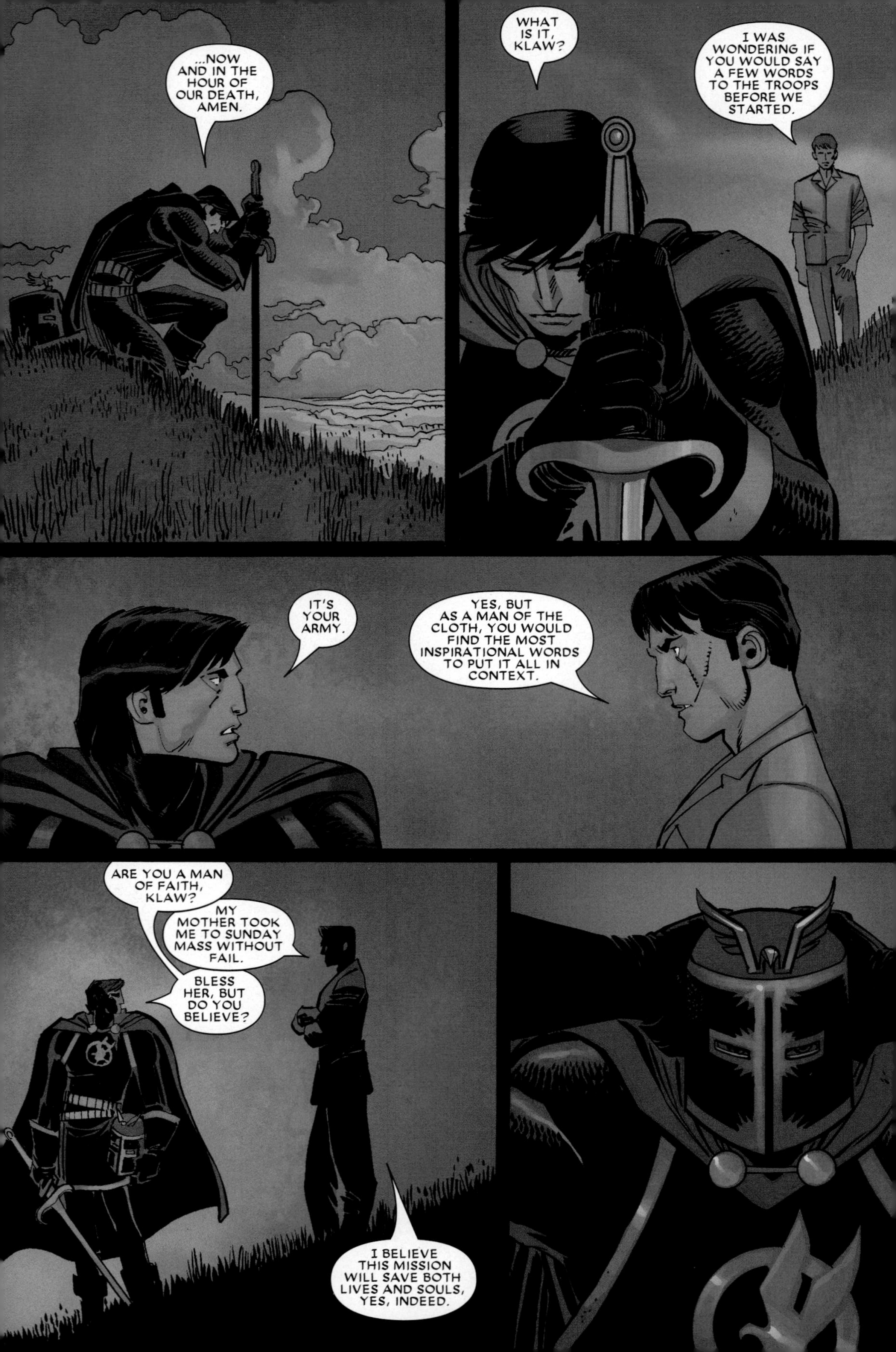
...NOW AND IN THE HOUR OF OUR DEATH, AMEN.
WHAT IS IT, KLAW?
I WAS WONDERING IF YOU WOULD SAY A FEW WORDS TO THE TROOPS BEFORE WE STARTED.
IT'S YOUR ARMY.
YES, BUT AS A MAN OF THE CLOTH, YOU WOULD FIND THE MOST INSPIRATIONAL WORDS TO PUT IT ALL IN CONTEXT.
ARE YOU A MAN OF FAITH, KLAW?
MY MOTHER TOOK ME TO SUNDAY MASS WITHOUT FAIL.
BLESS HER, BUT DO YOU BELIEVE?
I BELIEVE THIS MISSION WILL SAVE BOTH LIVES AND SOULS, YES, INDEED.

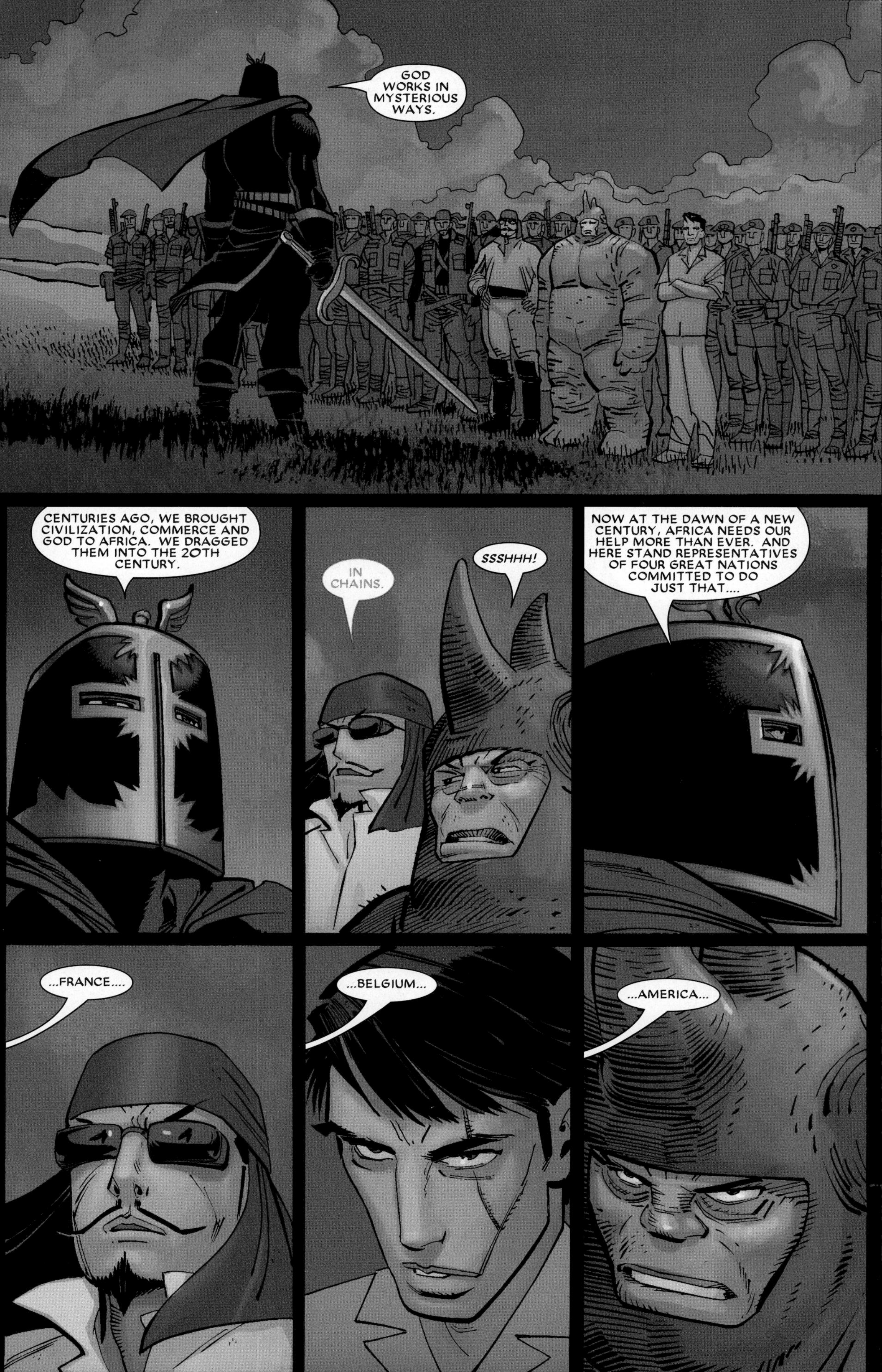
GOD WORKS IN MYSTERIOUS WAYS.
CENTURIES AGO, WE BROUGHT CIVILIZATION, COMMERCE AND GOD TO AFRICA. WE DRAGGED THEM INTO THE 20TH CENTURY.
IN CHAINS.
SSSHHH!
NOW AT THE DAWN OF A NEW CENTURY, AFRICA NEEDS OUR HELP MORE THAN EVER. AND HERE STAND REPRESENTATIVES OF FOUR GREAT NATIONS COMMITTED TO DO JUST THAT....
...FRANCE....
...BELGIUM...
...AMERICA...

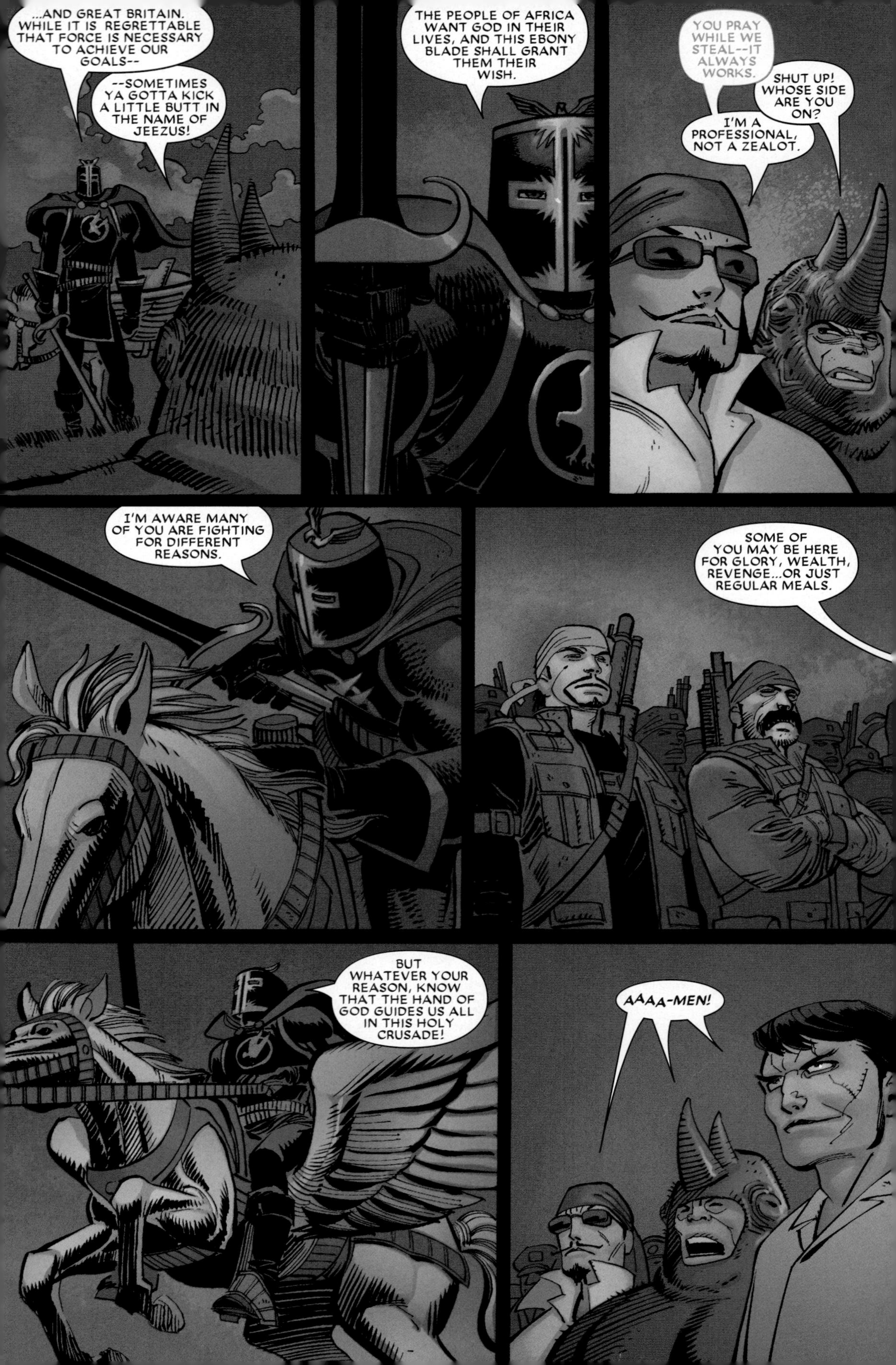
...AND GREAT BRITAIN. WHILE IT IS REGRETTABLE THAT FORCE IS NECESSARY TO ACHIEVE OUR GOALS--
--SOMETIMES YA GOTTA KICK A LITTLE BUTT IN THE NAME OF JEEZUS!
THE PEOPLE OF AFRICA WANT GOD IN THEIR LIVES, AND THIS EBONY BLADE SHALL GRANT THEM THEIR WISH.
YOU PRAY WHILE WE STEAL--IT ALWAYS WORKS.
SHUT UP! WHOSE SIDE ARE YOU ON?
I'M A PROFESSIONAL, NOT A ZEALOT.
I'M AWARE MANY OF YOU ARE FIGHTING FOR DIFFERENT REASONS.
SOME OF YOU MAY BE HERE FOR GLORY, WEALTH, REVENGE...OR JUST REGULAR MEALS.
BUT WHATEVER YOUR REASON, KNOW THAT THE HAND OF GOD GUIDES US ALL IN THIS HOLY CRUSADE!
AAAA-MEN!

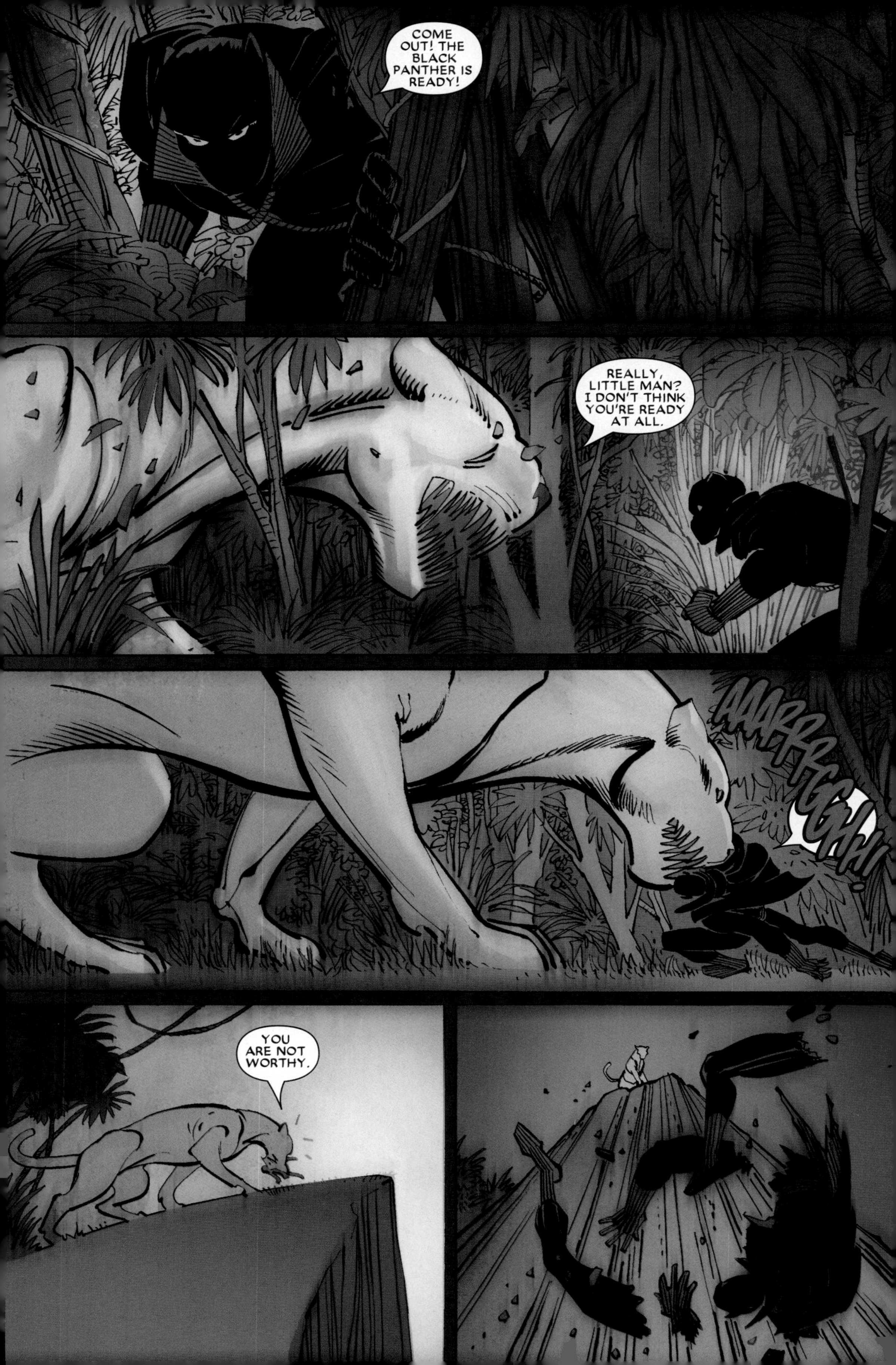
COME OUT! THE BLACK PANTHER IS READY!
REALLY, LITTLE MAN? I DON'T THINK YOU'RE READY AT ALL.
AAARRGGHH!
YOU ARE NOT WORTHY.

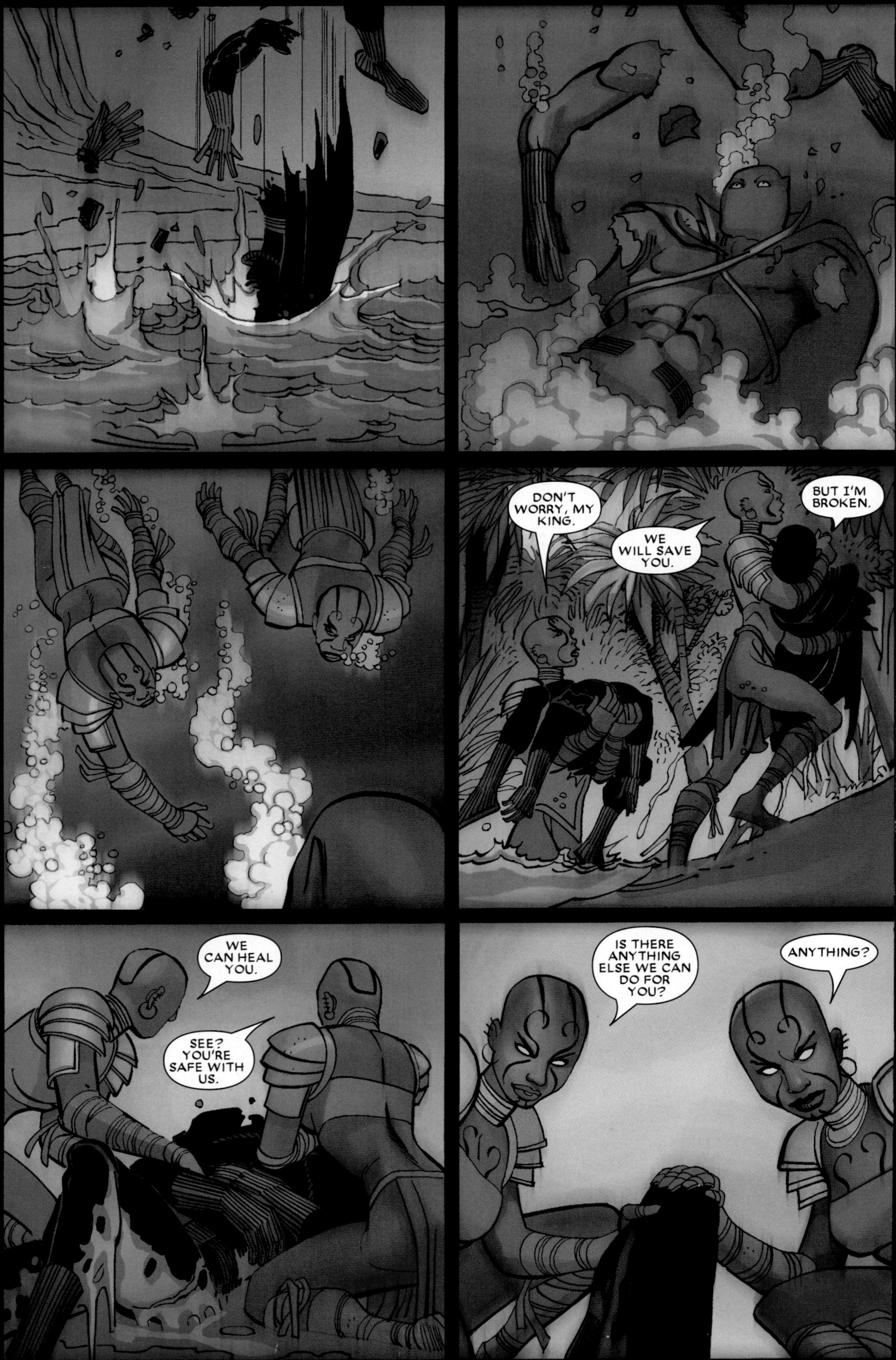
DON'T WORRY, MY KING.
WE WILL SAVE YOU.
BUT I'M BROKEN.
WE CAN HEAL YOU.
SEE? YOU'RE SAFE WITH US.
IS THERE ANYTHING ELSE WE CAN DO FOR YOU?
ANYTHING?

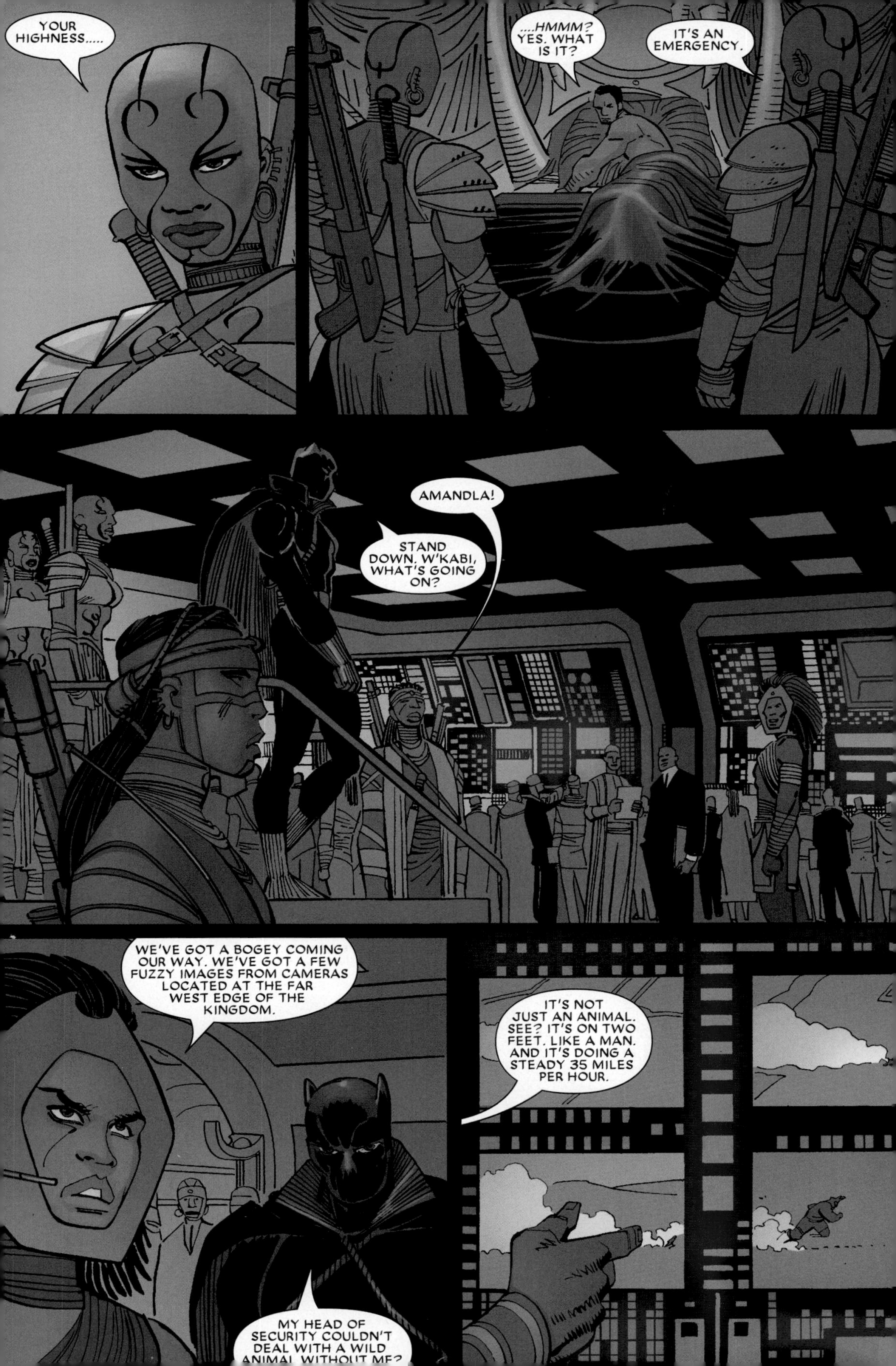
YOUR HIGHNESS.....
....HMMM? YES. WHAT IS IT?
IT'S AN EMERGENCY.
AMANDLA!
STAND DOWN. W'KABI, WHAT'S GOING ON?
WE'VE GOT A BOGEY COMING OUR WAY. WE'VE GOT A FEW FUZZY IMAGES FROM CAMERAS LOCATED AT THE FAR WEST EDGE OF THE KINGDOM.
IT'S NOT JUST AN ANIMAL. SEE? IT'S ON TWO FEET. LIKE A MAN. AND IT'S DOING A STEADY 35 MILES PER HOUR.
MY HEAD OF SECURITY COULDN'T DEAL WITH A WILD ANIMAL WITHOUT ME?

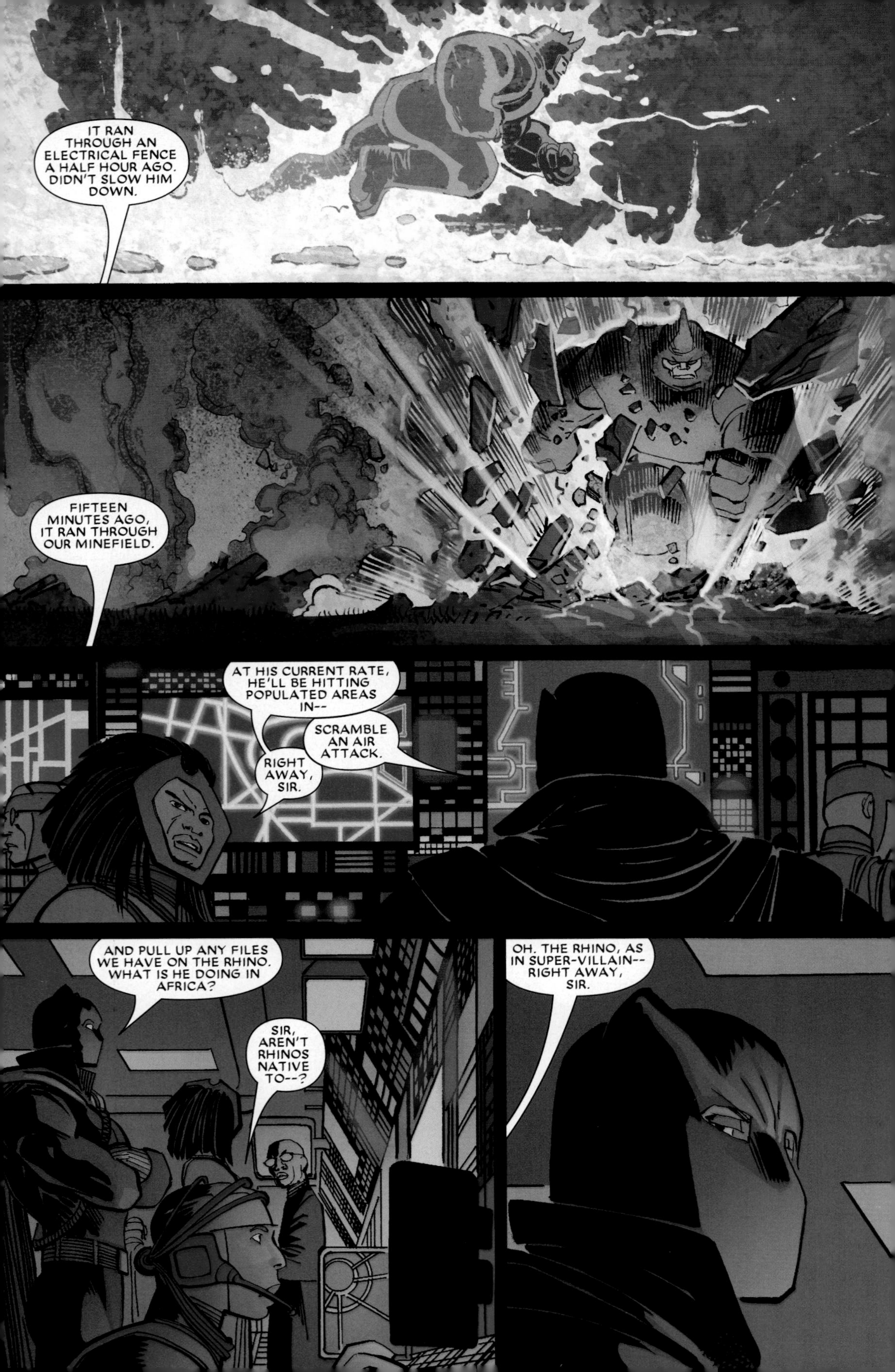
IT RAN THROUGH AN ELECTRICAL FENCE A HALF HOUR AGO. DIDN'T SLOW HIM DOWN.
FIFTEEN MINUTES AGO, IT RAN THROUGH OUR MINEFIELD.
AT HIS CURRENT RATE, HE'LL BE HITTING POPULATED AREAS IN--
SCRAMBLE AN AIR ATTACK.
RIGHT AWAY, SIR.
AND PULL UP ANY FILES WE HAVE ON THE RHINO. WHAT IS HE DOING IN AFRICA?
SIR, AREN'T RHINOS NATIVE TO--?
OH. THE RHINO, AS IN SUPER-VILLAIN-- RIGHT AWAY, SIR.

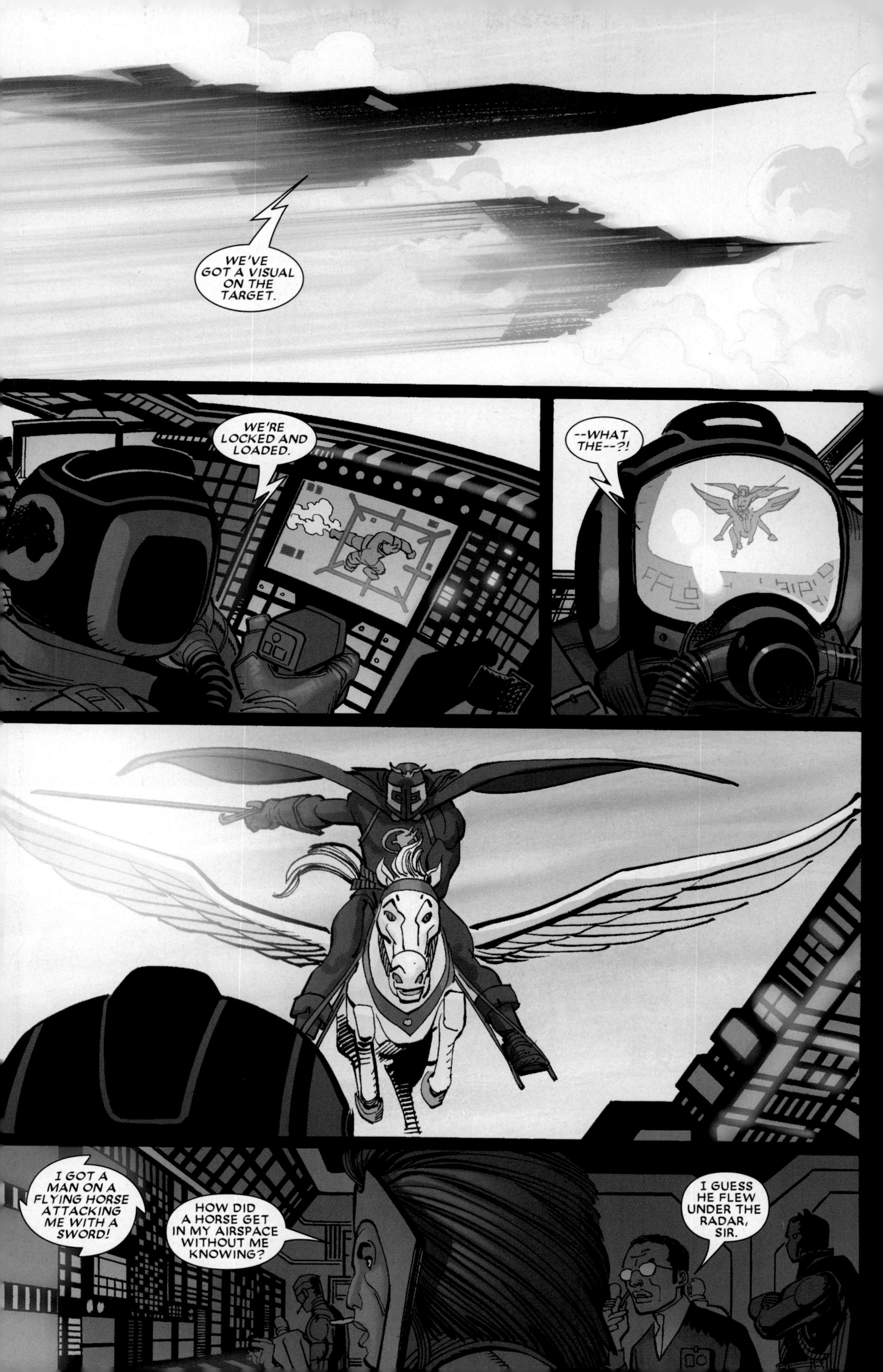
WE'VE GOT A VISUAL ON THE TARGET.
WE'RE LOCKED AND LOADED.
--WHAT THE--?!
I GOT A MAN ON A FLYING HORSE ATTACKING ME WITH A SWORD!
HOW DID A HORSE GET IN MY AIRSPACE WITHOUT ME KNOWING?
I GUESS HE FLEW UNDER THE RADAR, SIR.

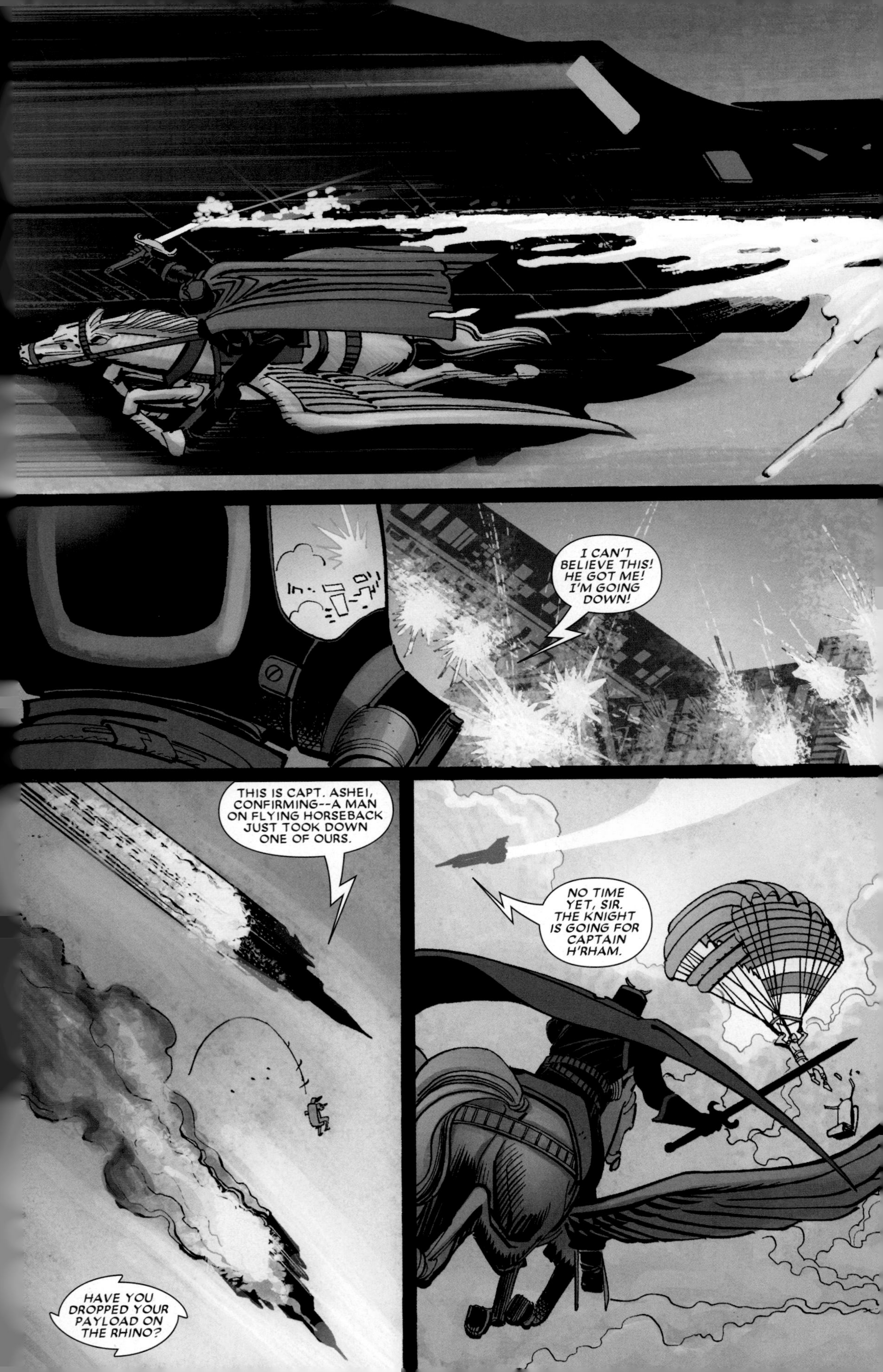
I CAN'T BELIEVE THIS! HE GOT ME! I'M GOING DOWN!
THIS IS CAPT. ASHEI, CONFIRMING--A MAN ON FLYING HORSEBACK JUST TOOK DOWN ONE OF OURS.
HAVE YOU DROPPED YOUR PAYLOAD ON THE RHINO?
NO TIME YET, SIR. THE KNIGHT IS GOING FOR CAPTAIN H'RHAM.

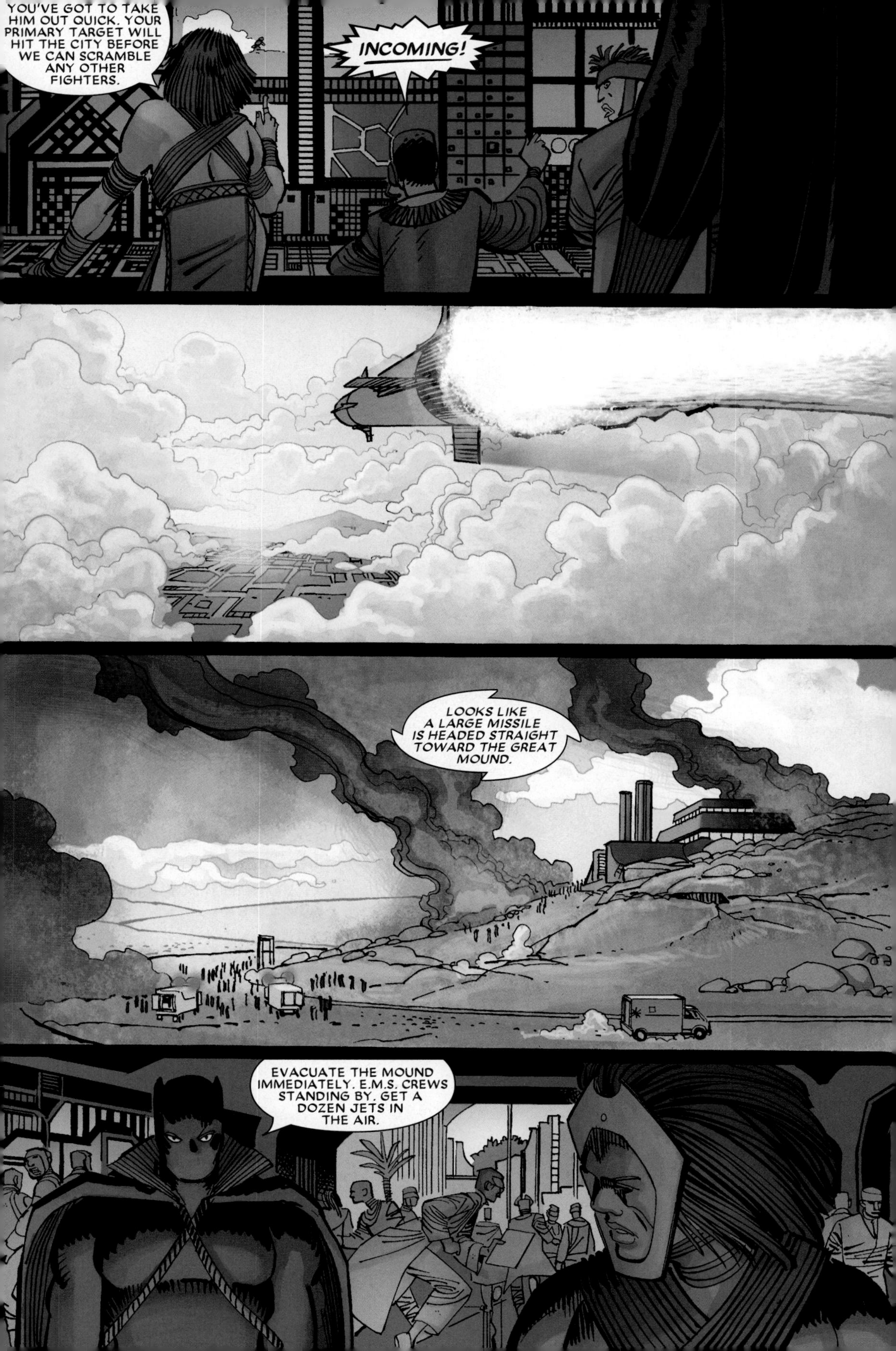
YOU'VE GOT TO TAKE HIM OUT QUICK. YOUR PRIMARY TARGET WILL HIT THE CITY BEFORE WE CAN SCRAMBLE ANY OTHER FIGHTERS.
INCOMING!
LOOKS LIKE A LARGE MISSILE IS HEADED STRAIGHT TOWARD THE GREAT MOUND.
EVACUATE THE MOUND IMMEDIATELY. E.M.S. CREWS STANDING BY. GET A DOZEN JETS IN THE AIR.

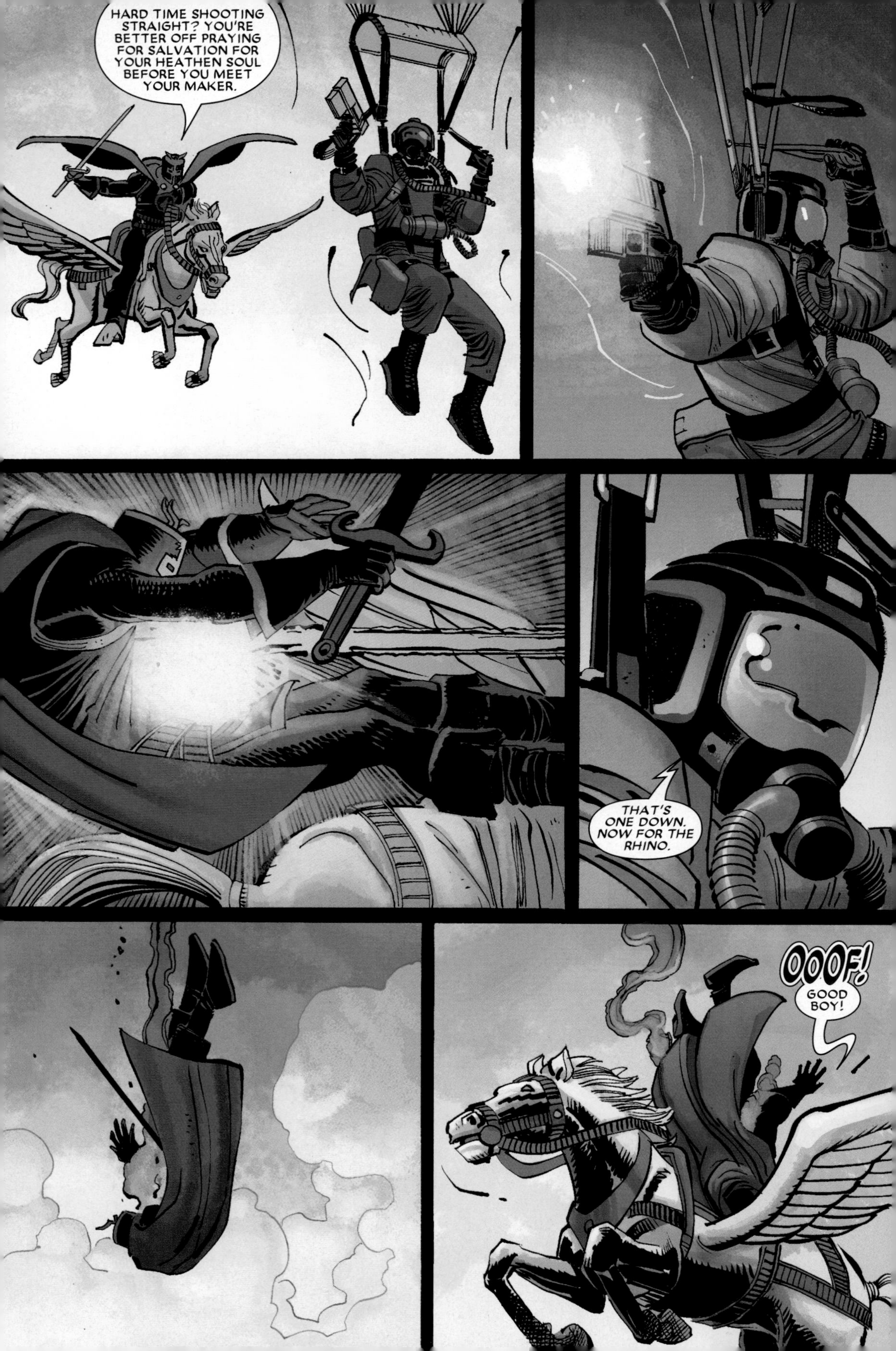
HARD TIME SHOOTING STRAIGHT? YOU'RE BETTER OFF PRAYING FOR SALVATION FOR YOUR HEATHEN SOUL BEFORE YOU MEET YOUR MAKER.
THAT'S ONE DOWN. NOW FOR THE RHINO.
OOOF!
GOOD BOY!

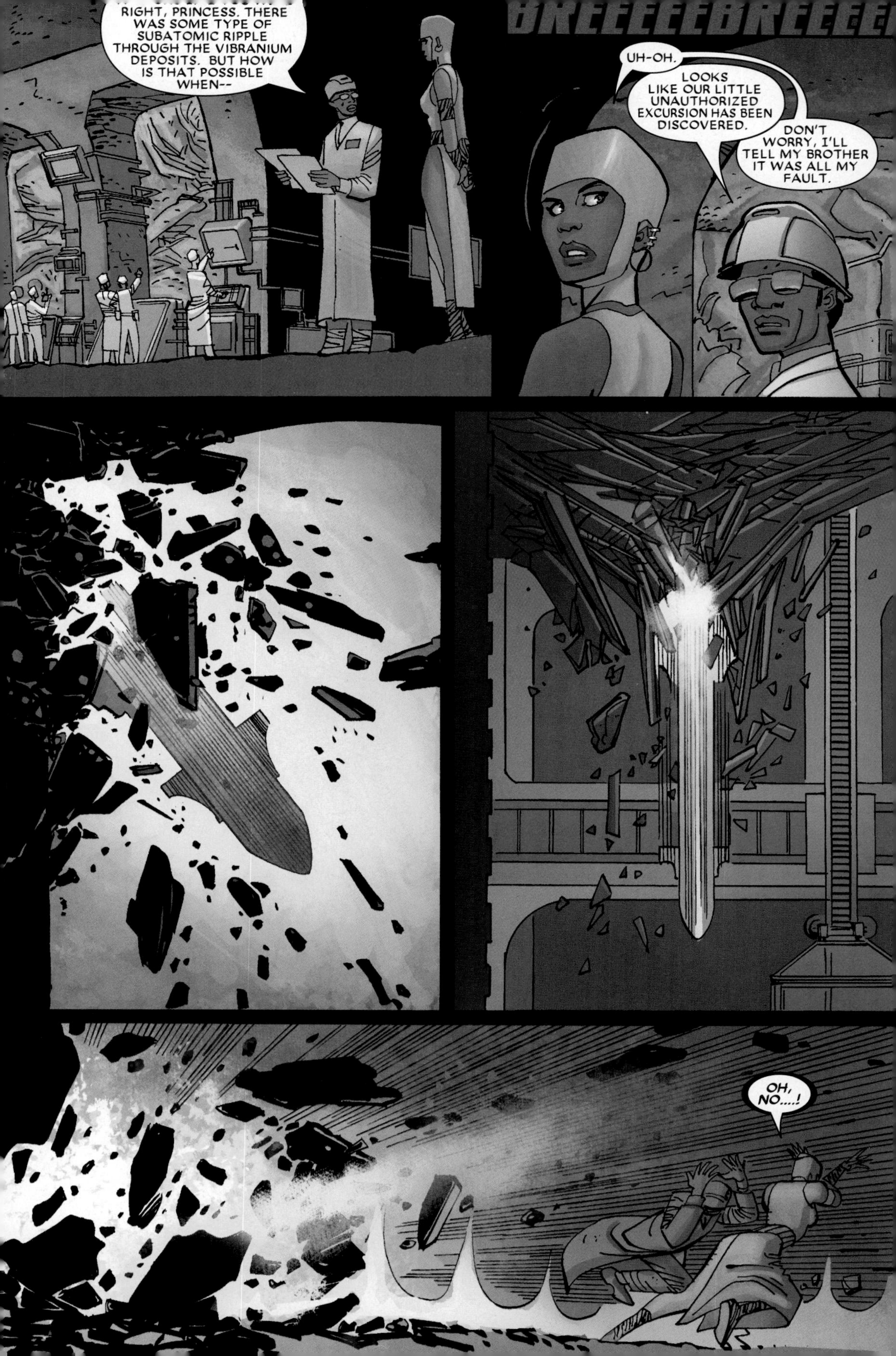
RIGHT, PRINCESS. THERE WAS SOME TYPE OF SUBATOMIC RIPPLE THROUGH THE VIBRANIUM DEPOSITS. BUT HOW IS THAT POSSIBLE WHEN--
BREEEEBREEEE
UH-OH.
LOOKS LIKE OUR LITTLE UNAUTHORIZED EXCURSION HAS BEEN DISCOVERED.
DON'T WORRY, I'LL TELL MY BROTHER IT WAS ALL MY FAULT.
OH, NO....!

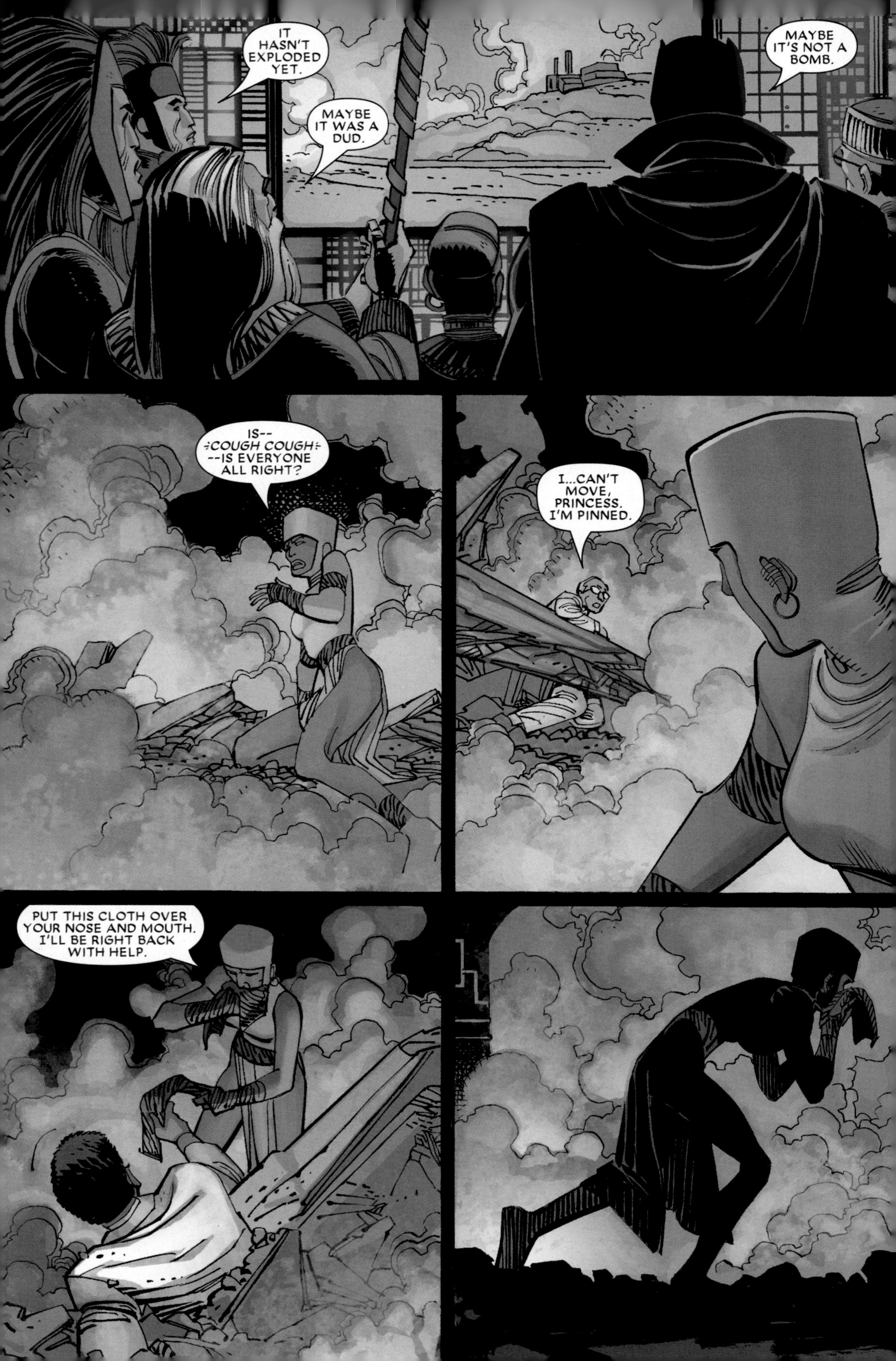
IT HASN'T EXPLODED YET.
MAYBE IT WAS A DUD.
MAYBE IT'S NOT A BOMB.
IS-- ≑COUGH COUGH≑ --IS EVERYONE ALL RIGHT?
I...CAN'T MOVE, PRINCESS. I'M PINNED.
PUT THIS CLOTH OVER YOUR NOSE AND MOUTH. I'LL BE RIGHT BACK WITH HELP.

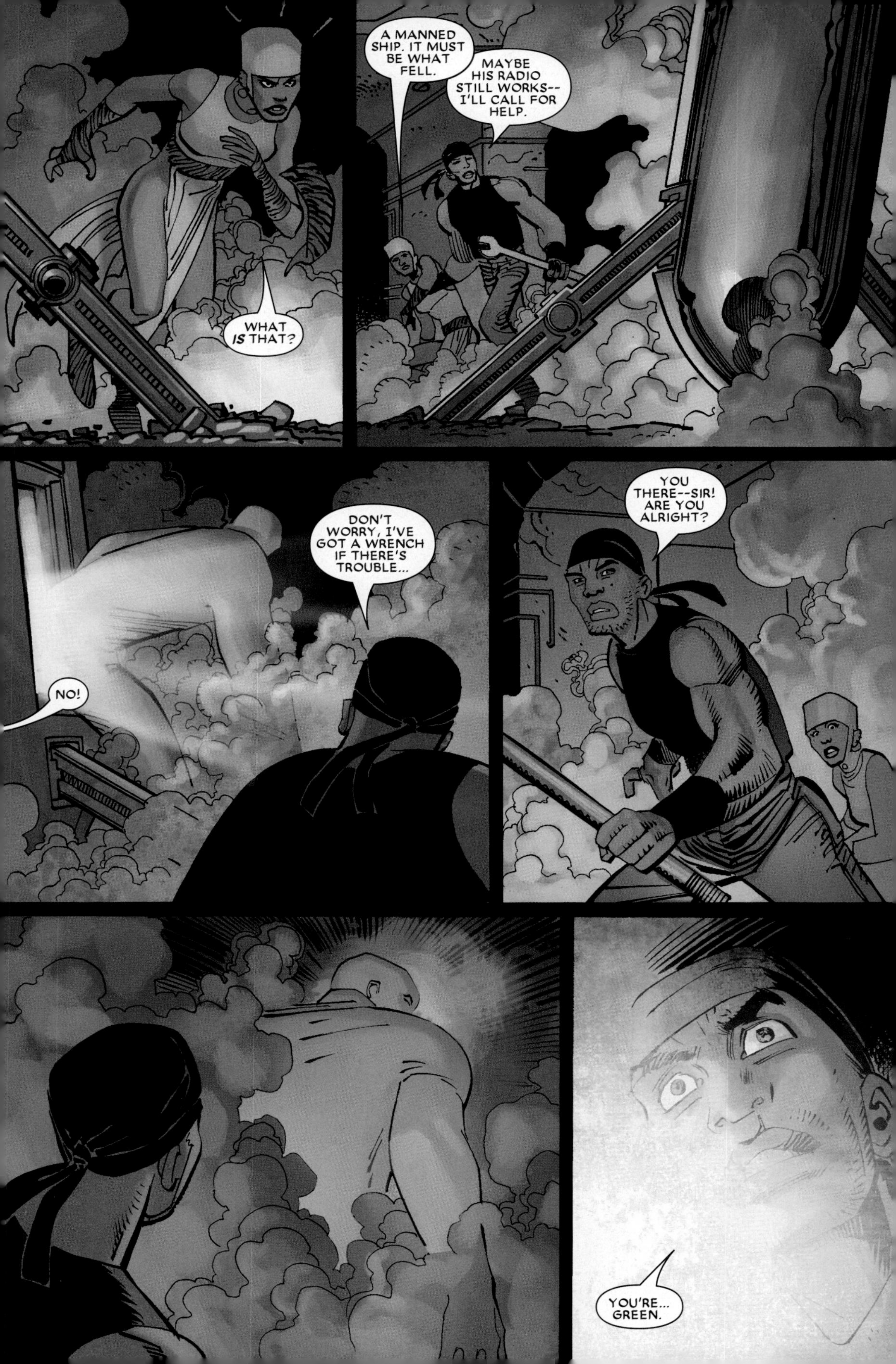
WHAT *IS* THAT?
A MANNED SHIP. IT MUST BE WHAT FELL.
MAYBE HIS RADIO STILL WORKS-- I'LL CALL FOR HELP.
DON'T WORRY, I'VE GOT A WRENCH IF THERE'S TROUBLE...
NO!
YOU THERE--SIR! ARE YOU ALRIGHT?
YOU'RE... GREEN.

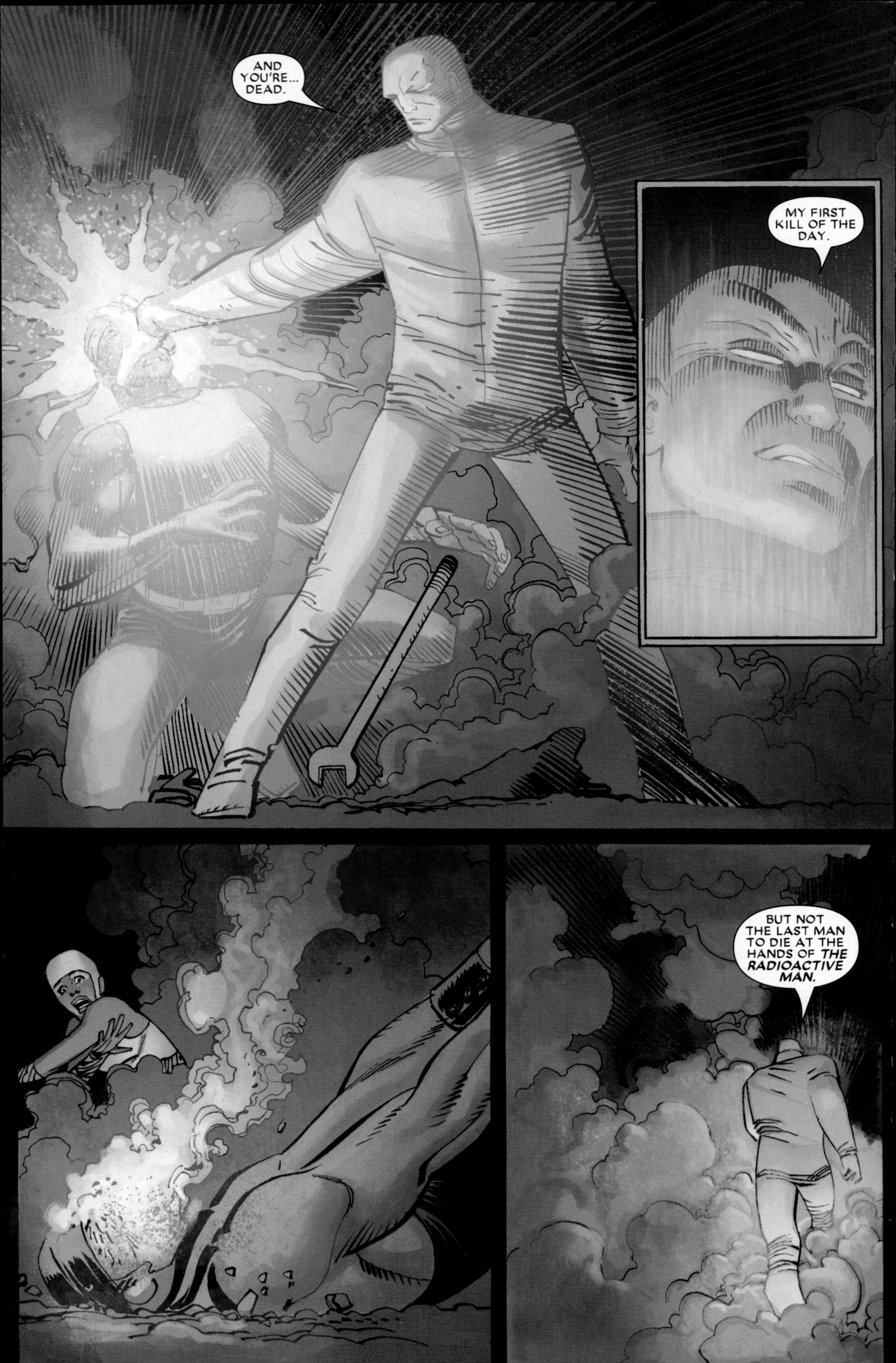
AND YOU'RE... DEAD.
MY FIRST KILL OF THE DAY.
BUT NOT THE LAST MAN TO DIE AT THE HANDS OF *THE RADIOACTIVE MAN.*

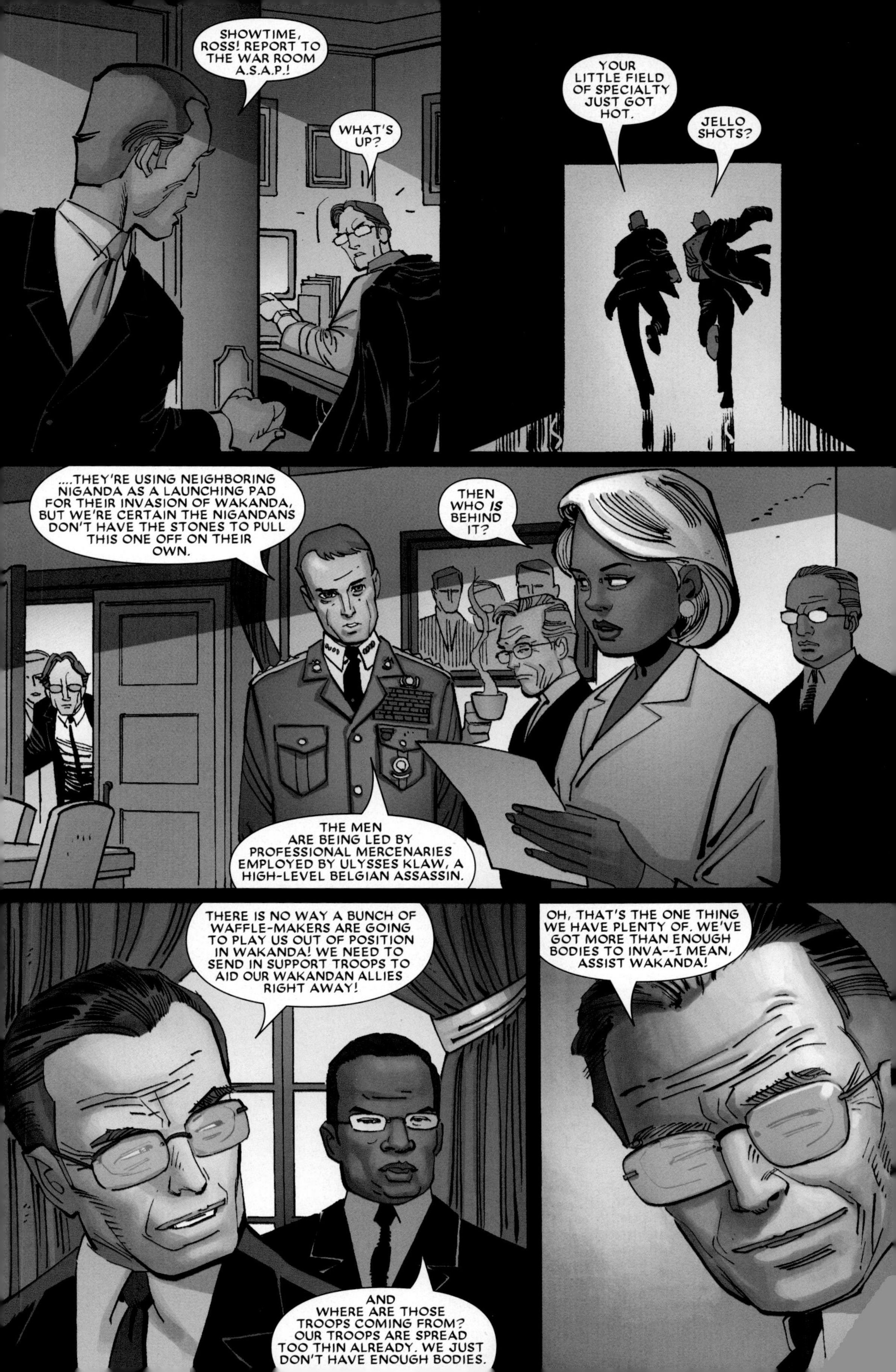
SHOWTIME, ROSS! REPORT TO THE WAR ROOM A.S.A.P.!
WHAT'S UP?
YOUR LITTLE FIELD OF SPECIALTY JUST GOT HOT.
JELLO SHOTS?
....THEY'RE USING NEIGHBORING NIGANDA AS A LAUNCHING PAD FOR THEIR INVASION OF WAKANDA, BUT WE'RE CERTAIN THE NIGANDANS DON'T HAVE THE STONES TO PULL THIS ONE OFF ON THEIR OWN.
THEN WHO *IS* BEHIND IT?
THE MEN ARE BEING LED BY PROFESSIONAL MERCENARIES EMPLOYED BY ULYSSES KLAW, A HIGH-LEVEL BELGIAN ASSASSIN.
THERE IS NO WAY A BUNCH OF WAFFLE-MAKERS ARE GOING TO PLAY US OUT OF POSITION IN WAKANDA! WE NEED TO SEND IN SUPPORT TROOPS TO AID OUR WAKANDAN ALLIES RIGHT AWAY!
AND WHERE ARE THOSE TROOPS COMING FROM? OUR TROOPS ARE SPREAD TOO THIN ALREADY. WE JUST DON'T HAVE ENOUGH BODIES.
OH, THAT'S THE ONE THING WE HAVE PLENTY OF. WE'VE GOT MORE THAN ENOUGH BODIES TO INVA--I MEAN, ASSIST WAKANDA!

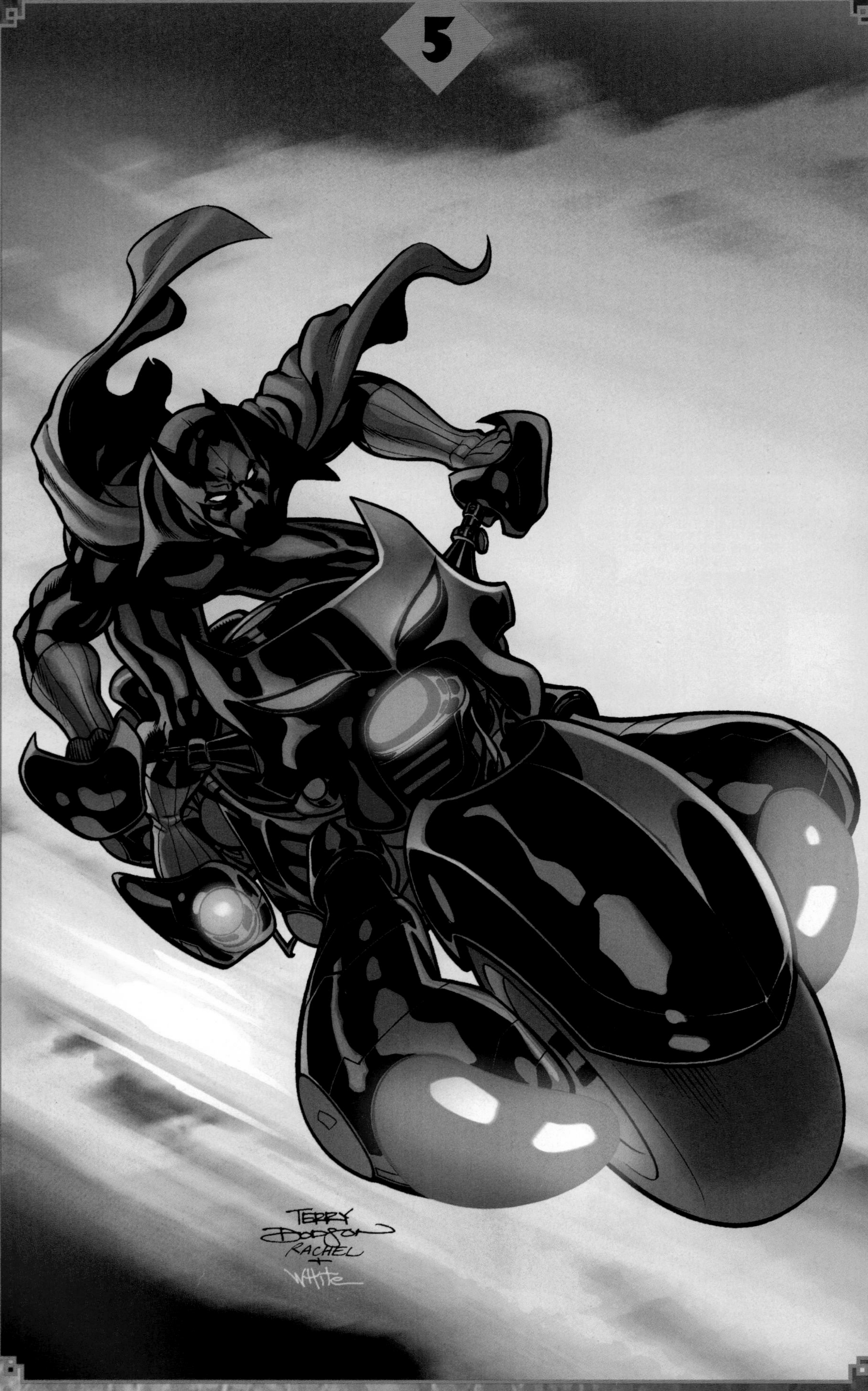
5
TERRY
DODSON
RACHEL
+
WHITE

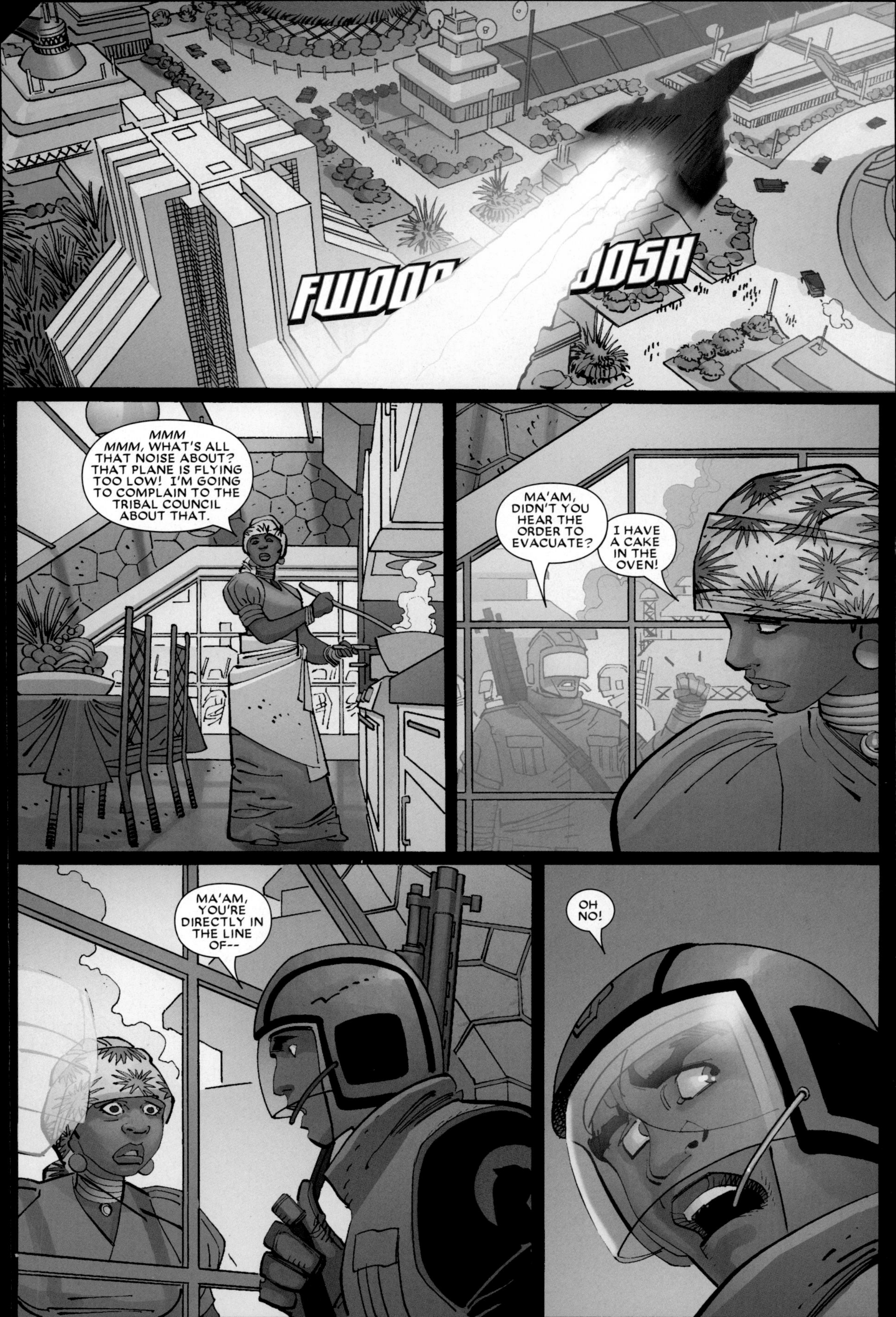
FWOOO
JOSH
MMM MMM, WHAT'S ALL THAT NOISE ABOUT? THAT PLANE IS FLYING TOO LOW! I'M GOING TO COMPLAIN TO THE TRIBAL COUNCIL ABOUT THAT.
MA'AM, DIDN'T YOU HEAR THE ORDER TO EVACUATE?
I HAVE A CAKE IN THE OVEN!
MA'AM, YOU'RE DIRECTLY IN THE LINE OF--
OH NO!

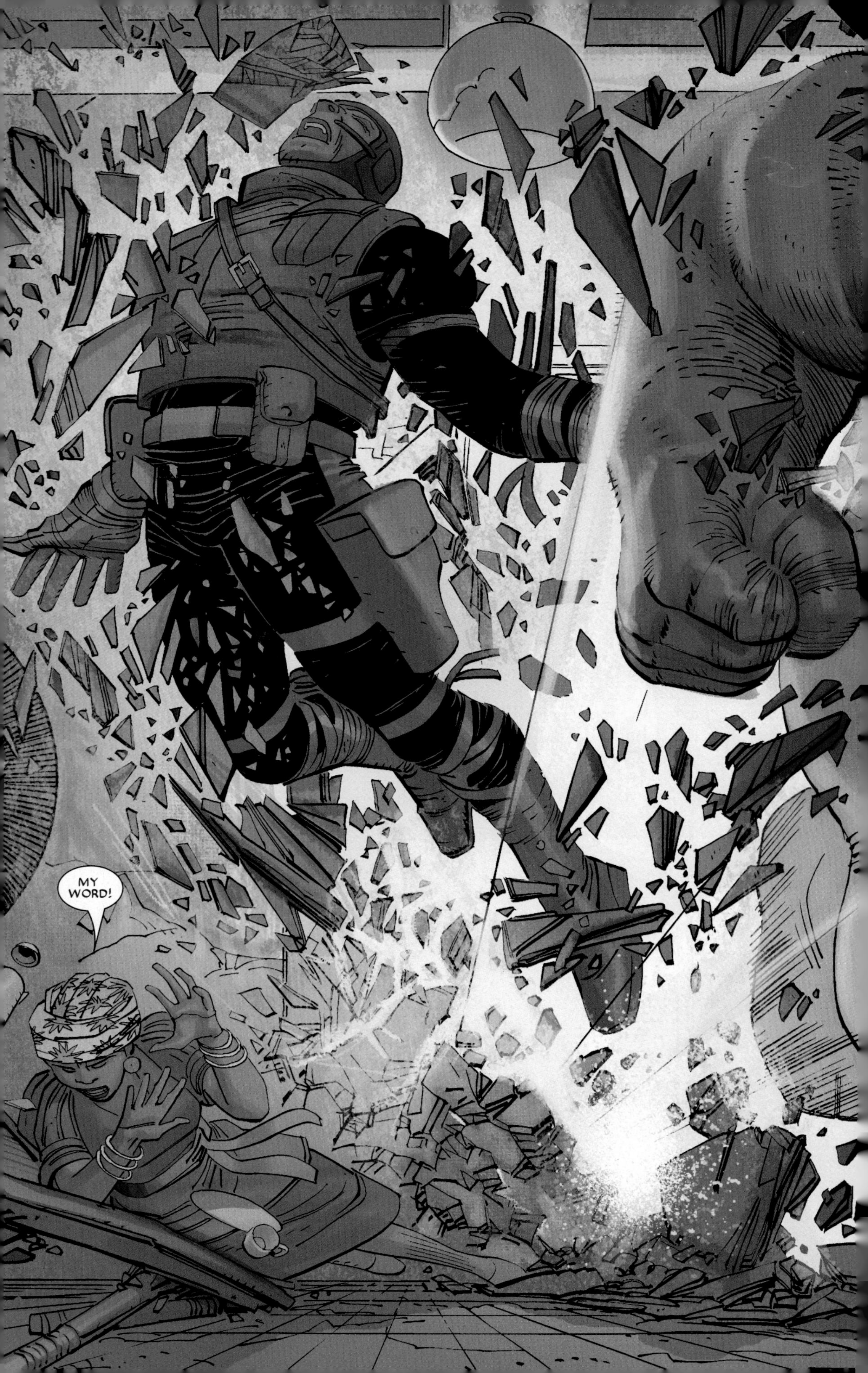
MY WORD!

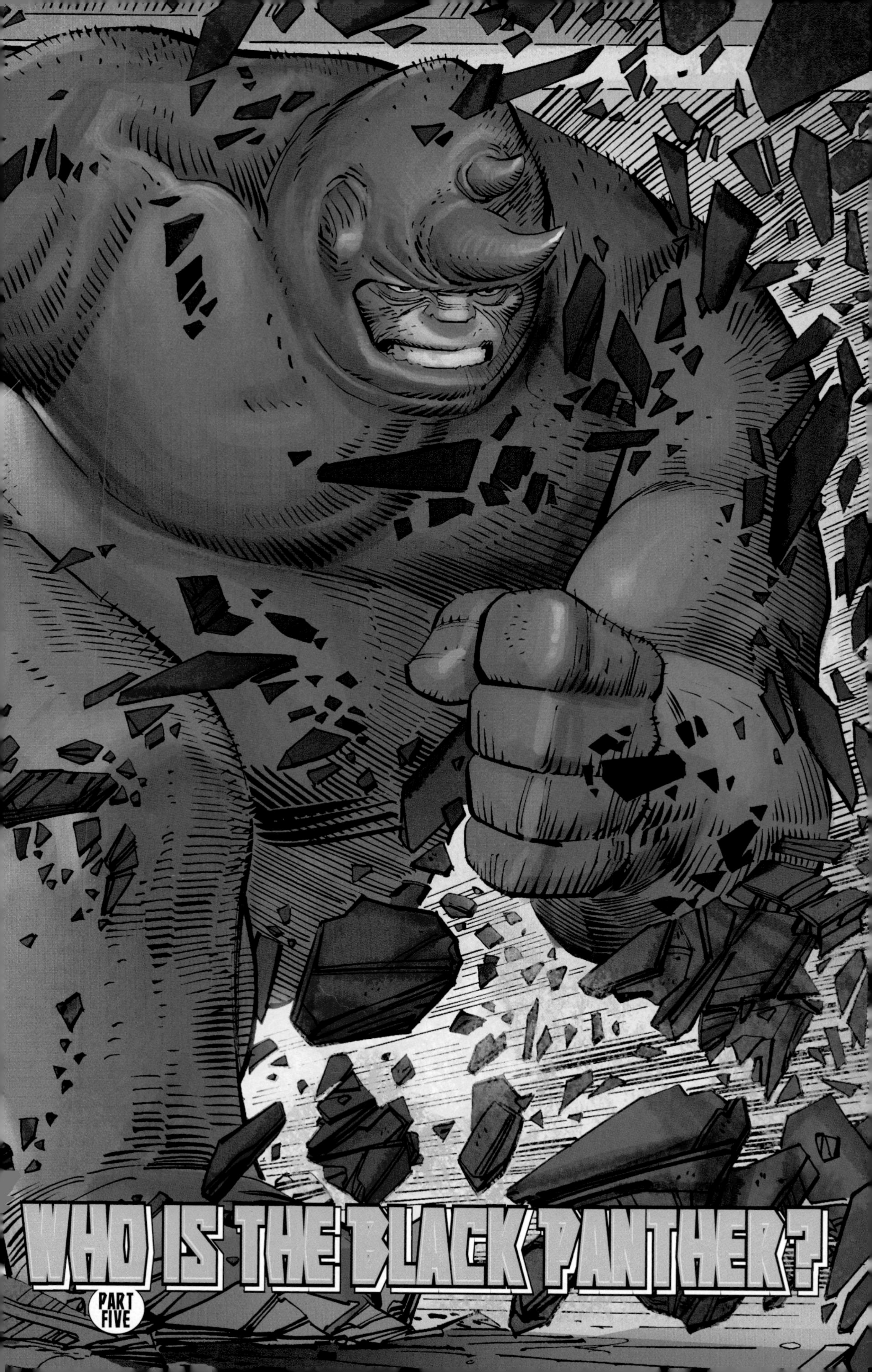
WHO IS THE BLACK PANTHER?
PART FIVE

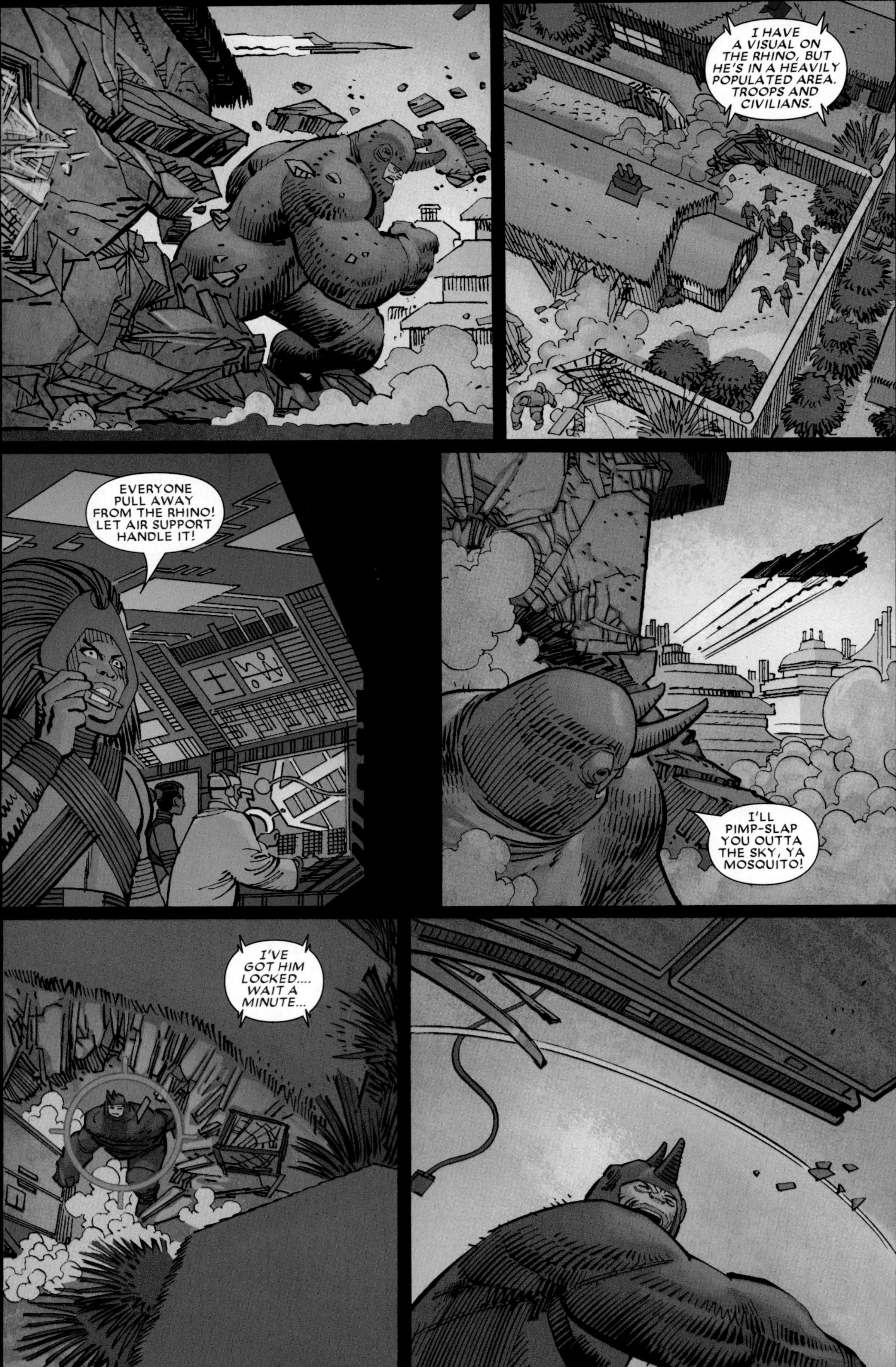
I HAVE A VISUAL ON THE RHINO, BUT HE'S IN A HEAVILY POPULATED AREA. TROOPS AND CIVILIANS.
EVERYONE PULL AWAY FROM THE RHINO! LET AIR SUPPORT HANDLE IT!
I'LL PIMP-SLAP YOU OUTTA THE SKY, YA MOSQUITO!
I'VE GOT HIM LOCKED.... WAIT A MINUTE...

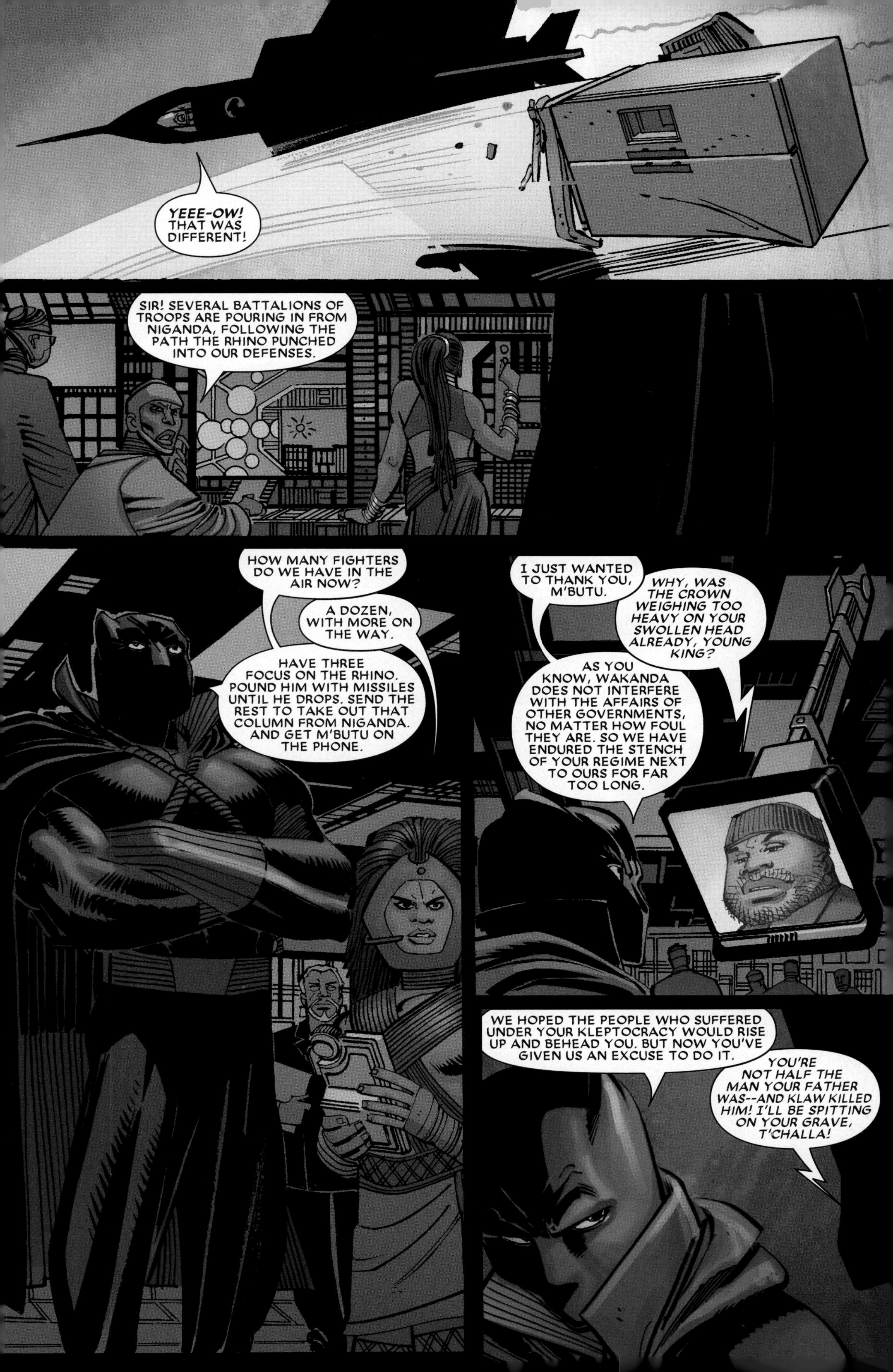
YEEE-OW! THAT WAS DIFFERENT!
SIR! SEVERAL BATTALIONS OF TROOPS ARE POURING IN FROM NIGANDA, FOLLOWING THE PATH THE RHINO PUNCHED INTO OUR DEFENSES.
HOW MANY FIGHTERS DO WE HAVE IN THE AIR NOW?
A DOZEN, WITH MORE ON THE WAY.
HAVE THREE FOCUS ON THE RHINO. POUND HIM WITH MISSILES UNTIL HE DROPS. SEND THE REST TO TAKE OUT THAT COLUMN FROM NIGANDA. AND GET M'BUTU ON THE PHONE.
I JUST WANTED TO THANK YOU, M'BUTU.
WHY, WAS THE CROWN WEIGHING TOO HEAVY ON YOUR SWOLLEN HEAD ALREADY, YOUNG KING?
AS YOU KNOW, WAKANDA DOES NOT INTERFERE WITH THE AFFAIRS OF OTHER GOVERNMENTS, NO MATTER HOW FOUL THEY ARE. SO WE HAVE ENDURED THE STENCH OF YOUR REGIME NEXT TO OURS FOR FAR TOO LONG.
WE HOPED THE PEOPLE WHO SUFFERED UNDER YOUR KLEPTOCRACY WOULD RISE UP AND BEHEAD YOU. BUT NOW YOU'VE GIVEN US AN EXCUSE TO DO IT.
YOU'RE NOT HALF THE MAN YOUR FATHER WAS--AND KLAW KILLED HIM! I'LL BE SPITTING ON YOUR GRAVE, T'CHALLA!

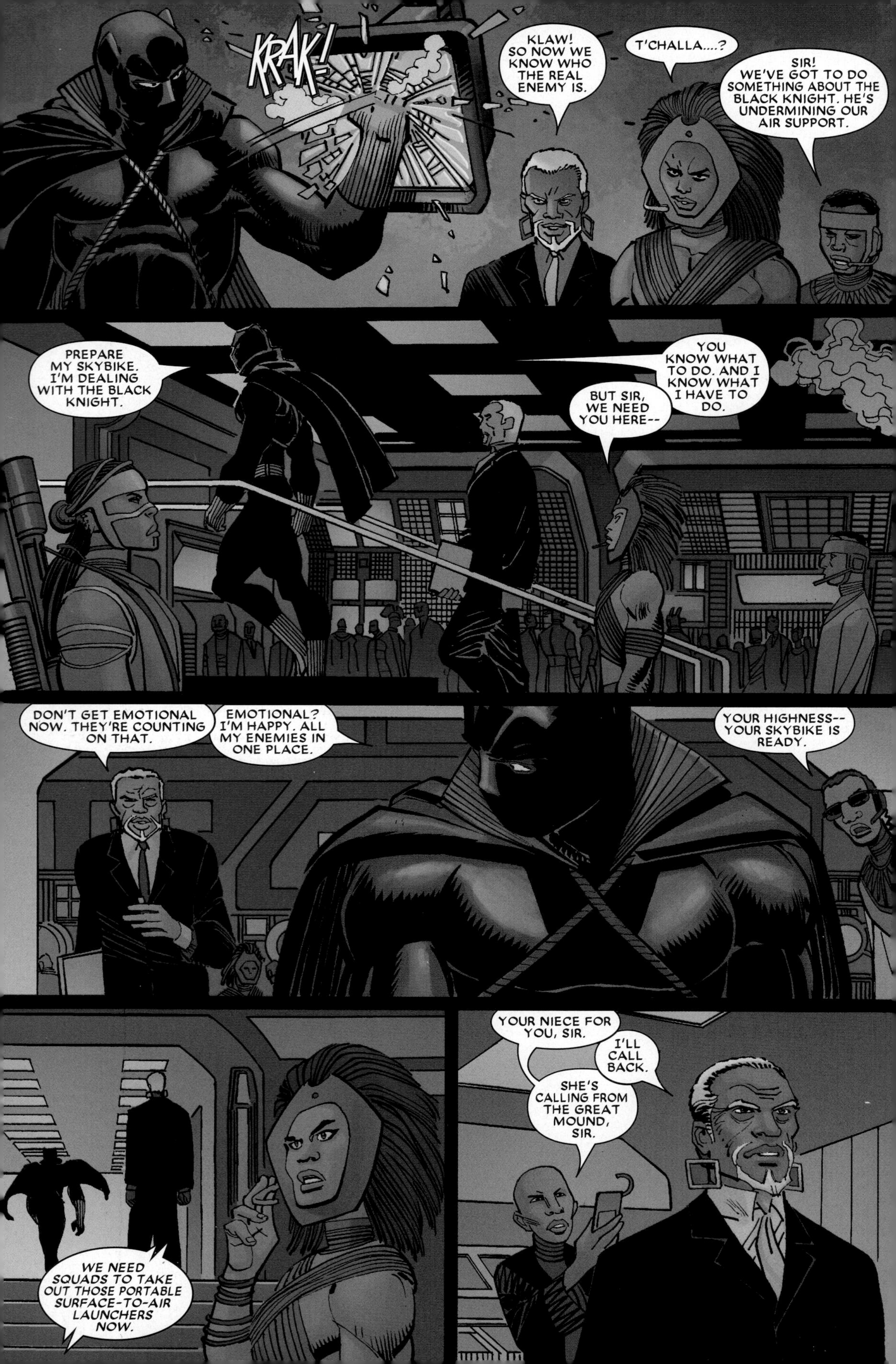
KRAK!
KLAW! SO NOW WE KNOW WHO THE REAL ENEMY IS.
T'CHALLA....?
SIR! WE'VE GOT TO DO SOMETHING ABOUT THE BLACK KNIGHT. HE'S UNDERMINING OUR AIR SUPPORT.
PREPARE MY SKYBIKE. I'M DEALING WITH THE BLACK KNIGHT.
BUT SIR, WE NEED YOU HERE--
YOU KNOW WHAT TO DO. AND I KNOW WHAT I HAVE TO DO.
DON'T GET EMOTIONAL NOW. THEY'RE COUNTING ON THAT.
EMOTIONAL? I'M HAPPY. ALL MY ENEMIES IN ONE PLACE.
YOUR HIGHNESS-- YOUR SKYBIKE IS READY.
WE NEED SQUADS TO TAKE OUT THOSE PORTABLE SURFACE-TO-AIR LAUNCHERS NOW.
YOUR NIECE FOR YOU, SIR.
I'LL CALL BACK.
SHE'S CALLING FROM THE GREAT MOUND, SIR.

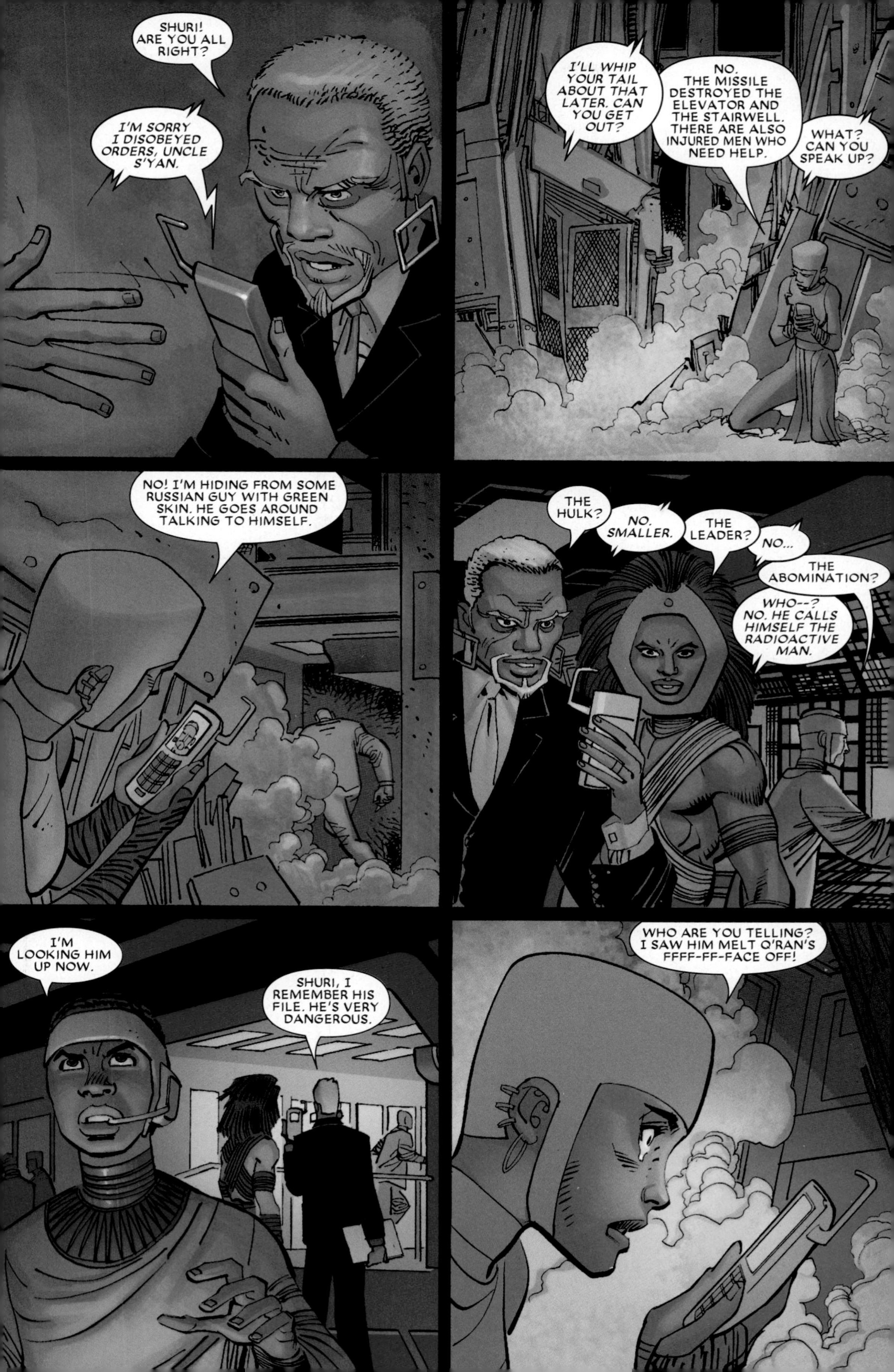
SHURI! ARE YOU ALL RIGHT?
I'M SORRY I DISOBEYED ORDERS, UNCLE S'YAN.
I'LL WHIP YOUR TAIL ABOUT THAT LATER. CAN YOU GET OUT?
NO. THE MISSILE DESTROYED THE ELEVATOR AND THE STAIRWELL. THERE ARE ALSO INJURED MEN WHO NEED HELP.
WHAT? CAN YOU SPEAK UP?
NO! I'M HIDING FROM SOME RUSSIAN GUY WITH GREEN SKIN. HE GOES AROUND TALKING TO HIMSELF.
THE HULK?
NO. SMALLER.
THE LEADER?
NO...
THE ABOMINATION?
WHO--? NO. HE CALLS HIMSELF THE RADIOACTIVE MAN.
I'M LOOKING HIM UP NOW.
SHURI, I REMEMBER HIS FILE. HE'S VERY DANGEROUS.
WHO ARE YOU TELLING? I SAW HIM MELT Q'RAN'S FFFF-FF-FACE OFF!

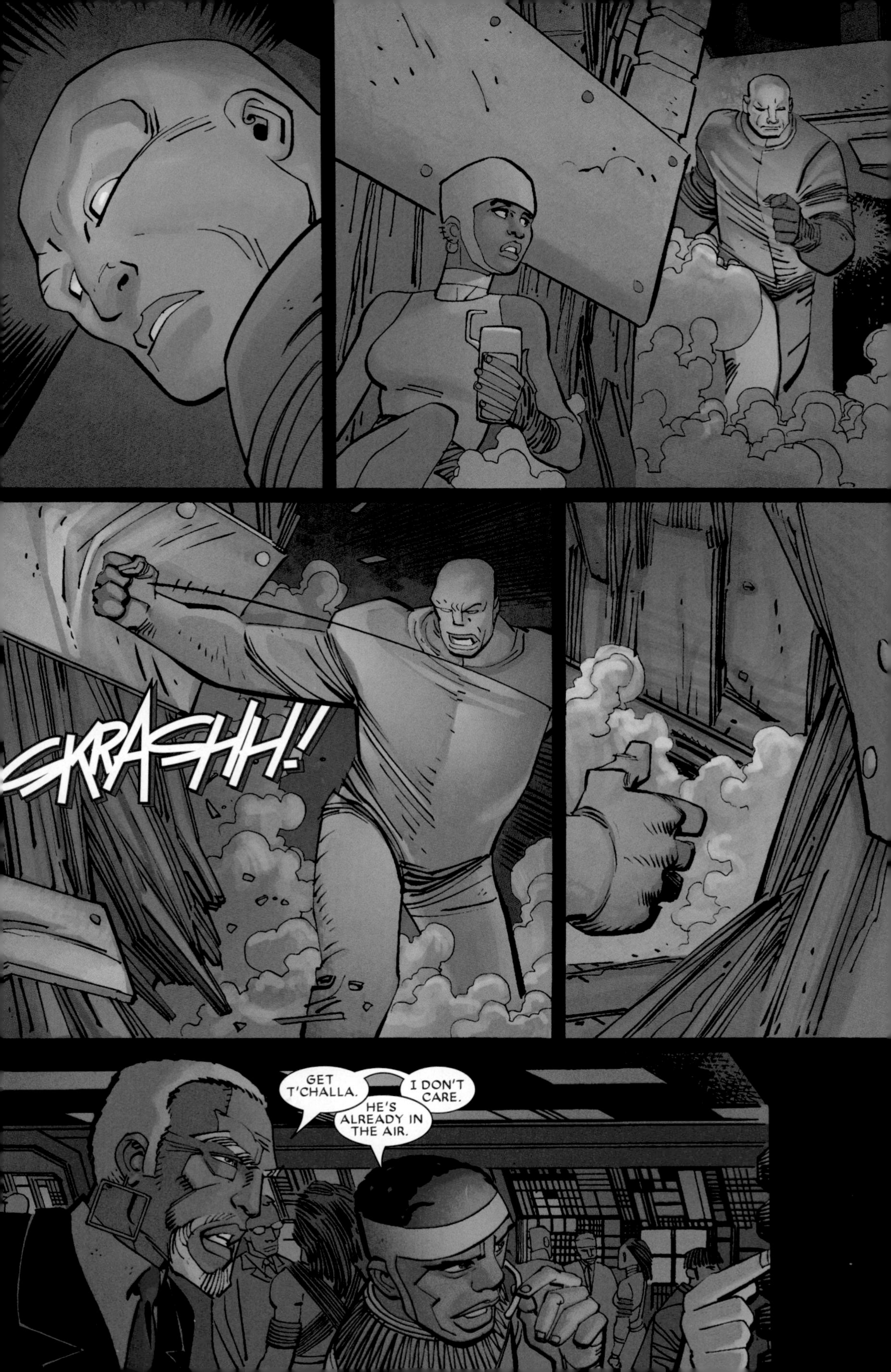
SKRASHH!
GET T'CHALLA.
I DON'T CARE.
HE'S ALREADY IN THE AIR.

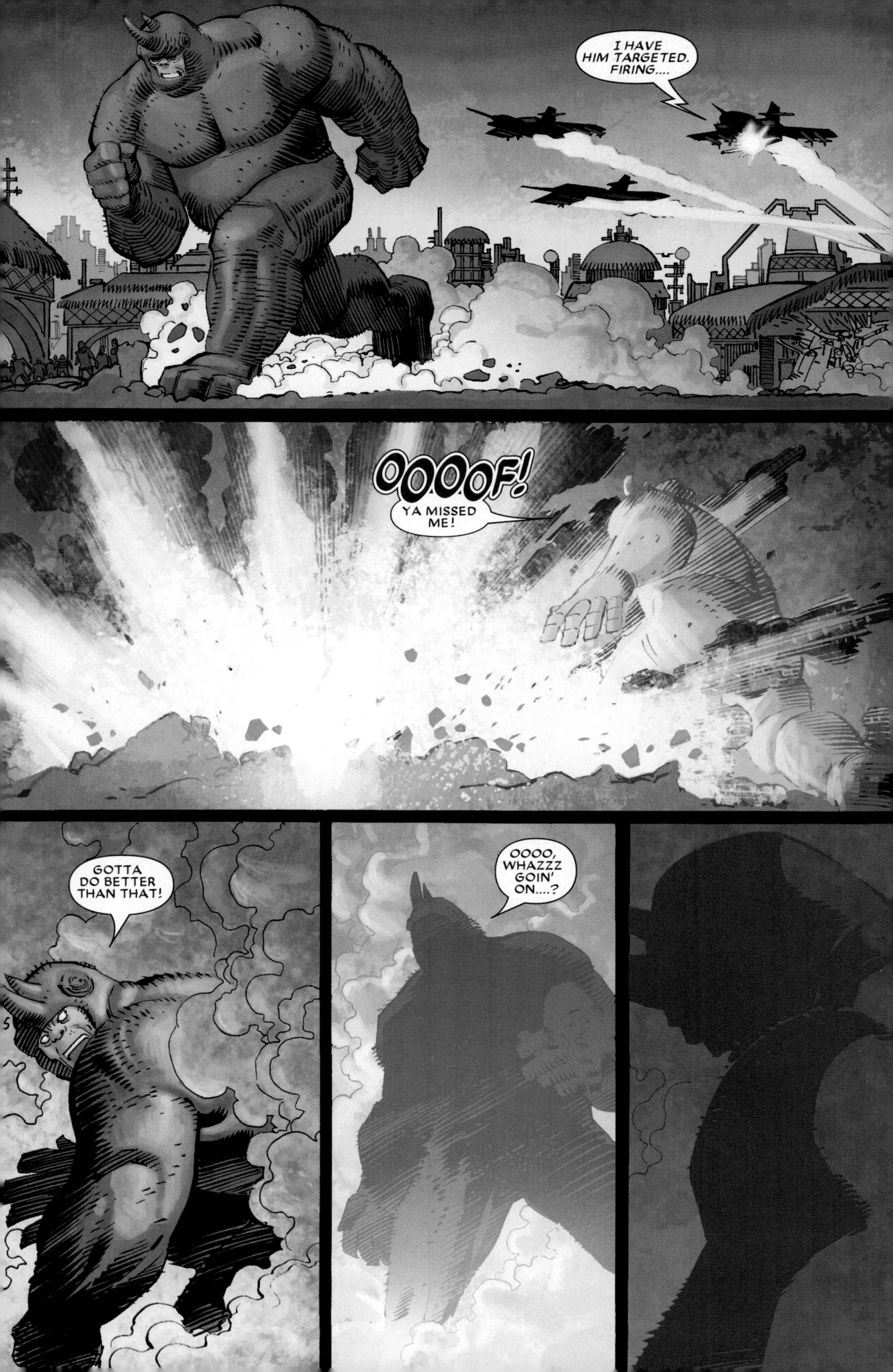
I HAVE HIM TARGETED. FIRING....
OOOOF!
YA MISSED ME!
GOTTA DO BETTER THAN THAT!
OOOO, WHAZZZ GOIN' ON....?

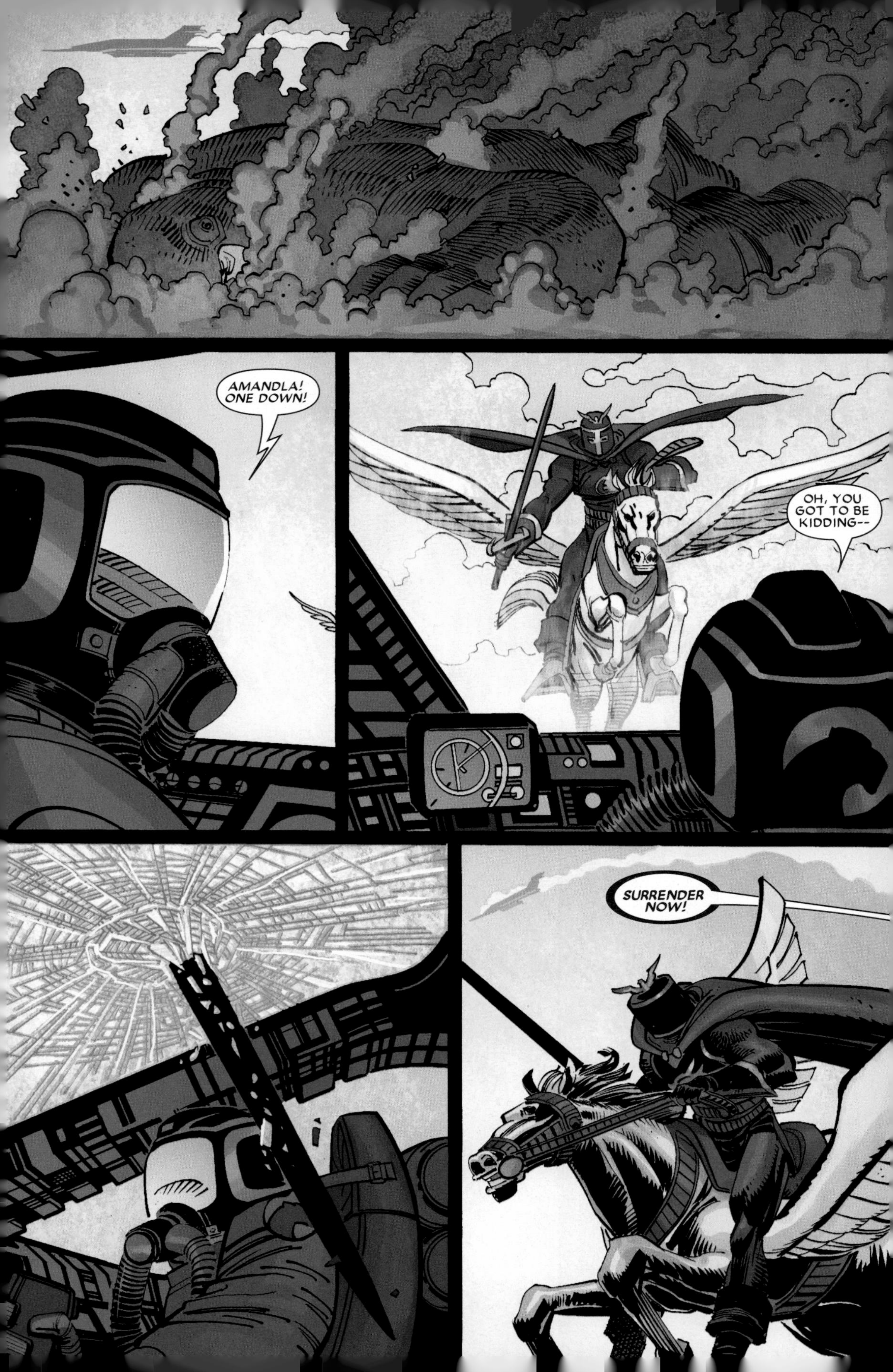
AMANDLA! ONE DOWN!
OH, YOU GOT TO BE KIDDING--
SURRENDER NOW!

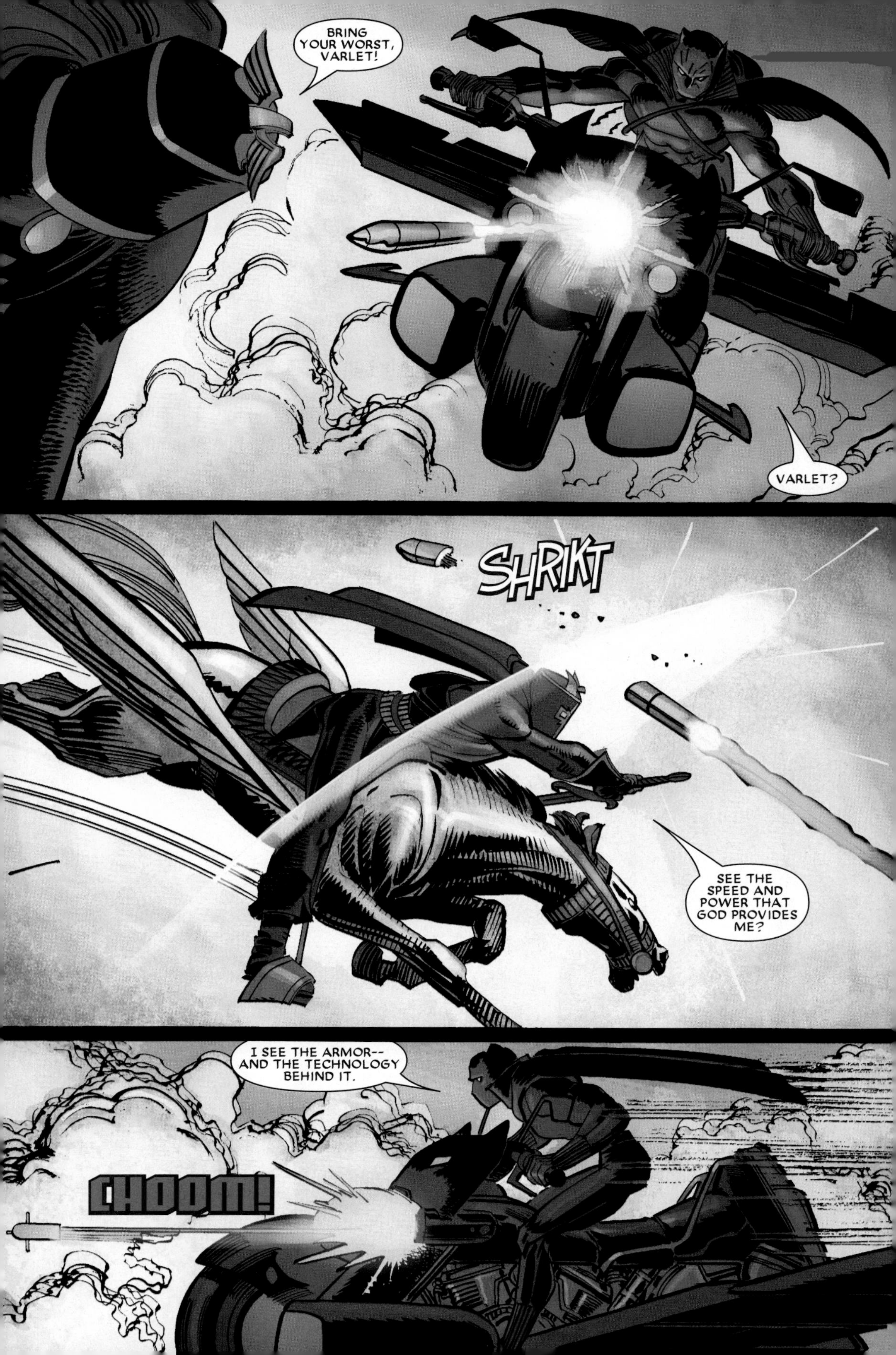
BRING YOUR WORST, VARLET!
VARLET?
SHRIKT
SEE THE SPEED AND POWER THAT GOD PROVIDES ME?
I SEE THE ARMOR-- AND THE TECHNOLOGY BEHIND IT.
CHOOM!

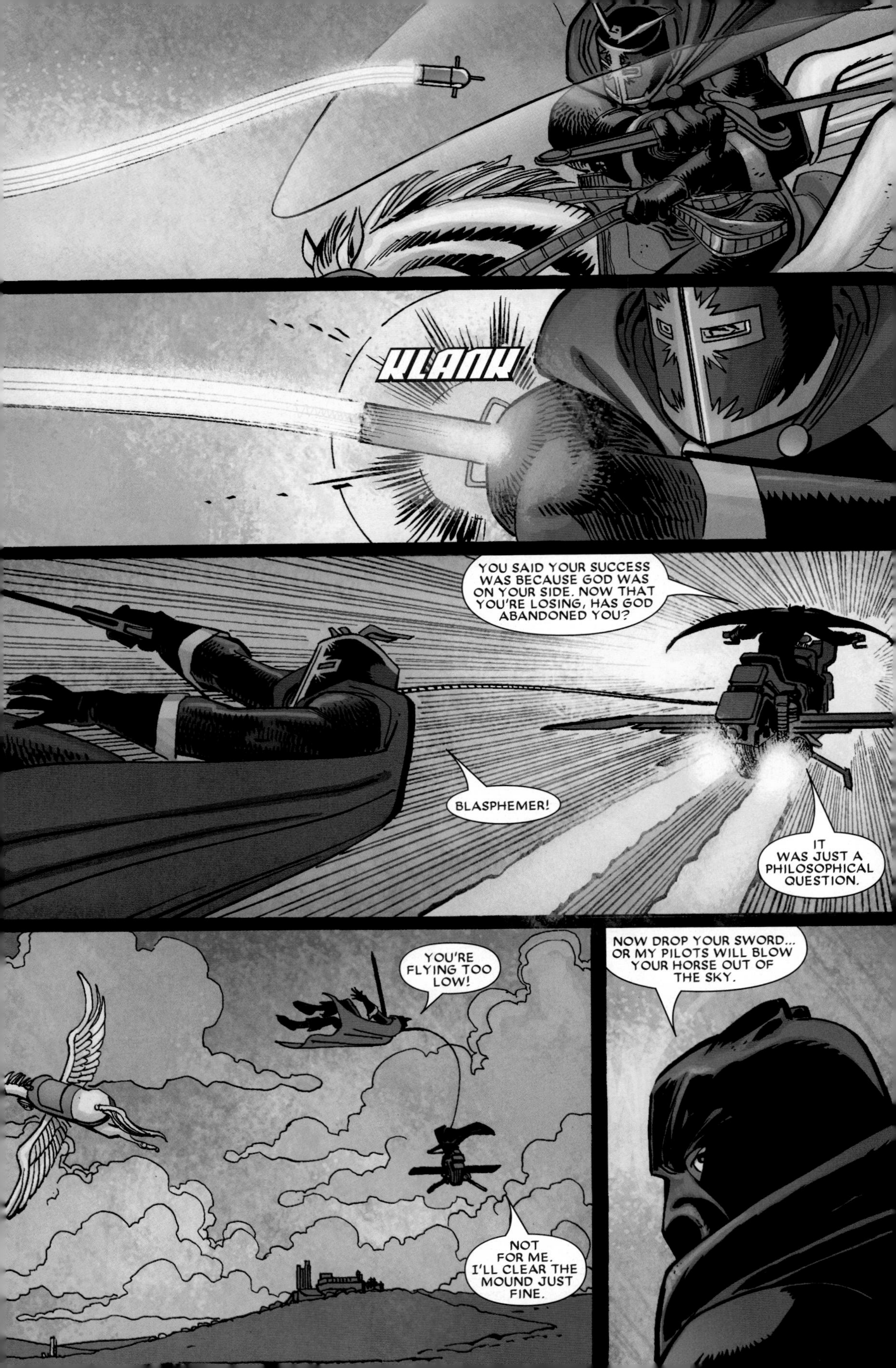
KLANK
YOU SAID YOUR SUCCESS WAS BECAUSE GOD WAS ON YOUR SIDE. NOW THAT YOU'RE LOSING, HAS GOD ABANDONED YOU?
BLASPHEMER!
IT WAS JUST A PHILOSOPHICAL QUESTION.
YOU'RE FLYING TOO LOW!
NOT FOR ME. I'LL CLEAR THE MOUND JUST FINE.
NOW DROP YOUR SWORD... OR MY PILOTS WILL BLOW YOUR HORSE OUT OF THE SKY.

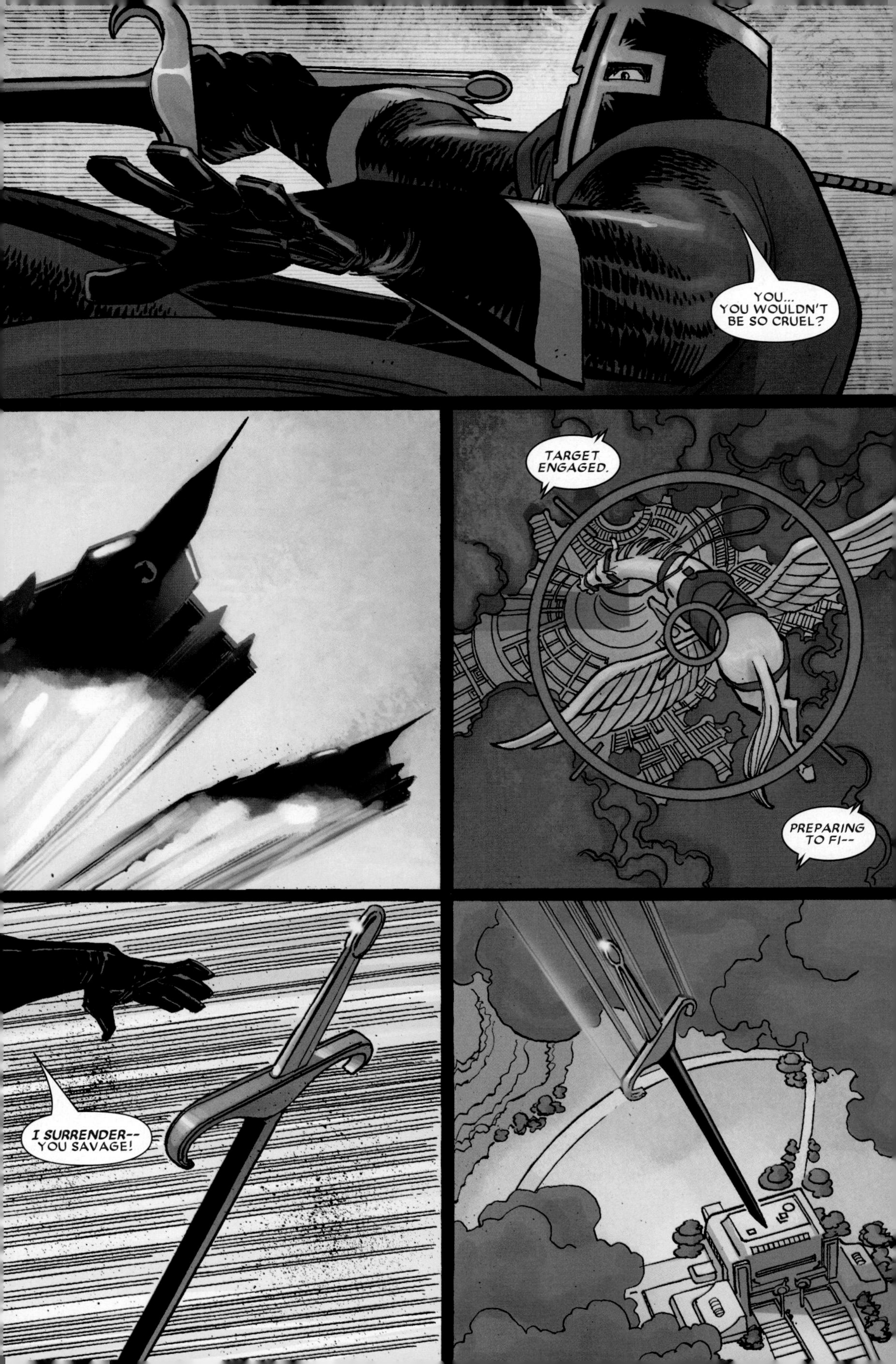
YOU... YOU WOULDN'T BE SO CRUEL?
TARGET ENGAGED.
PREPARING TO FI--
I SURRENDER-- YOU SAVAGE!

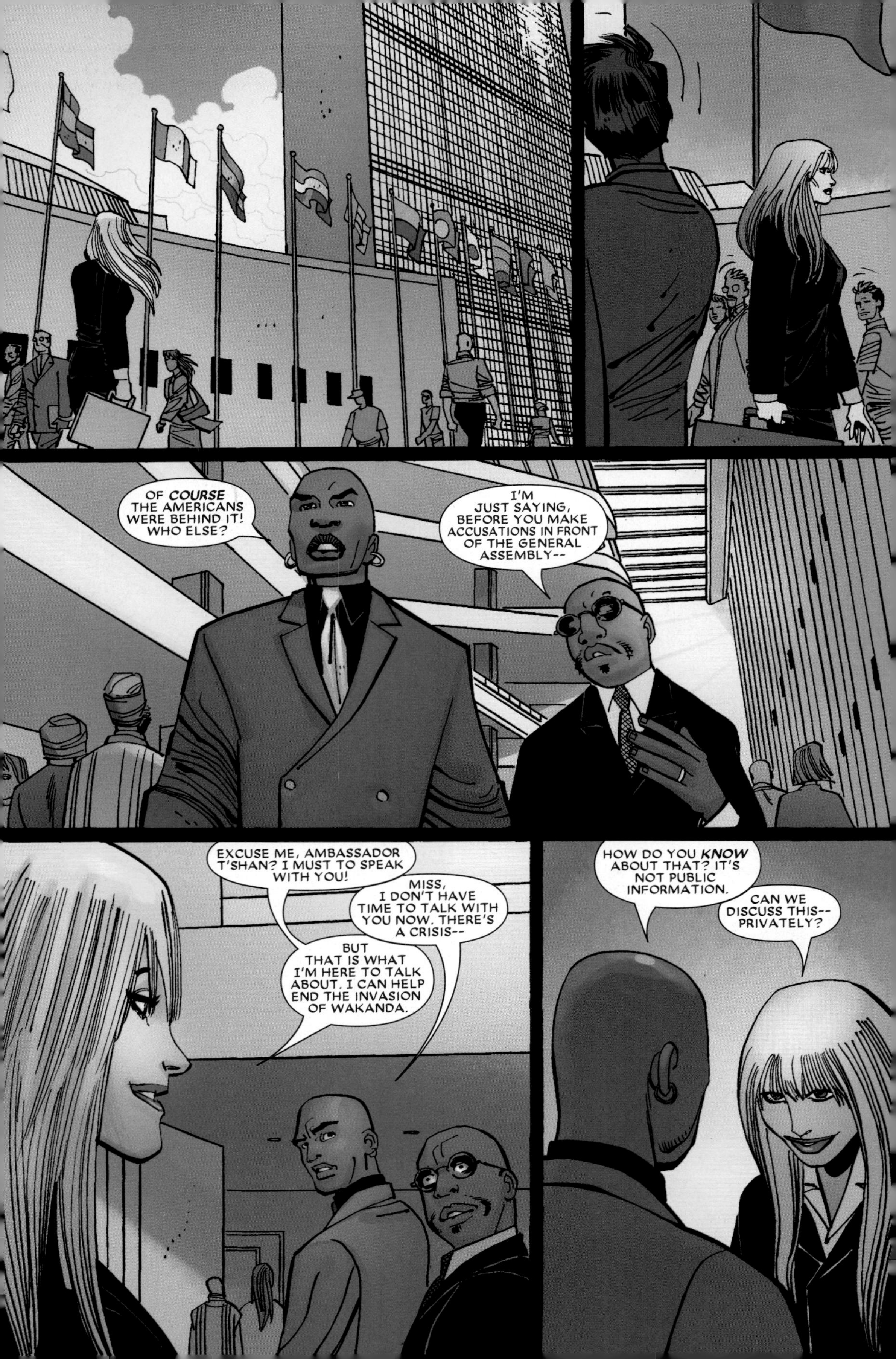
OF COURSE THE AMERICANS WERE BEHIND IT! WHO ELSE?
I'M JUST SAYING, BEFORE YOU MAKE ACCUSATIONS IN FRONT OF THE GENERAL ASSEMBLY--
EXCUSE ME, AMBASSADOR T'SHAN? I MUST TO SPEAK WITH YOU!
MISS, I DON'T HAVE TIME TO TALK WITH YOU NOW. THERE'S A CRISIS--
BUT THAT IS WHAT I'M HERE TO TALK ABOUT. I CAN HELP END THE INVASION OF WAKANDA.
HOW DO YOU KNOW ABOUT THAT? IT'S NOT PUBLIC INFORMATION.
CAN WE DISCUSS THIS-- PRIVATELY?

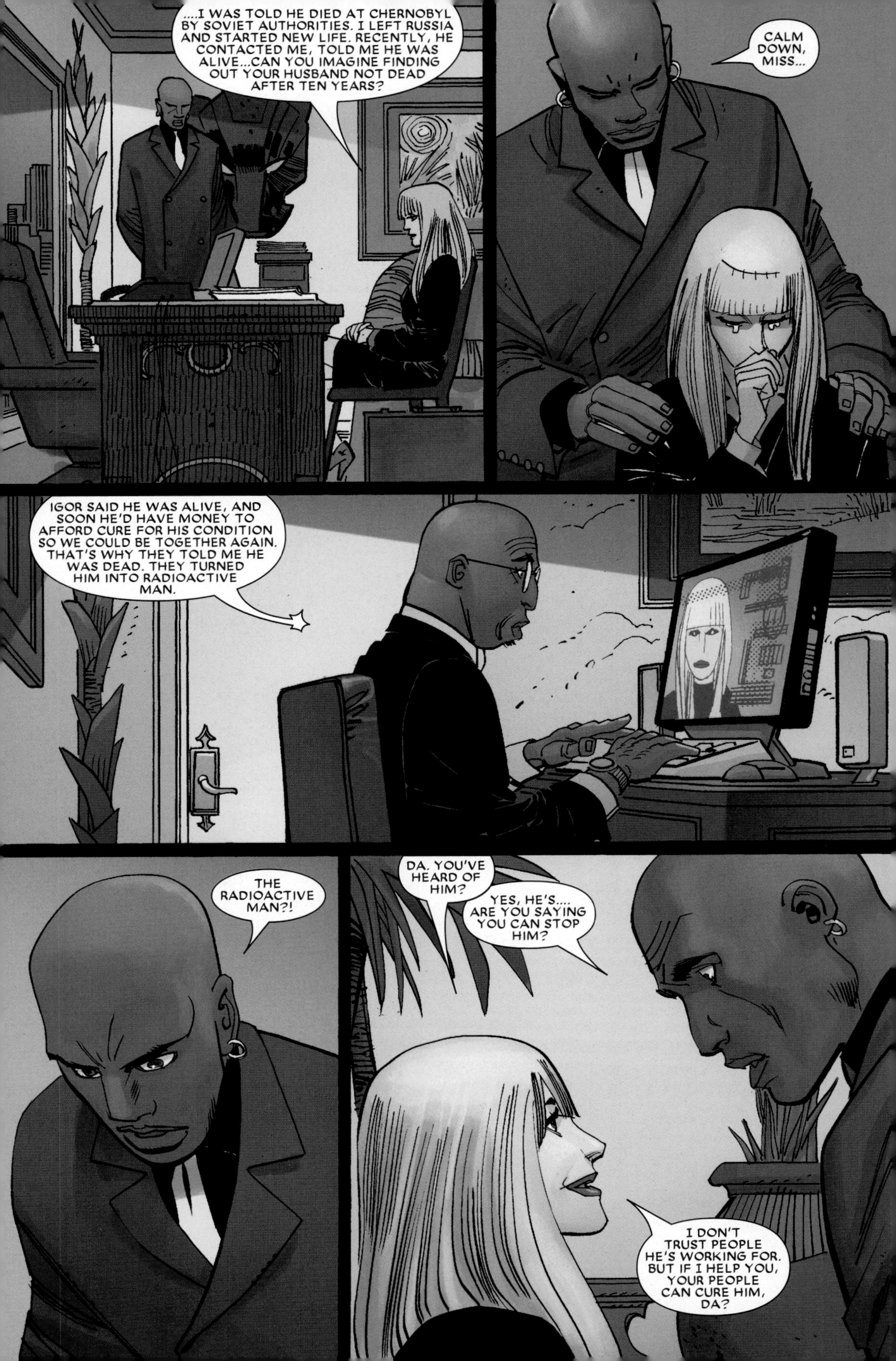
....I WAS TOLD HE DIED AT CHERNOBYL BY SOVIET AUTHORITIES. I LEFT RUSSIA AND STARTED NEW LIFE. RECENTLY, HE CONTACTED ME, TOLD ME HE WAS ALIVE...CAN YOU IMAGINE FINDING OUT YOUR HUSBAND NOT DEAD AFTER TEN YEARS?
CALM DOWN, MISS...
IGOR SAID HE WAS ALIVE, AND SOON HE'D HAVE MONEY TO AFFORD CURE FOR HIS CONDITION SO WE COULD BE TOGETHER AGAIN. THAT'S WHY THEY TOLD ME HE WAS DEAD. THEY TURNED HIM INTO RADIOACTIVE MAN.
THE RADIOACTIVE MAN?!
DA. YOU'VE HEARD OF HIM?
YES, HE'S.... ARE YOU SAYING YOU CAN STOP HIM?
I DON'T TRUST PEOPLE HE'S WORKING FOR. BUT IF I HELP YOU, YOUR PEOPLE CAN CURE HIM, DA?

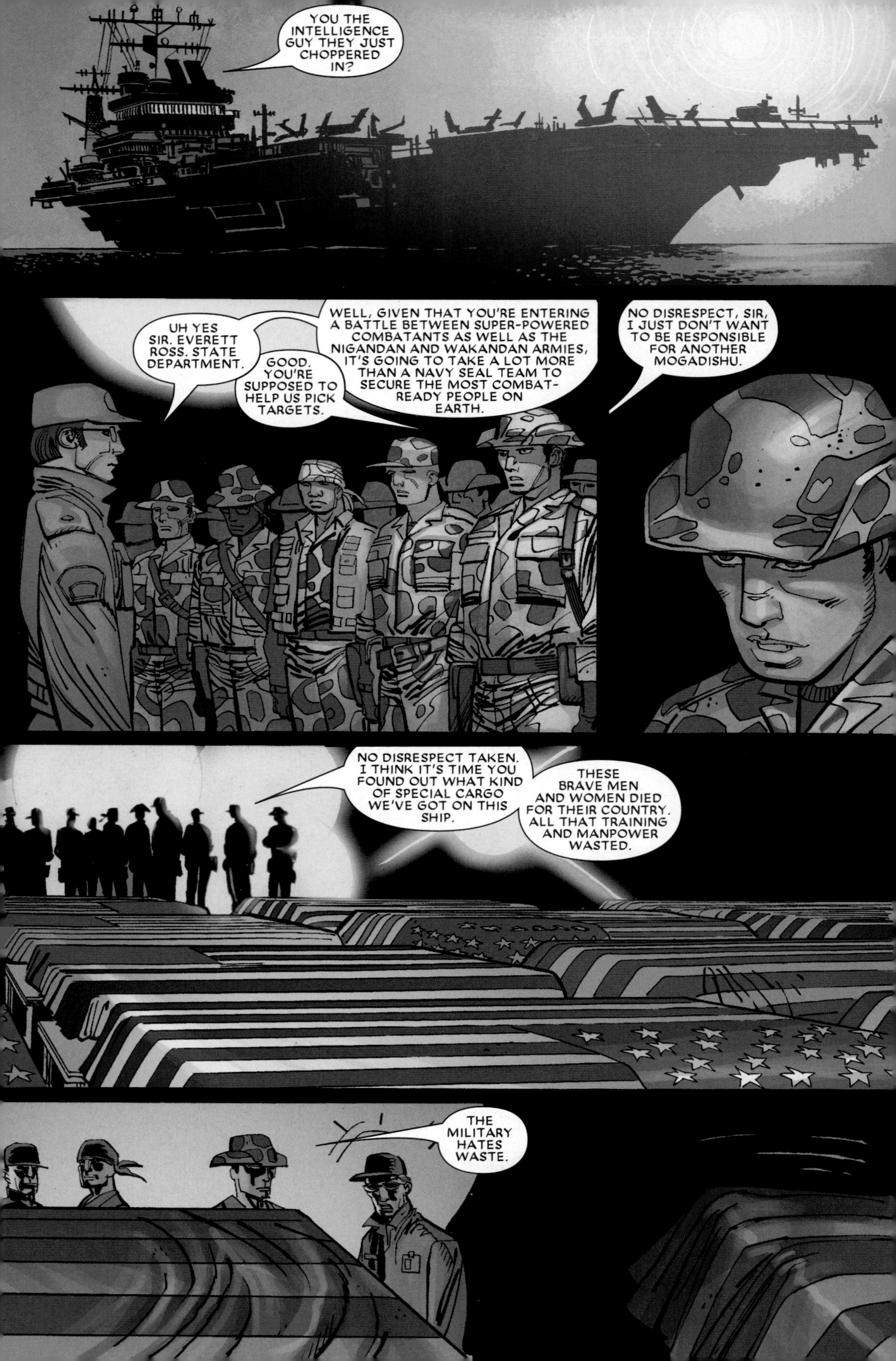
YOU THE INTELLIGENCE GUY THEY JUST CHOPPERED IN?
UH YES SIR. EVERETT ROSS. STATE DEPARTMENT.
GOOD. YOU'RE SUPPOSED TO HELP US PICK TARGETS.
WELL, GIVEN THAT YOU'RE ENTERING A BATTLE BETWEEN SUPER-POWERED COMBATANTS AS WELL AS THE NIGANDAN AND WAKANDAN ARMIES, IT'S GOING TO TAKE A LOT MORE THAN A NAVY SEAL TEAM TO SECURE THE MOST COMBAT-READY PEOPLE ON EARTH.
NO DISRESPECT, SIR, I JUST DON'T WANT TO BE RESPONSIBLE FOR ANOTHER MOGADISHU.
NO DISRESPECT TAKEN. I THINK IT'S TIME YOU FOUND OUT WHAT KIND OF SPECIAL CARGO WE'VE GOT ON THIS SHIP.
THESE BRAVE MEN AND WOMEN DIED FOR THEIR COUNTRY. ALL THAT TRAINING AND MANPOWER WASTED.
THE MILITARY HATES WASTE.

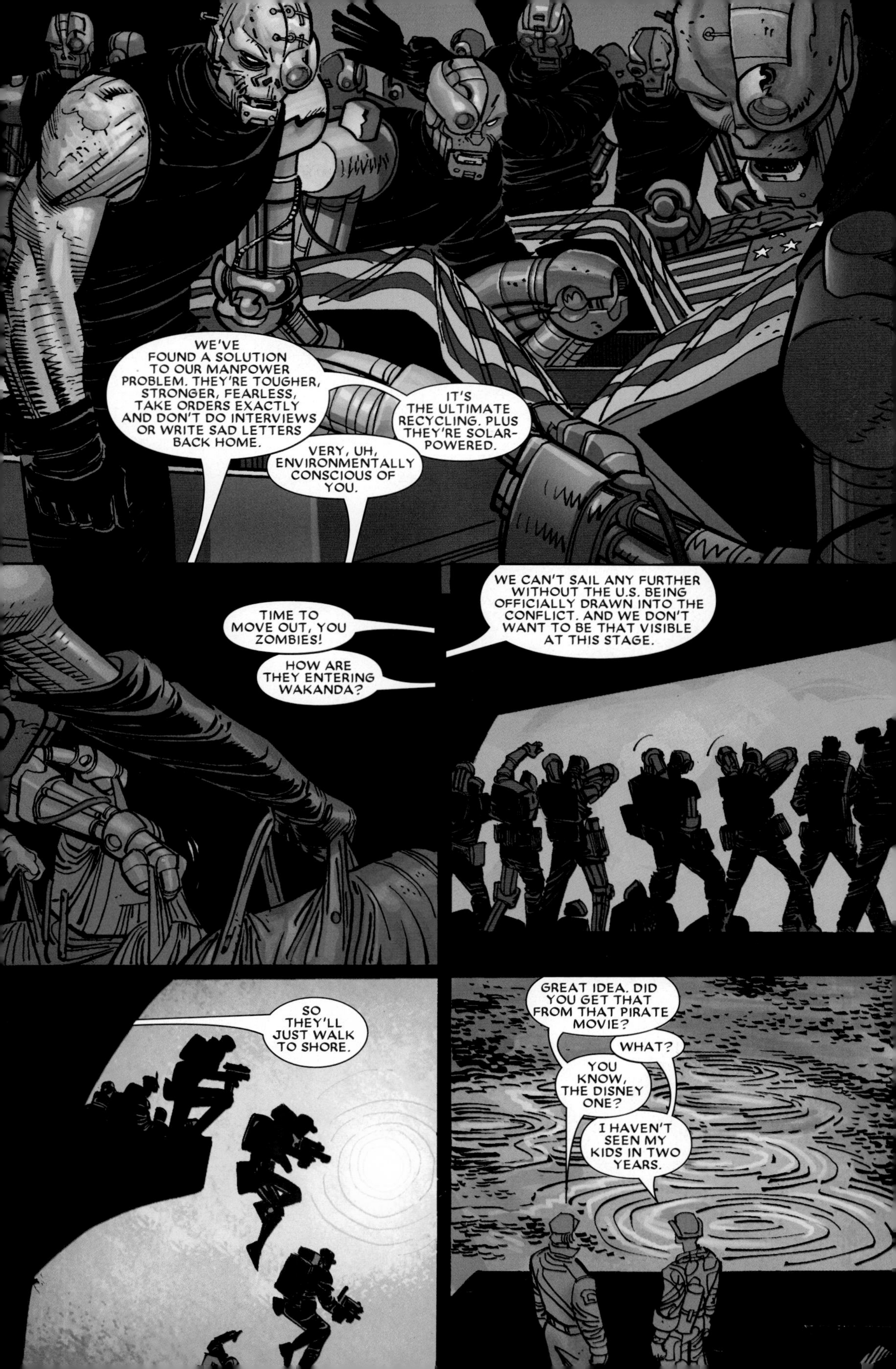

WE'VE FOUND A SOLUTION TO OUR MANPOWER PROBLEM. THEY'RE TOUGHER, STRONGER, FEARLESS, TAKE ORDERS EXACTLY AND DON'T DO INTERVIEWS OR WRITE SAD LETTERS BACK HOME.
IT'S THE ULTIMATE RECYCLING. PLUS THEY'RE SOLAR-POWERED.
VERY, UH, ENVIRONMENTALLY CONSCIOUS OF YOU.
TIME TO MOVE OUT, YOU ZOMBIES!
HOW ARE THEY ENTERING WAKANDA?
WE CAN'T SAIL ANY FURTHER WITHOUT THE U.S. BEING OFFICIALLY DRAWN INTO THE CONFLICT. AND WE DON'T WANT TO BE THAT VISIBLE AT THIS STAGE.
SO THEY'LL JUST WALK TO SHORE.
GREAT IDEA. DID YOU GET THAT FROM THAT PIRATE MOVIE?
WHAT?
YOU KNOW, THE DISNEY ONE?
I HAVEN'T SEEN MY KIDS IN TWO YEARS.

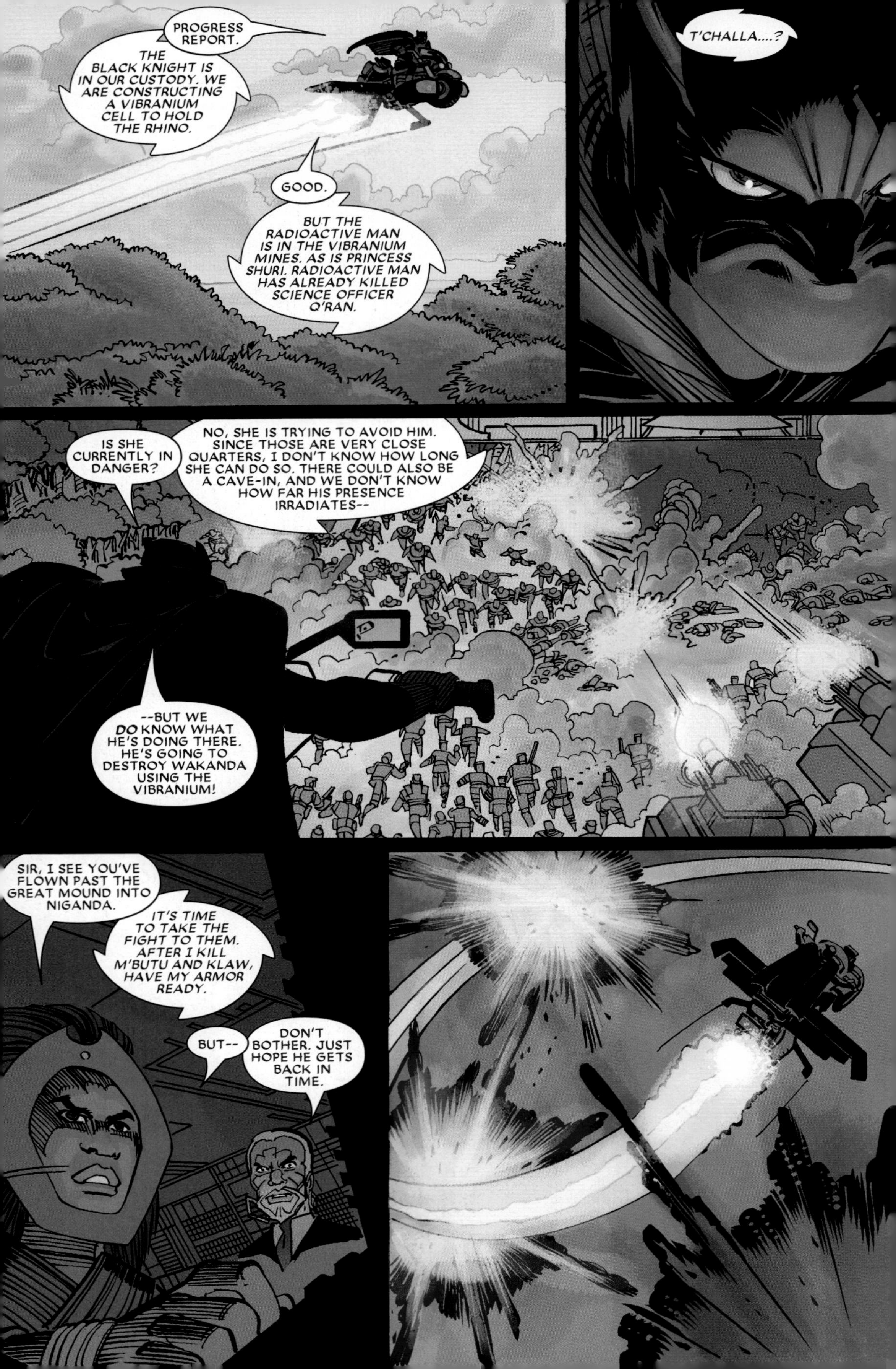
PROGRESS REPORT.
THE BLACK KNIGHT IS IN OUR CUSTODY. WE ARE CONSTRUCTING A VIBRANIUM CELL TO HOLD THE RHINO.
GOOD.
BUT THE RADIOACTIVE MAN IS IN THE VIBRANIUM MINES. AS IS PRINCESS SHURI. RADIOACTIVE MAN HAS ALREADY KILLED SCIENCE OFFICER Q'RAN.
T'CHALLA....?
IS SHE CURRENTLY IN DANGER?
NO, SHE IS TRYING TO AVOID HIM. SINCE THOSE ARE VERY CLOSE QUARTERS, I DON'T KNOW HOW LONG SHE CAN DO SO. THERE COULD ALSO BE A CAVE-IN, AND WE DON'T KNOW HOW FAR HIS PRESENCE IRRADIATES--
--BUT WE DO KNOW WHAT HE'S DOING THERE. HE'S GOING TO DESTROY WAKANDA USING THE VIBRANIUM!
SIR, I SEE YOU'VE FLOWN PAST THE GREAT MOUND INTO NIGANDA.
IT'S TIME TO TAKE THE FIGHT TO THEM. AFTER I KILL M'BUTU AND KLAW, HAVE MY ARMOR READY.
BUT--
DON'T BOTHER. JUST HOPE HE GETS BACK IN TIME.

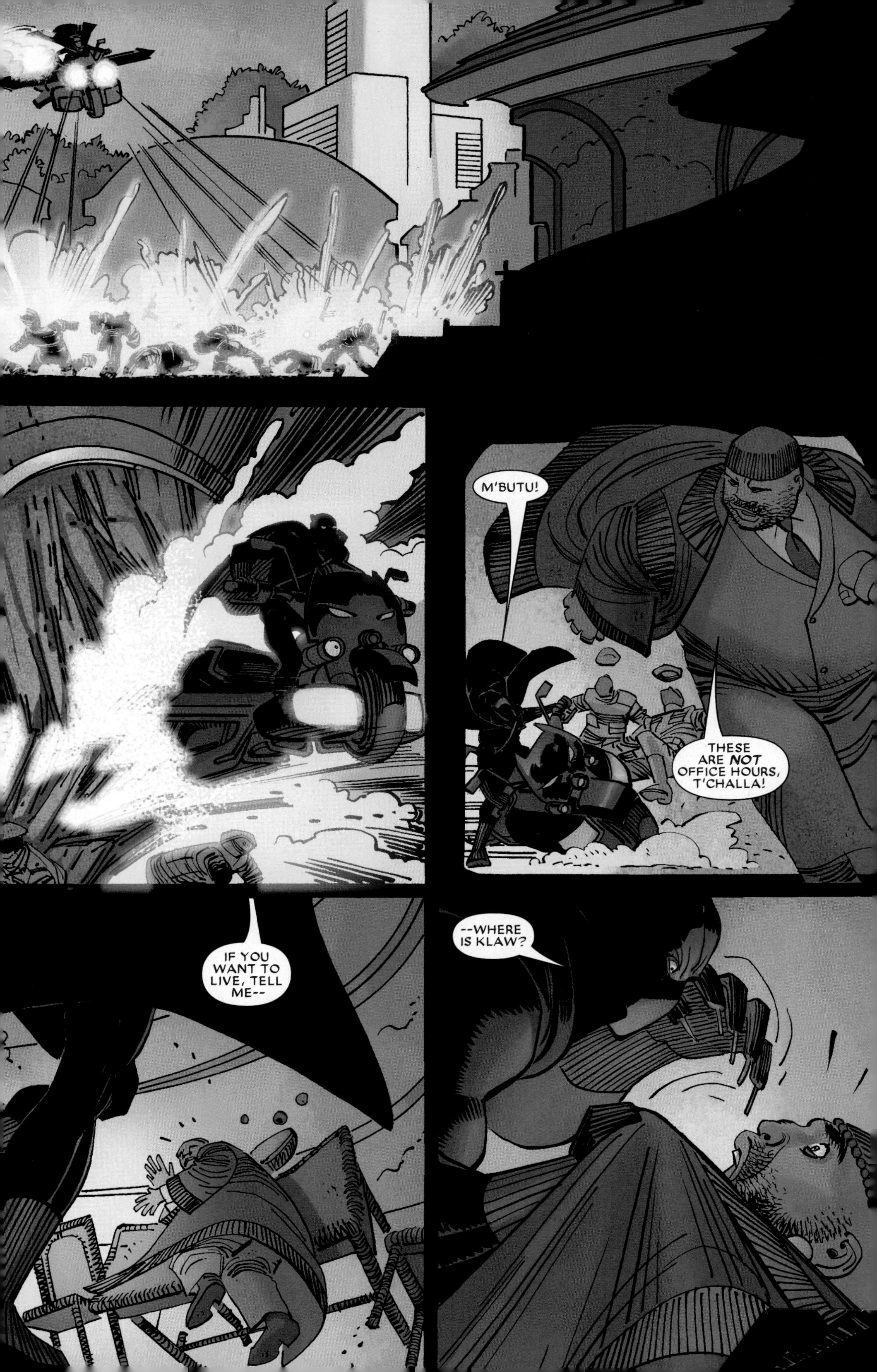
M'BUTU!
THESE ARE NOT OFFICE HOURS, T'CHALLA!
IF YOU WANT TO LIVE, TELL ME--
--WHERE IS KLAW?

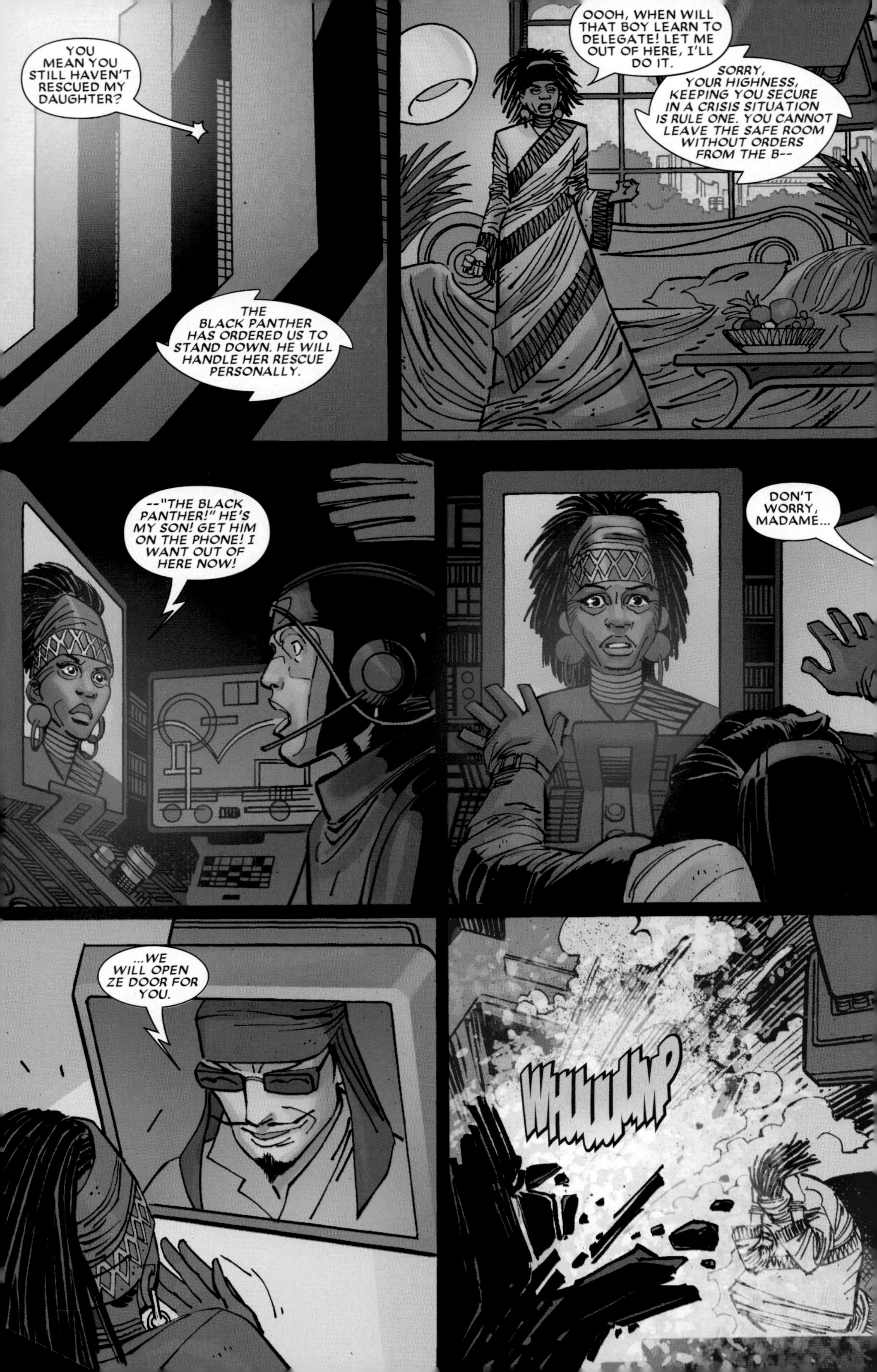

YOU MEAN YOU STILL HAVEN'T RESCUED MY DAUGHTER?
THE BLACK PANTHER HAS ORDERED US TO STAND DOWN. HE WILL HANDLE HER RESCUE PERSONALLY.
OOOH, WHEN WILL THAT BOY LEARN TO DELEGATE! LET ME OUT OF HERE, I'LL DO IT.
SORRY, YOUR HIGHNESS, KEEPING YOU SECURE IN A CRISIS SITUATION IS RULE ONE. YOU CANNOT LEAVE THE SAFE ROOM WITHOUT ORDERS FROM THE B--
--"THE BLACK PANTHER!" HE'S MY SON! GET HIM ON THE PHONE! I WANT OUT OF HERE NOW!
DON'T WORRY, MADAME...
...WE WILL OPEN ZE DOOR FOR YOU.
WHUUMP

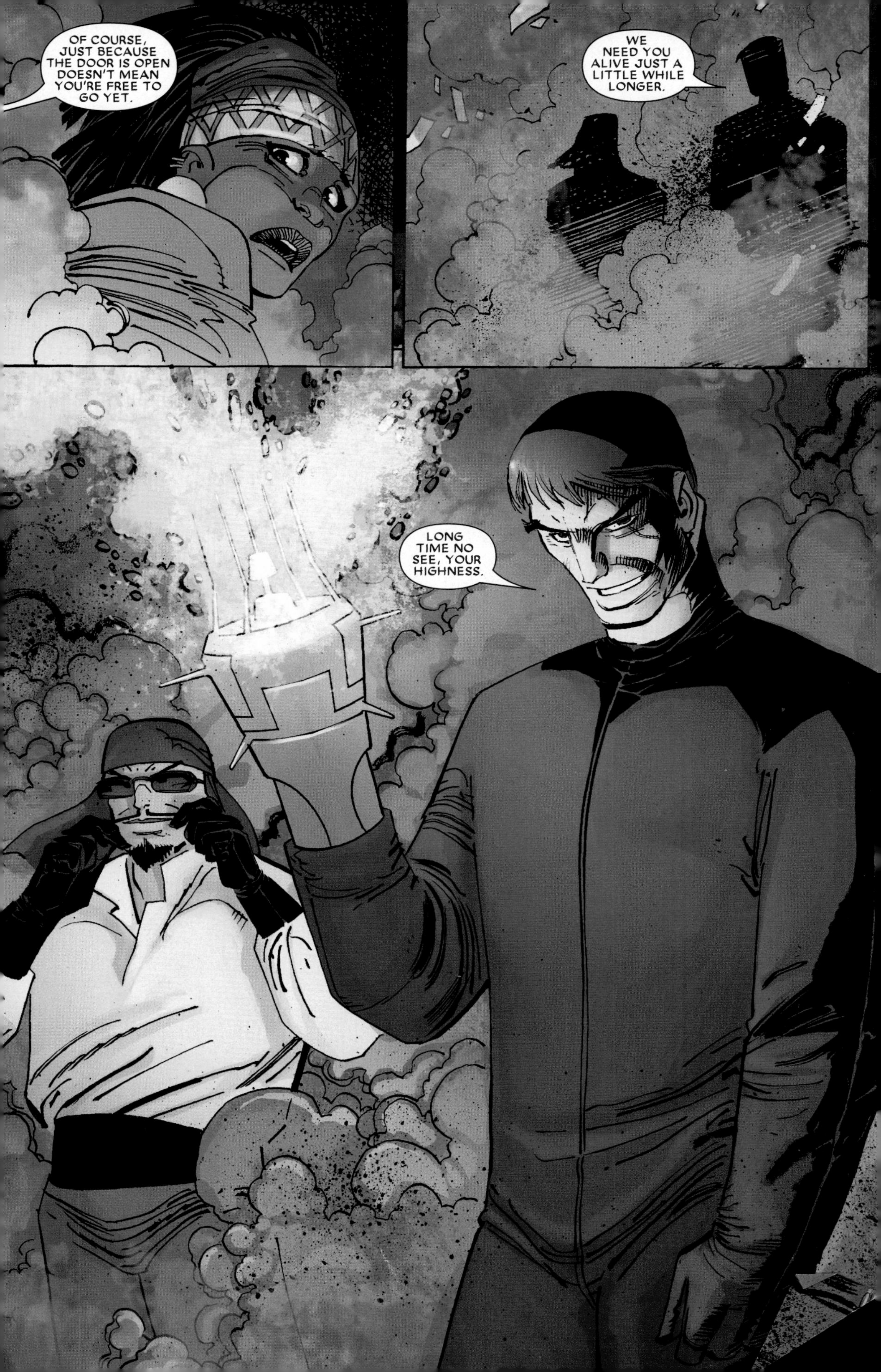
OF COURSE, JUST BECAUSE THE DOOR IS OPEN DOESN'T MEAN YOU'RE FREE TO GO YET.
WE NEED YOU ALIVE JUST A LITTLE WHILE LONGER.
LONG TIME NO SEE, YOUR HIGHNESS.

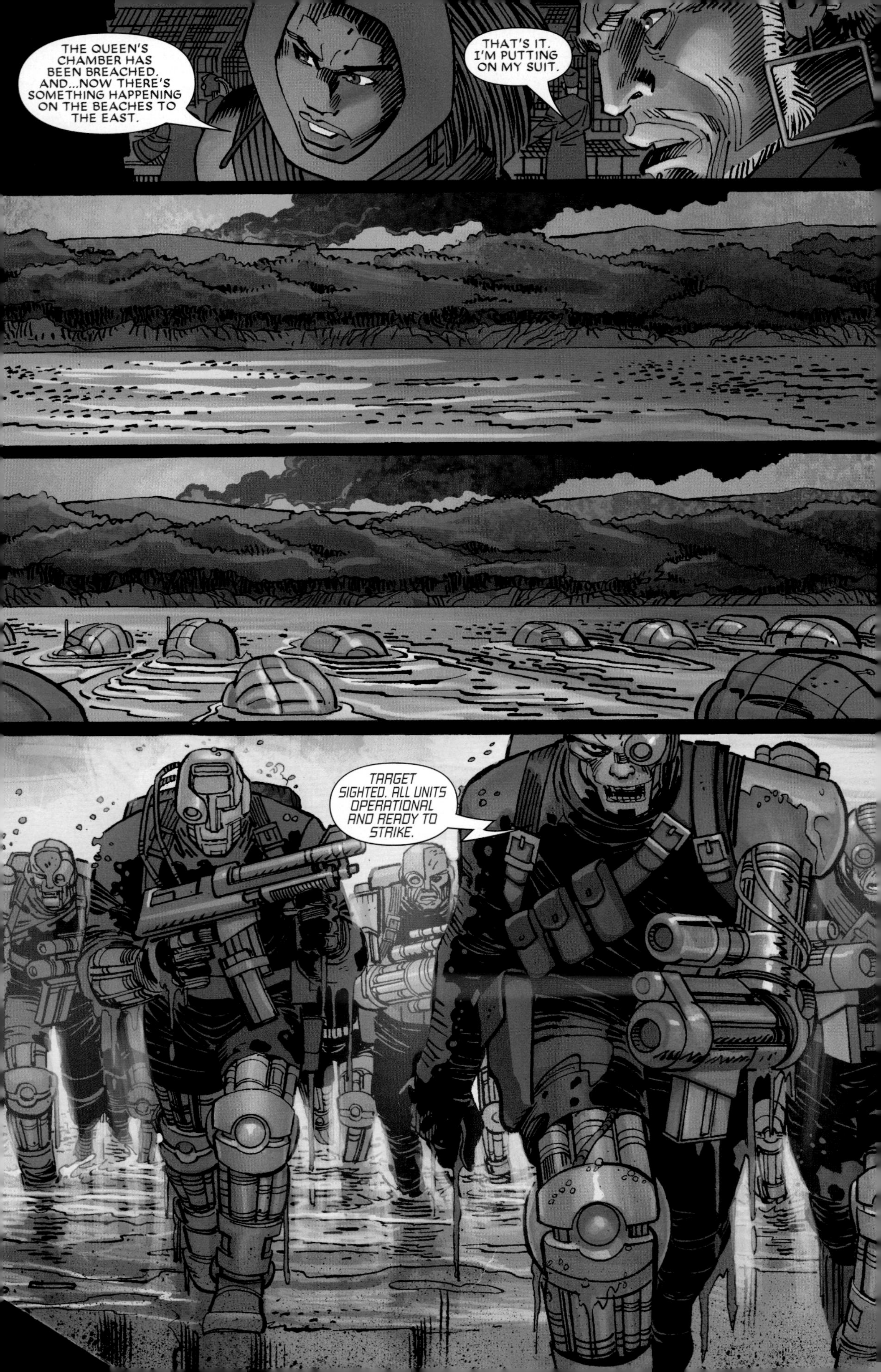
THE QUEEN'S CHAMBER HAS BEEN BREACHED. AND...NOW THERE'S SOMETHING HAPPENING ON THE BEACHES TO THE EAST.
THAT'S IT. I'M PUTTING ON MY SUIT.
TARGET SIGHTED. ALL UNITS OPERATIONAL AND READY TO STRIKE.

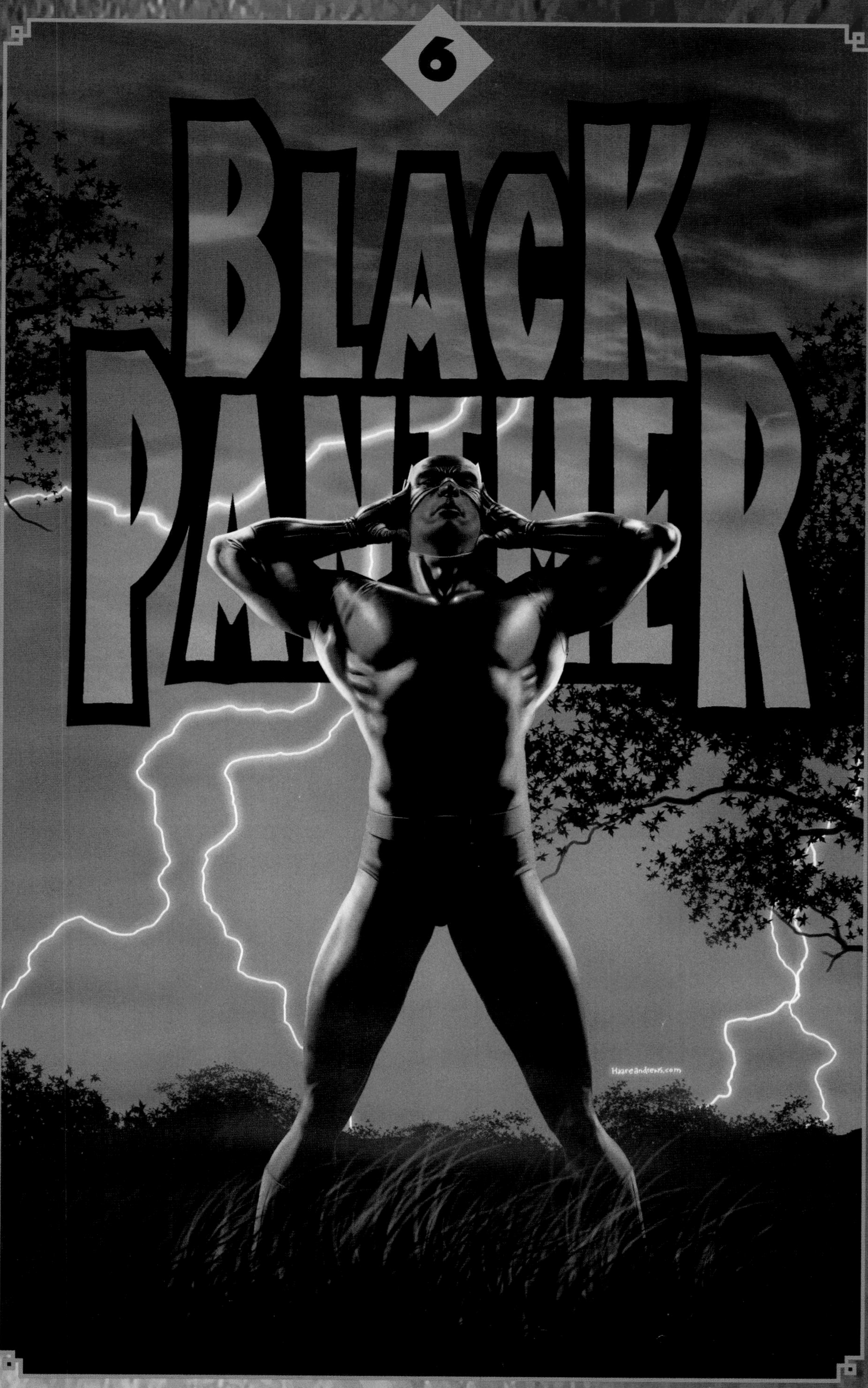
6
BLACK PANTHER
HaareAndrews.com

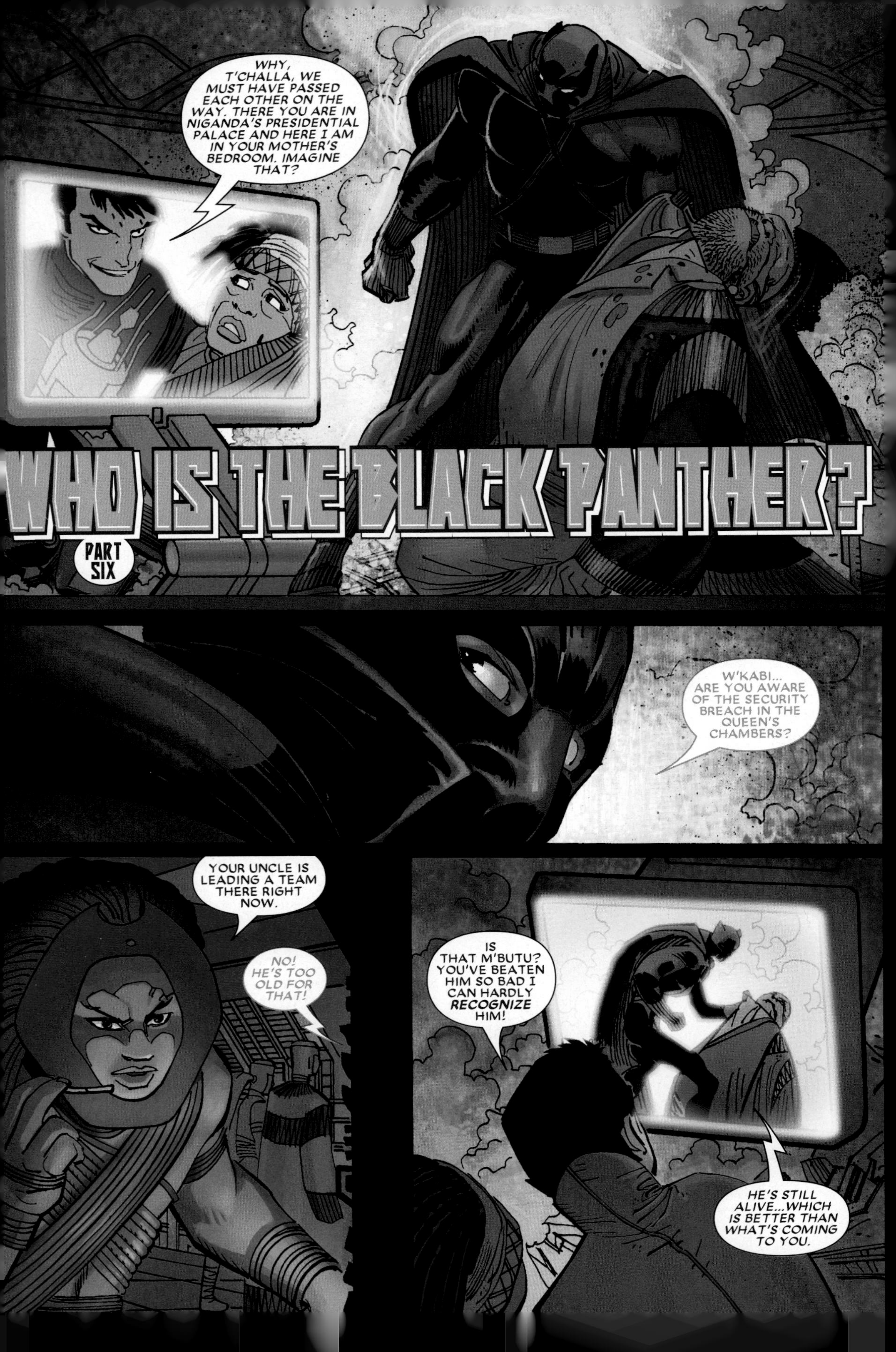
WHY, T'CHALLA, WE MUST HAVE PASSED EACH OTHER ON THE WAY. THERE YOU ARE IN NIGANDA'S PRESIDENTIAL PALACE AND HERE I AM IN YOUR MOTHER'S BEDROOM. IMAGINE THAT?
WHO IS THE BLACK PANTHER?
PART SIX
W'KABI... ARE YOU AWARE OF THE SECURITY BREACH IN THE QUEEN'S CHAMBERS?
YOUR UNCLE IS LEADING A TEAM THERE RIGHT NOW.
NO! HE'S TOO OLD FOR THAT!
IS THAT M'BUTU? YOU'VE BEATEN HIM SO BAD I CAN HARDLY RECOGNIZE HIM!
HE'S STILL ALIVE...WHICH IS BETTER THAN WHAT'S COMING TO YOU.

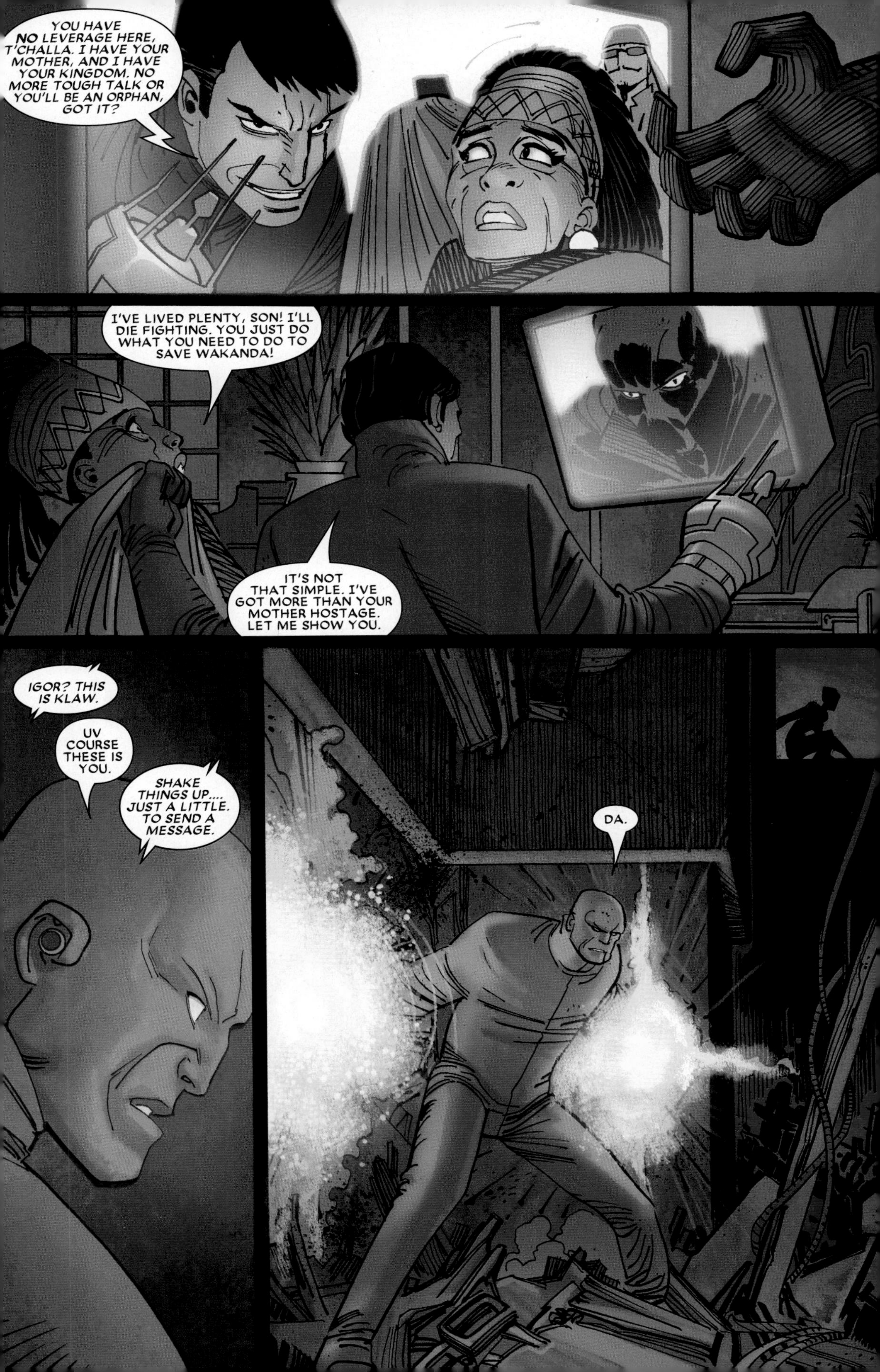
YOU HAVE NO LEVERAGE HERE, T'CHALLA. I HAVE YOUR MOTHER, AND I HAVE YOUR KINGDOM. NO MORE TOUGH TALK OR YOU'LL BE AN ORPHAN, GOT IT?
I'VE LIVED PLENTY, SON! I'LL DIE FIGHTING. YOU JUST DO WHAT YOU NEED TO DO TO SAVE WAKANDA!
IT'S NOT THAT SIMPLE. I'VE GOT MORE THAN YOUR MOTHER HOSTAGE. LET ME SHOW YOU.
IGOR? THIS IS KLAW.
UV COURSE THESE IS YOU.
SHAKE THINGS UP.... JUST A LITTLE. TO SEND A MESSAGE.
DA.

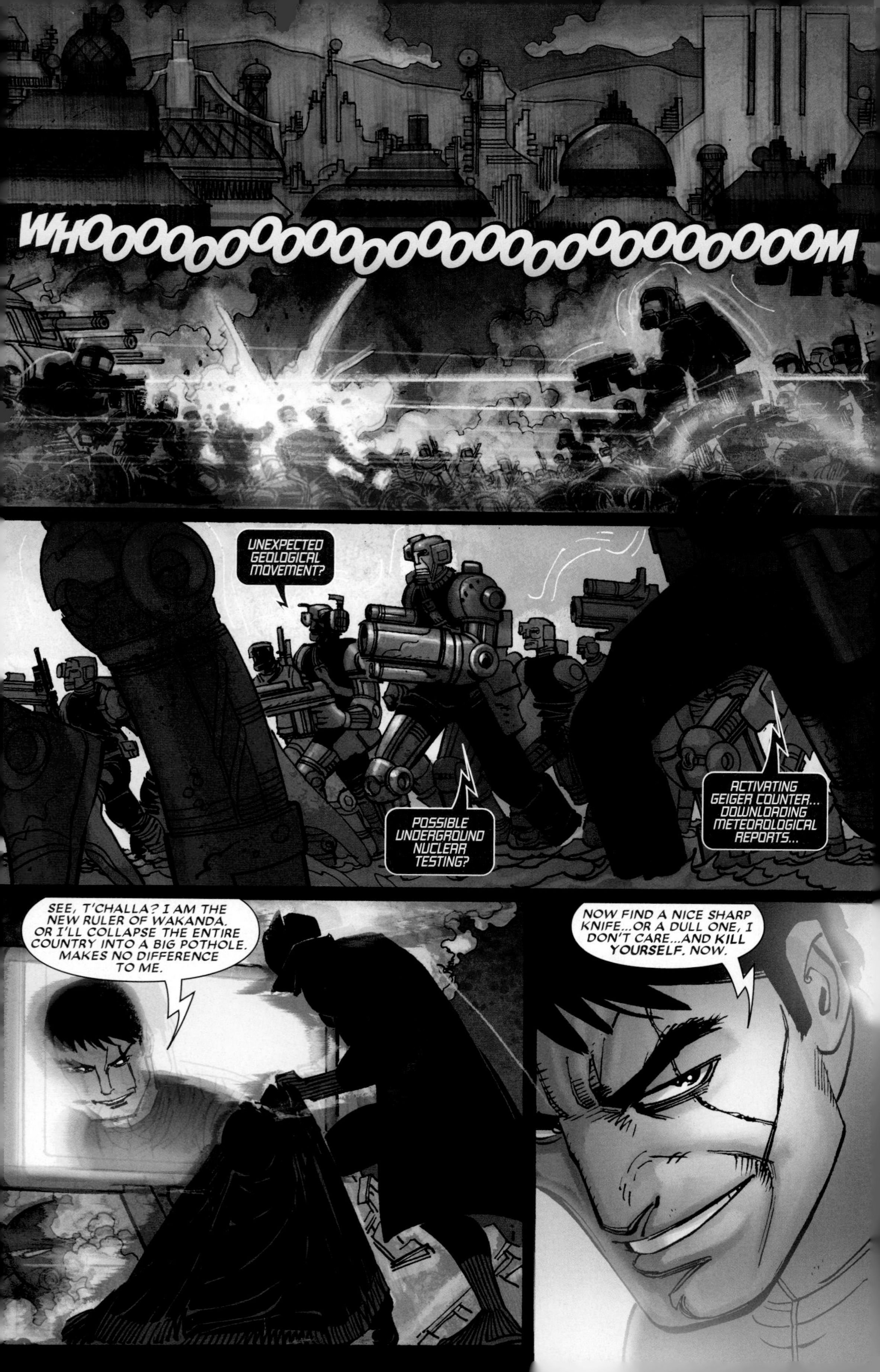
WHOOOOOOOOOOOOOOOOOOOOOOOOOOOM
UNEXPECTED GEOLOGICAL MOVEMENT?
POSSIBLE UNDERGROUND NUCLEAR TESTING?
ACTIVATING GEIGER COUNTER... DOWNLOADING METEOROLOGICAL REPORTS...
SEE, T'CHALLA? I AM THE NEW RULER OF WAKANDA. OR I'LL COLLAPSE THE ENTIRE COUNTRY INTO A BIG POTHOLE. MAKES NO DIFFERENCE TO ME.
NOW FIND A NICE SHARP KNIFE...OR A DULL ONE, I DON'T CARE...AND KILL YOURSELF. NOW.

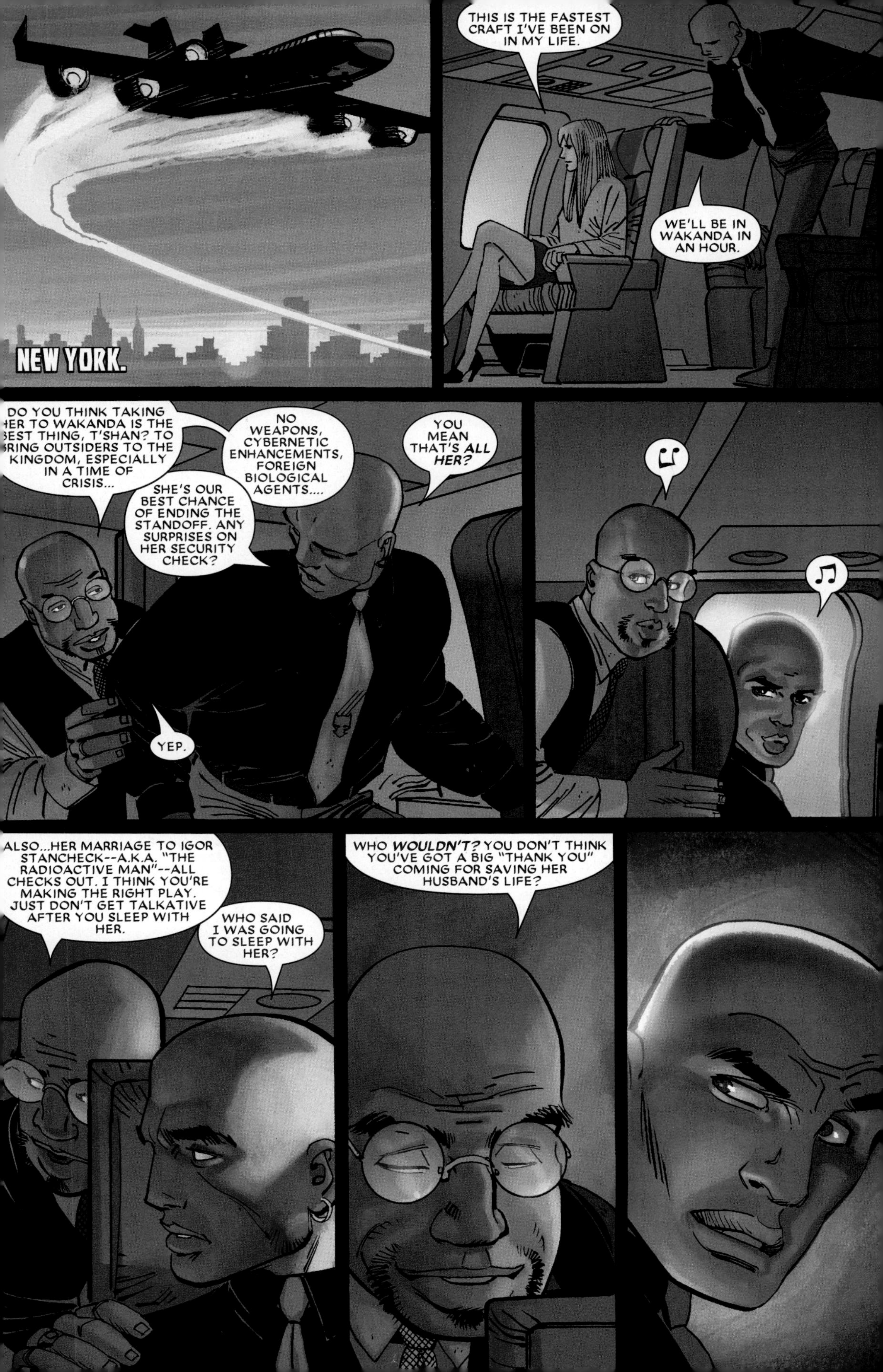
NEW YORK.
THIS IS THE FASTEST CRAFT I'VE BEEN ON IN MY LIFE.
WE'LL BE IN WAKANDA IN AN HOUR.
DO YOU THINK TAKING HER TO WAKANDA IS THE BEST THING, T'SHAN? TO BRING OUTSIDERS TO THE KINGDOM, ESPECIALLY IN A TIME OF CRISIS...
SHE'S OUR BEST CHANCE OF ENDING THE STANDOFF. ANY SURPRISES ON HER SECURITY CHECK?
NO WEAPONS, CYBERNETIC ENHANCEMENTS, FOREIGN BIOLOGICAL AGENTS....
YOU MEAN THAT'S ALL HER?
YEP.
ALSO...HER MARRIAGE TO IGOR STANCHECK--A.K.A. "THE RADIOACTIVE MAN"--ALL CHECKS OUT. I THINK YOU'RE MAKING THE RIGHT PLAY. JUST DON'T GET TALKATIVE AFTER YOU SLEEP WITH HER.
WHO SAID I WAS GOING TO SLEEP WITH HER?
WHO WOULDN'T? YOU DON'T THINK YOU'VE GOT A BIG "THANK YOU" COMING FOR SAVING HER HUSBAND'S LIFE?

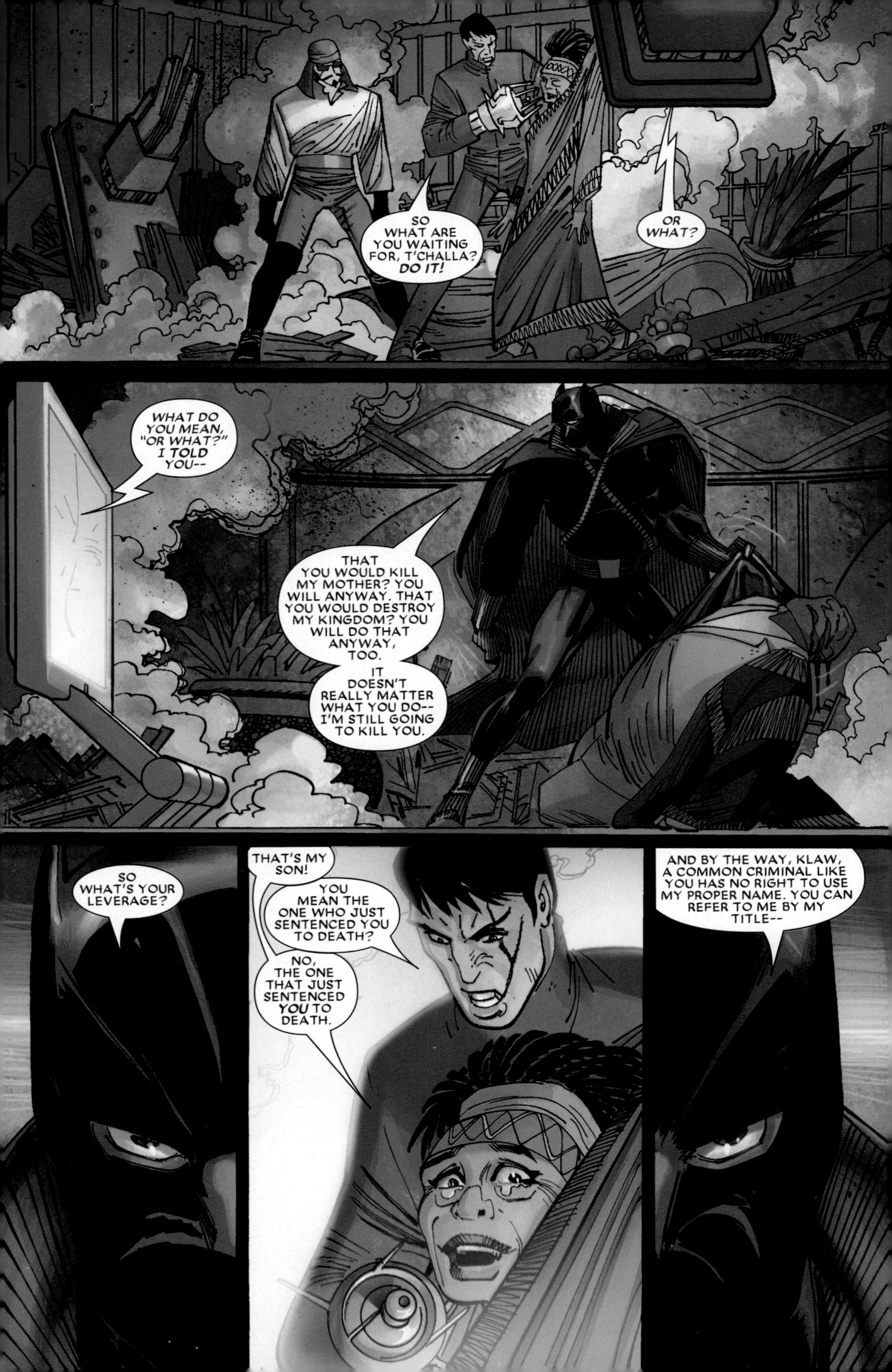
SO WHAT ARE YOU WAITING FOR, T'CHALLA? DO IT!
OR WHAT?
WHAT DO YOU MEAN, "OR WHAT?" I TOLD YOU--
THAT YOU WOULD KILL MY MOTHER? YOU WILL ANYWAY. THAT YOU WOULD DESTROY MY KINGDOM? YOU WILL DO THAT ANYWAY, TOO.
IT DOESN'T REALLY MATTER WHAT YOU DO-- I'M STILL GOING TO KILL YOU.
SO WHAT'S YOUR LEVERAGE?
THAT'S MY SON!
YOU MEAN THE ONE WHO JUST SENTENCED YOU TO DEATH?
NO, THE ONE THAT JUST SENTENCED YOU TO DEATH.
AND BY THE WAY, KLAW, A COMMON CRIMINAL LIKE YOU HAS NO RIGHT TO USE MY PROPER NAME. YOU CAN REFER TO ME BY MY TITLE--

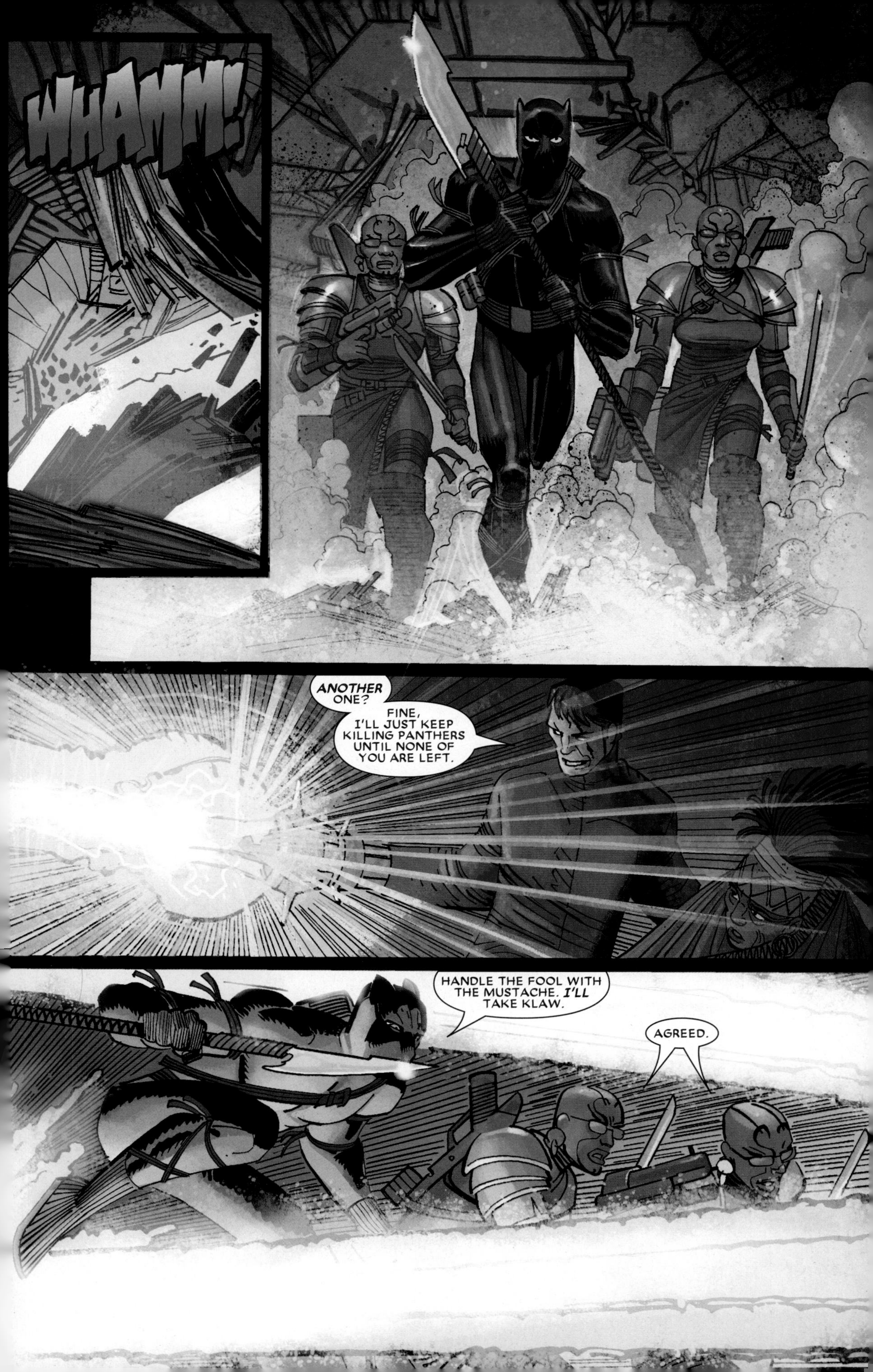
WHAMM!
ANOTHER ONE?
FINE, I'LL JUST KEEP KILLING PANTHERS UNTIL NONE OF YOU ARE LEFT.
HANDLE THE FOOL WITH THE MUSTACHE. I'LL TAKE KLAW.
AGREED.

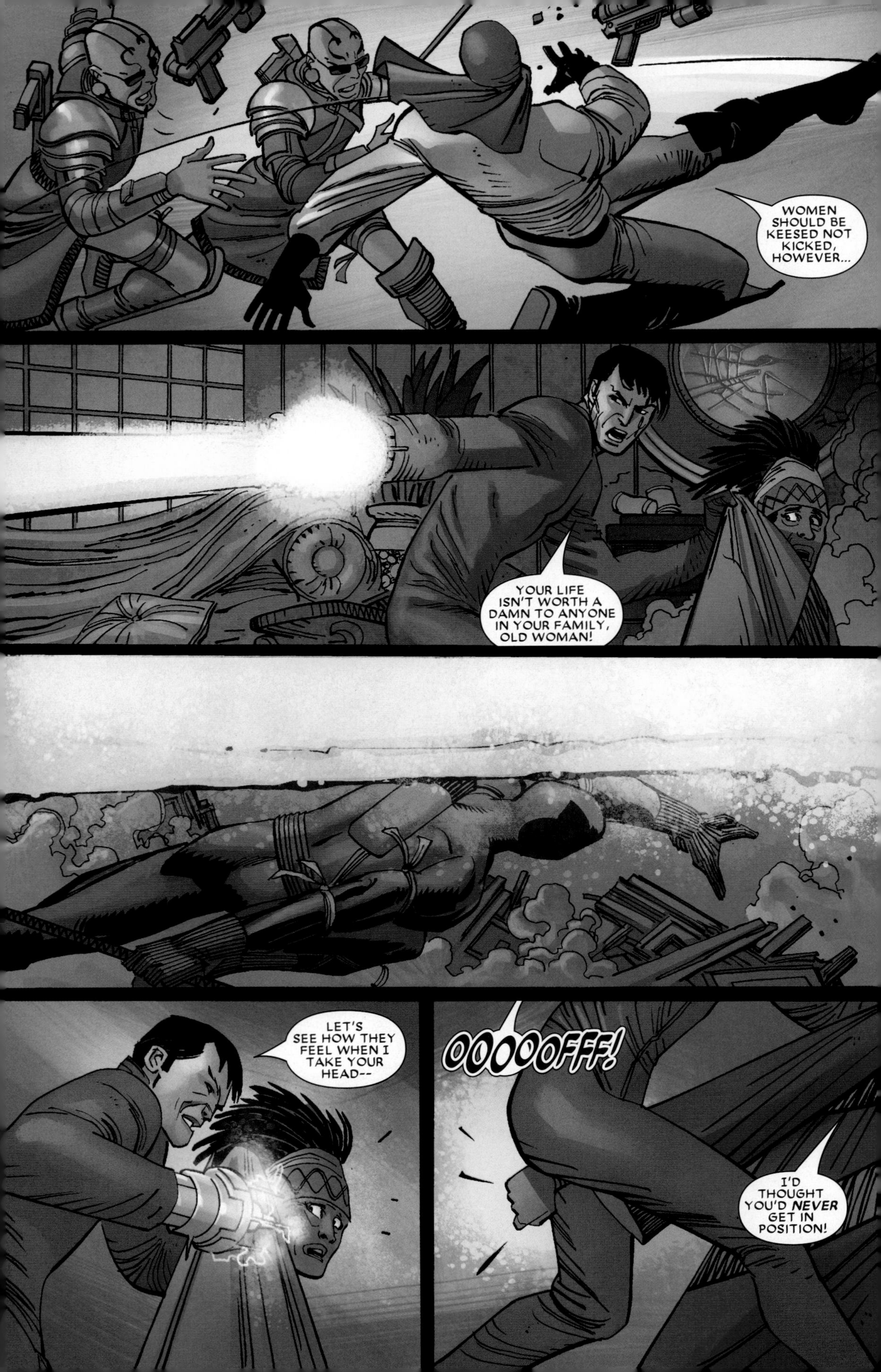
WOMEN SHOULD BE KEESED NOT KICKED, HOWEVER...
YOUR LIFE ISN'T WORTH A DAMN TO ANYONE IN YOUR FAMILY, OLD WOMAN!
LET'S SEE HOW THEY FEEL WHEN I TAKE YOUR HEAD--
OOOOOFFF!
I'D THOUGHT YOU'D *NEVER* GET IN POSITION!

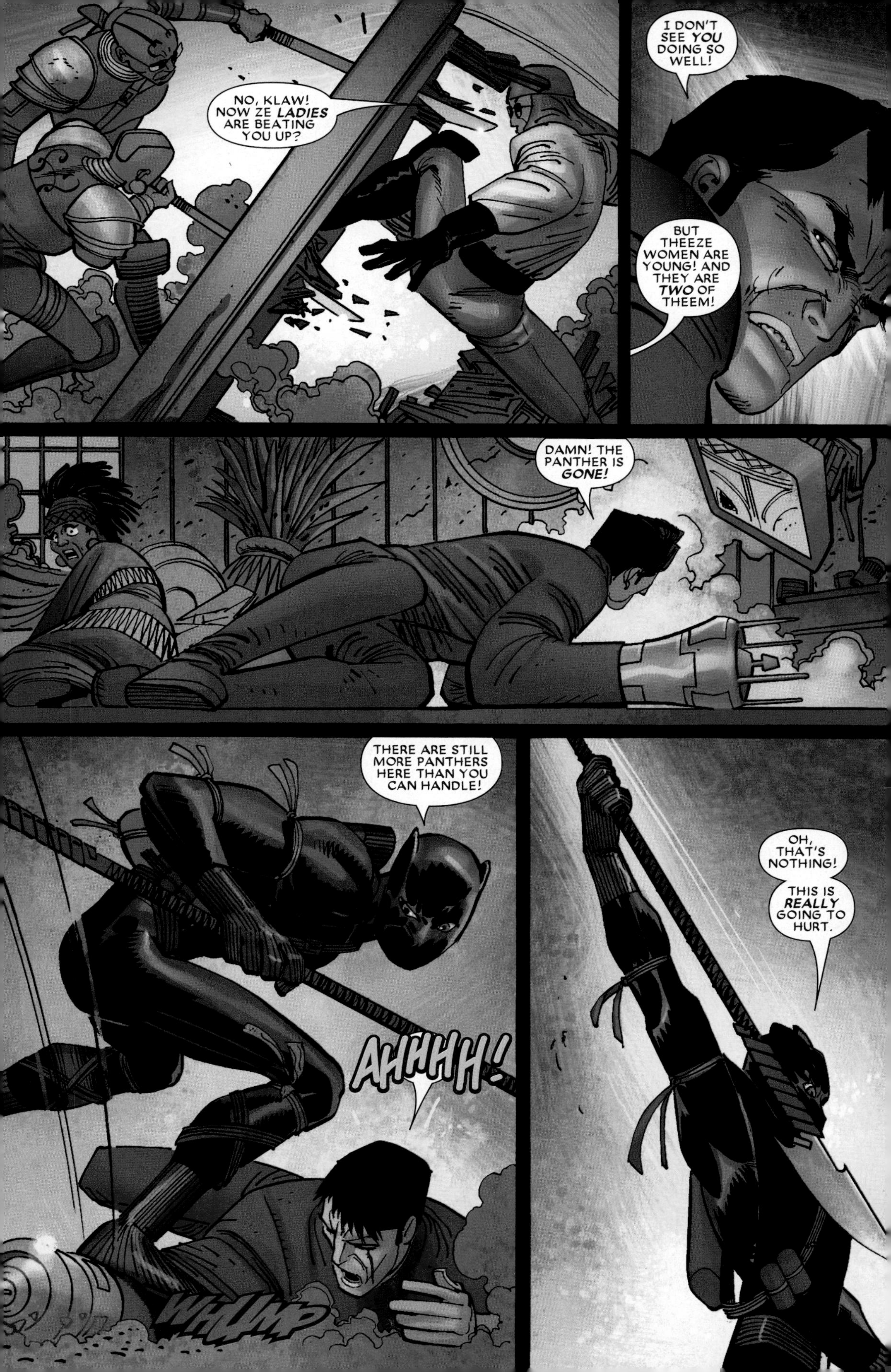

NO, KLAW! NOW ZE LADIES ARE BEATING YOU UP?
I DON'T SEE YOU DOING SO WELL!
BUT THEEZE WOMEN ARE YOUNG! AND THEY ARE TWO OF THEEM!
DAMN! THE PANTHER IS GONE!
THERE ARE STILL MORE PANTHERS HERE THAN YOU CAN HANDLE!
AHHHH!
WHUMP
OH, THAT'S NOTHING!
THIS IS REALLY GOING TO HURT.

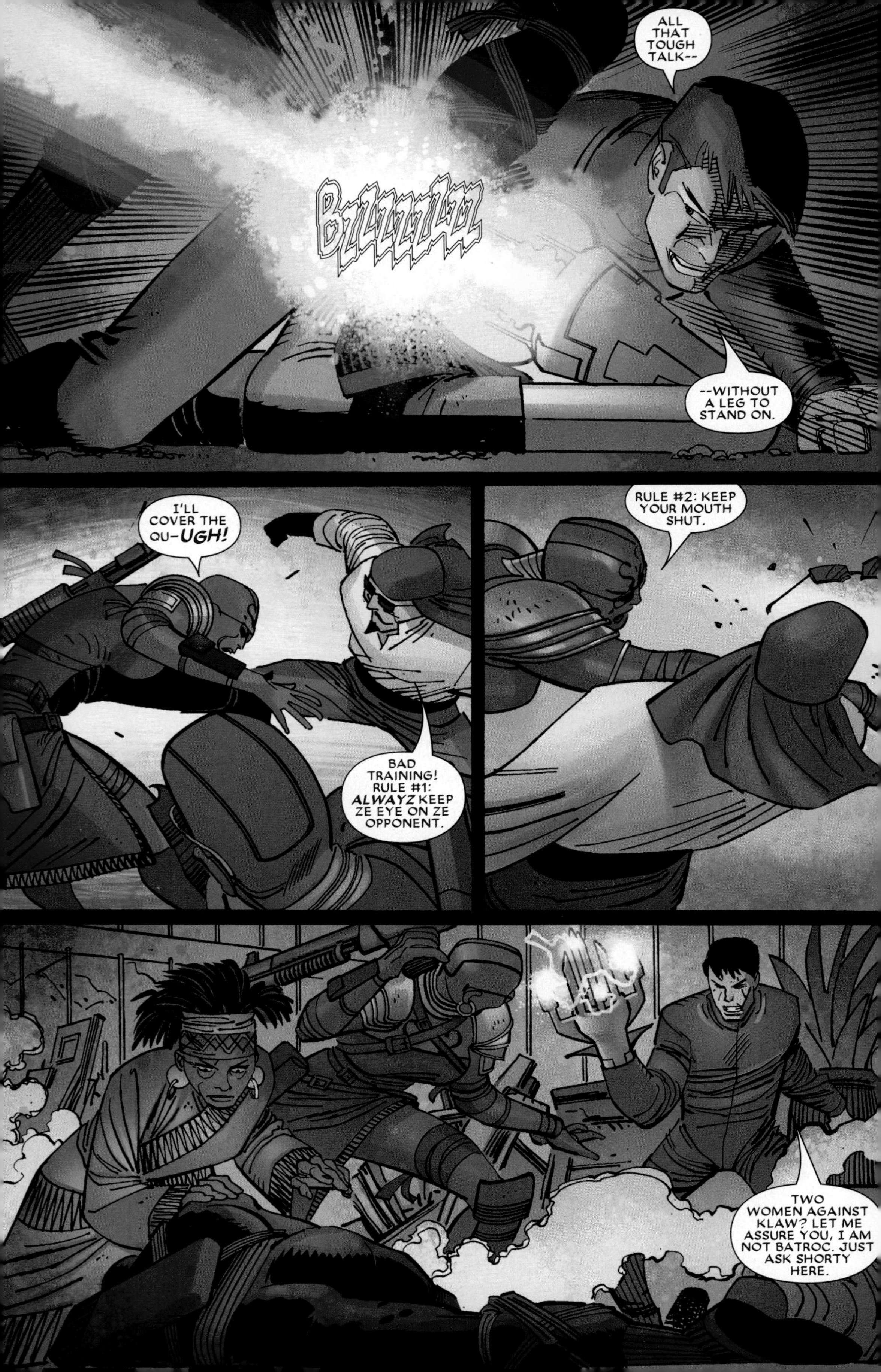
ALL THAT TOUGH TALK--
BZZZZZZZZ
--WITHOUT A LEG TO STAND ON.
I'LL COVER THE QU-UGH!
BAD TRAINING! RULE #1: ALWAYZ KEEP ZE EYE ON ZE OPPONENT.
RULE #2: KEEP YOUR MOUTH SHUT.
TWO WOMEN AGAINST KLAW? LET ME ASSURE YOU, I AM NOT BATROC. JUST ASK SHORTY HERE.

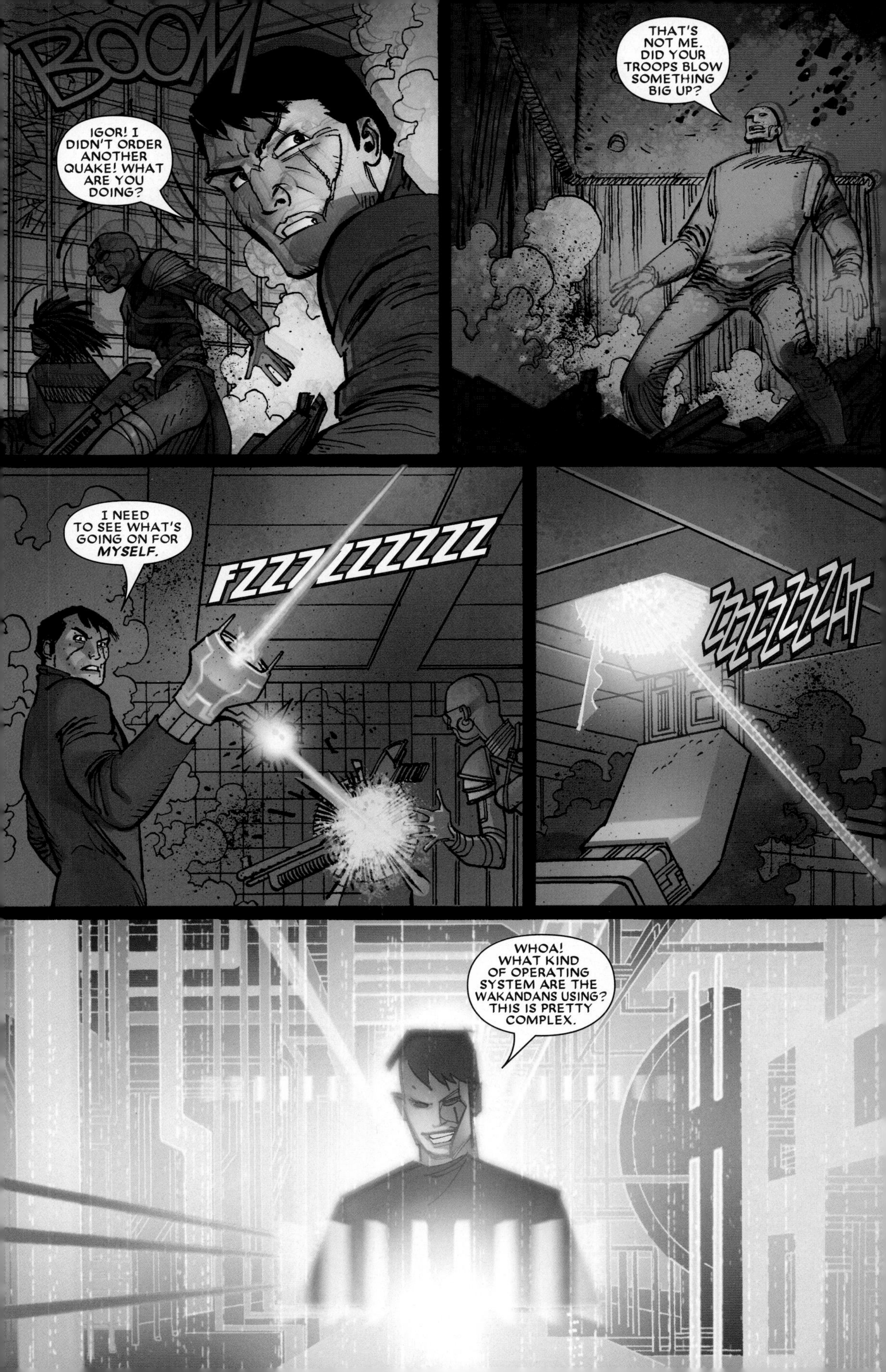
BOOM
IGOR! I DIDN'T ORDER ANOTHER QUAKE! WHAT ARE YOU DOING?
THAT'S NOT ME. DID YOUR TROOPS BLOW SOMETHING BIG UP?
I NEED TO SEE WHAT'S GOING ON FOR *MYSELF*.
FZZZZZZZZZZ
ZZZZZZZZAT
WHOA! WHAT KIND OF OPERATING SYSTEM ARE THE WAKANDANS USING? THIS IS PRETTY COMPLEX.

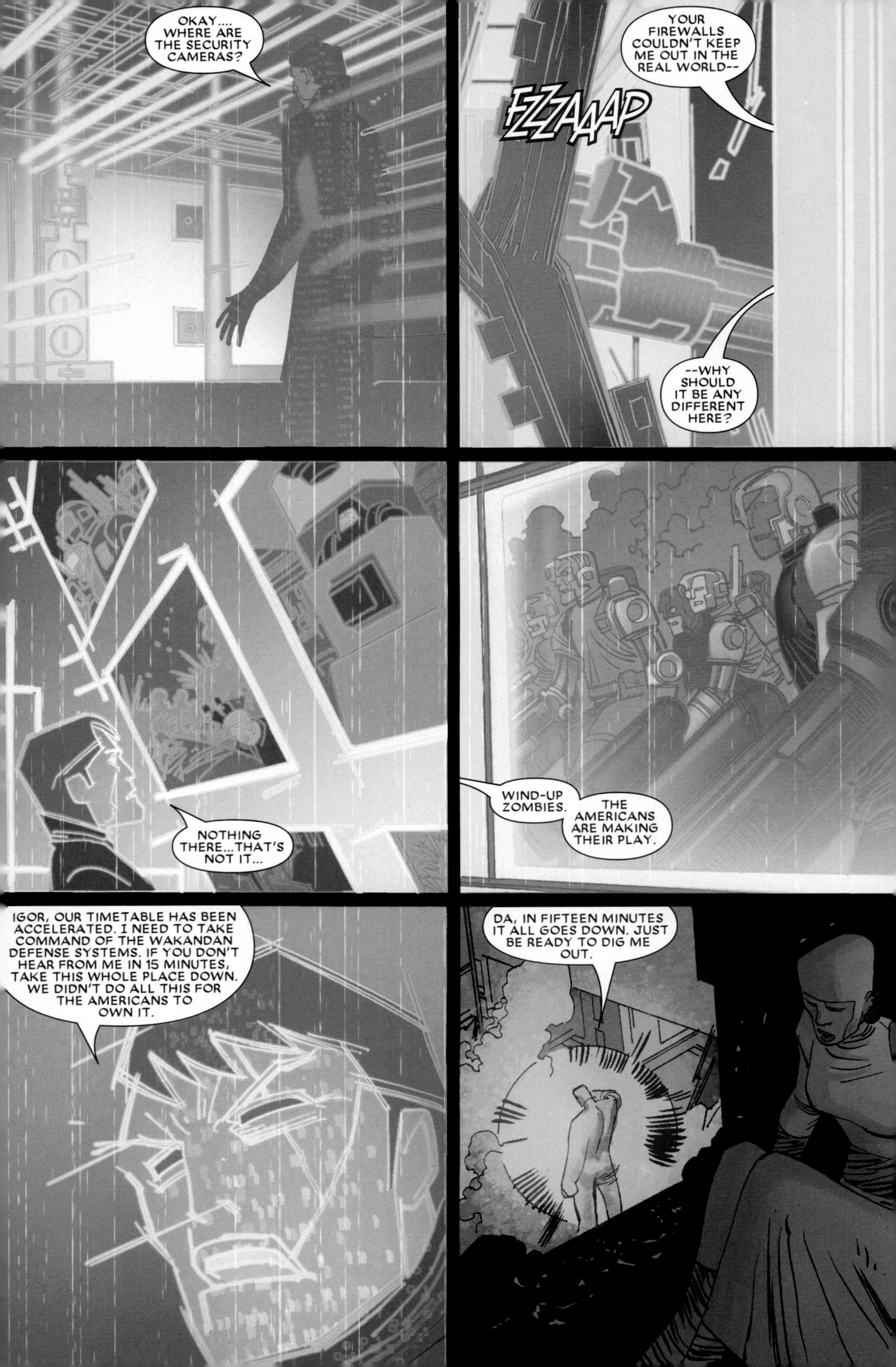
OKAY.... WHERE ARE THE SECURITY CAMERAS?
YOUR FIREWALLS COULDN'T KEEP ME OUT IN THE REAL WORLD--
EZZZAAAP
--WHY SHOULD IT BE ANY DIFFERENT HERE?
NOTHING THERE...THAT'S NOT IT...
WIND-UP ZOMBIES.
THE AMERICANS ARE MAKING THEIR PLAY.
IGOR, OUR TIMETABLE HAS BEEN ACCELERATED. I NEED TO TAKE COMMAND OF THE WAKANDAN DEFENSE SYSTEMS. IF YOU DON'T HEAR FROM ME IN 15 MINUTES, TAKE THIS WHOLE PLACE DOWN. WE DIDN'T DO ALL THIS FOR THE AMERICANS TO OWN IT.
DA, IN FIFTEEN MINUTES IT ALL GOES DOWN. JUST BE READY TO DIG ME OUT.

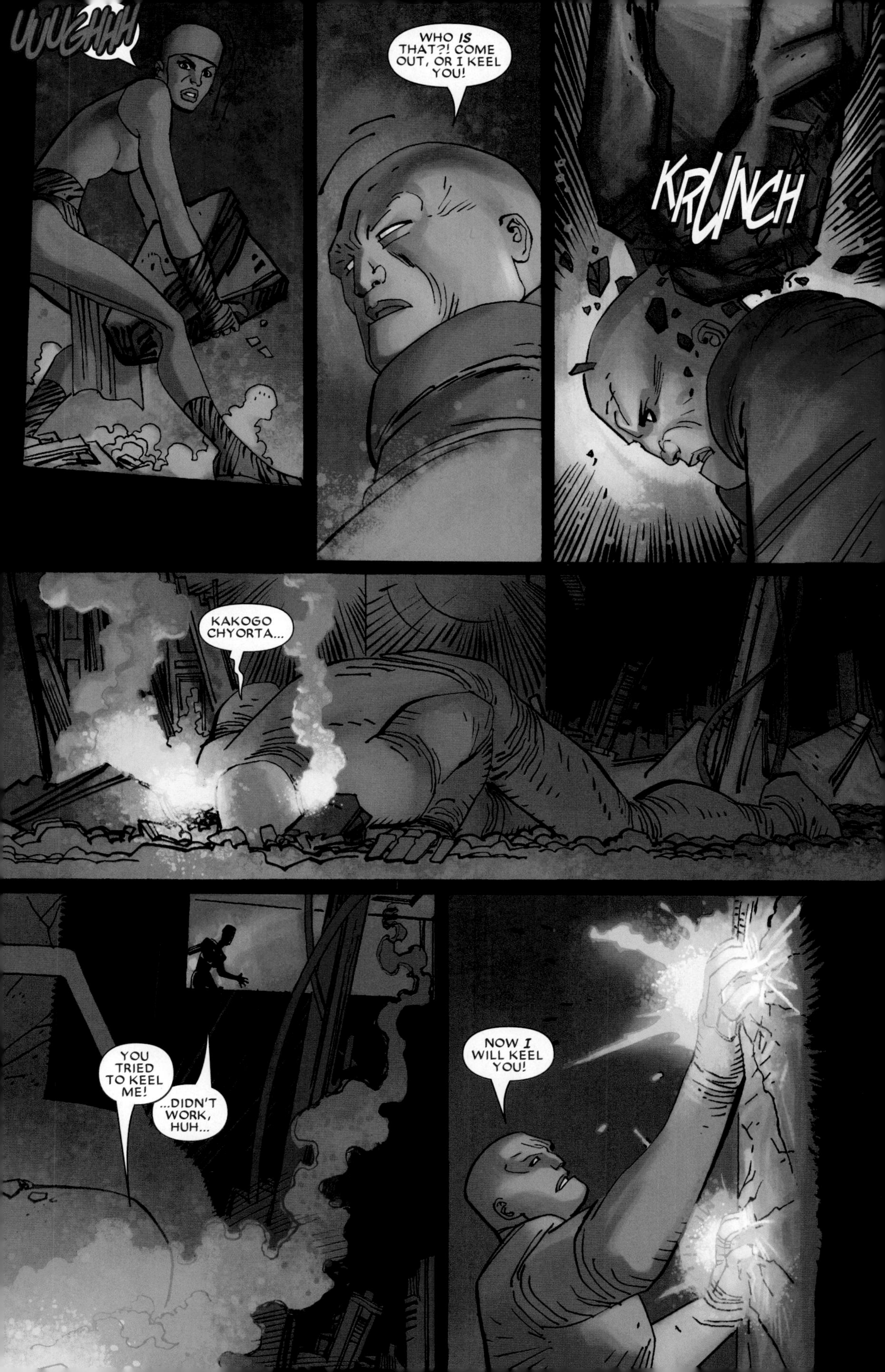
UUUGHHH
WHO IS THAT?! COME OUT, OR I KEEL YOU!
KRUNCH
KAKOGO CHYORTA...
YOU TRIED TO KEEL ME!
...DIDN'T WORK, HUH...
NOW I WILL KEEL YOU!

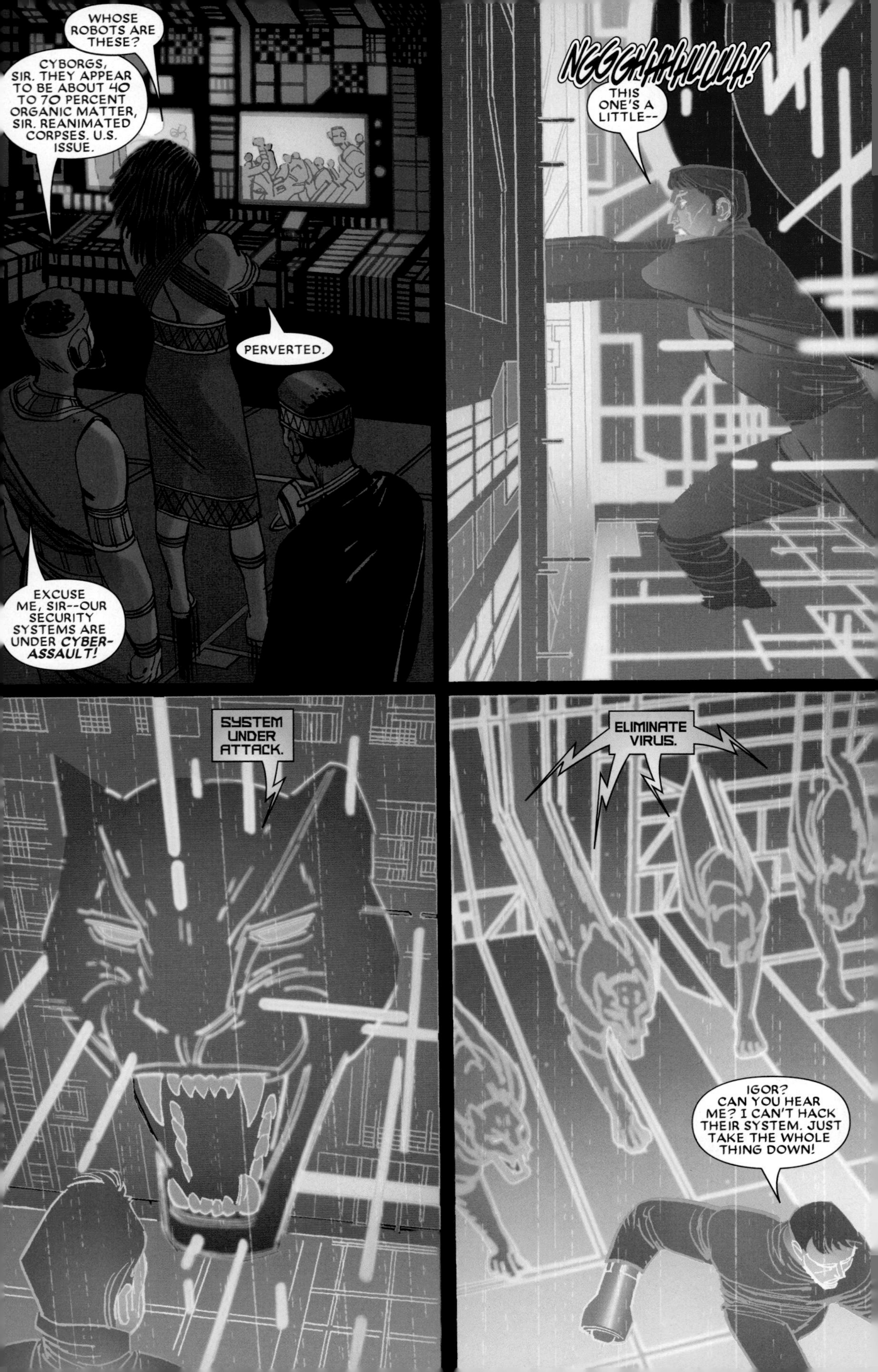
WHOSE ROBOTS ARE THESE?
CYBORGS, SIR. THEY APPEAR TO BE ABOUT 40 TO 70 PERCENT ORGANIC MATTER, SIR. REANIMATED CORPSES. U.S. ISSUE.
PERVERTED.
EXCUSE ME, SIR--OUR SECURITY SYSTEMS ARE UNDER *CYBER-ASSAULT!*
NGGGHAAHUUUH!
THIS ONE'S A LITTLE--
SYSTEM UNDER ATTACK.
ELIMINATE VIRUS.
IGOR? CAN YOU HEAR ME? I CAN'T HACK THEIR SYSTEM. JUST TAKE THE WHOLE THING DOWN!

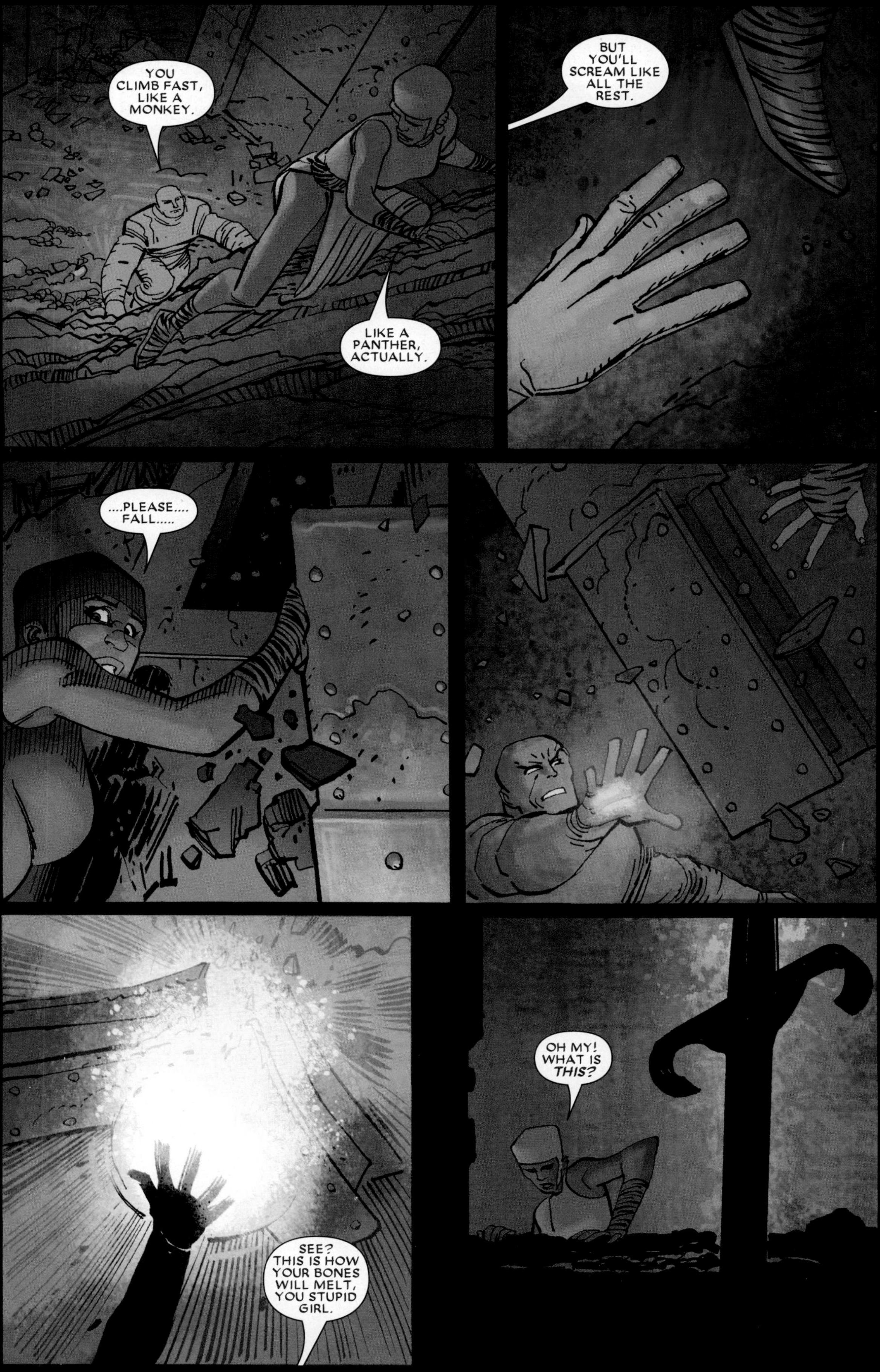
YOU CLIMB FAST, LIKE A MONKEY.
LIKE A PANTHER, ACTUALLY.
BUT YOU'LL SCREAM LIKE ALL THE REST.
....PLEASE.... FALL.....
SEE? THIS IS HOW YOUR BONES WILL MELT, YOU STUPID GIRL.
OH MY! WHAT IS *THIS?*

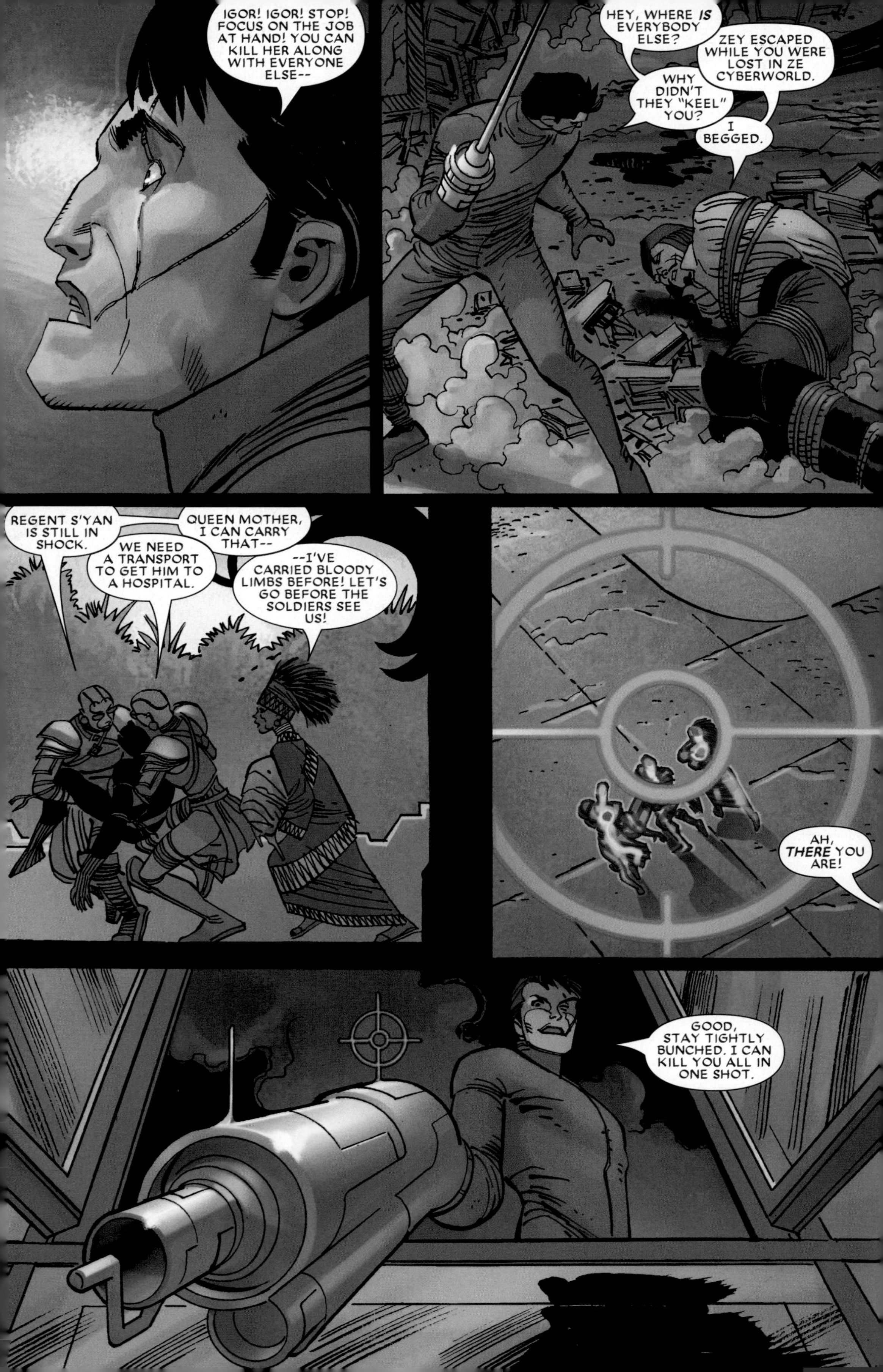
IGOR! IGOR! STOP! FOCUS ON THE JOB AT HAND! YOU CAN KILL HER ALONG WITH EVERYONE ELSE--
HEY, WHERE IS EVERYBODY ELSE?
ZEY ESCAPED WHILE YOU WERE LOST IN ZE CYBERWORLD.
WHY DIDN'T THEY "KEEL" YOU?
I BEGGED.
REGENT S'YAN IS STILL IN SHOCK.
WE NEED A TRANSPORT TO GET HIM TO A HOSPITAL.
QUEEN MOTHER, I CAN CARRY THAT--
--I'VE CARRIED BLOODY LIMBS BEFORE! LET'S GO BEFORE THE SOLDIERS SEE US!
AH, THERE YOU ARE!
GOOD, STAY TIGHTLY BUNCHED. I CAN KILL YOU ALL IN ONE SHOT.

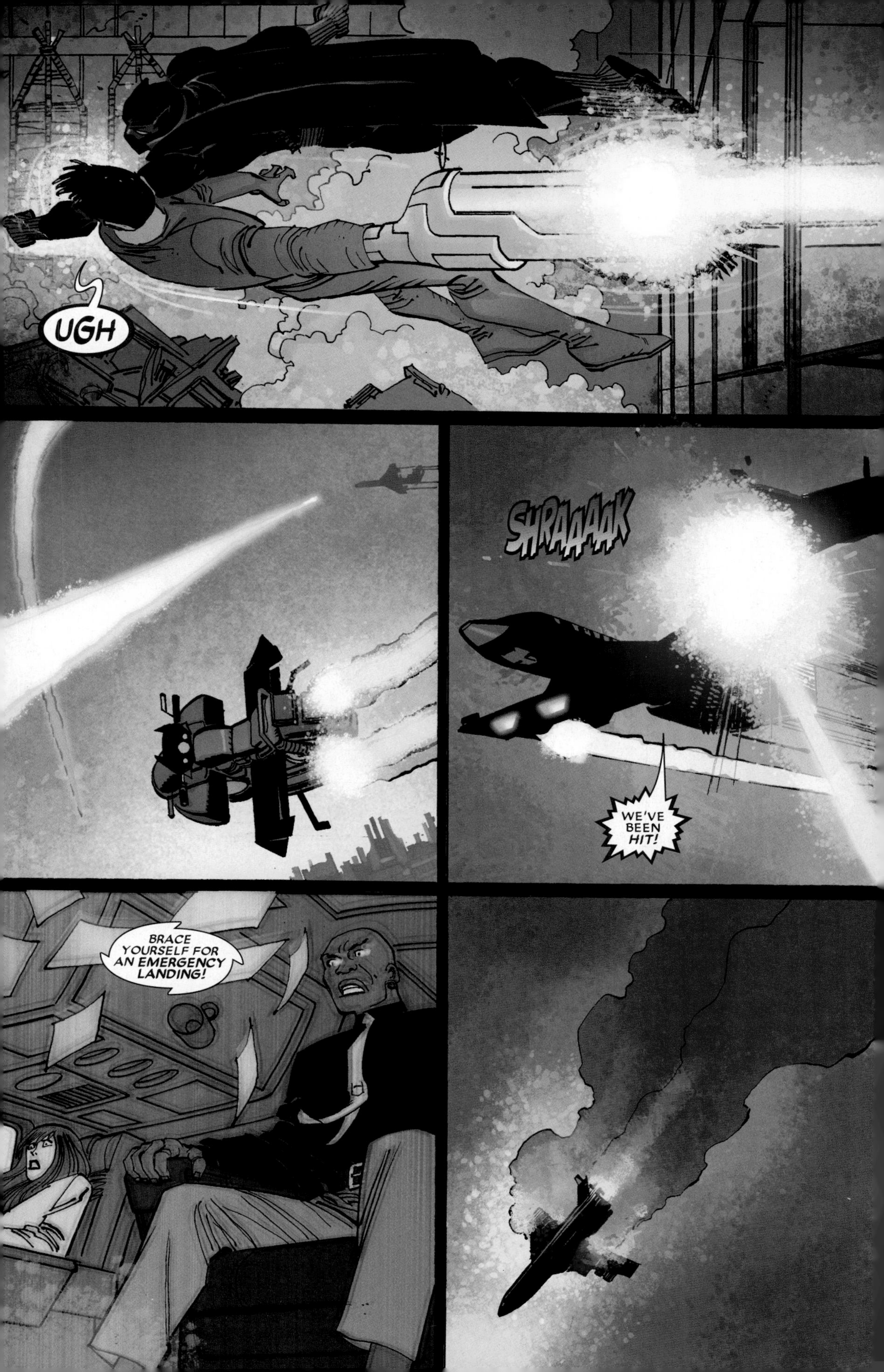
UGH
SHRAAAAK
WE'VE BEEN HIT!
BRACE YOURSELF FOR AN EMERGENCY LANDING!

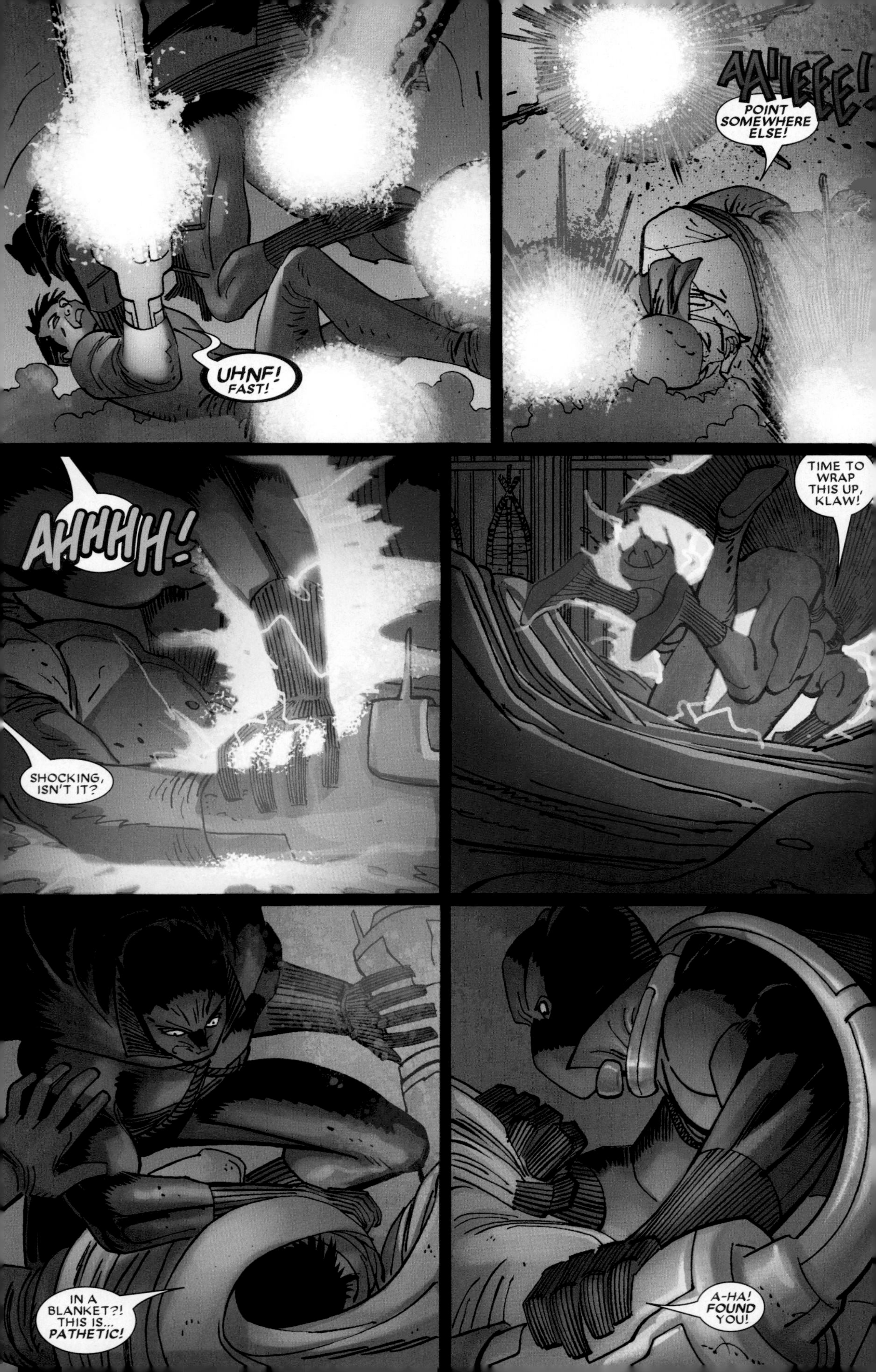
UHNF! FAST!
AA'IEEEE!
POINT SOMEWHERE ELSE!
AHHHH!
SHOCKING, ISN'T IT?
TIME TO WRAP THIS UP, KLAW!
IN A BLANKET?! THIS IS... PATHETIC!
A-HA! FOUND YOU!

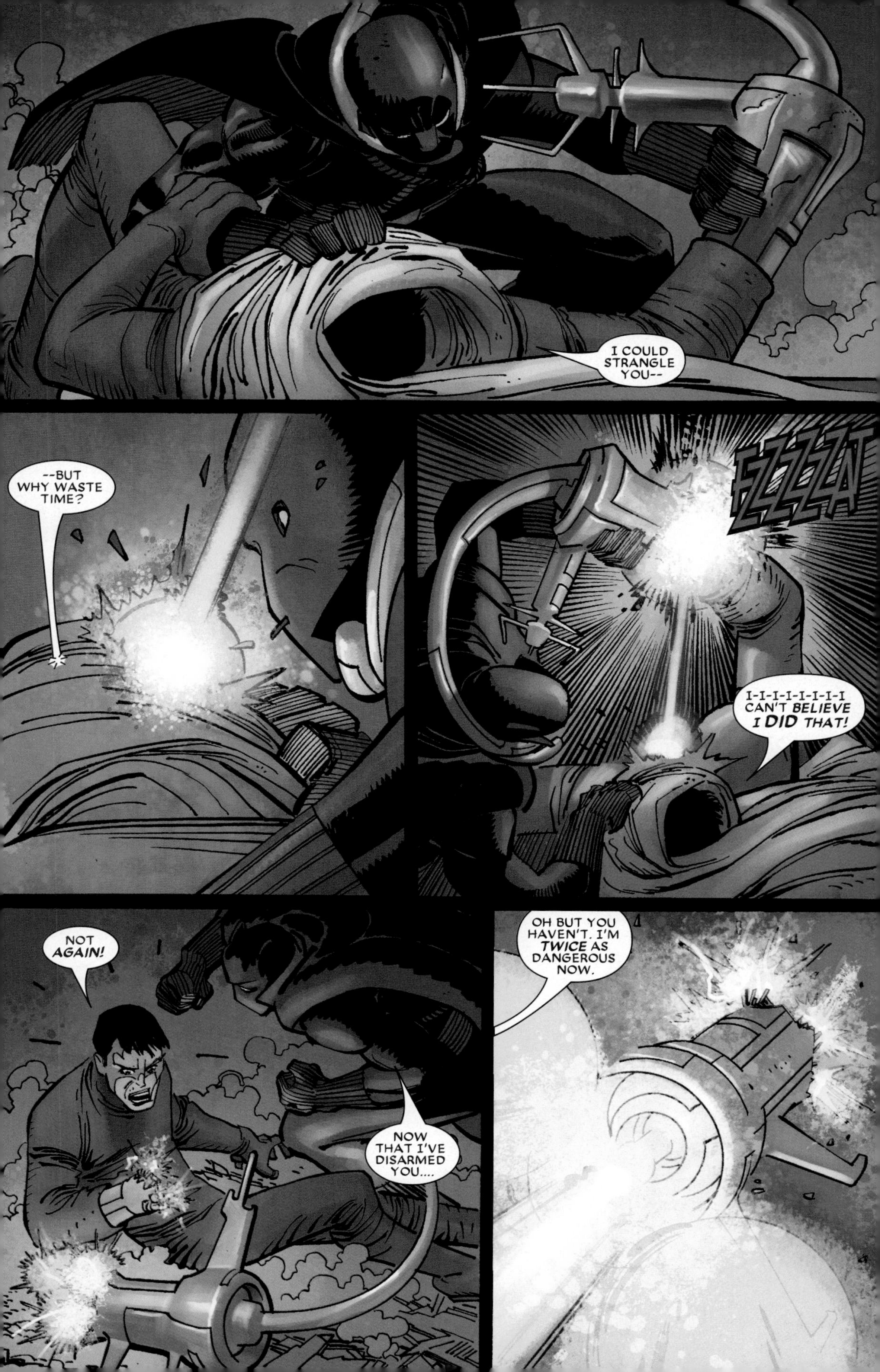
I COULD STRANGLE YOU--
--BUT WHY WASTE TIME?
EZZZZZAT
I-I-I-I-I-I-I-I CAN'T BELIEVE I DID THAT!
NOT AGAIN!
NOW THAT I'VE DISARMED YOU....
OH BUT YOU HAVEN'T. I'M TWICE AS DANGEROUS NOW.

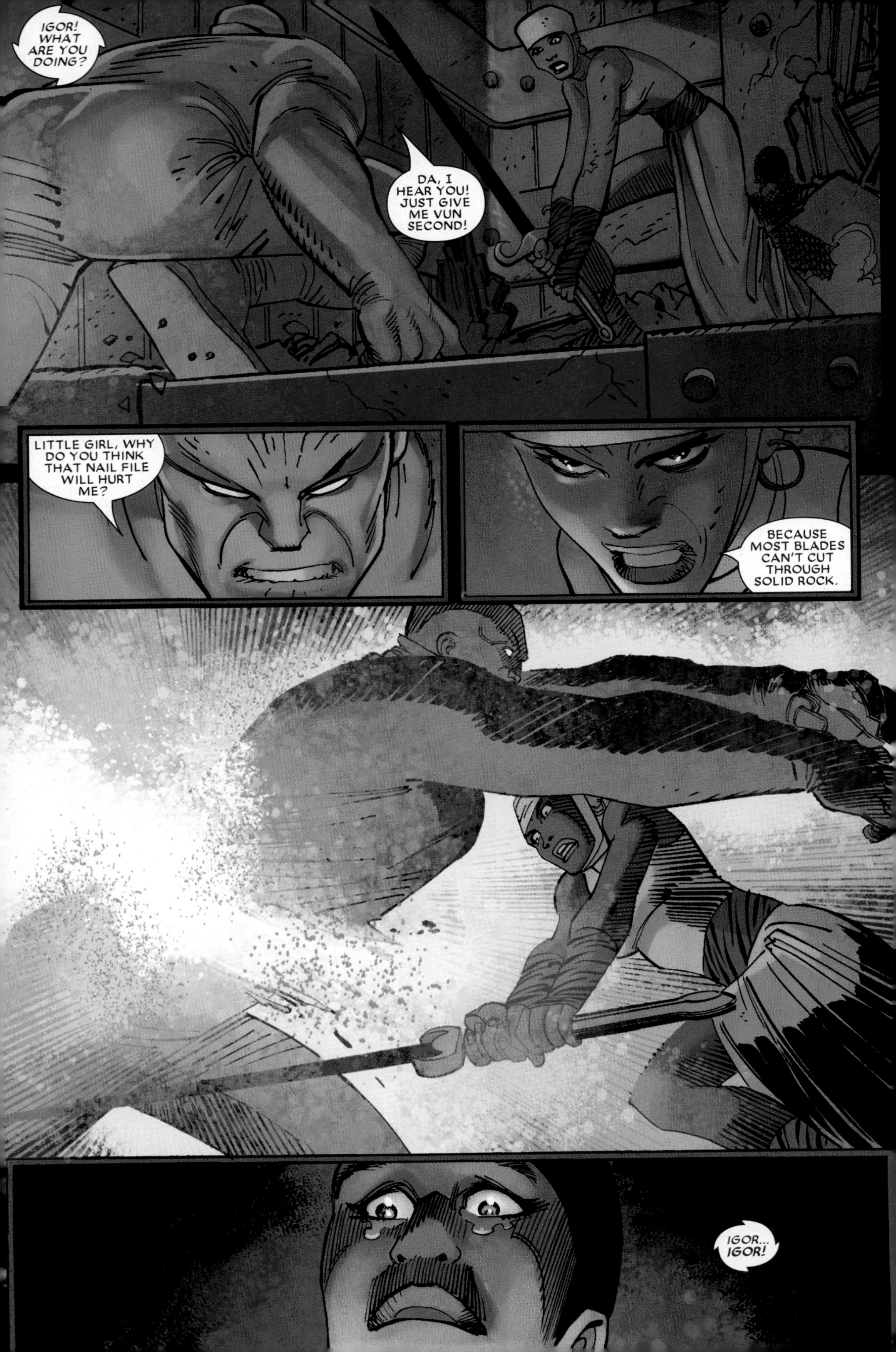
IGOR! WHAT ARE YOU DOING?
DA, I HEAR YOU! JUST GIVE ME VUN SECOND!
LITTLE GIRL, WHY DO YOU THINK THAT NAIL FILE WILL HURT ME?
BECAUSE MOST BLADES CAN'T CUT THROUGH SOLID ROCK.
IGOR... IGOR!

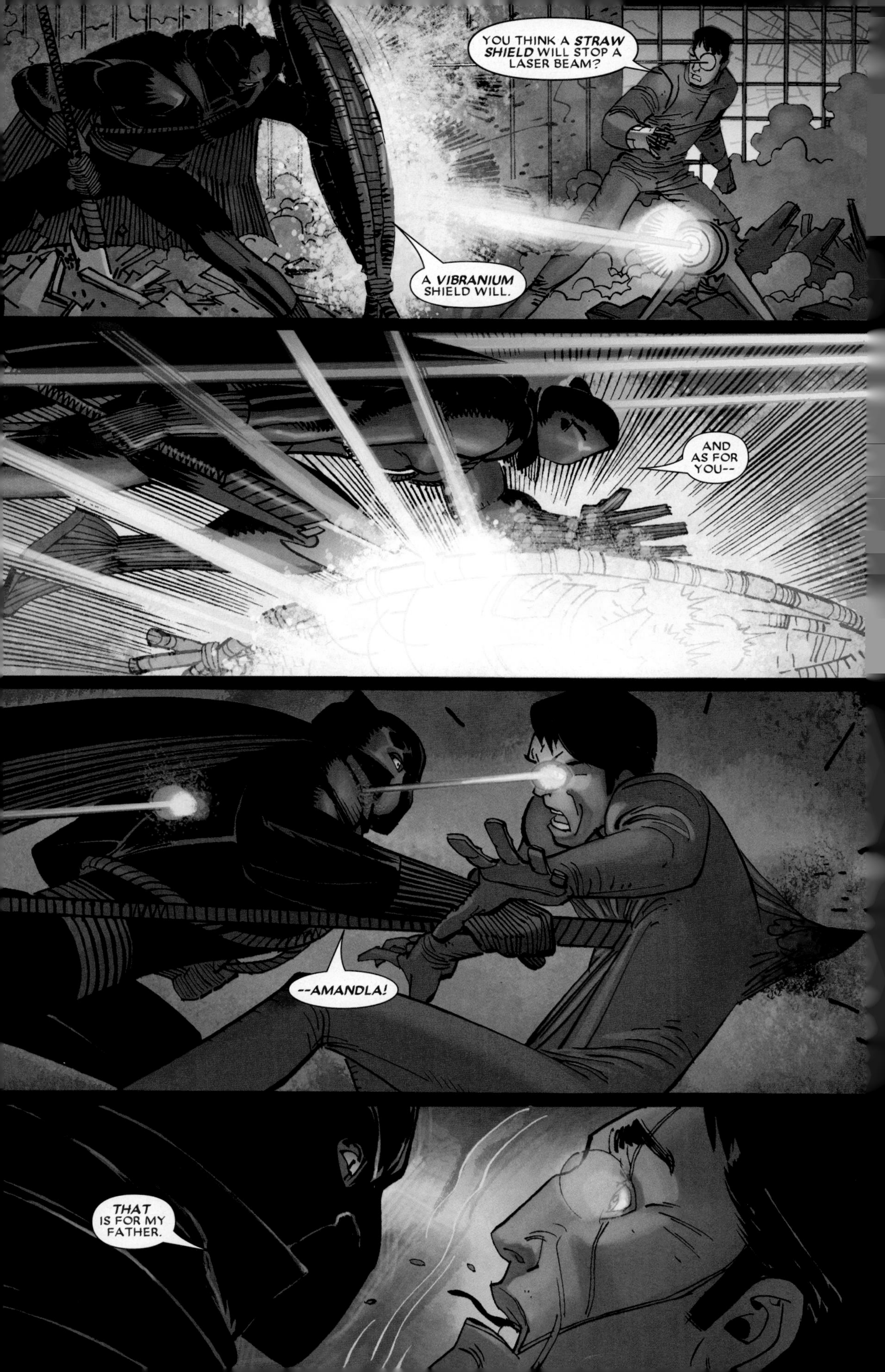
YOU THINK A STRAW SHIELD WILL STOP A LASER BEAM?
A VIBRANIUM SHIELD WILL.
AND AS FOR YOU--
--AMANDLA!
THAT IS FOR MY FATHER.

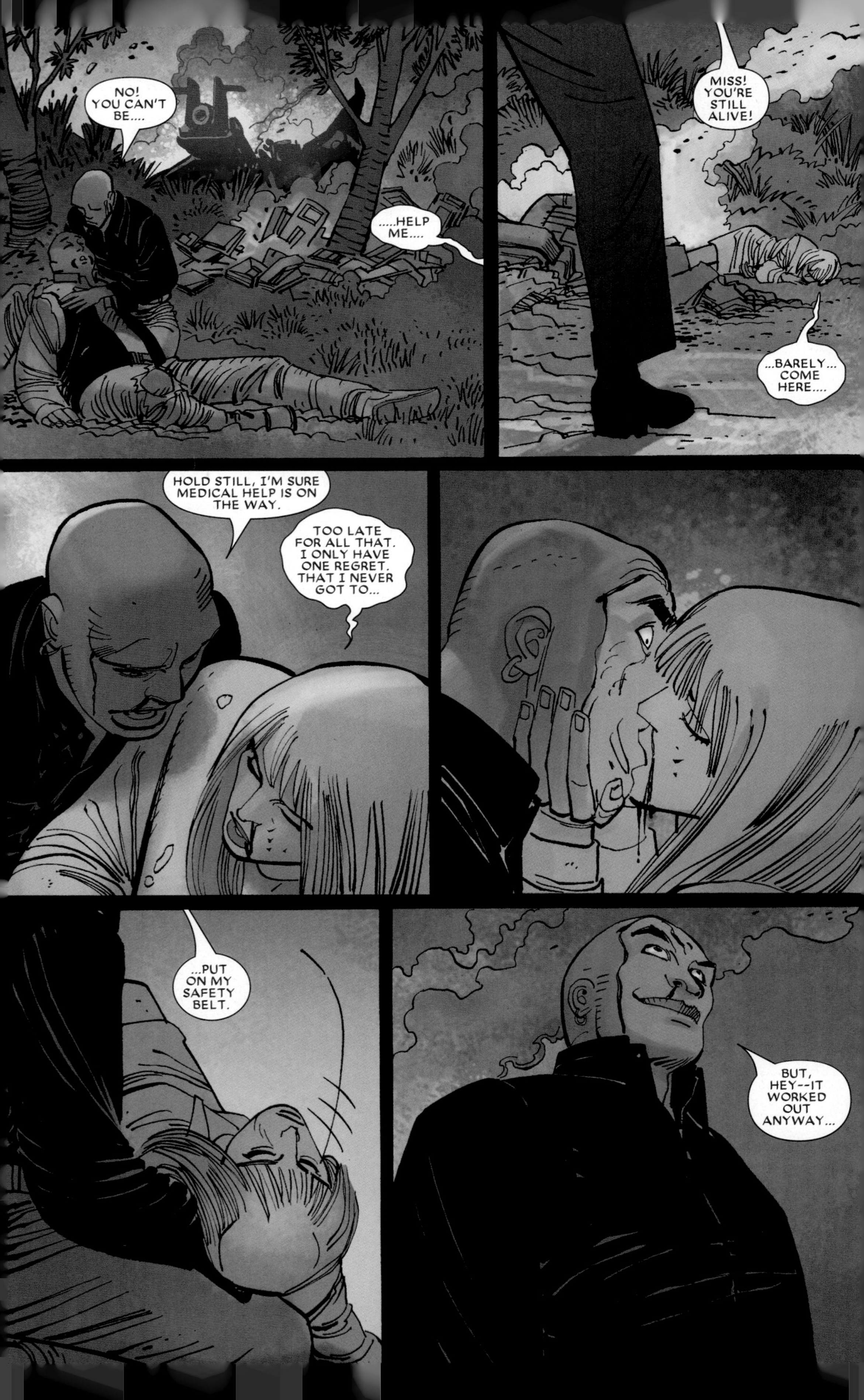
NO! YOU CAN'T BE....
.....HELP ME....
MISS! YOU'RE STILL ALIVE!
...BARELY... COME HERE....
HOLD STILL, I'M SURE MEDICAL HELP IS ON THE WAY.
TOO LATE FOR ALL THAT. I ONLY HAVE ONE REGRET. THAT I NEVER GOT TO...
...PUT ON MY SAFETY BELT.
BUT, HEY--IT WORKED OUT ANYWAY...

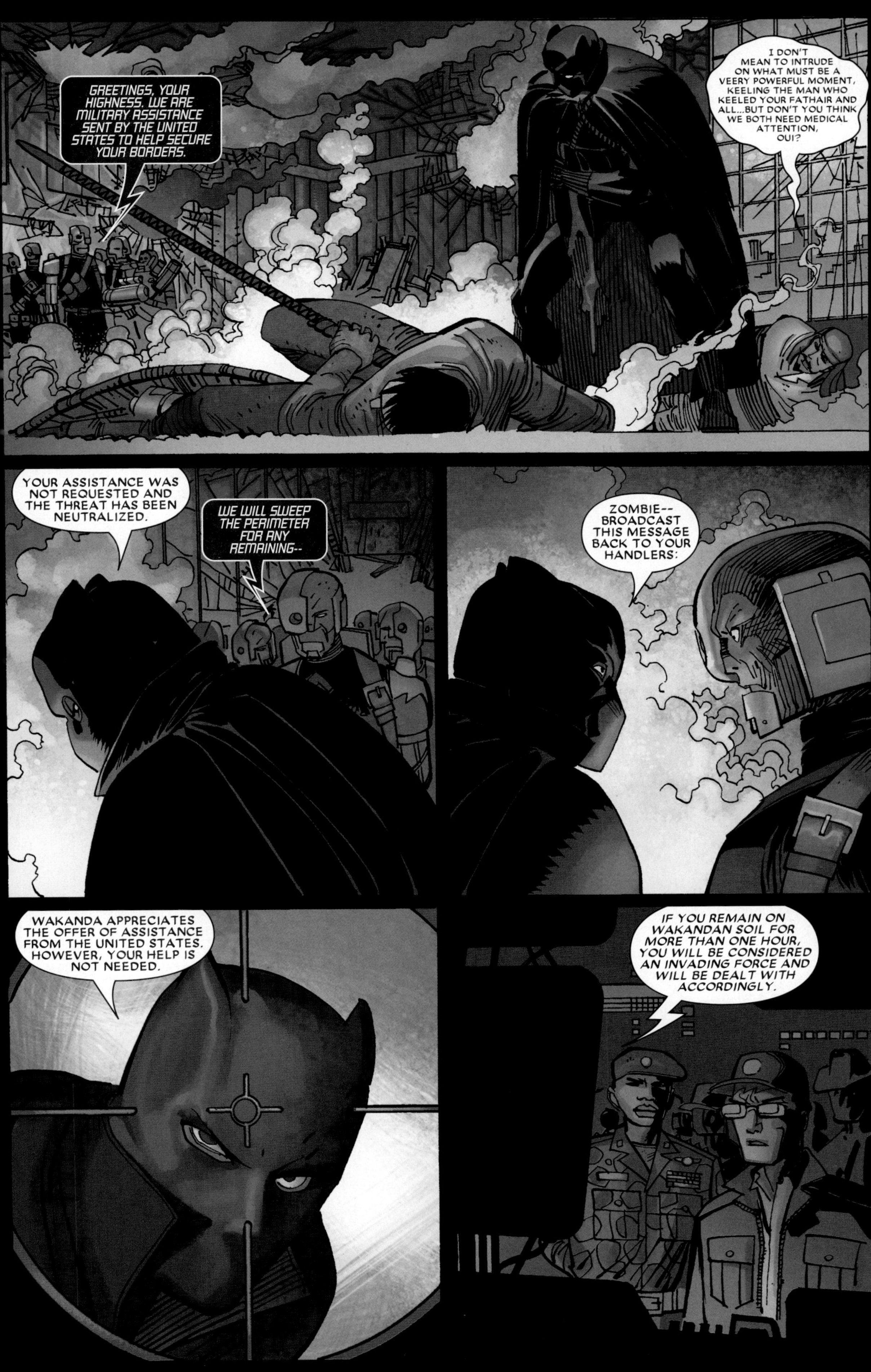
GREETINGS, YOUR HIGHNESS. WE ARE MILITARY ASSISTANCE SENT BY THE UNITED STATES TO HELP SECURE YOUR BORDERS.
I DON'T MEAN TO INTRUDE ON WHAT MUST BE A VEERY POWERFUL MOMENT, KEELING THE MAN WHO KEELED YOUR FATHAIR AND ALL...BUT DON'T YOU THINK WE BOTH NEED MEDICAL ATTENTION, OUI?
YOUR ASSISTANCE WAS NOT REQUESTED AND THE THREAT HAS BEEN NEUTRALIZED.
WE WILL SWEEP THE PERIMETER FOR ANY REMAINING--
ZOMBIE--BROADCAST THIS MESSAGE BACK TO YOUR HANDLERS:
WAKANDA APPRECIATES THE OFFER OF ASSISTANCE FROM THE UNITED STATES. HOWEVER, YOUR HELP IS NOT NEEDED.
IF YOU REMAIN ON WAKANDAN SOIL FOR MORE THAN ONE HOUR, YOU WILL BE CONSIDERED AN INVADING FORCE AND WILL BE DEALT WITH ACCORDINGLY.

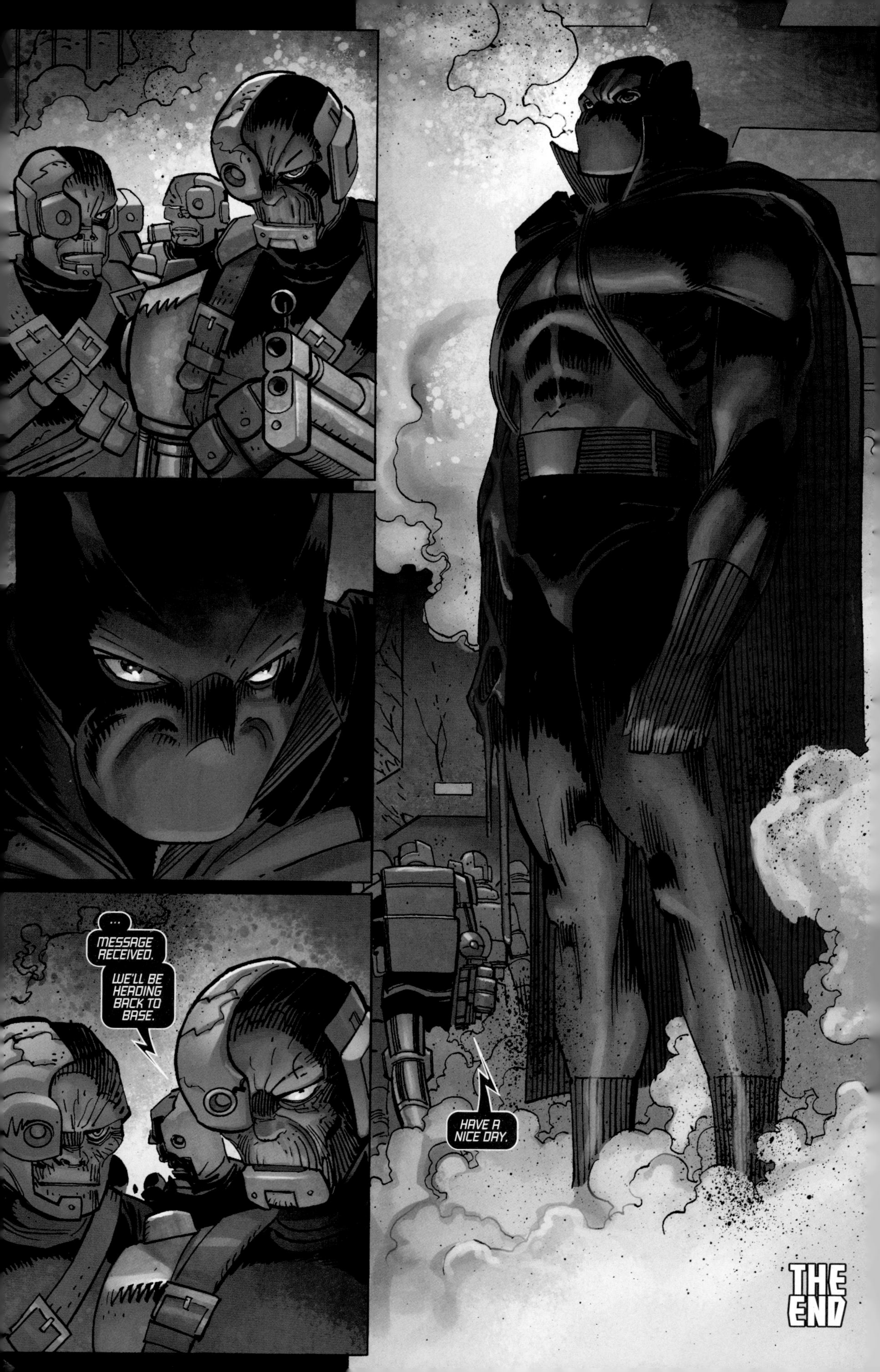
...
MESSAGE RECEIVED.
WE'LL BE HEADING BACK TO BASE.
HAVE A NICE DAY.
THE END

# BLACK PANTHER #1 • VARIANT COVER

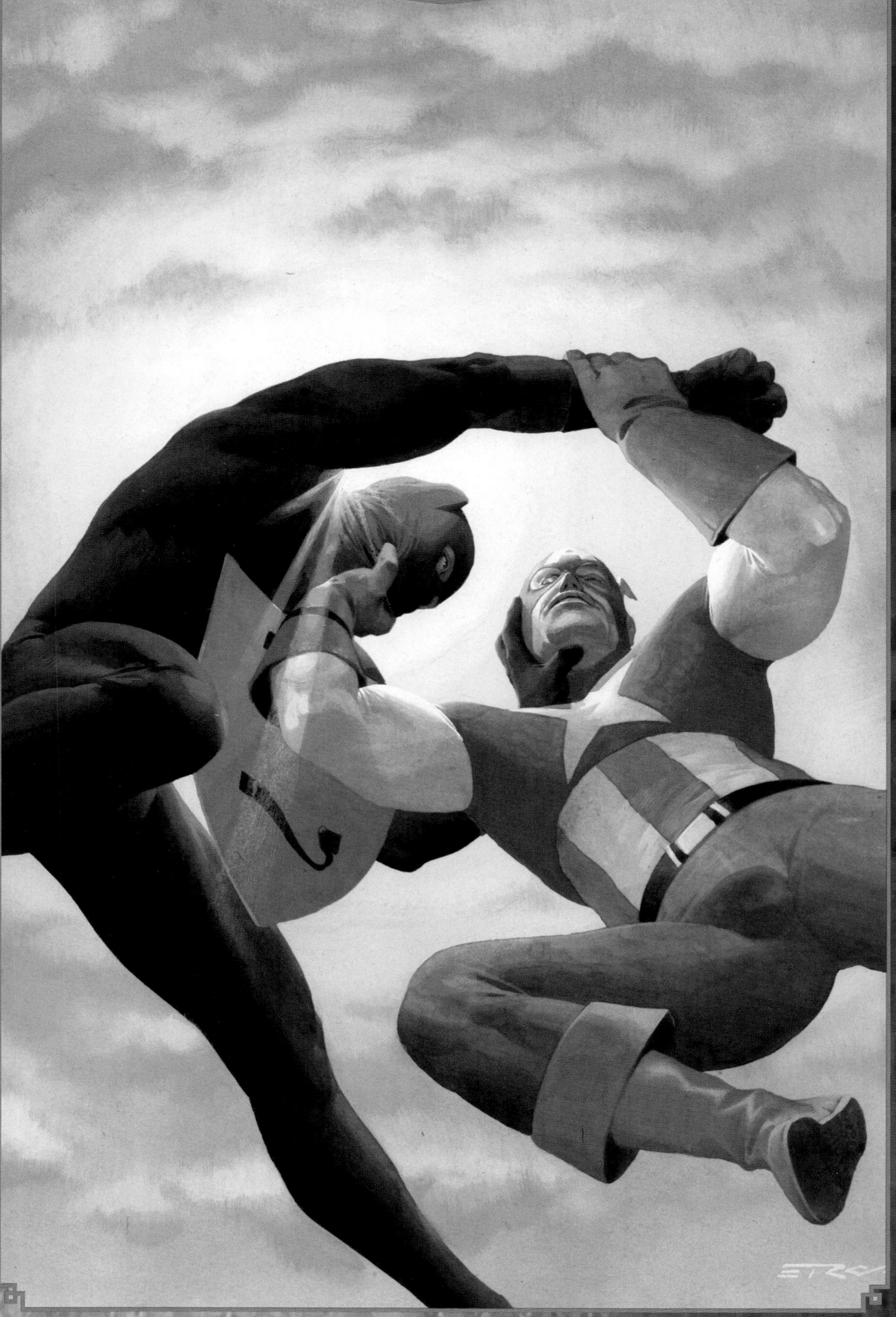

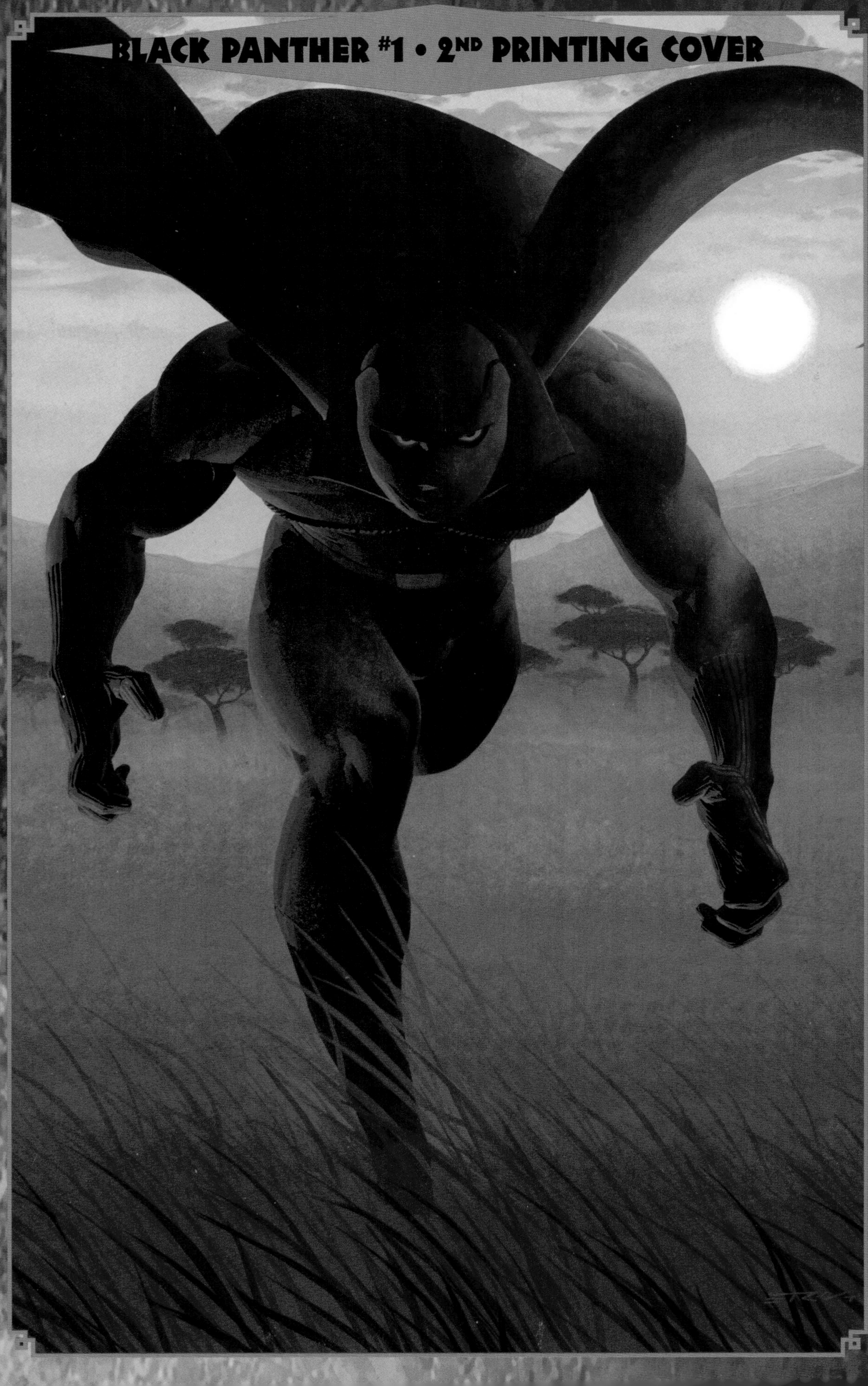
BLACK PANTHER #1 • 2ND PRINTING COVER

# THE BLACK PANTHER: A HISTORICAL OVERVIEW AND A LOOK TO THE FUTURE.
## BY REGINALD HUDLIN

When the Black Panther debuted in the '60s, he was so cool, so perfect a character in concept and execution it's hard to believe it was done by two white guys. But when the white guys in question were Stan Lee and Jack Kirby, then it makes sense. But to truly appreciate their achievement, it's worth putting it in context: No black super hero before or after the Black Panther is as cool as the Black Panther. Sure, others come close. Luke Cage is as brilliant a Marvel response to blaxploitation as Nick Fury, Agent of S.H.I.E.L.D. was to the James Bond/super spy trend. And the Milestone line of comics was wonderful and smart.

But the Black Panther is STILL The Man.

He's the king of his own country! He's rich! He's tough enough to defeat the Fantastic Four <u>and</u> Captain America! He's suave and sophisticated! He's got cool super-technology! And his name is...THE BLACK PANTHER. Just the name alone was so ahead of its time. (I wonder if the Black Panther Party in Oakland had gotten famous first, would Stan have used the name anyway? Well, he didn't change it, so double-kudos to him!)

The Panther's appearances in the Lee/Kirby issues of the FANTASTIC FOUR and CAPTAIN AMERICA were great, but nothing after that has been able to recapture the original magic. He never made much of an impression on me during any of his AVENGERS stints, and I never liked the McGregor-written series in JUNGLE ACTION. I even preferred the loopy but fun late Kirby series to McGregor's morose characters that endlessly droned on with overflowing captions with even more yakkety yakking. Enough already!

The Priest run on the PANTHER gave a much-needed shot in the arm to the character. His power level was restored to the point that the Panther had contingency plans to take on Galactus. Great! And he got two beautiful female bodyguards/concubines who can kick @$$. Great! He kicked it with fellow regents Namor and Doom. Great! He joined the Avengers to spy on them? The best idea yet!

The question is, how do we take the character to the next level?

Let's start by defining who he IS.

The Black Panther is the Black Captain America. He's the embodiment of the ideals of a people. As Americans, we feel good when we read Captain America because he reminds us of the potential of how good America can be, if, of course, we have the convictions to live by the principles the country was founded on. As a black person, the Black Panther should represent the fulfillment of the potential of the Motherland.

For a long time, the Black American equivalent of that ideal was represented by Sidney Poitier, a man who maintained his dignity even in degrading situations. But since the '80s, that ideal has shifted. In the post-integration, post-Reagan era, the new ideal is Spike Lee or Sean "Puffy" Combs, the artist/businessman hero who profits from his own cultural integrity. In other words, the man who has it all — the money, the politics and the cool and style of black culture.

What those celebrities named, along with Malcolm X, Miles Davis and Muhammad Ali, all have in common, is the knowledge that the act of being a black man in white America is an inherent act of rebellion. They are WILLING to be bad@$$es.

That's what hip hop is all about. Being a bad@$$. Everyone wants to be a bad@$$. That's why white kids have always loved black music — whether it's jazz, rock and roll or hip hop, black music is the music of bad@$$es, and plugging into that culture makes a suburban white kid feel like a bad@$$, too. And for a generation of white kids who have grown up without an "Elvis" — a white interpreter of black culture — their appreciation of edgy street culture is shocking even to me.

I say all this because the harder the Panther is, the more appealing he is to both black AND white audiences.

All we've got to do is let the Panther be who he is set up to be. After all, he's a Wakandan. Wakandans are so bad@$$ THEY'VE NEVER BEEN CONQUERED.

This is important. There are some countries that are like doormats — everybody's kicked their @$$ at one point or another. But there are other peoples in the world — Vietnam comes to mind — that kick the @$$ of everyone who messes with them, superpower or not.

The Wakandans are such people. I figure every 50 years or so, somebody tries to make a move on them, and they have to prove the point to that generation of would-be conquerors:

DON'T EVEN TRY IT!

The independence of the Wakandan people has got to be galling to the rest of the world for a lot of reasons. First of all, the rest of Africa has been carved up like a Christmas turkey. England, Germany, France, Belgium, the United States, the Soviet Union, Islamic and Christian invaders...so many empires have taken large chunks of land and resources for their own. Even after the independence movements of the '60s, any leader that was too competent got killed (like, say, Patrice Lumumba). So the colonial powers still controlled their territories through greedy thugs like Bokassa and Mubutu.

Not only does Wakanda's independence block the total dominance of Africa by colonial powers, its cultural evolution has gone unchecked for centuries. They were ahead of us a thousand years ago. And no one has colonized them, burned their books, erased their language, or broken their spirits.

Unfettered by the yoke of colonization, they have created a hi-tech, ecologically sound paradise that makes the rest of the world seem primitive by comparison. If the right company got their hands on their gadgets, their medicines, their R&D, they would vault themselves a century ahead of their competitors.

But the Wakandans can't be bought out. This isn't a bunch of starving orphans pimped by dictators who'll sell out for a sizable contribution to their Swiss bank account. Wakandans are led by the Black Panthers, a warrior cult that serves as the religious, political and military head of the country. That tower in the center of the country is like a big middle finger to the rest of the world — literally. Their borders are tightly shut and they deal with the world on their own terms...or not at all.

The first scene of the book would be in the 10th century. Start on some neighboring tribe walking across the savannah looking for its next conquest. They roll on Wakanda. But the Wakandans kick their @$$, using man-sized beartraps, crossbows and other technology that even Europeans didn't have at the time.

Cut to the turn of the century. The Boers have just finished conquering South Africa and are now moving on Wakanda. They've got rifles, they've got gatling guns. But the Wakandans have a magnetic based weapon that causes the Boer weapons to backfire, maiming and killing half their troops. The Panthers then move in, leaving one man alive, as they usually do, to spread the word — DON'T EVEN THINK ABOUT IT.

We see Captain America getting his butt whipped by T'Chaka during World War Two. Yeah, they will whip anybody's butt.

Okay, let me stop. I'm starting on scenes and I haven't even given an overview yet.

The first six issues of the book will be a re-telling of the Panther's origin. That hasn't been done during this incarnation of the Panther, and is the best way to set the tone for the book.

It will be a version without the Fantastic Four, much like the Lee/Kirby SILVER SURFER graphic novel from the '70s, which retold his origin without the FF's involvement in the story.

The first six issues will essentially be my version of what the BLACK PANTHER MOVIE should be. But no matter what happens with the movie, or if the movie ever happens, there will be a TPB that people can pick up and see the character done right. No matter how horrible the Joel Schumacher BATMAN movies are, they cannot erase the greatness of THE DARK KNIGHT RETURNS or BATMAN: YEAR ONE. Hopefully, this book will do the same for T'Challa.

I know some people at Marvel feel the Panther's base being in Africa is a problem. It shouldn't be. The Panther should move back and forth between Wakanda and the rest of the world the same way Thor moves between Asgard and Earth. He's an INTERNATIONAL player who's equally at home at the Davos Conference in Switzerland, meeting with Colin Powell in D.C., kicking it in Harlem with Bill Clinton and Al Sharpton, and brokering deals off the coast of Cuba with Fidel Castro and Prince Namor.

A great hero is defined by his villains. The Panther doesn't have his equivalents to Dr. Doom, the Red Skull, or Magneto. Instead he's got a guy wearing a white gorilla fur. I don't even know that loser's name, but he will never be seen inside the pages of the book I write.

Since the first story arc will be his origin, the main villain will be Klaw...but not the Murderous Master of Sound that he was in the 1960s. No way. Our villain is a South African who was named after his ancestor, who was one of the Boers who led the abortive attempt to invade Wakanda a century ago. In an act of revenge for the murder of his great-grandfather, and as part of a conspiracy to overthrow Wakanda, Klaw murdered T'Chaka. As he was about to kill the rest of the royal family, T'Challa, T'Chaka's son, blows Klaw's hand off, LITERALLY disarming him.

Now Klaw is equipped with a cybernetic hand that can turn into any number of murderous devices. He's invading Wakanda again, with a small commando squad of superpowered killers, to kill T'Challa and take over Wakanda.

But he's not the only person with the bright idea to invade Wakanda. Is the Panther ready to wage war at home — on multiple fronts?

And will he be betrayed from within?

Okay, that's not a whole pitch, but it's a start. I won't get into the second story arc with Cage, Shang-Chi, Photon and Storm...but that's gonna be even better.

— Reginald Hudlin

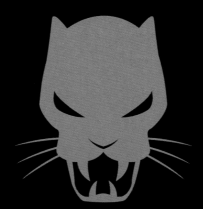

# BLACK PANTHER #1 COVER SKETCHES BY JOHN ROMITA JR.

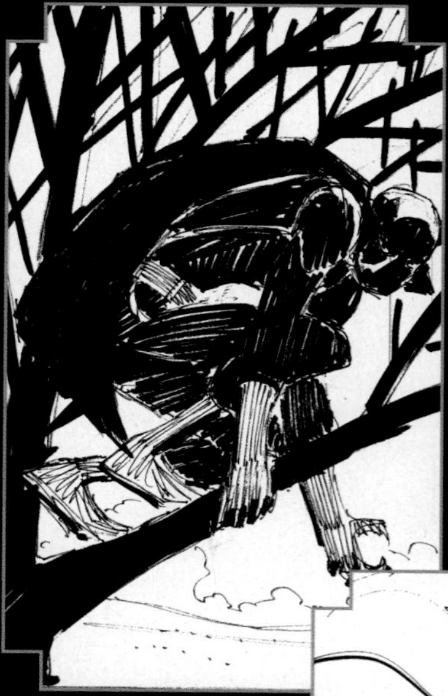

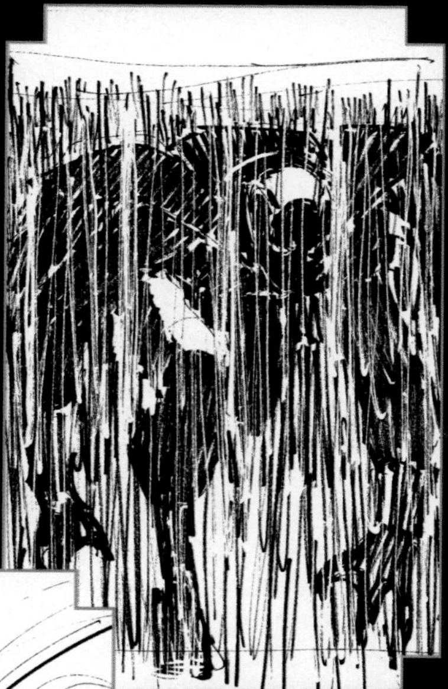

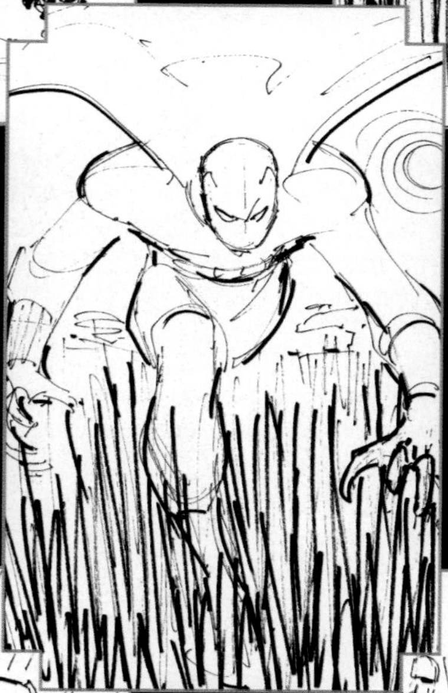

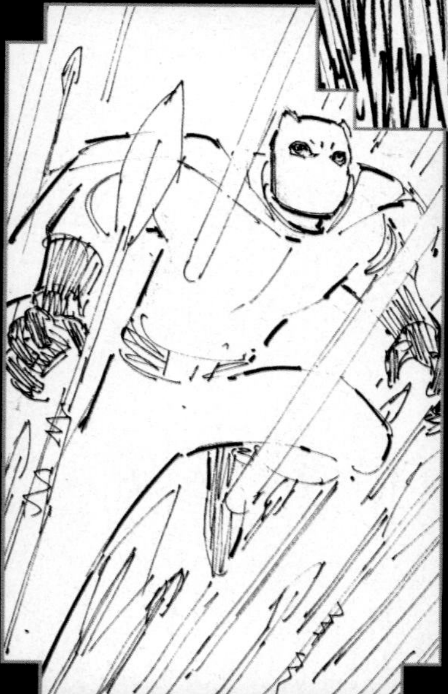

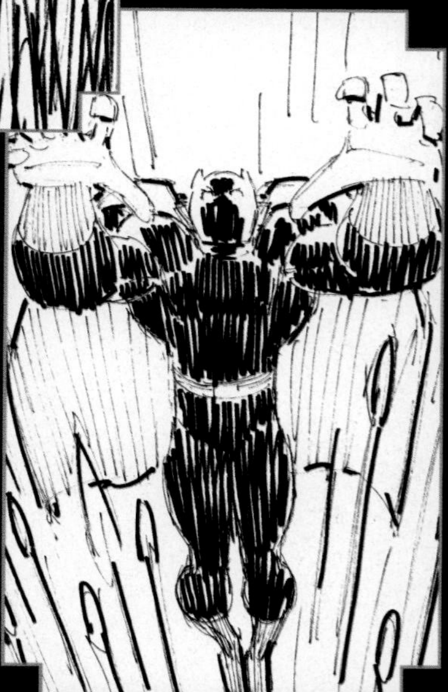

# BLACK PANTHER #1 COVER
## PENCILS BY JOHN ROMITA JR.
## INKS BY KLAUS JANSON

# BLACK PANTHER #2 COVER SKETCHES BY ESAD RIBIC

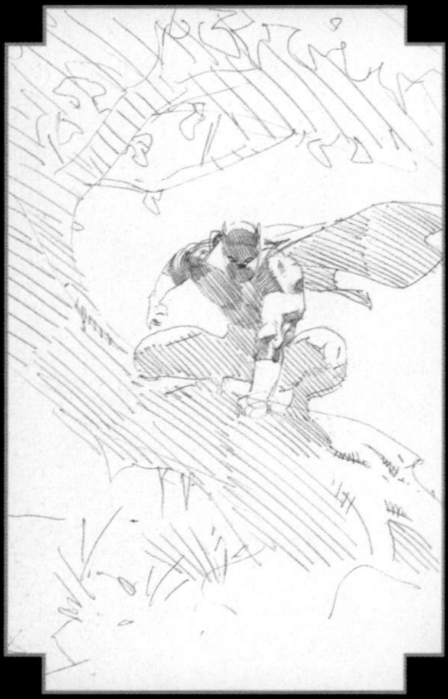
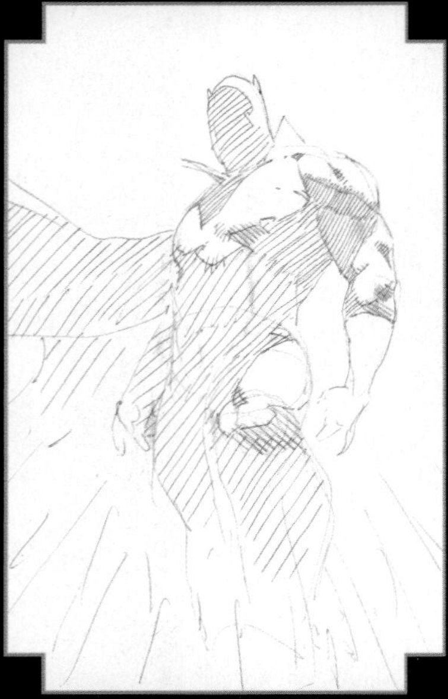
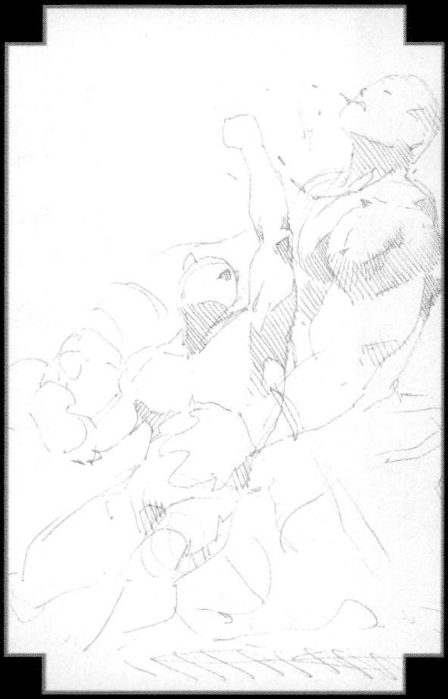

# BLACK PANTHER #6 COVER CONCEPTS BY KAARE ANDREWS

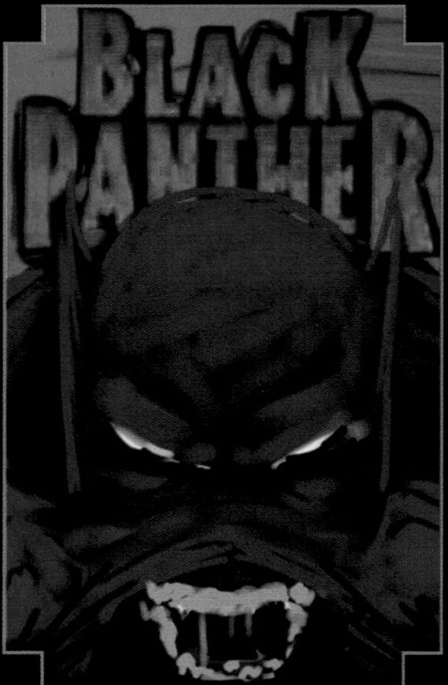
BLACK PANTHER
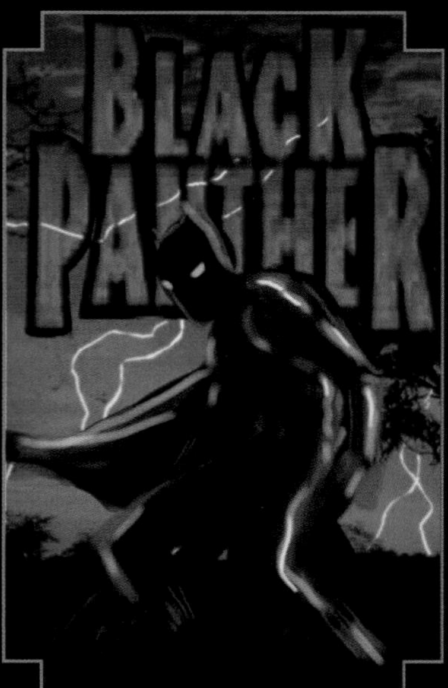
BLACK PANTHER
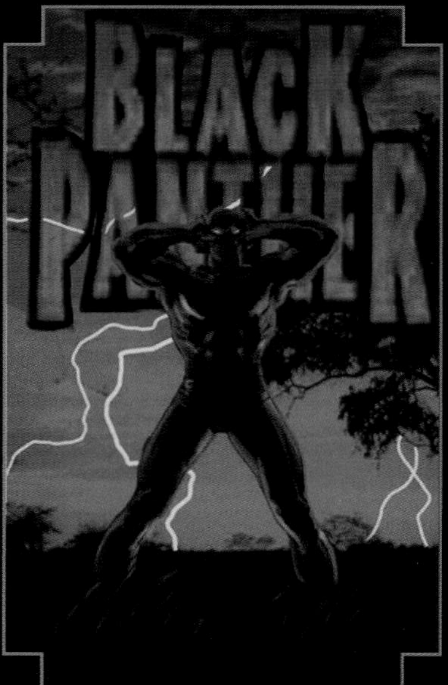
BLACK PANTHER

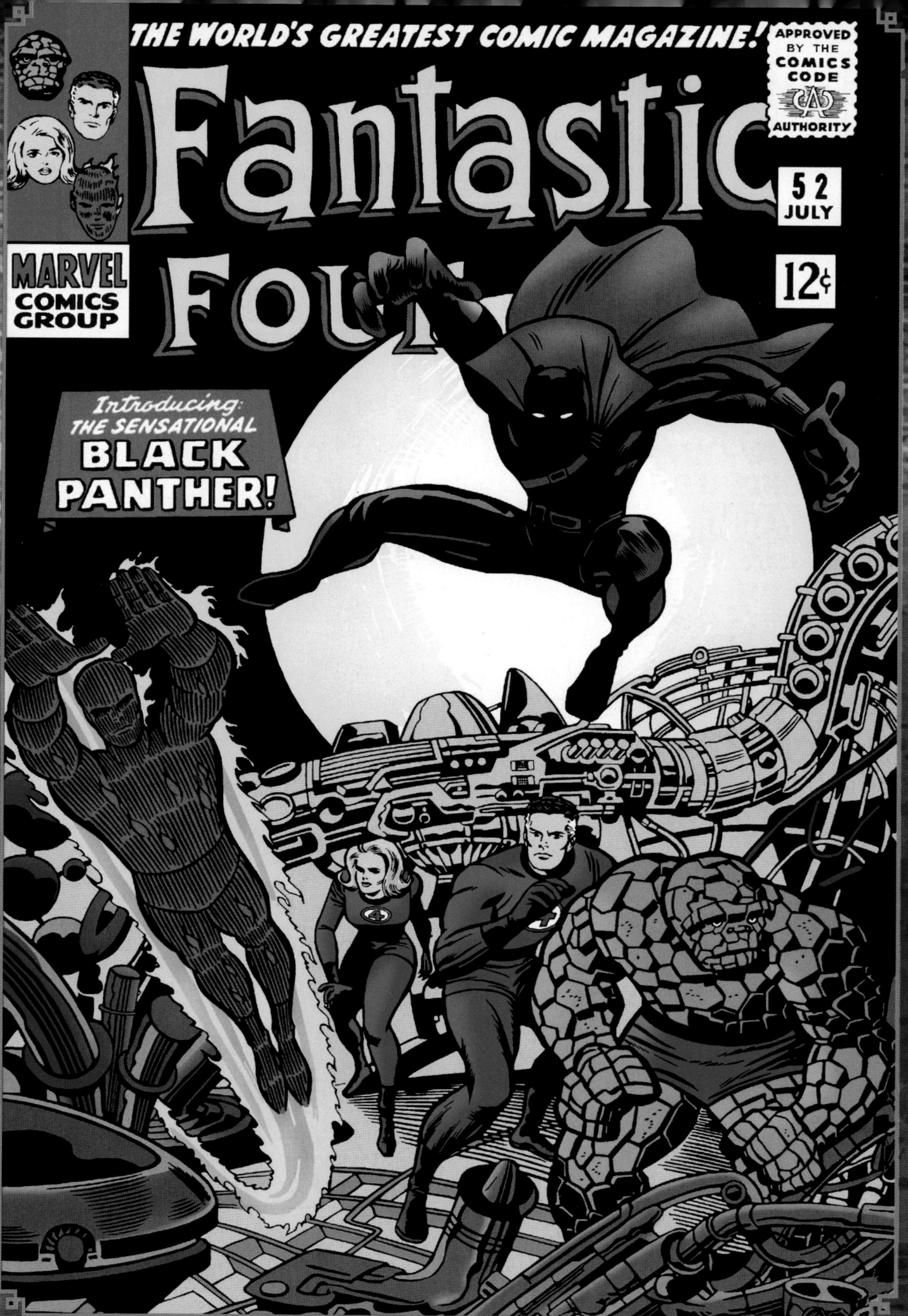
THE WORLD'S GREATEST COMIC MAGAZINE!
APPROVED BY THE COMICS CODE AUTHORITY
Fantastic Four
52
JULY
12¢
MARVEL COMICS GROUP
Introducing: THE SENSATIONAL BLACK PANTHER!

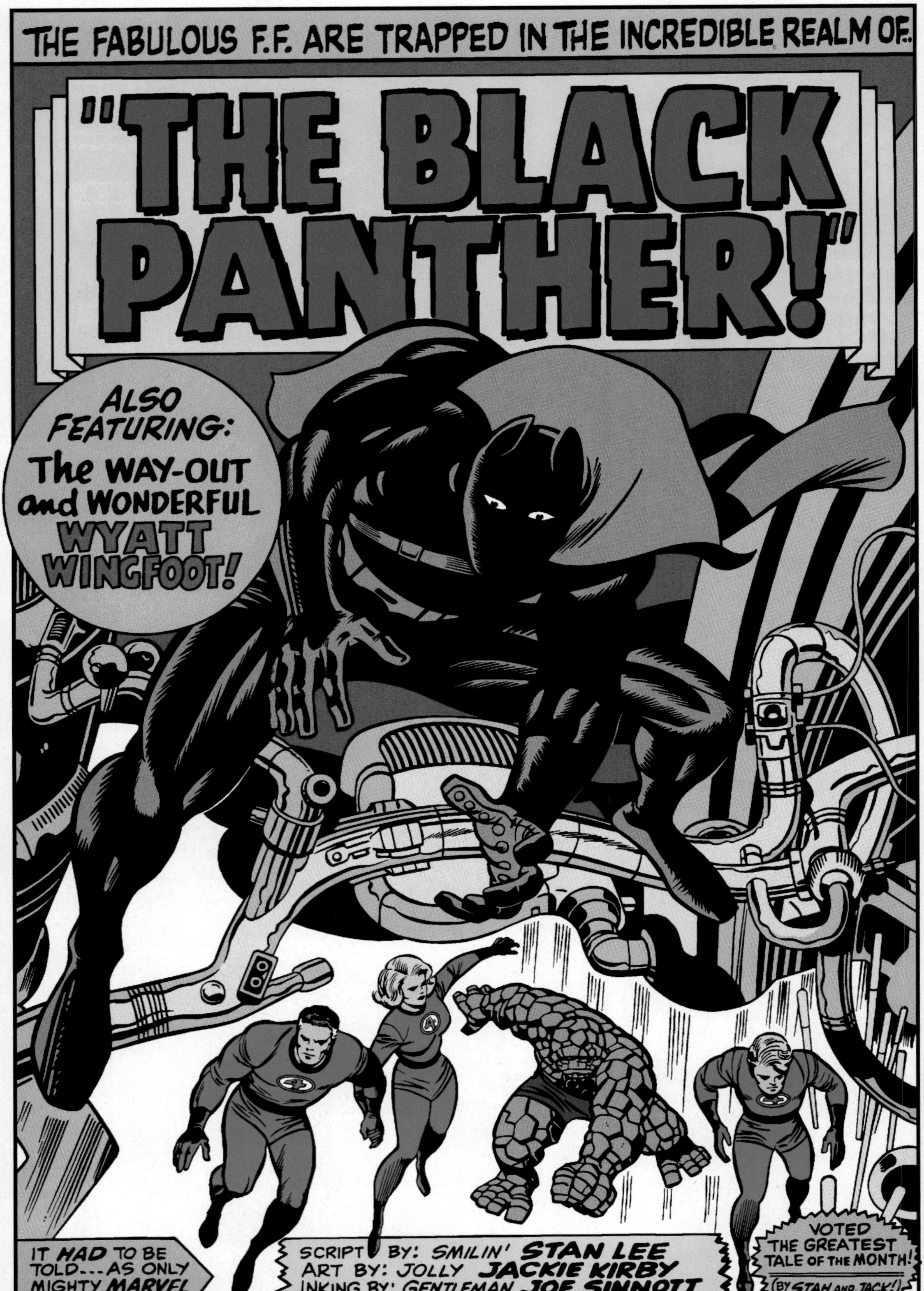
THE FABULOUS F.F. ARE TRAPPED IN THE INCREDIBLE REALM OF..
"THE BLACK PANTHER!"
ALSO FEATURING: The WAY-OUT and WONDERFUL WYATT WINGFOOT!
IT HAD TO BE TOLD...AS ONLY MIGHTY MARVEL COULD TELL IT!
SCRIPT BY: SMILIN' STAN LEE
ART BY: JOLLY JACKIE KIRBY
INKING BY: GENTLEMAN JOE SINNOTT
LETTERING BY: HAMMY SAMMY ROSEN
VOTED THE GREATEST TALE OF THE MONTH! (BY STAN AND JACK!)

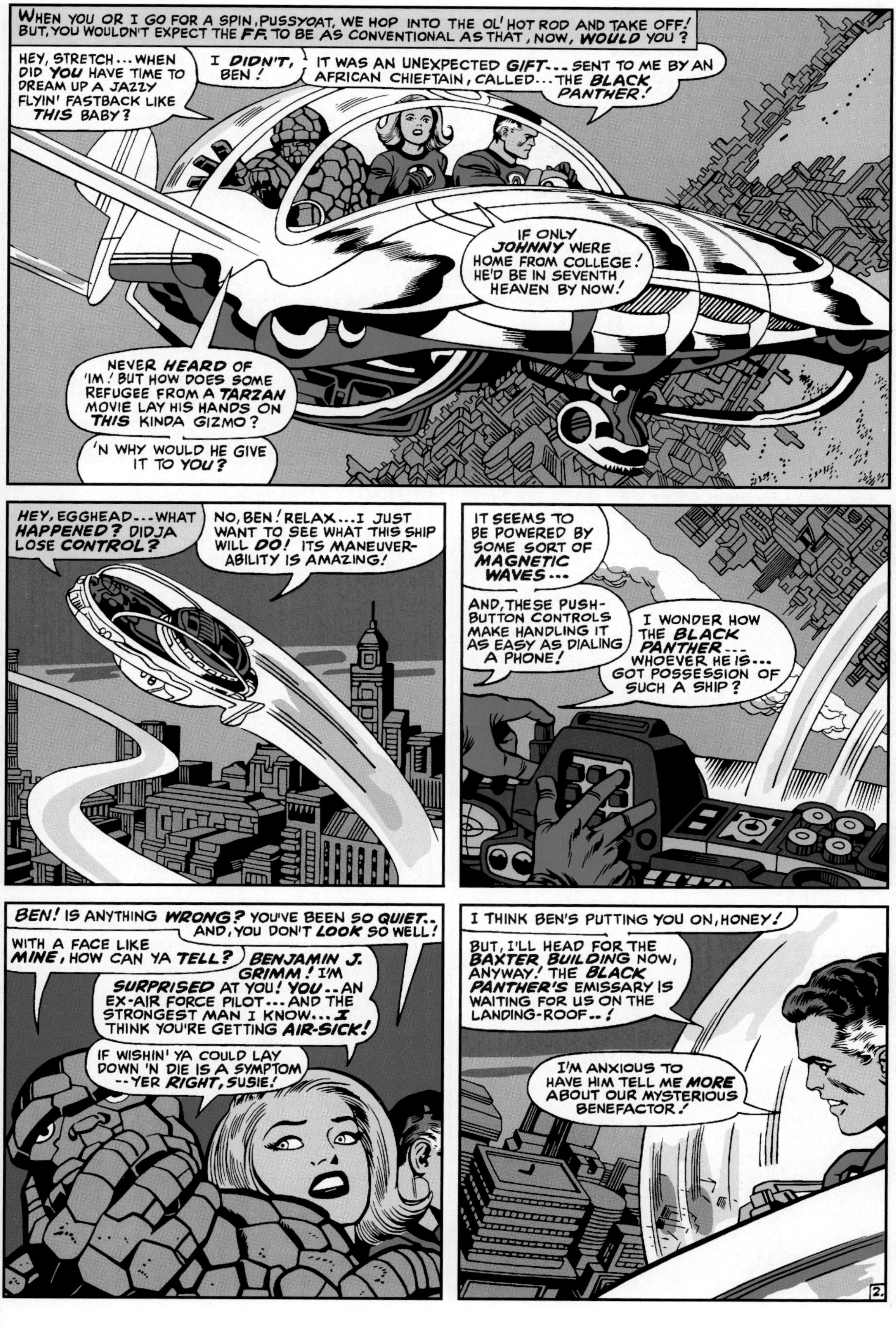

WHEN YOU OR I GO FOR A SPIN, PUSSYCAT, WE HOP INTO THE OL' HOT ROD AND TAKE OFF! BUT, YOU WOULDN'T EXPECT THE FF TO BE AS CONVENTIONAL AS THAT, NOW, WOULD YOU?
HEY, STRETCH... WHEN DID YOU HAVE TIME TO DREAM UP A JAZZY FLYIN' FASTBACK LIKE THIS BABY?
I DIDN'T, BEN!
IT WAS AN UNEXPECTED GIFT--- SENT TO ME BY AN AFRICAN CHIEFTAIN, CALLED... THE BLACK PANTHER!
IF ONLY JOHNNY WERE HOME FROM COLLEGE! HE'D BE IN SEVENTH HEAVEN BY NOW!
NEVER HEARD OF 'IM! BUT HOW DOES SOME REFUGEE FROM A TARZAN MOVIE LAY HIS HANDS ON THIS KINDA GIZMO?
'N WHY WOULD HE GIVE IT TO YOU?
HEY, EGGHEAD... WHAT HAPPENED? DIDJA LOSE CONTROL?
NO, BEN! RELAX... I JUST WANT TO SEE WHAT THIS SHIP WILL DO! ITS MANEUVERABILITY IS AMAZING!
IT SEEMS TO BE POWERED BY SOME SORT OF MAGNETIC WAVES...
AND, THESE PUSH-BUTTON CONTROLS MAKE HANDLING IT AS EASY AS DIALING A PHONE!
I WONDER HOW THE BLACK PANTHER... WHOEVER HE IS... GOT POSSESSION OF SUCH A SHIP?
BEN! IS ANYTHING WRONG? YOU'VE BEEN SO QUIET.. AND, YOU DON'T LOOK SO WELL!
WITH A FACE LIKE MINE, HOW CAN YA TELL?
BENJAMIN J. GRIMM! I'M SURPRISED AT YOU! YOU.. AN EX-AIR FORCE PILOT... AND THE STRONGEST MAN I KNOW... I THINK YOU'RE GETTING AIR-SICK!
IF WISHIN' YA COULD LAY DOWN 'N DIE IS A SYMPTOM --YER RIGHT, SUSIE!
I THINK BEN'S PUTTING YOU ON, HONEY!
BUT, I'LL HEAD FOR THE BAXTER BUILDING NOW, ANYWAY! THE BLACK PANTHER'S EMISSARY IS WAITING FOR US ON THE LANDING-ROOF..!
I'M ANXIOUS TO HAVE HIM TELL ME MORE ABOUT OUR MYSTERIOUS BENEFACTOR!

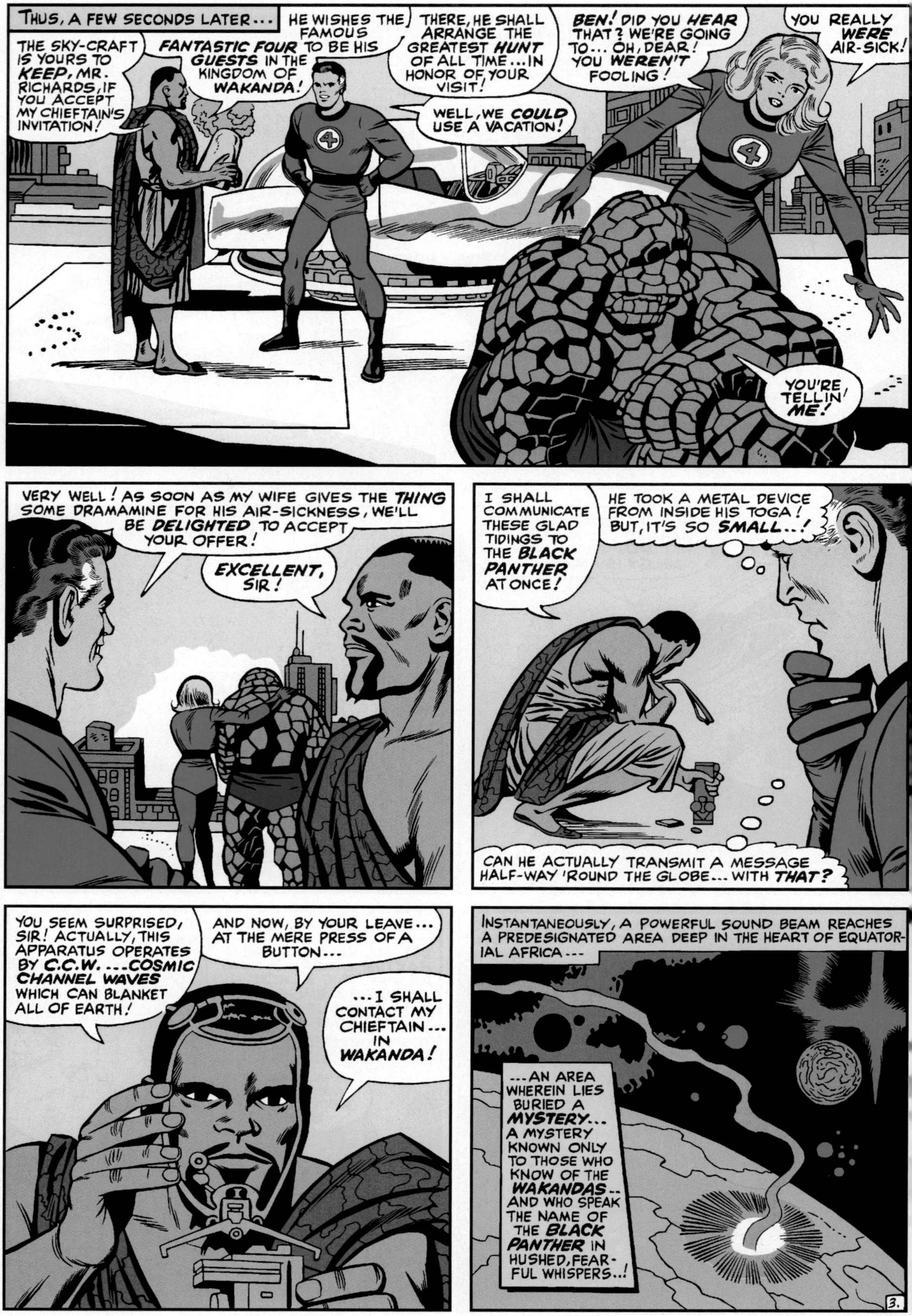
THUS, A FEW SECONDS LATER...
THE SKY-CRAFT IS YOURS TO KEEP, MR. RICHARDS, IF YOU ACCEPT MY CHIEFTAIN'S INVITATION!
HE WISHES THE FAMOUS FANTASTIC FOUR TO BE HIS GUESTS IN THE KINGDOM OF WAKANDA!
THERE, HE SHALL ARRANGE THE GREATEST HUNT OF ALL TIME...IN HONOR OF YOUR VISIT!
WELL, WE COULD USE A VACATION!
BEN! DID YOU HEAR THAT? WE'RE GOING TO... OH, DEAR! YOU WEREN'T FOOLING!
YOU REALLY WERE AIR-SICK!
YOU'RE TELLIN' ME!
VERY WELL! AS SOON AS MY WIFE GIVES THE THING SOME DRAMAMINE FOR HIS AIR-SICKNESS, WE'LL BE DELIGHTED TO ACCEPT YOUR OFFER!
EXCELLENT, SIR!
I SHALL COMMUNICATE THESE GLAD TIDINGS TO THE BLACK PANTHER AT ONCE!
HE TOOK A METAL DEVICE FROM INSIDE HIS TOGA! BUT, IT'S SO SMALL..!
CAN HE ACTUALLY TRANSMIT A MESSAGE HALF-WAY 'ROUND THE GLOBE... WITH THAT?
YOU SEEM SURPRISED, SIR! ACTUALLY, THIS APPARATUS OPERATES BY C.C.W. ...COSMIC CHANNEL WAVES WHICH CAN BLANKET ALL OF EARTH!
AND NOW, BY YOUR LEAVE... AT THE MERE PRESS OF A BUTTON...
...I SHALL CONTACT MY CHIEFTAIN... IN WAKANDA!
INSTANTANEOUSLY, A POWERFUL SOUND BEAM REACHES A PREDESIGNATED AREA DEEP IN THE HEART OF EQUATORIAL AFRICA---
---AN AREA WHEREIN LIES BURIED A MYSTERY... A MYSTERY KNOWN ONLY TO THOSE WHO KNOW OF THE WAKANDAS.. AND WHO SPEAK THE NAME OF THE BLACK PANTHER IN HUSHED, FEARFUL WHISPERS..!
3.

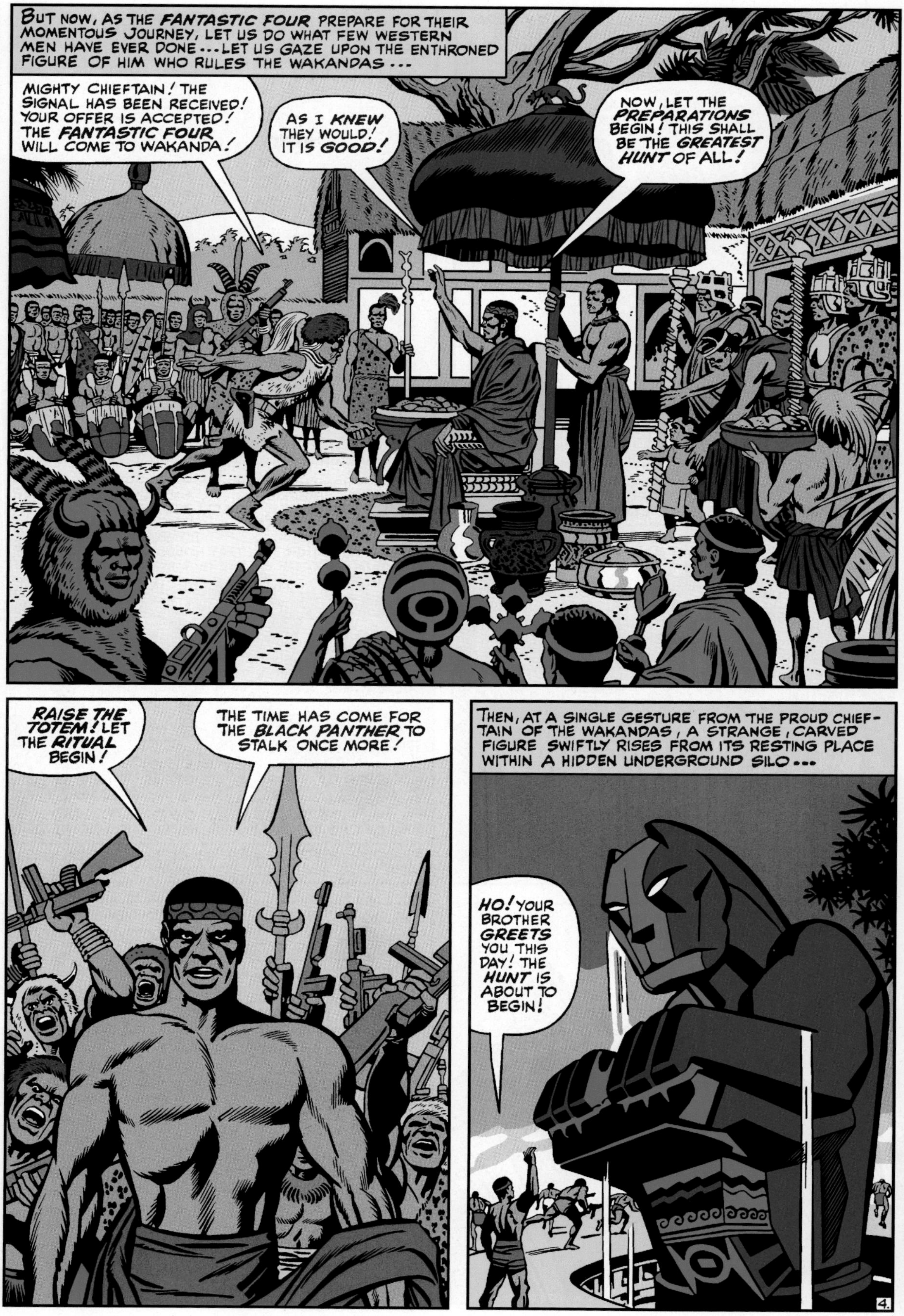

BUT NOW, AS THE *FANTASTIC FOUR* PREPARE FOR THEIR MOMENTOUS JOURNEY, LET US DO WHAT FEW WESTERN MEN HAVE EVER DONE... LET US GAZE UPON THE ENTHRONED FIGURE OF HIM WHO RULES THE WAKANDAS...
MIGHTY CHIEFTAIN! THE SIGNAL HAS BEEN RECEIVED! YOUR OFFER IS ACCEPTED! THE *FANTASTIC FOUR* WILL COME TO WAKANDA!
AS I *KNEW* THEY WOULD! IT IS *GOOD!*
NOW, LET THE *PREPARATIONS* BEGIN! THIS SHALL BE THE *GREATEST HUNT* OF ALL!
*RAISE THE TOTEM!* LET THE *RITUAL* BEGIN!
THE TIME HAS COME FOR THE *BLACK PANTHER* TO STALK ONCE MORE!
THEN, AT A SINGLE GESTURE FROM THE PROUD CHIEFTAIN OF THE WAKANDAS, A STRANGE, CARVED FIGURE SWIFTLY RISES FROM ITS RESTING PLACE WITHIN A HIDDEN UNDERGROUND SILO...
*HO!* YOUR BROTHER *GREETS* YOU THIS DAY! THE *HUNT* IS ABOUT TO BEGIN!
4.

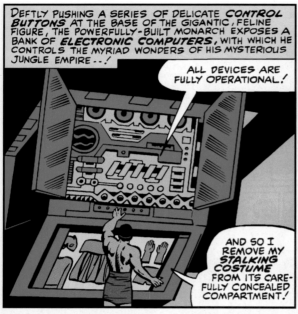

DEFTLY PUSHING A SERIES OF DELICATE *CONTROL BUTTONS* AT THE BASE OF THE GIGANTIC, FELINE FIGURE, THE POWERFULLY-BUILT MONARCH EXPOSES A BANK OF *ELECTRONIC COMPUTERS*, WITH WHICH HE CONTROLS THE MYRIAD WONDERS OF HIS MYSTERIOUS JUNGLE EMPIRE--!

ALL DEVICES ARE FULLY OPERATIONAL!

AND SO I REMOVE MY *STALKING COSTUME* FROM ITS CAREFULLY CONCEALED COMPARTMENT!

NOW, LET THE FANTASTIC FOUR *COME!*

THE *BLACK PANTHER* SHALL GREET THEM... AS THEY HAVE NEVER BEEN GREETED BEFORE!

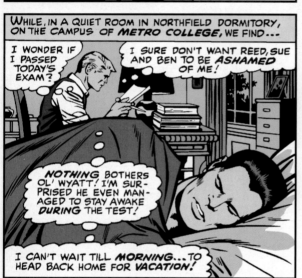

WHILE, IN A QUIET ROOM IN NORTHFIELD DORMITORY, ON THE CAMPUS OF *METRO COLLEGE*, WE FIND...

I WONDER IF I PASSED TODAY'S EXAM?

I SURE DON'T WANT REED, SUE AND BEN TO BE *ASHAMED* OF ME!

*NOTHING* BOTHERS OL' WYATT! I'M SURPRISED HE EVEN MANAGED TO STAY AWAKE *DURING* THE TEST!

I CAN'T WAIT TILL *MORNING*...TO HEAD BACK HOME FOR *VACATION!*

IT'S HARD...HARDER THAN I *THOUGHT* IT WOULD BE...TO CONCENTRATE ON MY COURSES... WHEN I CAN'T GET *CRYSTAL* OUT OF MY MIND!

BUT, I'VE GOT TO KEEP *TRYING!* UNTIL REED CAN FIND SOME WAY TO BREAK THE *BARRIER* THAT HOLDS HER PRISONER,* THERE'S NOTHING I CAN DO!

NOTHING BUT HOPE...AND DREAM...AND PRAY!

I'VE GOT TO SNAP *OUT* OF IT...AND I *WILL!* IF ONLY THE *EVENINGS* WEREN'T SO LONG...!

* IF YOU MISSED F.F. #48, DON'T TELL US! YOU KNOW HOW UPSET WE GET! ... SHAKY STAN.

HEY!! HOLY HANNAH!! WHAT THE...?!!

SURPRISE!

HIYA, JOE COLLEGE. WHAT'S THE GOOD WORD, LITTLE ITTY BITTY BUDDY?

I'LL ITTY BITTY BUDDY *YOU*, YOU BLUE-EYED BIRDBRAIN!!

I *KNOWED* YA'D BE AS GOOD-NATURED AS EVER, JUNIOR!

*LEGGO*, BEFORE I GIVE YOU A HOT-FOOT BETWEEN WHERE YOUR *EARS* OUGHTTA BE!

5

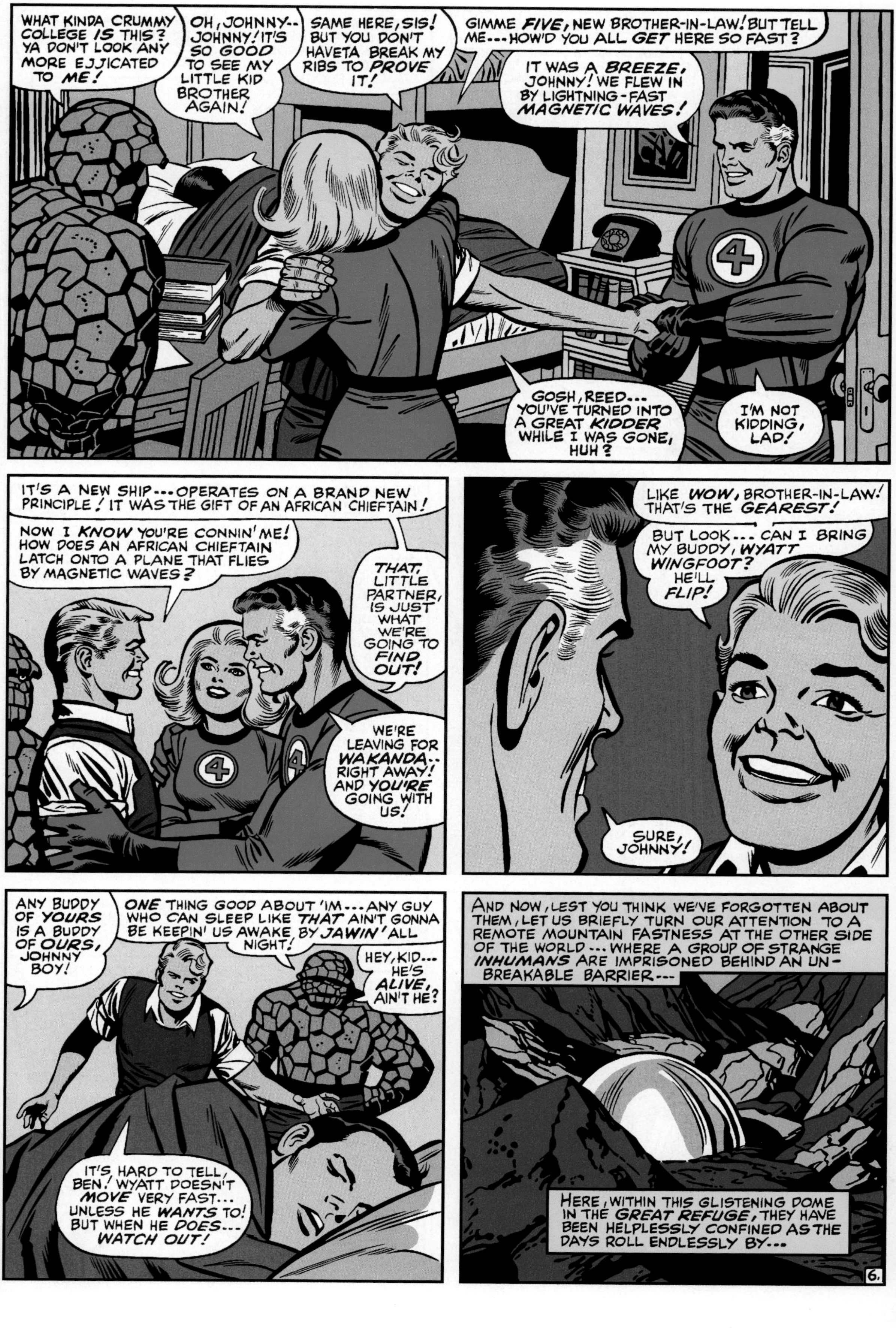
WHAT KINDA CRUMMY COLLEGE IS THIS? YA DON'T LOOK ANY MORE EJJICATED TO ME!
OH, JOHNNY-- JOHNNY! IT'S SO GOOD TO SEE MY LITTLE KID BROTHER AGAIN!
SAME HERE, SIS! BUT YOU DON'T HAVETA BREAK MY RIBS TO PROVE IT!
GIMME FIVE, NEW BROTHER-IN-LAW! BUT TELL ME--- HOW'D YOU ALL GET HERE SO FAST?
IT WAS A BREEZE, JOHNNY! WE FLEW IN BY LIGHTNING-FAST MAGNETIC WAVES!
GOSH, REED--- YOU'VE TURNED INTO A GREAT KIDDER WHILE I WAS GONE, HUH?
I'M NOT KIDDING, LAD!
IT'S A NEW SHIP---OPERATES ON A BRAND NEW PRINCIPLE! IT WAS THE GIFT OF AN AFRICAN CHIEFTAIN!
NOW I KNOW YOU'RE CONNIN' ME! HOW DOES AN AFRICAN CHIEFTAIN LATCH ONTO A PLANE THAT FLIES BY MAGNETIC WAVES?
THAT, LITTLE PARTNER, IS JUST WHAT WE'RE GOING TO FIND OUT!
WE'RE LEAVING FOR WAKANDA-- RIGHT AWAY! AND YOU'RE GOING WITH US!
LIKE WOW, BROTHER-IN-LAW! THAT'S THE GEAREST!
BUT LOOK--- CAN I BRING MY BUDDY, WYATT WINGFOOT? HE'LL FLIP!
SURE, JOHNNY!
ANY BUDDY OF YOURS IS A BUDDY OF OURS, JOHNNY BOY!
ONE THING GOOD ABOUT 'IM--- ANY GUY WHO CAN SLEEP LIKE THAT AIN'T GONNA BE KEEPIN' US AWAKE BY JAWIN' ALL NIGHT!
HEY, KID--- HE'S ALIVE, AIN'T HE?
IT'S HARD TO TELL, BEN! WYATT DOESN'T MOVE VERY FAST--- UNLESS HE WANTS TO! BUT WHEN HE DOES--- WATCH OUT!
AND NOW, LEST YOU THINK WE'VE FORGOTTEN ABOUT THEM, LET US BRIEFLY TURN OUR ATTENTION TO A REMOTE MOUNTAIN FASTNESS AT THE OTHER SIDE OF THE WORLD--- WHERE A GROUP OF STRANGE INHUMANS ARE IMPRISONED BEHIND AN UN-BREAKABLE BARRIER---
HERE, WITHIN THIS GLISTENING DOME IN THE GREAT REFUGE, THEY HAVE BEEN HELPLESSLY CONFINED AS THE DAYS ROLL ENDLESSLY BY---
6.

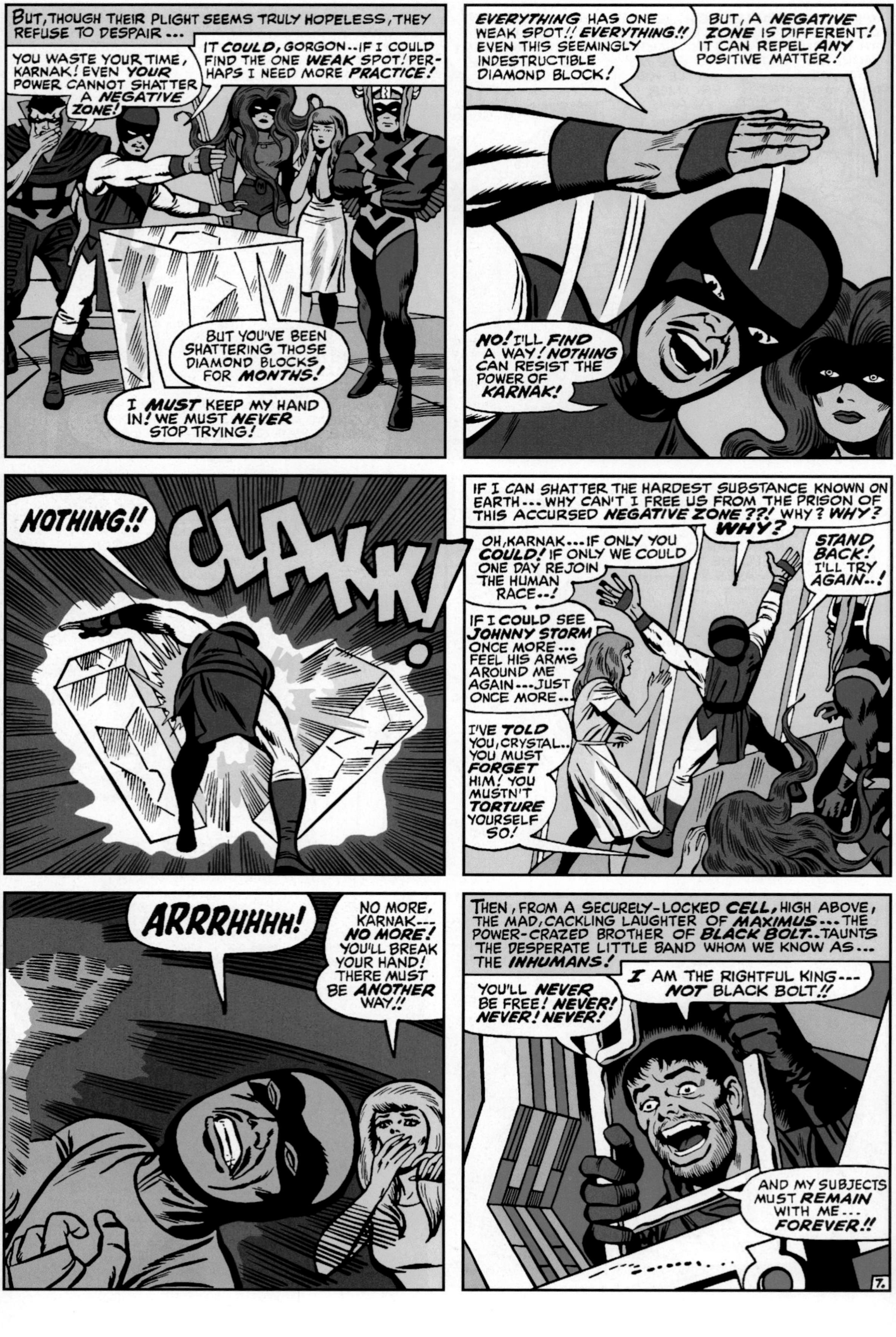

BUT, THOUGH THEIR PLIGHT SEEMS TRULY HOPELESS, THEY REFUSE TO DESPAIR...
YOU WASTE YOUR TIME, KARNAK! EVEN YOUR POWER CANNOT SHATTER A NEGATIVE ZONE!
IT COULD, GORGON..IF I COULD FIND THE ONE WEAK SPOT! PERHAPS I NEED MORE PRACTICE!
BUT YOU'VE BEEN SHATTERING THOSE DIAMOND BLOCKS FOR MONTHS!
I MUST KEEP MY HAND IN! WE MUST NEVER STOP TRYING!
EVERYTHING HAS ONE WEAK SPOT!! EVERYTHING!! EVEN THIS SEEMINGLY INDESTRUCTIBLE DIAMOND BLOCK!
BUT, A NEGATIVE ZONE IS DIFFERENT! IT CAN REPEL ANY POSITIVE MATTER!
NO! I'LL FIND A WAY! NOTHING CAN RESIST THE POWER OF KARNAK!
NOTHING!!
CLAKK!
IF I CAN SHATTER THE HARDEST SUBSTANCE KNOWN ON EARTH... WHY CAN'T I FREE US FROM THE PRISON OF THIS ACCURSED NEGATIVE ZONE??! WHY? WHY? WHY?
OH, KARNAK... IF ONLY YOU COULD! IF ONLY WE COULD ONE DAY REJOIN THE HUMAN RACE..!
STAND BACK! I'LL TRY AGAIN..!
IF I COULD SEE JOHNNY STORM ONCE MORE... FEEL HIS ARMS AROUND ME AGAIN...JUST ONCE MORE...
I'VE TOLD YOU, CRYSTAL.. YOU MUST FORGET HIM! YOU MUSTN'T TORTURE YOURSELF SO!
ARRRHHHH!
NO MORE, KARNAK--- NO MORE! YOU'LL BREAK YOUR HAND! THERE MUST BE ANOTHER WAY!!
THEN, FROM A SECURELY-LOCKED CELL, HIGH ABOVE, THE MAD, CACKLING LAUGHTER OF MAXIMUS... THE POWER-CRAZED BROTHER OF BLACK BOLT.. TAUNTS THE DESPERATE LITTLE BAND WHOM WE KNOW AS... THE INHUMANS!
YOU'LL NEVER BE FREE! NEVER! NEVER! NEVER!
I AM THE RIGHTFUL KING--- NOT BLACK BOLT!!
AND MY SUBJECTS MUST REMAIN WITH ME--- FOREVER!!

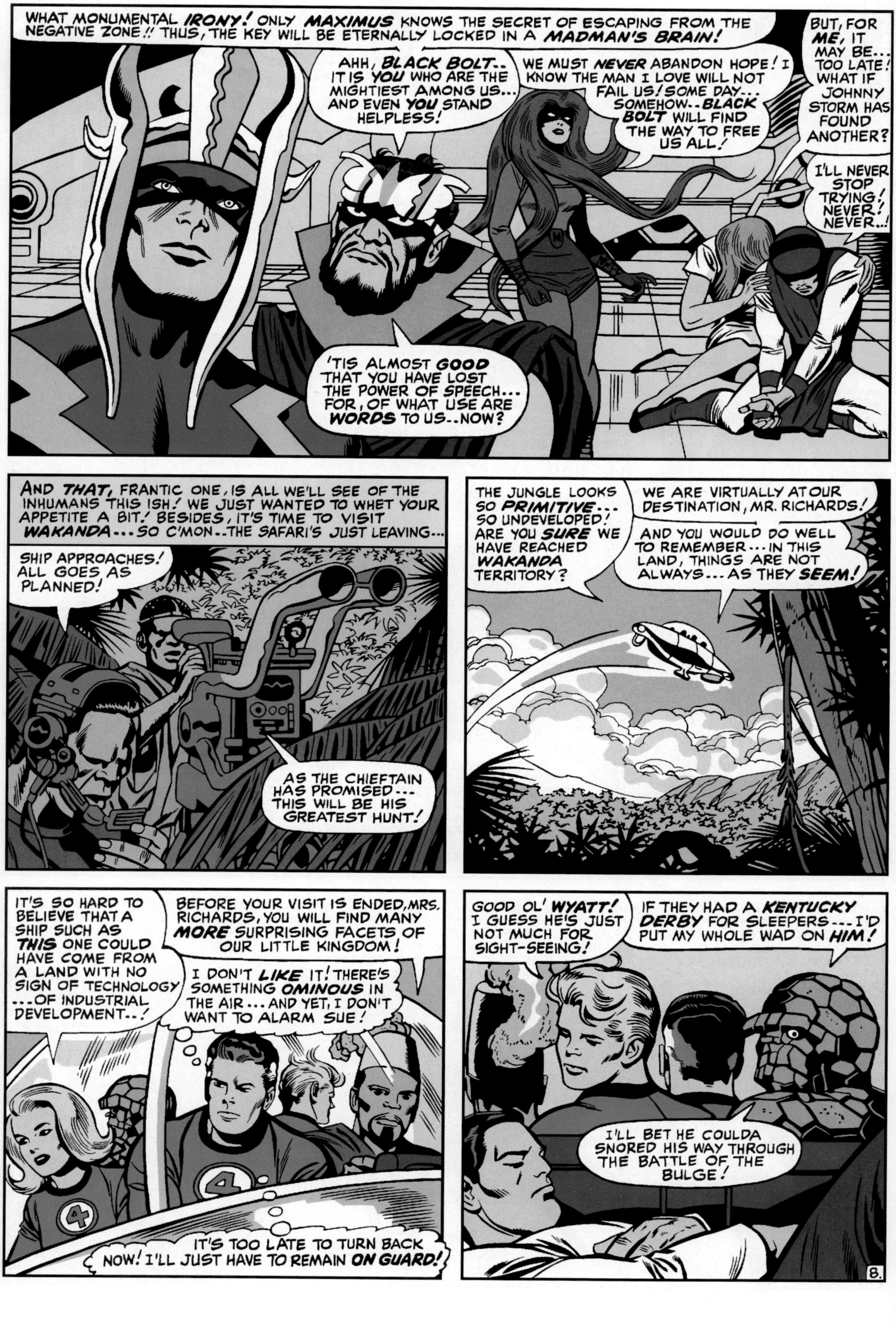

WHAT MONUMENTAL IRONY! ONLY MAXIMUS KNOWS THE SECRET OF ESCAPING FROM THE NEGATIVE ZONE!! THUS, THE KEY WILL BE ETERNALLY LOCKED IN A MADMAN'S BRAIN!
AHH, BLACK BOLT.. IT IS YOU WHO ARE THE MIGHTIEST AMONG US... AND EVEN YOU STAND HELPLESS!
'TIS ALMOST GOOD THAT YOU HAVE LOST THE POWER OF SPEECH... FOR, OF WHAT USE ARE WORDS TO US..NOW?
WE MUST NEVER ABANDON HOPE! I KNOW THE MAN I LOVE WILL NOT FAIL US! SOME DAY... SOMEHOW..BLACK BOLT WILL FIND THE WAY TO FREE US ALL!
BUT, FOR ME, IT MAY BE... TOO LATE! WHAT IF JOHNNY STORM HAS FOUND ANOTHER?
I'LL NEVER STOP TRYING! NEVER! NEVER..!
AND THAT, FRANTIC ONE, IS ALL WE'LL SEE OF THE INHUMANS THIS ISH! WE JUST WANTED TO WHET YOUR APPETITE A BIT! BESIDES, IT'S TIME TO VISIT WAKANDA... SO C'MON..THE SAFARI'S JUST LEAVING...
SHIP APPROACHES! ALL GOES AS PLANNED!
AS THE CHIEFTAIN HAS PROMISED... THIS WILL BE HIS GREATEST HUNT!
THE JUNGLE LOOKS SO PRIMITIVE... SO UNDEVELOPED! ARE YOU SURE WE HAVE REACHED WAKANDA TERRITORY?
WE ARE VIRTUALLY AT OUR DESTINATION, MR. RICHARDS!
AND YOU WOULD DO WELL TO REMEMBER... IN THIS LAND, THINGS ARE NOT ALWAYS... AS THEY SEEM!
IT'S SO HARD TO BELIEVE THAT A SHIP SUCH AS THIS ONE COULD HAVE COME FROM A LAND WITH NO SIGN OF TECHNOLOGY ...OF INDUSTRIAL DEVELOPMENT..!
BEFORE YOUR VISIT IS ENDED, MRS. RICHARDS, YOU WILL FIND MANY MORE SURPRISING FACETS OF OUR LITTLE KINGDOM!
I DON'T LIKE IT! THERE'S SOMETHING OMINOUS IN THE AIR... AND YET, I DON'T WANT TO ALARM SUE!
IT'S TOO LATE TO TURN BACK NOW! I'LL JUST HAVE TO REMAIN ON GUARD!
GOOD OL' WYATT! I GUESS HE'S JUST NOT MUCH FOR SIGHT-SEEING!
IF THEY HAD A KENTUCKY DERBY FOR SLEEPERS --- I'D PUT MY WHOLE WAD ON HIM!
I'LL BET HE COULDA SNORED HIS WAY THROUGH THE BATTLE OF THE BULGE!
8.

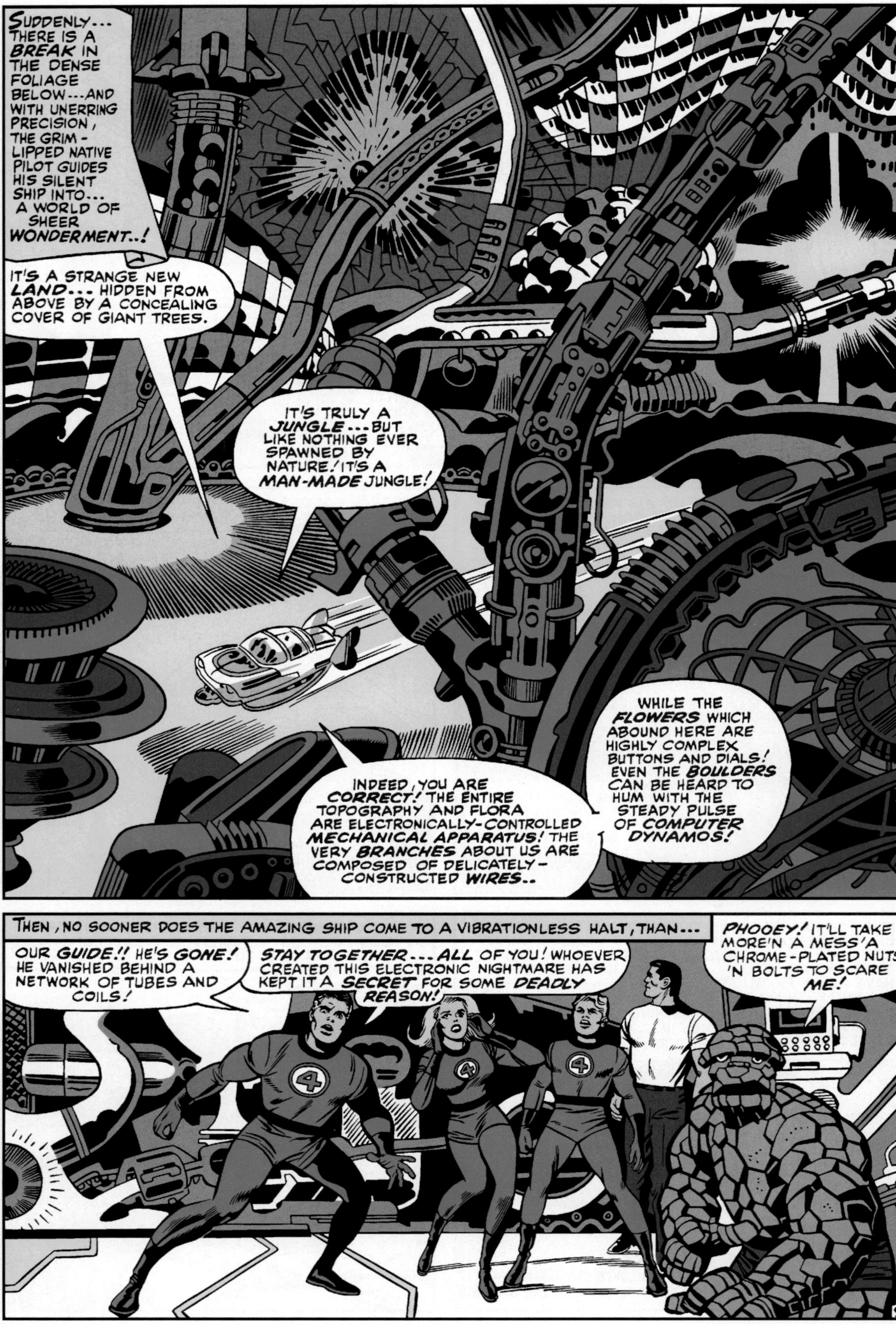
SUDDENLY... THERE IS A BREAK IN THE DENSE FOLIAGE BELOW---AND WITH UNERRING PRECISION, THE GRIM-LIPPED NATIVE PILOT GUIDES HIS SILENT SHIP INTO... A WORLD OF SHEER WONDERMENT..!
IT'S A STRANGE NEW LAND... HIDDEN FROM ABOVE BY A CONCEALING COVER OF GIANT TREES.
IT'S TRULY A JUNGLE---BUT LIKE NOTHING EVER SPAWNED BY NATURE! IT'S A MAN-MADE JUNGLE!
INDEED, YOU ARE CORRECT! THE ENTIRE TOPOGRAPHY AND FLORA ARE ELECTRONICALLY-CONTROLLED MECHANICAL APPARATUS! THE VERY BRANCHES ABOUT US ARE COMPOSED OF DELICATELY-CONSTRUCTED WIRES..
WHILE THE FLOWERS WHICH ABOUND HERE ARE HIGHLY COMPLEX BUTTONS AND DIALS! EVEN THE BOULDERS CAN BE HEARD TO HUM WITH THE STEADY PULSE OF COMPUTER DYNAMOS!
THEN, NO SOONER DOES THE AMAZING SHIP COME TO A VIBRATIONLESS HALT, THAN...
OUR GUIDE!! HE'S GONE! HE VANISHED BEHIND A NETWORK OF TUBES AND COILS!
STAY TOGETHER...ALL OF YOU! WHOEVER CREATED THIS ELECTRONIC NIGHTMARE HAS KEPT IT A SECRET FOR SOME DEADLY REASON!
PHOOEY! IT'LL TAKE MORE'N A MESS'A CHROME-PLATED NUTS 'N BOLTS TO SCARE ME!
9.

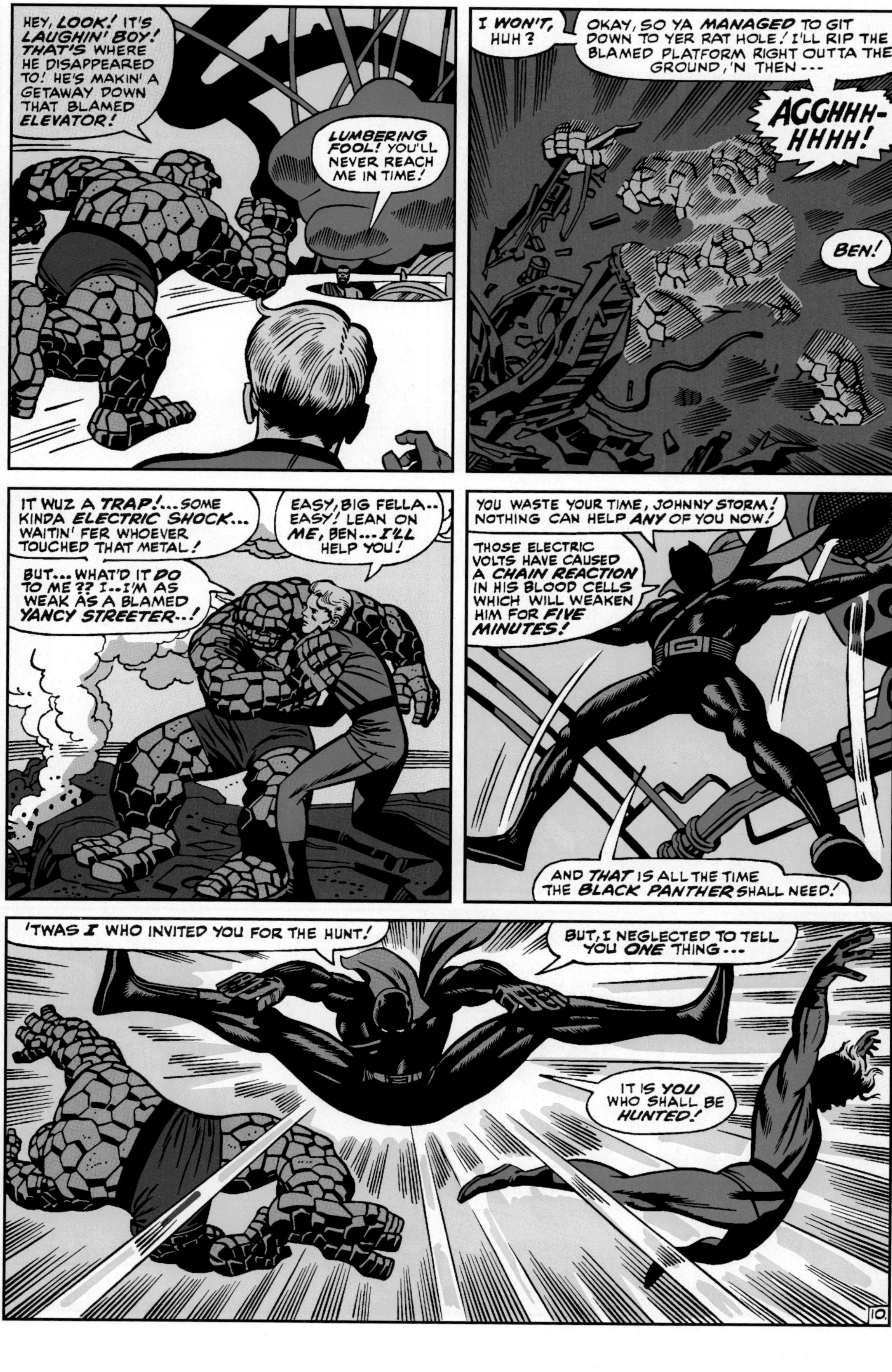
HEY, LOOK! IT'S LAUGHIN' BOY! THAT'S WHERE HE DISAPPEARED TO! HE'S MAKIN' A GETAWAY DOWN THAT BLAMED ELEVATOR!
LUMBERING FOOL! YOU'LL NEVER REACH ME IN TIME!
I WON'T, HUH?
OKAY, SO YA MANAGED TO GIT DOWN TO YER RAT HOLE! I'LL RIP THE BLAMED PLATFORM RIGHT OUTTA THE GROUND, 'N THEN ---
AGGHHH-HHHH!
BEN!
IT WUZ A TRAP!... SOME KINDA ELECTRIC SHOCK... WAITIN' FER WHOEVER TOUCHED THAT METAL!
EASY, BIG FELLA.. EASY! LEAN ON ME, BEN... I'LL HELP YOU!
BUT... WHAT'D IT DO TO ME?? I--I'M AS WEAK AS A BLAMED YANCY STREETER..!
YOU WASTE YOUR TIME, JOHNNY STORM! NOTHING CAN HELP ANY OF YOU NOW!
THOSE ELECTRIC VOLTS HAVE CAUSED A CHAIN REACTION IN HIS BLOOD CELLS WHICH WILL WEAKEN HIM FOR FIVE MINUTES!
AND THAT IS ALL THE TIME THE BLACK PANTHER SHALL NEED!
'TWAS I WHO INVITED YOU FOR THE HUNT!
BUT, I NEGLECTED TO TELL YOU ONE THING ---
IT IS YOU WHO SHALL BE HUNTED!
10.

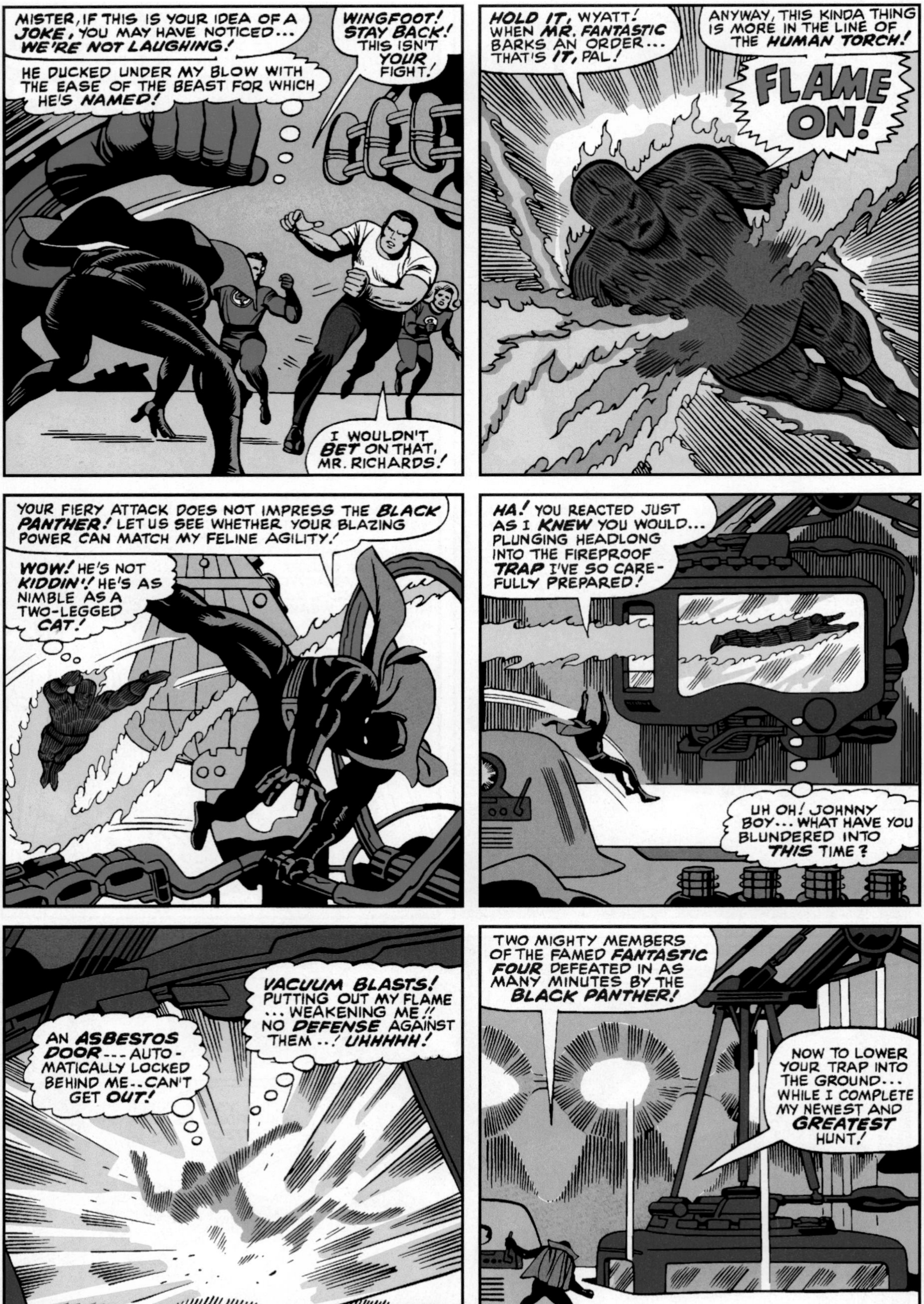

MISTER, IF THIS IS YOUR IDEA OF A JOKE, YOU MAY HAVE NOTICED... WE'RE NOT LAUGHING!
HE DUCKED UNDER MY BLOW WITH THE EASE OF THE BEAST FOR WHICH HE'S NAMED!
WINGFOOT! STAY BACK! THIS ISN'T YOUR FIGHT!
I WOULDN'T BET ON THAT, MR. RICHARDS!
HOLD IT, WYATT! WHEN MR. FANTASTIC BARKS AN ORDER... THAT'S IT, PAL!
ANYWAY, THIS KINDA THING IS MORE IN THE LINE OF THE HUMAN TORCH!
FLAME ON!
YOUR FIERY ATTACK DOES NOT IMPRESS THE BLACK PANTHER! LET US SEE WHETHER YOUR BLAZING POWER CAN MATCH MY FELINE AGILITY!
WOW! HE'S NOT KIDDIN'! HE'S AS NIMBLE AS A TWO-LEGGED CAT!
HA! YOU REACTED JUST AS I KNEW YOU WOULD... PLUNGING HEADLONG INTO THE FIREPROOF TRAP I'VE SO CAREFULLY PREPARED!
UH OH! JOHNNY BOY... WHAT HAVE YOU BLUNDERED INTO THIS TIME?
AN ASBESTOS DOOR--- AUTOMATICALLY LOCKED BEHIND ME.. CAN'T GET OUT!
VACUUM BLASTS! PUTTING OUT MY FLAME ... WEAKENING ME!! NO DEFENSE AGAINST THEM ..! UHHHHH!
TWO MIGHTY MEMBERS OF THE FAMED FANTASTIC FOUR DEFEATED IN AS MANY MINUTES BY THE BLACK PANTHER!
NOW TO LOWER YOUR TRAP INTO THE GROUND... WHILE I COMPLETE MY NEWEST AND GREATEST HUNT!

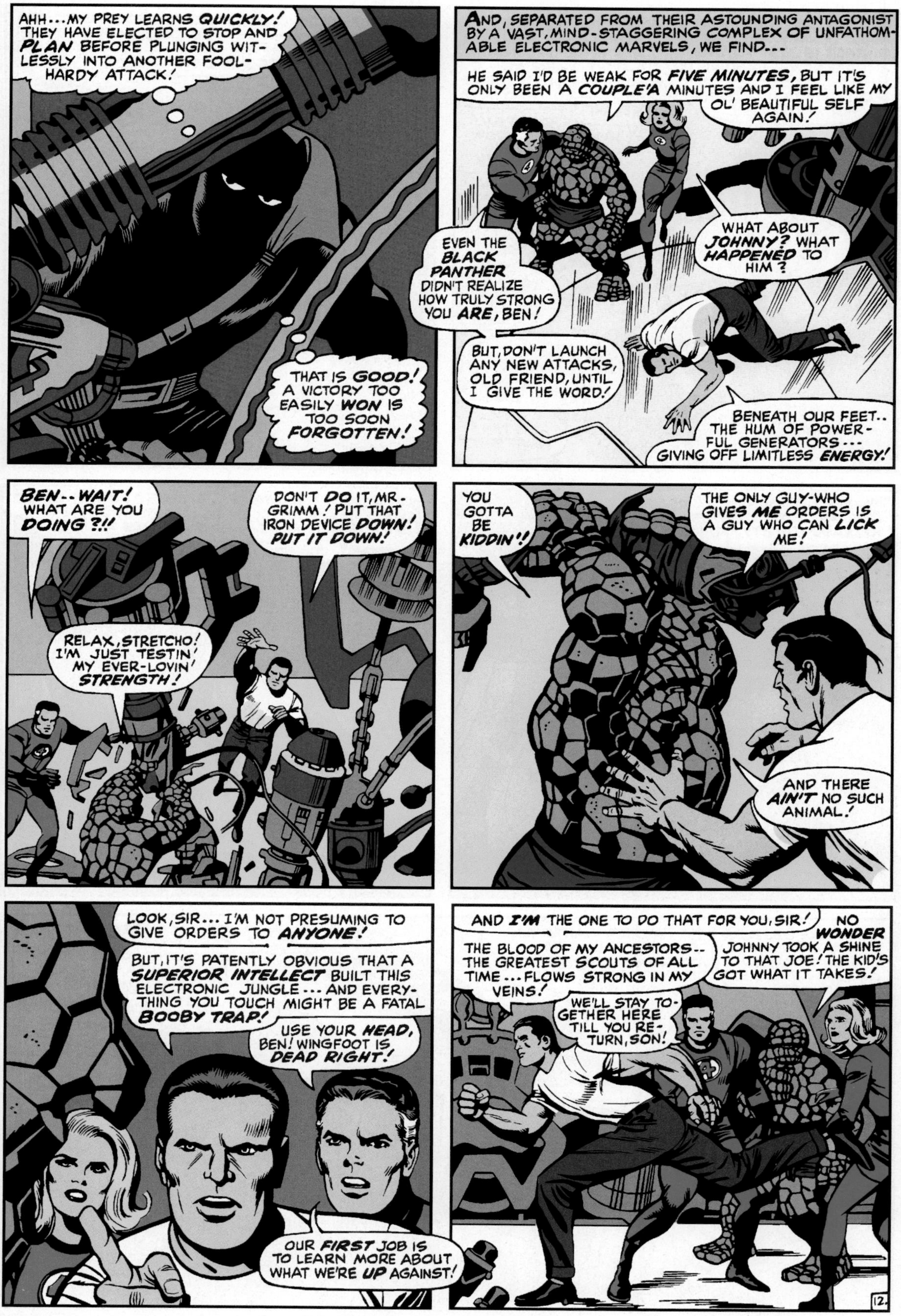
AHH... MY PREY LEARNS QUICKLY! THEY HAVE ELECTED TO STOP AND PLAN BEFORE PLUNGING WITLESSLY INTO ANOTHER FOOLHARDY ATTACK!
THAT IS GOOD! A VICTORY TOO EASILY WON IS TOO SOON FORGOTTEN!
AND, SEPARATED FROM THEIR ASTOUNDING ANTAGONIST BY A VAST, MIND-STAGGERING COMPLEX OF UNFATHOMABLE ELECTRONIC MARVELS, WE FIND...
HE SAID I'D BE WEAK FOR FIVE MINUTES, BUT IT'S ONLY BEEN A COUPLE'A MINUTES AND I FEEL LIKE MY OL' BEAUTIFUL SELF AGAIN!
EVEN THE BLACK PANTHER DIDN'T REALIZE HOW TRULY STRONG YOU ARE, BEN!
WHAT ABOUT JOHNNY? WHAT HAPPENED TO HIM?
BUT, DON'T LAUNCH ANY NEW ATTACKS, OLD FRIEND, UNTIL I GIVE THE WORD!
BENEATH OUR FEET.. THE HUM OF POWERFUL GENERATORS --- GIVING OFF LIMITLESS ENERGY!
BEN--WAIT! WHAT ARE YOU DOING ?!!
DON'T DO IT, MR. GRIMM! PUT THAT IRON DEVICE DOWN! PUT IT DOWN!
RELAX, STRETCHO! I'M JUST TESTIN' MY EVER-LOVIN' STRENGTH!
YOU GOTTA BE KIDDIN'!
THE ONLY GUY-WHO GIVES ME ORDERS IS A GUY WHO CAN LICK ME!
AND THERE AIN'T NO SUCH ANIMAL!
LOOK, SIR... I'M NOT PRESUMING TO GIVE ORDERS TO ANYONE!
BUT, IT'S PATENTLY OBVIOUS THAT A SUPERIOR INTELLECT BUILT THIS ELECTRONIC JUNGLE... AND EVERYTHING YOU TOUCH MIGHT BE A FATAL BOOBY TRAP!
USE YOUR HEAD, BEN! WINGFOOT IS DEAD RIGHT!
OUR FIRST JOB IS TO LEARN MORE ABOUT WHAT WE'RE UP AGAINST!
AND I'M THE ONE TO DO THAT FOR YOU, SIR!
THE BLOOD OF MY ANCESTORS-- THE GREATEST SCOUTS OF ALL TIME... FLOWS STRONG IN MY VEINS!
NO WONDER JOHNNY TOOK A SHINE TO THAT JOE! THE KID'S GOT WHAT IT TAKES!
WE'LL STAY TOGETHER HERE TILL YOU RETURN, SON!
12.

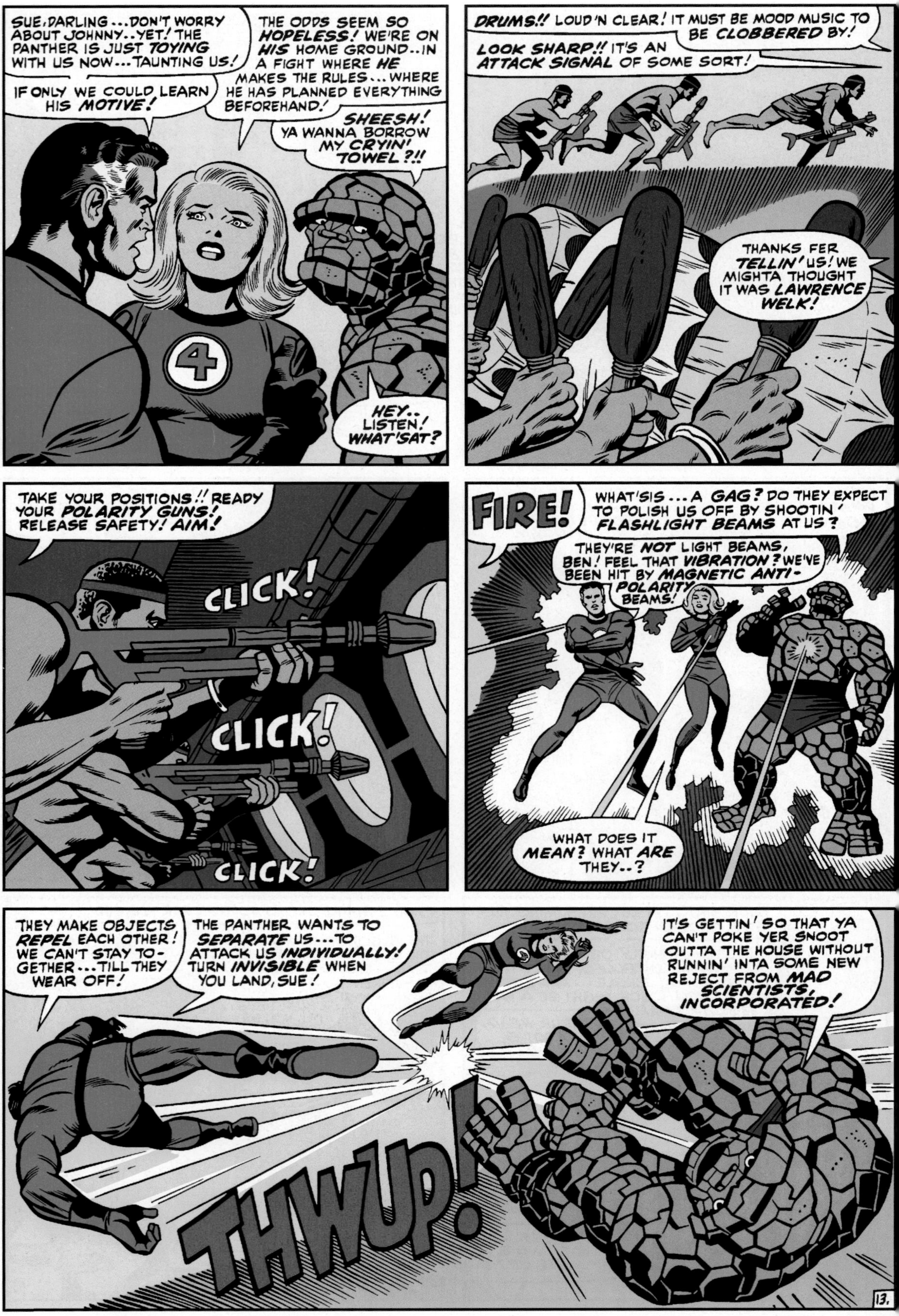
SUE, DARLING ... DON'T WORRY ABOUT JOHNNY.. YET! THE PANTHER IS JUST TOYING WITH US NOW ... TAUNTING US!
IF ONLY WE COULD LEARN HIS MOTIVE!
THE ODDS SEEM SO HOPELESS! WE'RE ON HIS HOME GROUND..IN A FIGHT WHERE HE MAKES THE RULES ... WHERE HE HAS PLANNED EVERYTHING BEFOREHAND!
SHEESH! YA WANNA BORROW MY CRYIN' TOWEL ?!!
HEY.. LISTEN! WHAT'SAT?
DRUMS!! LOUD 'N CLEAR! IT MUST BE MOOD MUSIC TO BE CLOBBERED BY!
LOOK SHARP!! IT'S AN ATTACK SIGNAL OF SOME SORT!
THANKS FER TELLIN' US! WE MIGHTA THOUGHT IT WAS LAWRENCE WELK!
TAKE YOUR POSITIONS!! READY YOUR POLARITY GUNS! RELEASE SAFETY! AIM!
CLICK!
CLICK!
CLICK!
FIRE!
WHAT'SIS ... A GAG? DO THEY EXPECT TO POLISH US OFF BY SHOOTIN' FLASHLIGHT BEAMS AT US?
THEY'RE NOT LIGHT BEAMS, BEN! FEEL THAT VIBRATION? WE'VE BEEN HIT BY MAGNETIC ANTI-POLARITY BEAMS!
WHAT DOES IT MEAN? WHAT ARE THEY..?
THEY MAKE OBJECTS REPEL EACH OTHER! WE CAN'T STAY TO-GETHER ... TILL THEY WEAR OFF!
THE PANTHER WANTS TO SEPARATE US ... TO ATTACK US INDIVIDUALLY! TURN INVISIBLE WHEN YOU LAND, SUE!
IT'S GETTIN' SO THAT YA CAN'T POKE YER SNOOT OUTTA THE HOUSE WITHOUT RUNNIN' INTA SOME NEW REJECT FROM MAD SCIENTISTS, INCORPORATED!
THWUP!
13.

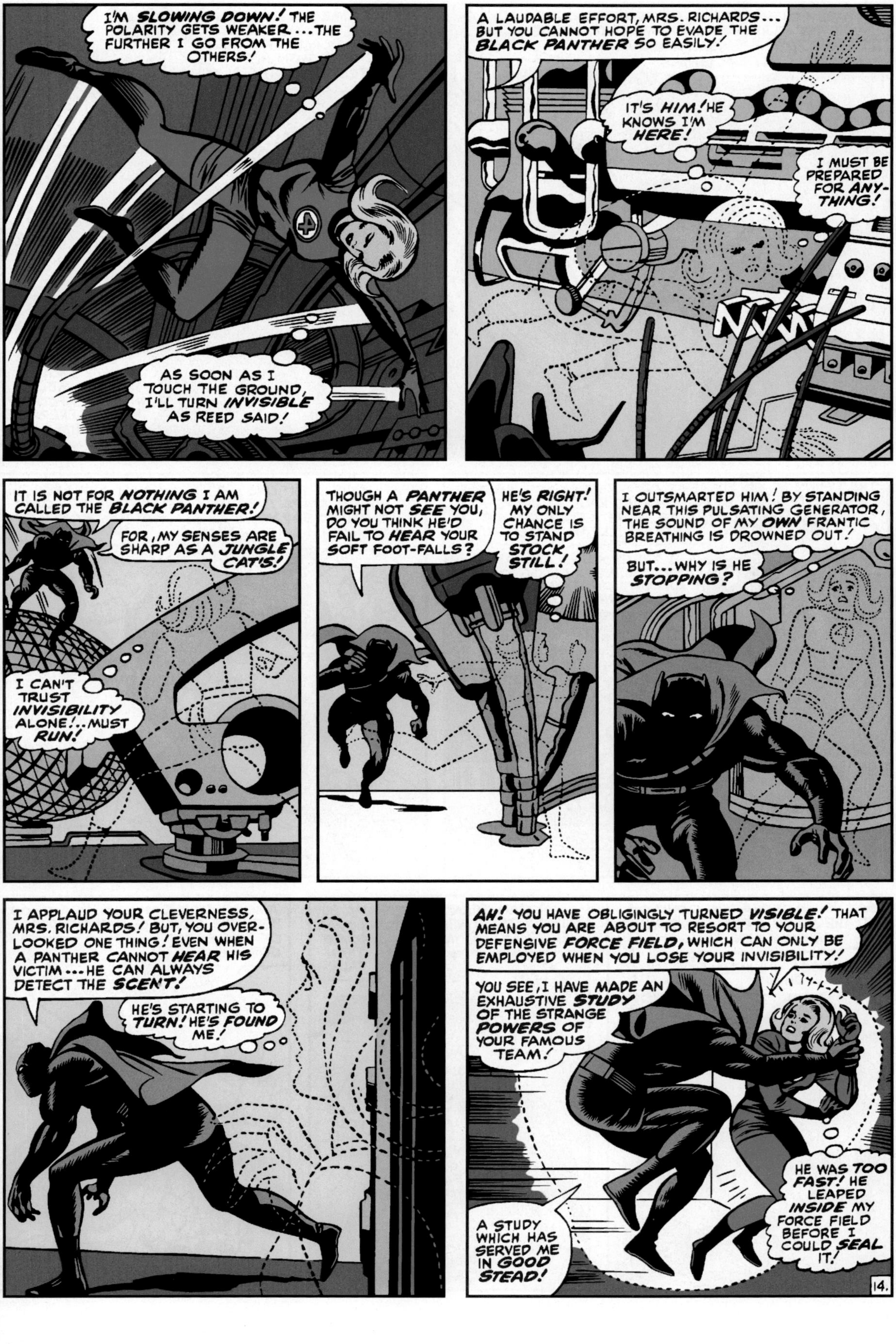

I'M SLOWING DOWN! THE POLARITY GETS WEAKER...THE FURTHER I GO FROM THE OTHERS!
AS SOON AS I TOUCH THE GROUND, I'LL TURN INVISIBLE AS REED SAID!
A LAUDABLE EFFORT, MRS. RICHARDS... BUT YOU CANNOT HOPE TO EVADE THE BLACK PANTHER SO EASILY!
IT'S HIM! HE KNOWS I'M HERE!
I MUST BE PREPARED FOR ANYTHING!
IT IS NOT FOR NOTHING I AM CALLED THE BLACK PANTHER!
FOR, MY SENSES ARE SHARP AS A JUNGLE CAT'S!
I CAN'T TRUST INVISIBILITY ALONE!..MUST RUN!
THOUGH A PANTHER MIGHT NOT SEE YOU, DO YOU THINK HE'D FAIL TO HEAR YOUR SOFT FOOT-FALLS?
HE'S RIGHT! MY ONLY CHANCE IS TO STAND STOCK STILL!
I OUTSMARTED HIM! BY STANDING NEAR THIS PULSATING GENERATOR, THE SOUND OF MY OWN FRANTIC BREATHING IS DROWNED OUT!
BUT...WHY IS HE STOPPING?
I APPLAUD YOUR CLEVERNESS, MRS. RICHARDS! BUT, YOU OVERLOOKED ONE THING! EVEN WHEN A PANTHER CANNOT HEAR HIS VICTIM...HE CAN ALWAYS DETECT THE SCENT!
HE'S STARTING TO TURN! HE'S FOUND ME!
AH! YOU HAVE OBLIGINGLY TURNED VISIBLE! THAT MEANS YOU ARE ABOUT TO RESORT TO YOUR DEFENSIVE FORCE FIELD, WHICH CAN ONLY BE EMPLOYED WHEN YOU LOSE YOUR INVISIBILITY!
YOU SEE, I HAVE MADE AN EXHAUSTIVE STUDY OF THE STRANGE POWERS OF YOUR FAMOUS TEAM!
A STUDY WHICH HAS SERVED ME IN GOOD STEAD!
HE WAS TOO FAST! HE LEAPED INSIDE MY FORCE FIELD BEFORE I COULD SEAL IT!
14.

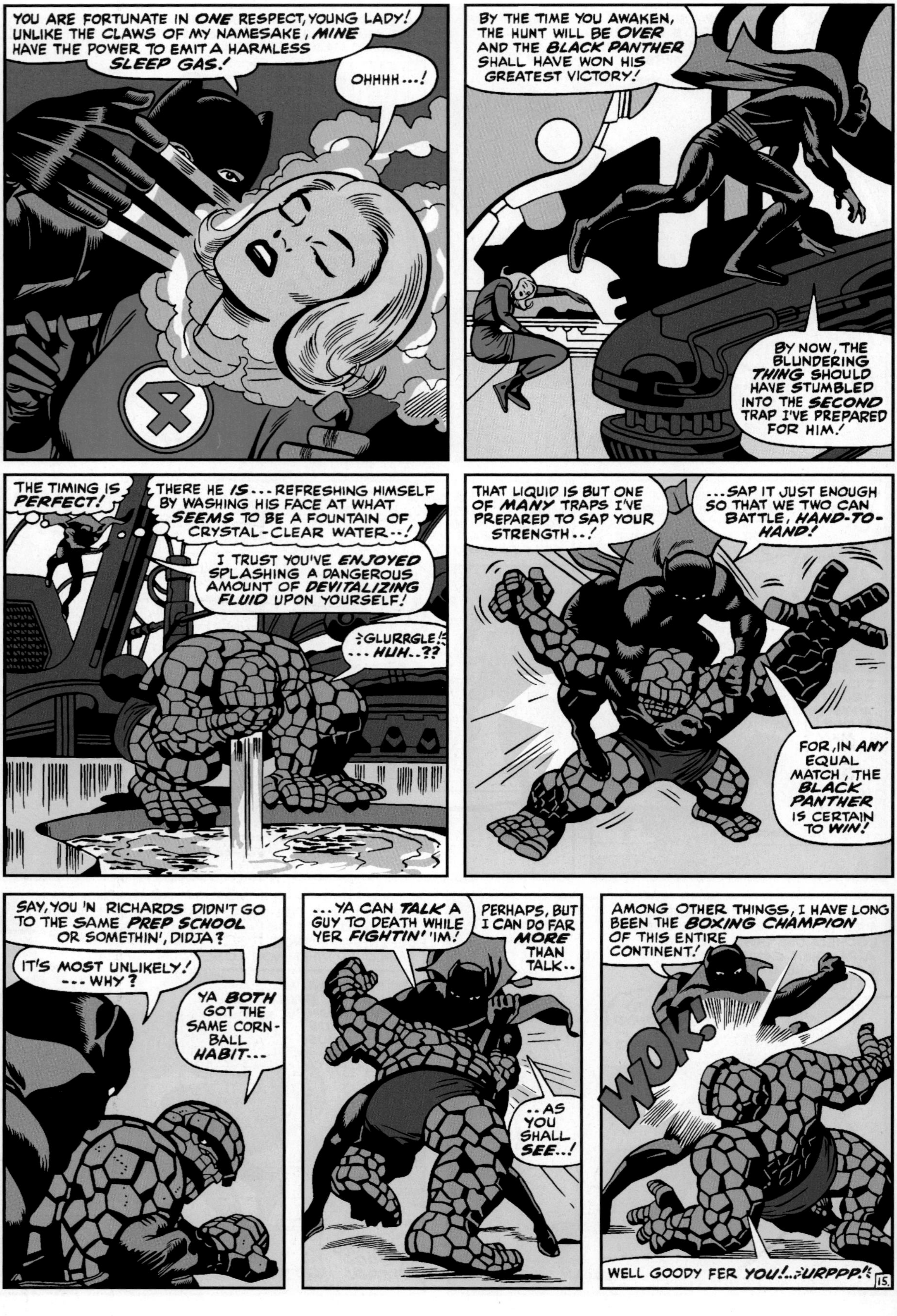
YOU ARE FORTUNATE IN ONE RESPECT, YOUNG LADY! UNLIKE THE CLAWS OF MY NAMESAKE, MINE HAVE THE POWER TO EMIT A HARMLESS SLEEP GAS!
OHHHH...!
BY THE TIME YOU AWAKEN, THE HUNT WILL BE OVER AND THE BLACK PANTHER SHALL HAVE WON HIS GREATEST VICTORY!
BY NOW, THE BLUNDERING THING SHOULD HAVE STUMBLED INTO THE SECOND TRAP I'VE PREPARED FOR HIM!
THE TIMING IS PERFECT!
THERE HE IS... REFRESHING HIMSELF BY WASHING HIS FACE AT WHAT SEEMS TO BE A FOUNTAIN OF CRYSTAL-CLEAR WATER--!
I TRUST YOU'VE ENJOYED SPLASHING A DANGEROUS AMOUNT OF DEVITALIZING FLUID UPON YOURSELF!
GLURRGLE!! ... HUH..??
THAT LIQUID IS BUT ONE OF MANY TRAPS I'VE PREPARED TO SAP YOUR STRENGTH..!
...SAP IT JUST ENOUGH SO THAT WE TWO CAN BATTLE, HAND-TO-HAND!
FOR, IN ANY EQUAL MATCH, THE BLACK PANTHER IS CERTAIN TO WIN!
SAY, YOU 'N RICHARDS DIDN'T GO TO THE SAME PREP SCHOOL OR SOMETHIN', DIDJA?
IT'S MOST UNLIKELY! --- WHY?
YA BOTH GOT THE SAME CORN-BALL HABIT...
...YA CAN TALK A GUY TO DEATH WHILE YER FIGHTIN' 'IM!
PERHAPS, BUT I CAN DO FAR MORE THAN TALK..
..AS YOU SHALL SEE..!
AMONG OTHER THINGS, I HAVE LONG BEEN THE BOXING CHAMPION OF THIS ENTIRE CONTINENT!
WOK!
WELL GOODY FER YOU!..URPPP!
15.

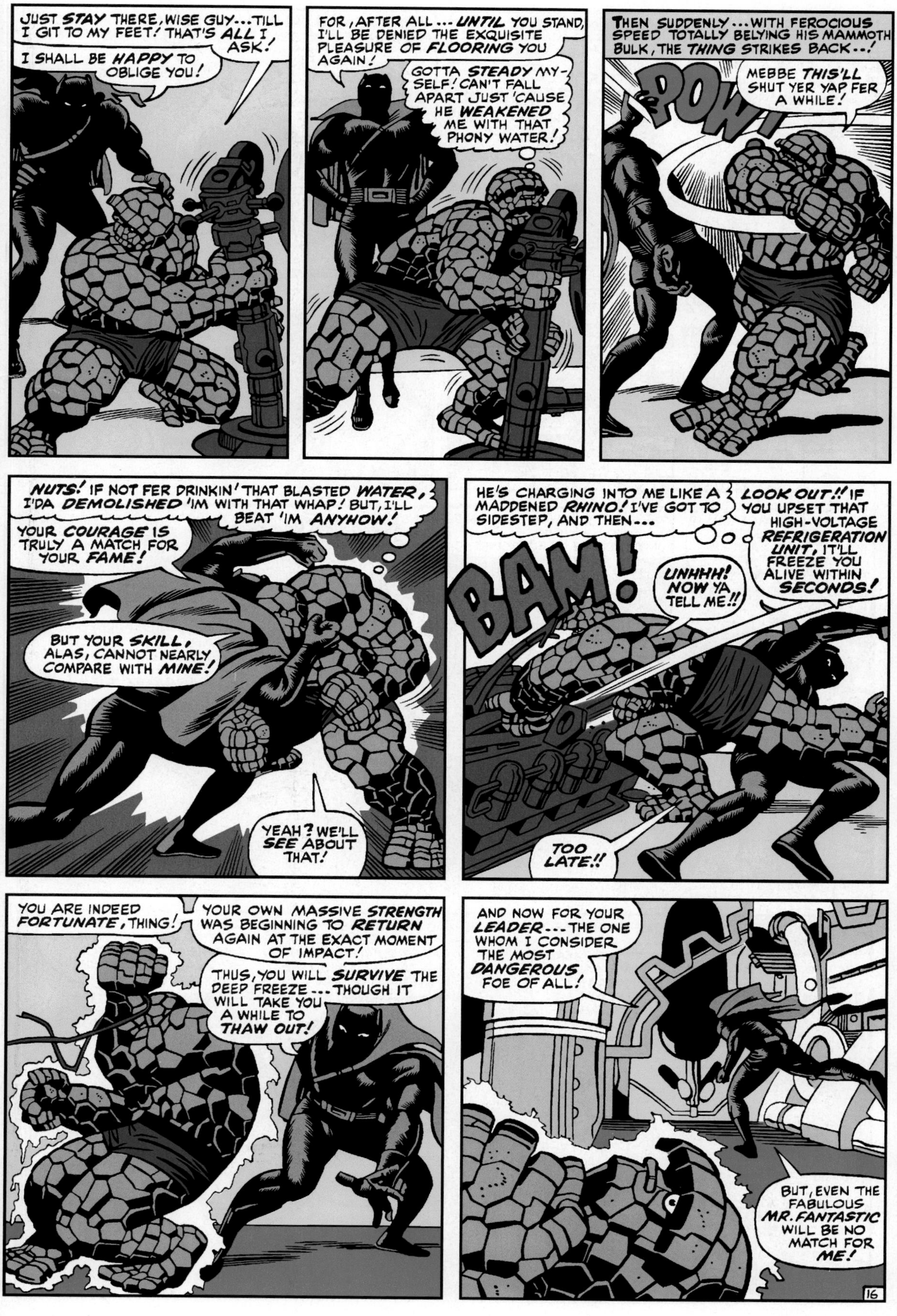
JUST STAY THERE, WISE GUY... TILL I GIT TO MY FEET! THAT'S ALL I ASK!
I SHALL BE HAPPY TO OBLIGE YOU!
FOR, AFTER ALL... UNTIL YOU STAND, I'LL BE DENIED THE EXQUISITE PLEASURE OF FLOORING YOU AGAIN!
GOTTA STEADY MY-SELF! CAN'T FALL APART JUST 'CAUSE HE WEAKENED ME WITH THAT PHONY WATER!
THEN SUDDENLY... WITH FEROCIOUS SPEED TOTALLY BELYING HIS MAMMOTH BULK, THE THING STRIKES BACK..!
POW
MEBBE THIS'LL SHUT YER YAP FER A WHILE!
NUTS! IF NOT FER DRINKIN' THAT BLASTED WATER, I'DA DEMOLISHED 'IM WITH THAT WHAP! BUT, I'LL BEAT 'IM ANYHOW!
YOUR COURAGE IS TRULY A MATCH FOR YOUR FAME!
BUT YOUR SKILL, ALAS, CANNOT NEARLY COMPARE WITH MINE!
YEAH? WE'LL SEE ABOUT THAT!
HE'S CHARGING INTO ME LIKE A MADDENED RHINO! I'VE GOT TO SIDESTEP, AND THEN...
LOOK OUT!! IF YOU UPSET THAT HIGH-VOLTAGE REFRIGERATION UNIT, IT'LL FREEZE YOU ALIVE WITHIN SECONDS!
BAM!
UNHHH! NOW YA TELL ME!!
TOO LATE!!
YOU ARE INDEED FORTUNATE, THING!
YOUR OWN MASSIVE STRENGTH WAS BEGINNING TO RETURN AGAIN AT THE EXACT MOMENT OF IMPACT!
THUS, YOU WILL SURVIVE THE DEEP FREEZE... THOUGH IT WILL TAKE YOU A WHILE TO THAW OUT!
AND NOW FOR YOUR LEADER... THE ONE WHOM I CONSIDER THE MOST DANGEROUS FOE OF ALL!
BUT, EVEN THE FABULOUS MR. FANTASTIC WILL BE NO MATCH FOR ME!
16

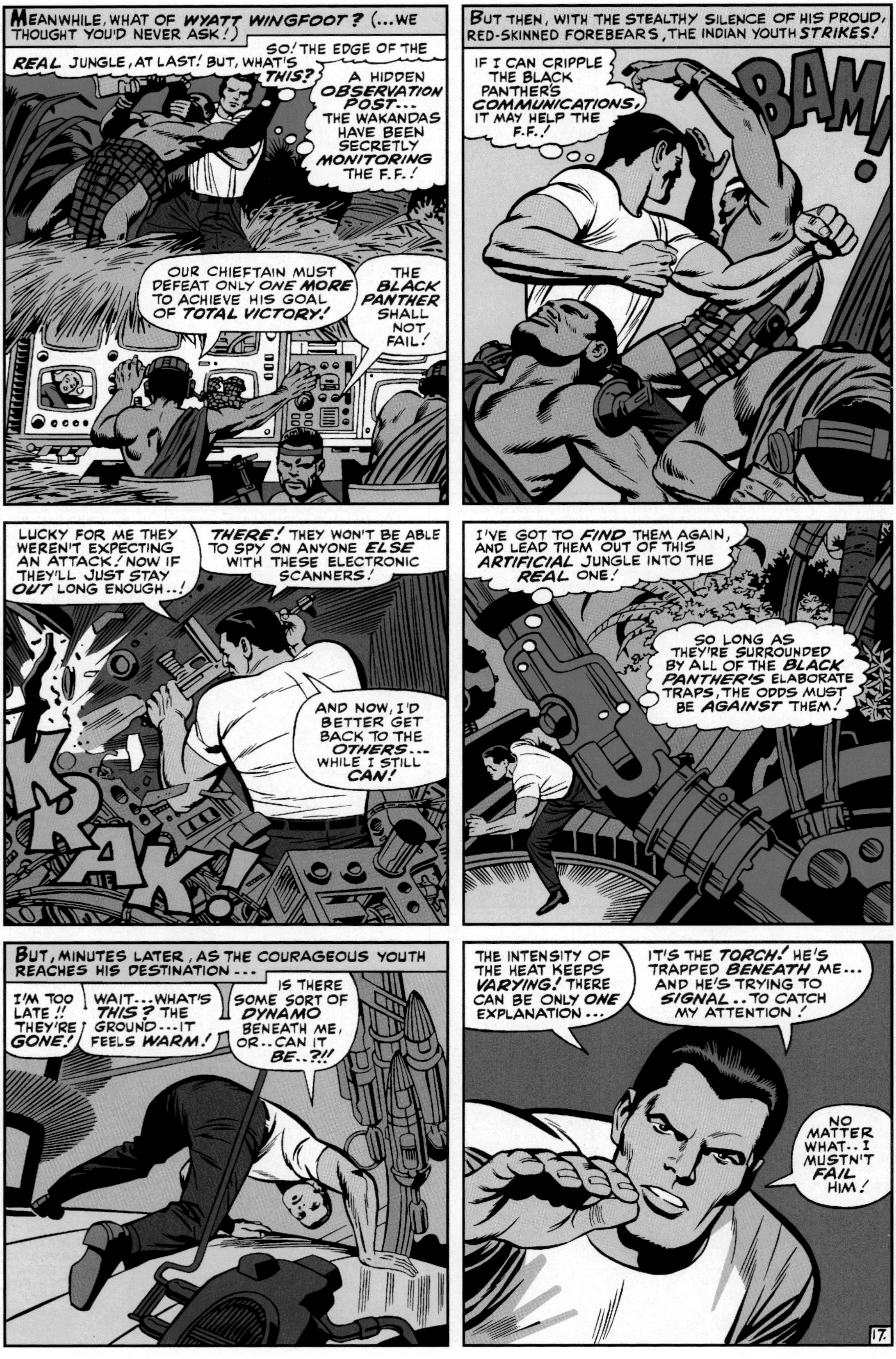
MEANWHILE, WHAT OF WYATT WINGFOOT? (...WE THOUGHT YOU'D NEVER ASK!)
SO! THE EDGE OF THE REAL JUNGLE, AT LAST! BUT, WHAT'S THIS?
A HIDDEN OBSERVATION POST... THE WAKANDAS HAVE BEEN SECRETLY MONITORING THE F.F.!
OUR CHIEFTAIN MUST DEFEAT ONLY ONE MORE TO ACHIEVE HIS GOAL OF TOTAL VICTORY!
THE BLACK PANTHER SHALL NOT FAIL!
BUT THEN, WITH THE STEALTHY SILENCE OF HIS PROUD, RED-SKINNED FOREBEARS, THE INDIAN YOUTH STRIKES!
IF I CAN CRIPPLE THE BLACK PANTHER'S COMMUNICATIONS, IT MAY HELP THE F.F.!
BAM!
LUCKY FOR ME THEY WEREN'T EXPECTING AN ATTACK! NOW IF THEY'LL JUST STAY OUT LONG ENOUGH..!
THERE! THEY WON'T BE ABLE TO SPY ON ANYONE ELSE WITH THESE ELECTRONIC SCANNERS!
AND NOW, I'D BETTER GET BACK TO THE OTHERS... WHILE I STILL CAN!
KRAK!
I'VE GOT TO FIND THEM AGAIN, AND LEAD THEM OUT OF THIS ARTIFICIAL JUNGLE INTO THE REAL ONE!
SO LONG AS THEY'RE SURROUNDED BY ALL OF THE BLACK PANTHER'S ELABORATE TRAPS, THE ODDS MUST BE AGAINST THEM!
BUT, MINUTES LATER, AS THE COURAGEOUS YOUTH REACHES HIS DESTINATION...
I'M TOO LATE!! THEY'RE GONE!
WAIT...WHAT'S THIS? THE GROUND...IT FEELS WARM!
IS THERE SOME SORT OF DYNAMO BENEATH ME, OR..CAN IT BE..?!!
THE INTENSITY OF THE HEAT KEEPS VARYING! THERE CAN BE ONLY ONE EXPLANATION...
IT'S THE TORCH! HE'S TRAPPED BENEATH ME... AND HE'S TRYING TO SIGNAL.. TO CATCH MY ATTENTION!
NO MATTER WHAT.. I MUSTN'T FAIL HIM!
17.

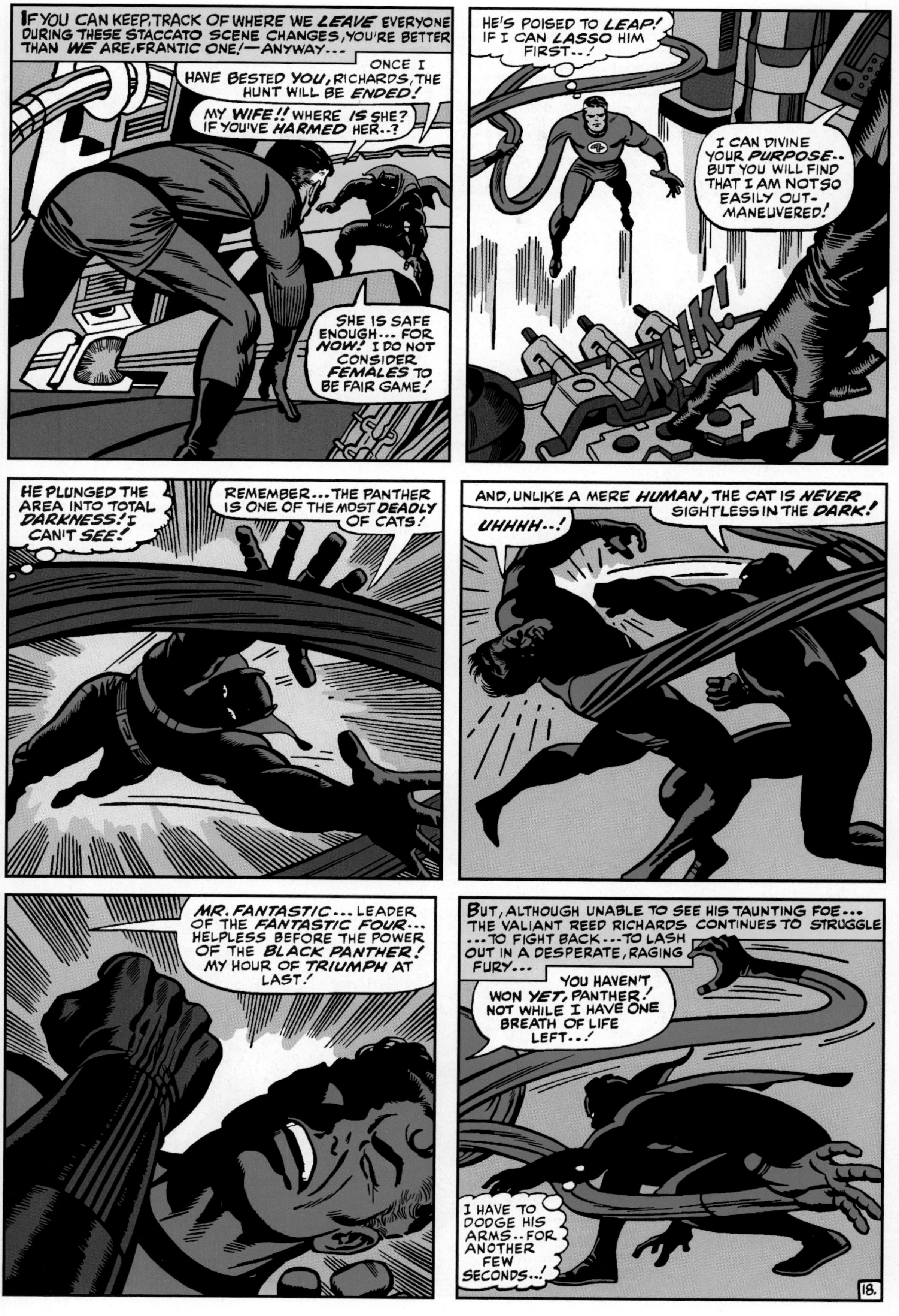
IF YOU CAN KEEP TRACK OF WHERE WE LEAVE EVERYONE DURING THESE STACCATO SCENE CHANGES, YOU'RE BETTER THAN WE ARE, FRANTIC ONE! — ANYWAY...
ONCE I HAVE BESTED YOU, RICHARDS, THE HUNT WILL BE ENDED!
MY WIFE!! WHERE IS SHE? IF YOU'VE HARMED HER..?
SHE IS SAFE ENOUGH... FOR NOW! I DO NOT CONSIDER FEMALES TO BE FAIR GAME!
HE'S POISED TO LEAP! IF I CAN LASSO HIM FIRST..!
I CAN DIVINE YOUR PURPOSE.. BUT YOU WILL FIND THAT I AM NOT SO EASILY OUT-MANEUVERED!
KLIK!
HE PLUNGED THE AREA INTO TOTAL DARKNESS! I CAN'T SEE!
REMEMBER... THE PANTHER IS ONE OF THE MOST DEADLY OF CATS!
AND, UNLIKE A MERE HUMAN, THE CAT IS NEVER SIGHTLESS IN THE DARK!
UHHHH..!
MR. FANTASTIC... LEADER OF THE FANTASTIC FOUR... HELPLESS BEFORE THE POWER OF THE BLACK PANTHER! MY HOUR OF TRIUMPH AT LAST!
BUT, ALTHOUGH UNABLE TO SEE HIS TAUNTING FOE... THE VALIANT REED RICHARDS CONTINUES TO STRUGGLE ...TO FIGHT BACK...TO LASH OUT IN A DESPERATE, RAGING FURY...
YOU HAVEN'T WON YET, PANTHER! NOT WHILE I HAVE ONE BREATH OF LIFE LEFT..!
I HAVE TO DODGE HIS ARMS.. FOR ANOTHER FEW SECONDS..!
18.

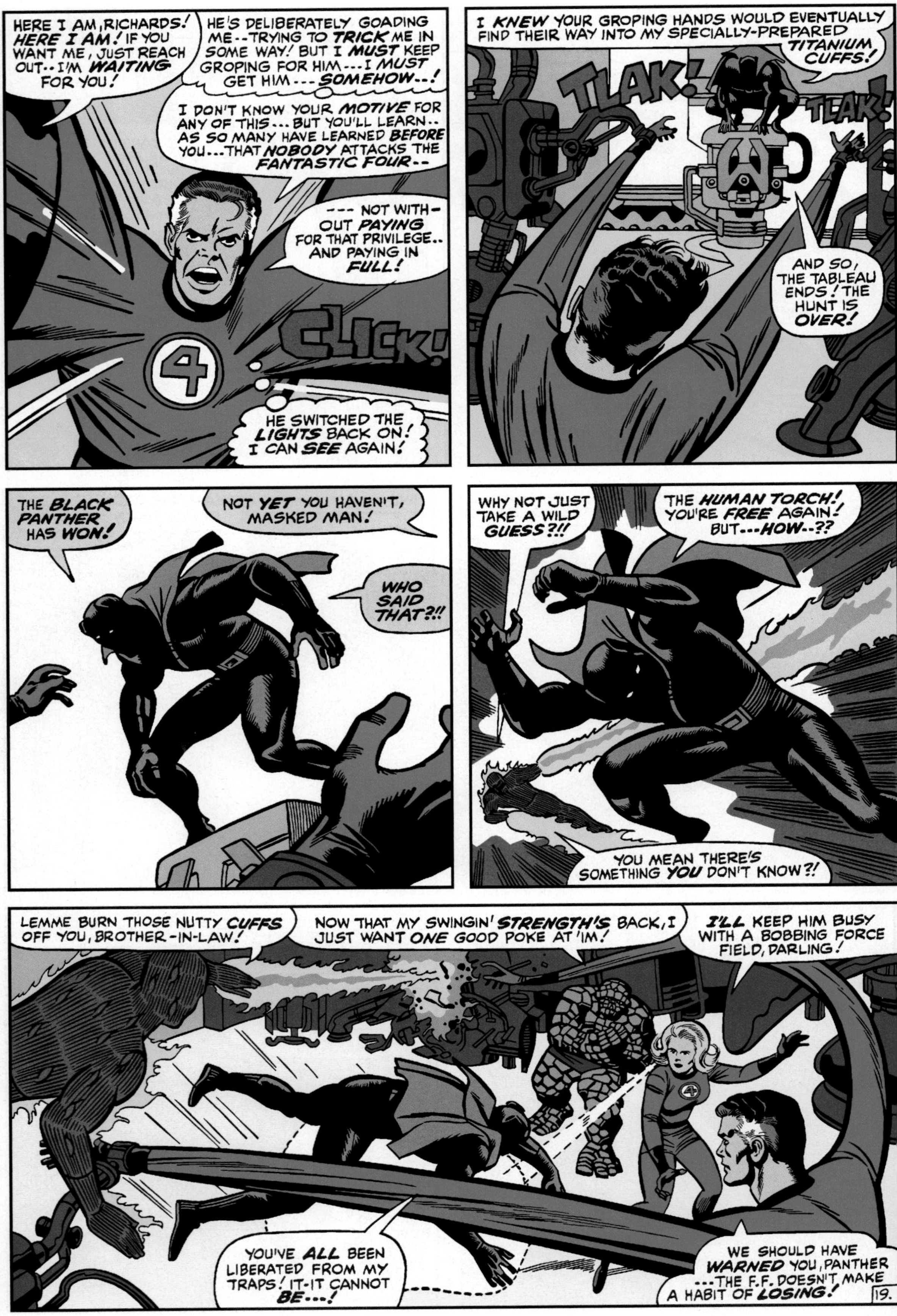
HERE I AM, RICHARDS! HERE I AM! IF YOU WANT ME, JUST REACH OUT-- I'M WAITING FOR YOU!
HE'S DELIBERATELY GOADING ME--TRYING TO TRICK ME IN SOME WAY! BUT I MUST KEEP GROPING FOR HIM---I MUST GET HIM---SOMEHOW--!
I DON'T KNOW YOUR MOTIVE FOR ANY OF THIS... BUT YOU'LL LEARN.. AS SO MANY HAVE LEARNED BEFORE YOU...THAT NOBODY ATTACKS THE FANTASTIC FOUR--
---NOT WITH-OUT PAYING FOR THAT PRIVILEGE.. AND PAYING IN FULL!
CLICK!
HE SWITCHED THE LIGHTS BACK ON! I CAN SEE AGAIN!
I KNEW YOUR GROPING HANDS WOULD EVENTUALLY FIND THEIR WAY INTO MY SPECIALLY-PREPARED TITANIUM CUFFS!
TLAK!
TLAK!
AND SO, THE TABLEAU ENDS! THE HUNT IS OVER!
THE BLACK PANTHER HAS WON!
NOT YET YOU HAVEN'T, MASKED MAN!
WHO SAID THAT?!!
WHY NOT JUST TAKE A WILD GUESS?!!
THE HUMAN TORCH! YOU'RE FREE AGAIN! BUT---HOW--??
YOU MEAN THERE'S SOMETHING YOU DON'T KNOW?!
LEMME BURN THOSE NUTTY CUFFS OFF YOU, BROTHER-IN-LAW!
NOW THAT MY SWINGIN' STRENGTH'S BACK, I JUST WANT ONE GOOD POKE AT 'IM!
I'LL KEEP HIM BUSY WITH A BOBBING FORCE FIELD, DARLING!
YOU'VE ALL BEEN LIBERATED FROM MY TRAPS! IT-IT CANNOT BE...!
WE SHOULD HAVE WARNED YOU, PANTHER ...THE F.F. DOESN'T MAKE A HABIT OF LOSING!
19.

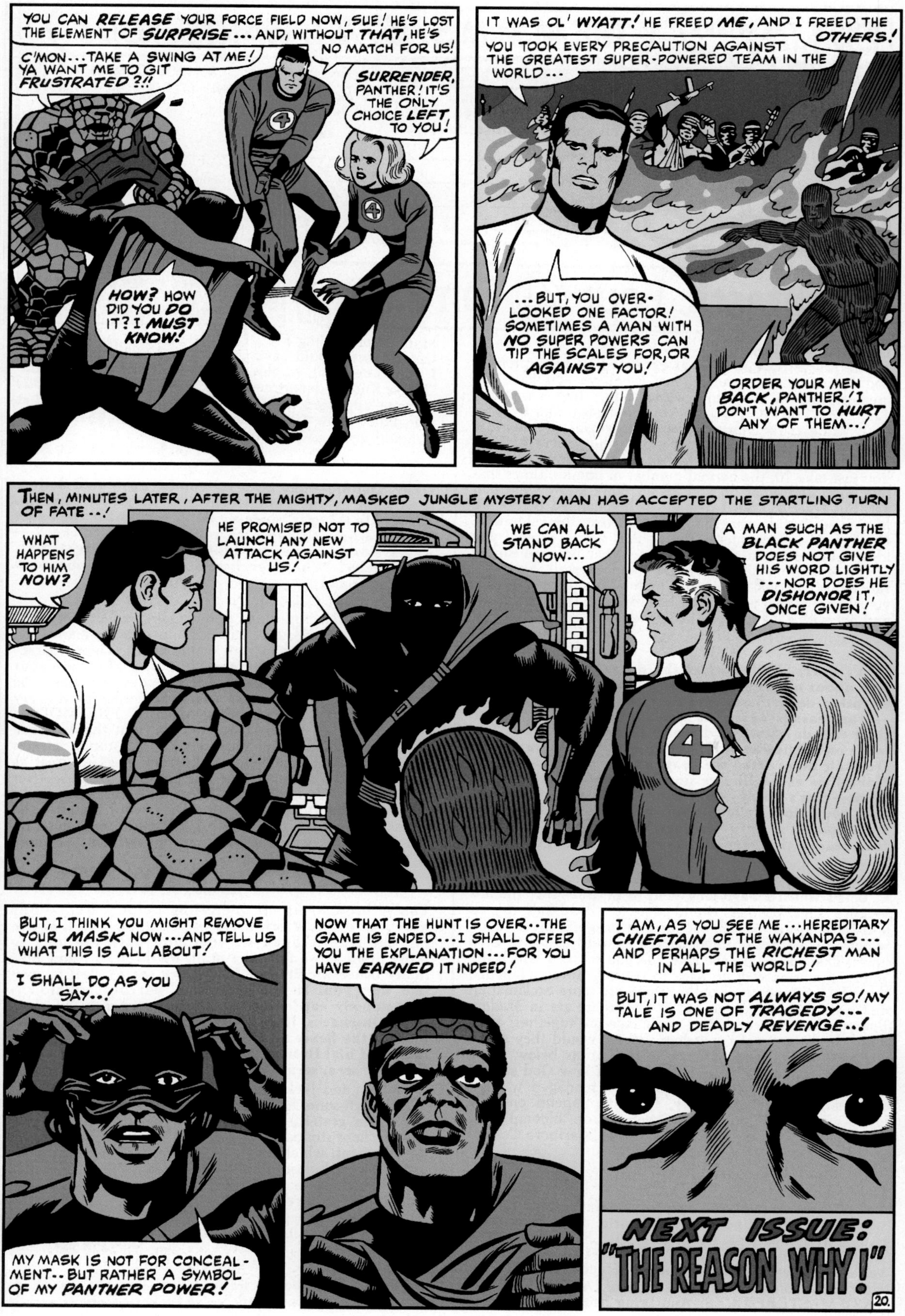

YOU CAN RELEASE YOUR FORCE FIELD NOW, SUE! HE'S LOST THE ELEMENT OF SURPRISE... AND, WITHOUT THAT, HE'S NO MATCH FOR US!
C'MON... TAKE A SWING AT ME! YA WANT ME TO GIT FRUSTRATED?!!
SURRENDER, PANTHER! IT'S THE ONLY CHOICE LEFT TO YOU!
HOW? HOW DID YOU DO IT? I MUST KNOW!
IT WAS OL' WYATT! HE FREED ME, AND I FREED THE OTHERS!
YOU TOOK EVERY PRECAUTION AGAINST THE GREATEST SUPER-POWERED TEAM IN THE WORLD...
...BUT, YOU OVER-LOOKED ONE FACTOR! SOMETIMES A MAN WITH NO SUPER POWERS CAN TIP THE SCALES FOR, OR AGAINST YOU!
ORDER YOUR MEN BACK, PANTHER! I DON'T WANT TO HURT ANY OF THEM..!
THEN, MINUTES LATER, AFTER THE MIGHTY, MASKED JUNGLE MYSTERY MAN HAS ACCEPTED THE STARTLING TURN OF FATE..!
WHAT HAPPENS TO HIM NOW?
HE PROMISED NOT TO LAUNCH ANY NEW ATTACK AGAINST US!
WE CAN ALL STAND BACK NOW...
A MAN SUCH AS THE BLACK PANTHER DOES NOT GIVE HIS WORD LIGHTLY ...NOR DOES HE DISHONOR IT, ONCE GIVEN!
BUT, I THINK YOU MIGHT REMOVE YOUR MASK NOW...AND TELL US WHAT THIS IS ALL ABOUT!
I SHALL DO AS YOU SAY..!
MY MASK IS NOT FOR CONCEAL-MENT.. BUT RATHER A SYMBOL OF MY PANTHER POWER!
NOW THAT THE HUNT IS OVER..THE GAME IS ENDED...I SHALL OFFER YOU THE EXPLANATION...FOR YOU HAVE EARNED IT INDEED!
I AM, AS YOU SEE ME...HEREDITARY CHIEFTAIN OF THE WAKANDAS... AND PERHAPS THE RICHEST MAN IN ALL THE WORLD!
BUT, IT WAS NOT ALWAYS SO! MY TALE IS ONE OF TRAGEDY... AND DEADLY REVENGE..!
NEXT ISSUE: "THE REASON WHY!"
20.

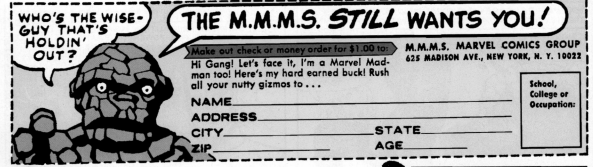

# Fantastic Four ④ Fan Page

Send letters to: LEE and KIRBY
THE MARVEL COMICS GROUP
SECOND FLOOR 625 MADISON AV.
NEW YORK 10022 N. Y.

Dear Stan and Jack,

The Marvel Comic Co. has exceeded all past, present, and future comic organizations. I believe you have the greatest staff in the comic world today. In my opinion, THE FANTASTIC FOUR is your best mag, and lives up to its name as the world's greatest magazine. I think it is disgraceful, though, about your subscription prices. $1.75—! Do you think that money grows on trees or something? You just take 10, the normal number of comics, times that tidy sum, and what do you get? I don't know what *you* get, but *I* get $17.50! I demand it be changed before we Marvel readers do something drastic. Next, the Inhumans. How could you do such a thing? It is horrible, what you idiots have done to the Inhumans. What is the meaning of the separation between Johnny and Crystal? Also, it is ridiculous that you never told us how Black Bolt lost his voice! I am asking you to please answer this letter seriously, and not with a joke, as you usually do.

Phillip Pearson, Box 95
Kendrick, Idaho

**Don't worry, Phil — after the devastating things you said about us, who can joke? Unfortunately, our subscription department says they can't alter their prices — for reasons which *we* don't understand any more than *you* do! But, we'd really prefer you to buy our mags on the newsstands anyway—it gets you out in the fresh air more often that way, and we wanna keep you Marvelites as healthy as possible! As for Johnny and Chris—don't worry—they won't be separated forever! And you know we'll tell you how Black Bolt lost his voice sooner or later—in fact, we're kicking around a few ideas on that very subject right now. That's it, tiger!**

Dear Stan and Jack,

Just finished reading the latest F.F. and have confirmed a belief which I have long held to be true—that the adventure comic business would come to a dead halt, dry up and blow away were it not for one insignificant adjunct, which is as necessary to comicdom as word balloons. Give up?!? That's it! That's the sine qua non without which the public might as well go back to reading novels (horrible thought!). Do you realize that there are more exclamation marks in the above issue (473) than there are in *Madam Bovary, the Bible,* and *War and Peace* put together? Hats off to the letterers of comicdom. Where would they all be without the skill and patience to make dots below lines? Even the commonly accepted version of how God started to make the universe (Fiat Lux) was managed without exclamations. Is it necessary, then, to append one (at least) after every "crummp," "twanng," or "bloomp"?

Garlad Storrow, Marlboro College
Marlboro, Vt.

**Wow! Yep! It sure is! Zowie!**

Dear Stan and Jack,

I've been meaning to write to you since 1963, but always put it off. But now, it's either write or go crazy. Your two newest creations are great. COLLECTORS' ITEM CLASSICS and FANTASY MASTERPIECES are both very good ideas. I have about 30 of your fantasy mags. How about doing the complete series of Dr. Doom in FANTASY MASTERPIECES? And bring back the Tomorrow Man. After reading F.F., I realize that you guys are nuts! Only Marvel would have a guy named Silver Surfer! But, I think he's great. In closing, I have news for you. In the "Didja Know" department, you stated that the *first* Doc Strange appeared in IRON MAN, which is right. What you didn't know is that he appeared in ish #41. I think I should get a no-prize for that.

Don Jarvis, 45 Lawn Ave.,
Warwick, R. I.

**Okay, Donnie—one no-prize comin' up—we'll deliver it as soon as our Fantasti-car gets its yearly tune-up. (The only thing is, since we don't remember the exact ish—and haven't any back number copies to check— we have to take your word for it that you're right! But, that's okay! Who ever heard of a Marvel madman being wrong?)**

Dear Stan and Jack,

Between Galactus, the Watcher, Odin, and Eternity, you have lost me completely. There are now far too many "all-powerful" characters in your comic books. These characters, though they make for exciting stories, also make your tales unbelievable. This is fine if a reader only buys one or two of your titles, but, as a fan who buys almost every comic you produce (excluding MILLIE THE MODEL and RAWHIDE KID), I can tell you that the existence of too many omnipotent characters in your stories detracts from the realism that helps make your mags as great as they are, and also ruins your less powerful villains. After all, if the F.F. manages to defeat Galactus, how could they ever have trouble defeating Dr. Doom? So, after the threat of Galactus is over, let's get back to some good ol' one-issue fights with the old sparring partners. No more of these all-powerful cats, dig?

Larry Bush, 134-25 166th Place
Jamaica, N. Y.

**You've brought up an interesting point, Larry — one which we'd like a few more opinions on—and, knowing our frantic ones, we shouldn't have too long to wait! Soon as we tally the mail, we'll letcha know how many other meditating Marvelites see eyeball to eyeball with you. In the meantime, our own opinion is that nobody can embellish those nutty universe-shattering menaces like King Kirby can; and we just haven't the heart to stifle that awesome artistic imagination of his! Besides, *we* flip over that kind of yarn! But, que sera, sera!**

Dear Stan and Jack,

Although some fans seem to dislike your continued stories, I am grateful to you for printing them in the first place. These stories allow you time for plot and character development, which heightens the reader's interest in the story. Before I close, I must comment on F.F. #48, which concludes the adventure with the Inhumans. It was a great story, but I wasn't satisfied with the way Johnny Storm and Crystal were treated. Stan, whatever you do, those two must be reunited. Long live the M.M.M.S.

J. W. Goodwin, Jr., 2426 Belvedere
Wilmington, N. C.

**Amen, J. W.! And, as we told Phil Pearson elsewhere on this page, if you think we've forgotten about cuddly**

**Chris—don't believe it! We don't yet know where, when, or even how — but in the name of Ben's Aunt Petunia, we pledge that Johnny and Crystal will meet again! Unfortunately, we don't yet know whether it will be a happy or tragic meeting (not that we'd give it away if we *did* know!), but bear with us, and we'll find out together!**

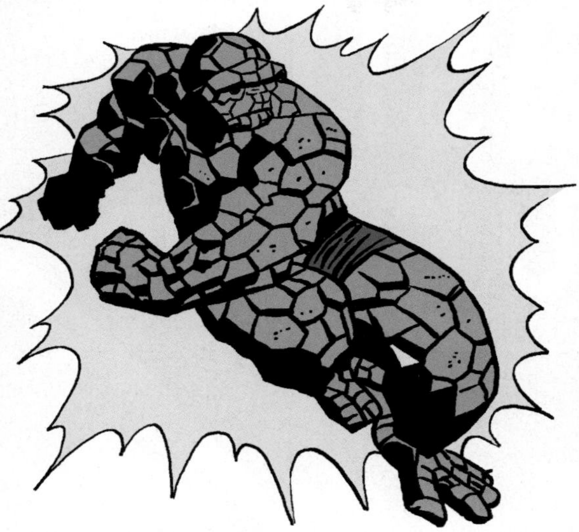

Dear Stan and Jack,

Three of us here at Haverford College have recently been overwhelmed by the astounding brilliance of the Hulk and his cohorts. As for the Fantastic Four, no words can express our awesome admiration at their amazing adventures. The three of us do a weekly rock'n'roll show on the campus radio station, WHRC. In a glorious attempt to add more prestige to our weekly performance and to appeal to the more cultured denizens of the college community, we have usurped the titles of our three favorite Marvel characters—the Hulk, the Human Torch, and Doctor Doom. Local consensus of opinion indicates that our show is definitely CLOBBERIN TIME. We praise and applaud the persistently powerful personality portraits which you potently promulgate in your perennially pandemonious paper. We pose a puzzler, however—what accounts for the gratuitous, garish, gross greenness of the Hulk? 'Nuff said! FLAME ON!

Dave "Torch" Wieck, John "Hulk" Stuart,
Vernon "Doom" Haskell
Haverford College, Haverford, Penna.

**So, you wanna know why our incredible, iconoclastic, inveterate rampager is green, eh? The answer happens to be simplicity itself, lads—think how silly he'd look if his skin was *purple!***

Dear Stan and Jack,

Just read FANTASTIC FOUR #49—excellent, as usual. The F.F. have come a long way. They've left the world of comics, and entered the world of pure fantasy—and I must say I love it! Ever since the Frightful Four incident started, and then the Inhumans (who *must* have their own mag), on down to Galactus . . . The F.F. have pioneered the world of science fiction. Like all your unique creations, they have a technique all their own, and it is unexcelled in the field of comic books—or in any form of literature. You may or may not realize it, but (in my unabashed opinion), you have created a team of super-heroes so different that they are the world's greatest science fiction creations, and I commend you, Stan, and you, Jack, for creating them.

Eugene Bearringer, 508 Eleanor
Toledo, Ohio

**We're sorry that your natural reticence has inhibited you somewhat so that you weren't able to be as effusive in your praise as you might otherwise have been, Gene—but we get the message anyway, pal—thanks a heap!**

Dear Stan and Jack,

I was just sitting here at my desk, and I thought I'd take a break from reading my F.F. mag by writing you a letter. Mainly, I want to say that I go ape over your use of photographs. Two other things—for the first time, in #48, one of your heroes needed a shave, and the "Silver Surfer" is a corny name. In some of your comics, I've seen you use full-page pictures. I like these very much, but I was wondering if you could make pictures the full length of the mag? Get what I mean? This way, the action pictures would be twice as good. Say, I dig your FANTASY MASTERPIECES magazine! That fab photo of ol' Stan gave me an idea. Since this magazine shows the early work of your artists, how about having a photo of one of these guys in every ish, telling about the stories?

Doug Nikkel, 43 Rainbow Dr.
Humboldt, Iowa

**Good idea, Doug. But, we can't do it every ish, or we'd run out of photos before you can say Yancy Street! However, we'll do it once in a while, shooting for the element of *surprise*, as usual! Y'know, it's a funny thing — about a half dozen liltin' letters so far have also referred to the Silver Surfer as a corny name. Yet, we can still remember how we patted each other on the back when we made it up—we thought it was an inspiration! It just goes to prove—the more you know, the more you realize how little you know! (But, darn it, we still think it's a groovy name!)**

Dear Stan and Jack,

Congratulations on a job well-done, referring to your complete line of Marvel Comics. My interest in comics, which dates back to 1940, lagged terribly till you fellows went to work in earnest: how your competitors must be tossing and turning at night, wondering what on earth happened. I wonder if they realize that a good share of their plight is as much their *own* fault as the "fault" of the fabulous Marvel staff! They were a lazy bunch, weren't they? They actually didn't give a fig for the readers; but look at them now!— letters pages , fancy blurbs, guest stars, the whole works. A great many heads must have rolled! Now, before I become too long-winded, I'd like to submit *my* suggestion list; something, undoubtedly, which you boys get mighty bored at receiving in the old mail bag . . . First, drop the westerns; you've far too much talent to waste on these. And second, you boys have the only limitless, unmatched—no pun intended—character in the field of comics with the Human Torch. Your competitors would simply go out of their minds trying to duplicate him. In fact, he can not be duplicated, much less imitated. I can see it now—each company desperately trying to outdo a magazine titled simply, THE HUMAN TORCH. They'd turn up with Fireball; the Flaming Being; Torchman; and heaven only knows what else. No kidding, the Human Torch, in a magazine of his own, would take the nation by storm, leaving the other companies limp. Third, you'd dazzle your readers, and gain a few thousand in the bargain, if you'd have a war between Sub-Mariner and the Human Torch. Conflict between these two is too much of a "natural" to be discarded, don't you agree? Lastly, it constantly amazes me to watch Captain America sail along with no change in uniform—I suspicion that you have a sentimental attachment to Cap. You fellows deserve many compliments, and, I observe on your letters pages, you're getting quite a few. Keep up the MARVELous work.

Donald J. Brown, 1407 Alexander
Colorado Springs, Colo.

**Thanks, Don. You've swelled our heads, inflated our egos, and given us eyestrain! So, the least we can do is tell you that we think THE HUMAN TORCH would be a great mag — and, if we ever get the time — who knows? But, till then—we *do* have a dozen or so other titles that we're still pushin'—and it won't make us the least bit angry if you buy *them* by the carload! See ya!**

NEXT ISH: Mighty Marvel does it again! You'll thrill to the origin of the Black Panther—and meet the astounding Mr. Klaw ! You'll cheer the spectacle and surprises from Stan and Jack at their imaginative best! And you'll be able to smile with satisfaction, in years to come, when they ask if you were a part of the magnificent, magical Marvel Age of Comics! So, don't miss the eerie excitement that awaits you in F.F. #53 — it's merely the greatest! 'Nuff said!

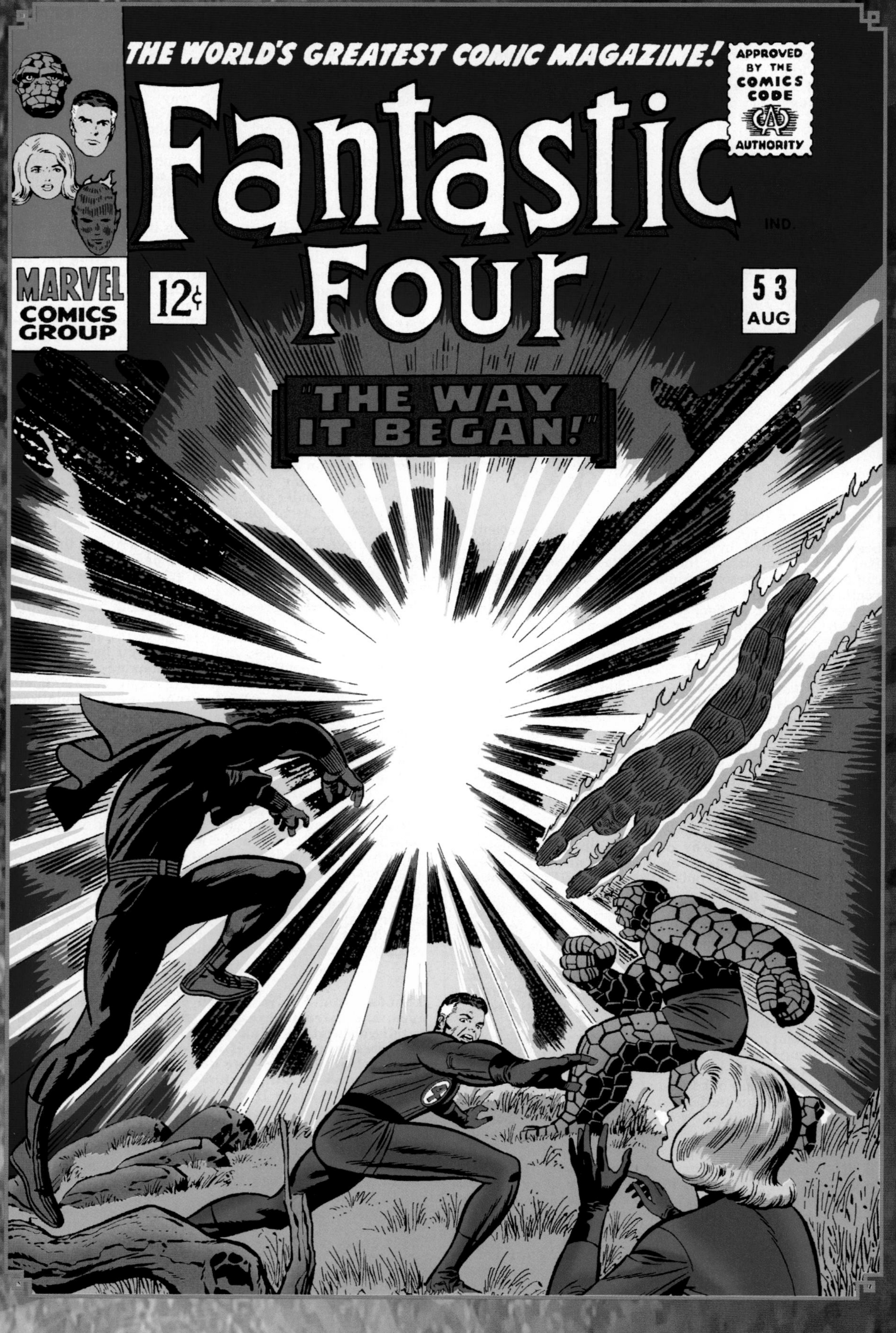
THE WORLD'S GREATEST COMIC MAGAZINE!
APPROVED BY THE COMICS CODE AUTHORITY
Fantastic Four
IND.
MARVEL COMICS GROUP
12¢
53 AUG
"THE WAY IT BEGAN!"

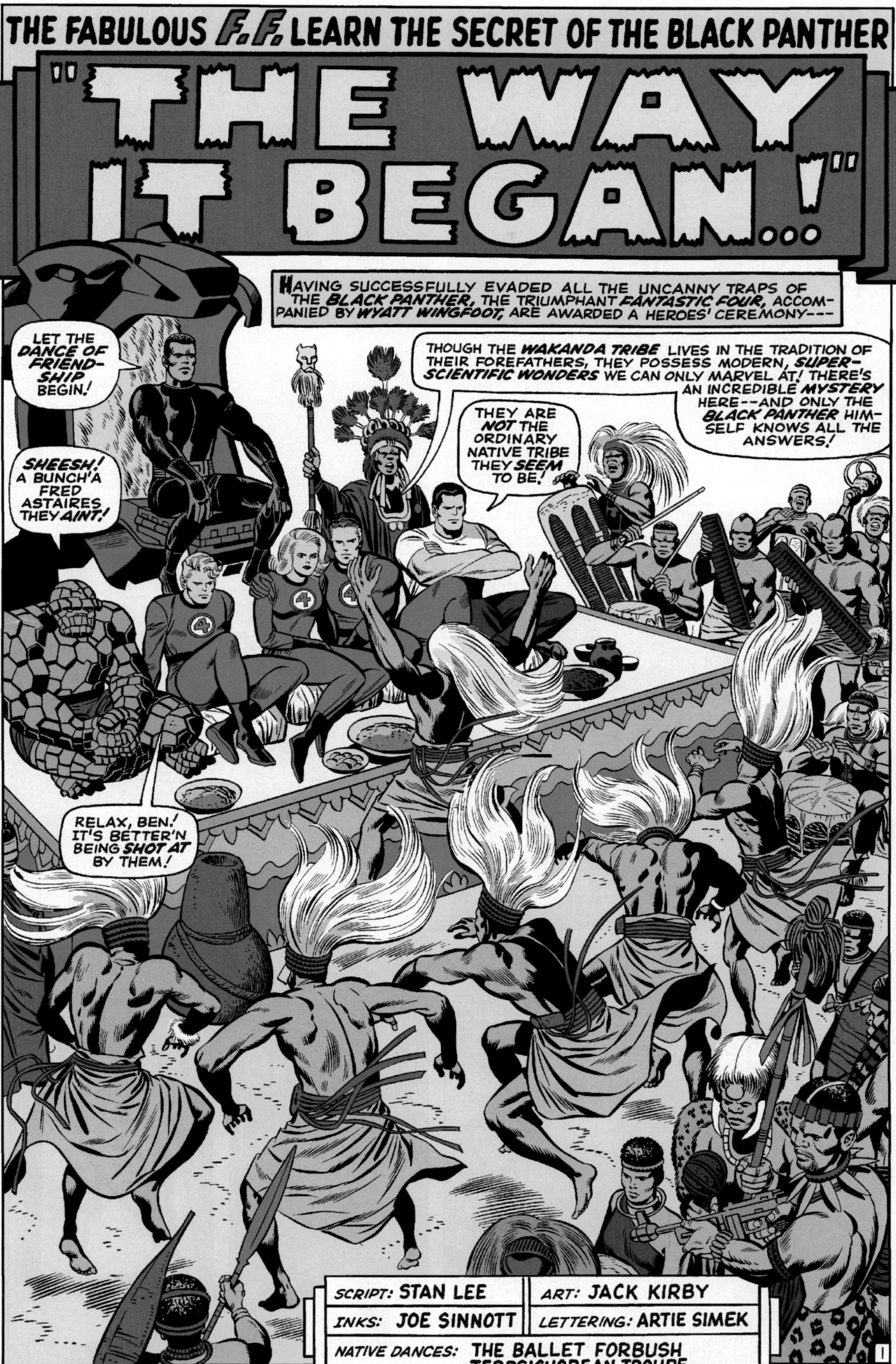
THE FABULOUS F.F. LEARN THE SECRET OF THE BLACK PANTHER
"THE WAY IT BEGAN...!"
HAVING SUCCESSFULLY EVADED ALL THE UNCANNY TRAPS OF THE BLACK PANTHER, THE TRIUMPHANT FANTASTIC FOUR, ACCOMPANIED BY WYATT WINGFOOT, ARE AWARDED A HEROES' CEREMONY---
LET THE DANCE OF FRIENDSHIP BEGIN!
THOUGH THE WAKANDA TRIBE LIVES IN THE TRADITION OF THEIR FOREFATHERS, THEY POSSESS MODERN, SUPER-SCIENTIFIC WONDERS WE CAN ONLY MARVEL AT! THERE'S AN INCREDIBLE MYSTERY HERE--AND ONLY THE BLACK PANTHER HIMSELF KNOWS ALL THE ANSWERS!
THEY ARE NOT THE ORDINARY NATIVE TRIBE THEY SEEM TO BE!
SHEESH! A BUNCH'A FRED ASTAIRES THEY AIN'T!
RELAX, BEN! IT'S BETTER'N BEING SHOT AT BY THEM!
SCRIPT: STAN LEE
ART: JACK KIRBY
INKS: JOE SINNOTT
LETTERING: ARTIE SIMEK
NATIVE DANCES: THE BALLET FORBUSH TERPSICHOREAN TROUPE
1

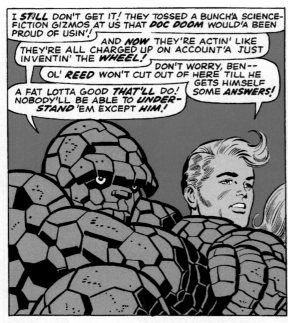

I **STILL** don't get it! They tossed a bunch'a science-fiction gizmos at us that **DOC DOOM** would'a been proud of usin'!

And **NOW** they're actin' like they're all charged up on account'a just inventin' the **WHEEL!**

Don't worry, Ben-- ol' **REED** won't cut out of here till he gets himself some **ANSWERS!**

A fat lotta good **THAT'LL** do! Nobody'll be able to **UNDER-STAND** 'em except **HIM!**

Awright, break it up--**BREAK IT UP!** What're ya all **GAPIN'** at, anyway?

Aintcha never seen a bashful, blue-eyed **THING** before?!!

**LET'S GO, BEN!** The Black Panther is inviting us to his **PRIVATE QUARTERS!**

**WOW!** Wotta pad! I'll bet even Hugh Hefner couldn't improve on **THIS** layout!

**MAN!** If ya **GOTTA** live in the jungle, this sure is the way ta **DO** it! There must be a lotta **DOUGH** in Black Pantherin'!

Still **ANOTHER** example of the old and the new, darling! Look at that elaborate **STEREO** music system--complete with **TAPE RECORDER!**

I just can't **BELIEVE** we're in the heart of the jungle!

My guests and I do not wish to be disturbed!

You seem **PUZZLED** by what you have seen! You **SHOULDN'T** be!

After all, I can **AFFORD** to pamper myself--to indulge my every whim-- enjoy every luxury! I'm one of the **RICHEST MEN** in the world!

Remember, I've seen, I **BELIEVE** you! But, there's **MORE** to your story than mere **WEALTH**--

You are **PERCEPTIVE** indeed, Richards!

Actually, the Black Panther lives under a tragic **CURSE!**

But, my tale really begins with the spear and shield of my father--**T'CHAKA,** the warrior king!

2

BUT, EVEN AS THE DRAMATIC **BLACK PANTHER** BEGINS HIS REVELATION, TWO MEMBERS OF THE **TERRITORIAL PATROL** COME UPON A STAGGERING DISCOVERY--

THE ENTIRE AREA SEEMS TO HAVE BEEN *RIPPED UP*-- AS THOUGH BY *GIANT HANDS!* THERE ARE NO ANIMALS--NO BIRDS!! EVERY FORM OF LIFE HAS BEEN *FRIGHTENED AWAY!*

AND THESE HOLES IN THE GROUND-- IMPOSSIBLE THOUGH IT SEEMS, THEY CAN ONLY BE *TRACKS*-- THE FOOTPRINTS OF SOME *GARGANTUAN* CREATURE!

CAN IT BE THAT THE RUMORS OF MONSTROUS BEASTS ROAMING THE JUNGLE ARE *TRUE?!!*

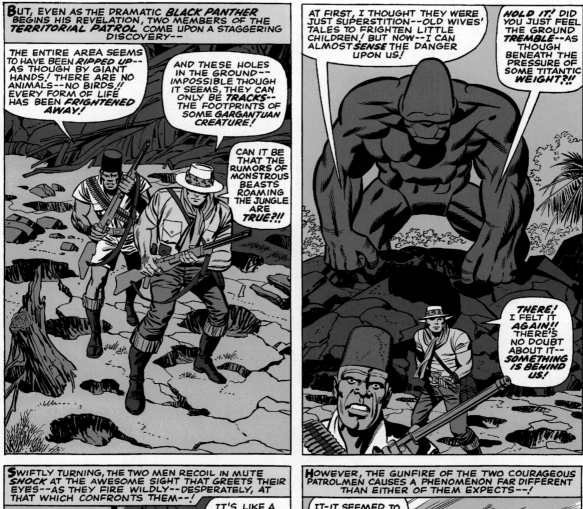

AT FIRST, I THOUGHT THEY WERE JUST SUPERSTITION--OLD WIVES' TALES TO FRIGHTEN LITTLE CHILDREN! BUT NOW--I CAN ALMOST *SENSE* THE DANGER UPON US!

*HOLD IT!* DID YOU JUST FEEL THE GROUND *TREMBLE*--AS THOUGH BENEATH THE PRESSURE OF SOME *TITANIC WEIGHT?!!*

*THERE!* I FELT IT *AGAIN!!* THERE'S NO DOUBT ABOUT IT-- SOMETHING IS BEHIND US!

SWIFTLY TURNING, THE TWO MEN RECOIL IN MUTE *SHOCK* AT THE AWESOME SIGHT THAT GREETS THEIR EYES--AS THEY FIRE WILDLY--DESPERATELY, AT THAT WHICH CONFRONTS THEM--!

IT'S LIKE A GIGANTIC *GORILLA*--AN UNBELIEVABLE CRIMSON ANTHROPOID!!

CRAK!

CRAK

KEEP FIRING! OUR ONLY CHANCE IS TO FRIGHTEN HIM AWAY WITH OUR GUNSHOTS!! IT'S *TOO LATE* TO RUN!

HOWEVER, THE GUNFIRE OF THE TWO COURAGEOUS PATROLMEN CAUSES A PHENOMENON FAR *DIFFERENT* THAN EITHER OF THEM EXPECTS--!

IT--IT SEEMED TO *EXPLODE*--RIGHT BEFORE OUR EYES!!

IT'S IMPOSSIBLE! IT *CAN'T BE*--!

AND YET-- *I* SAW IT, TOO!

3

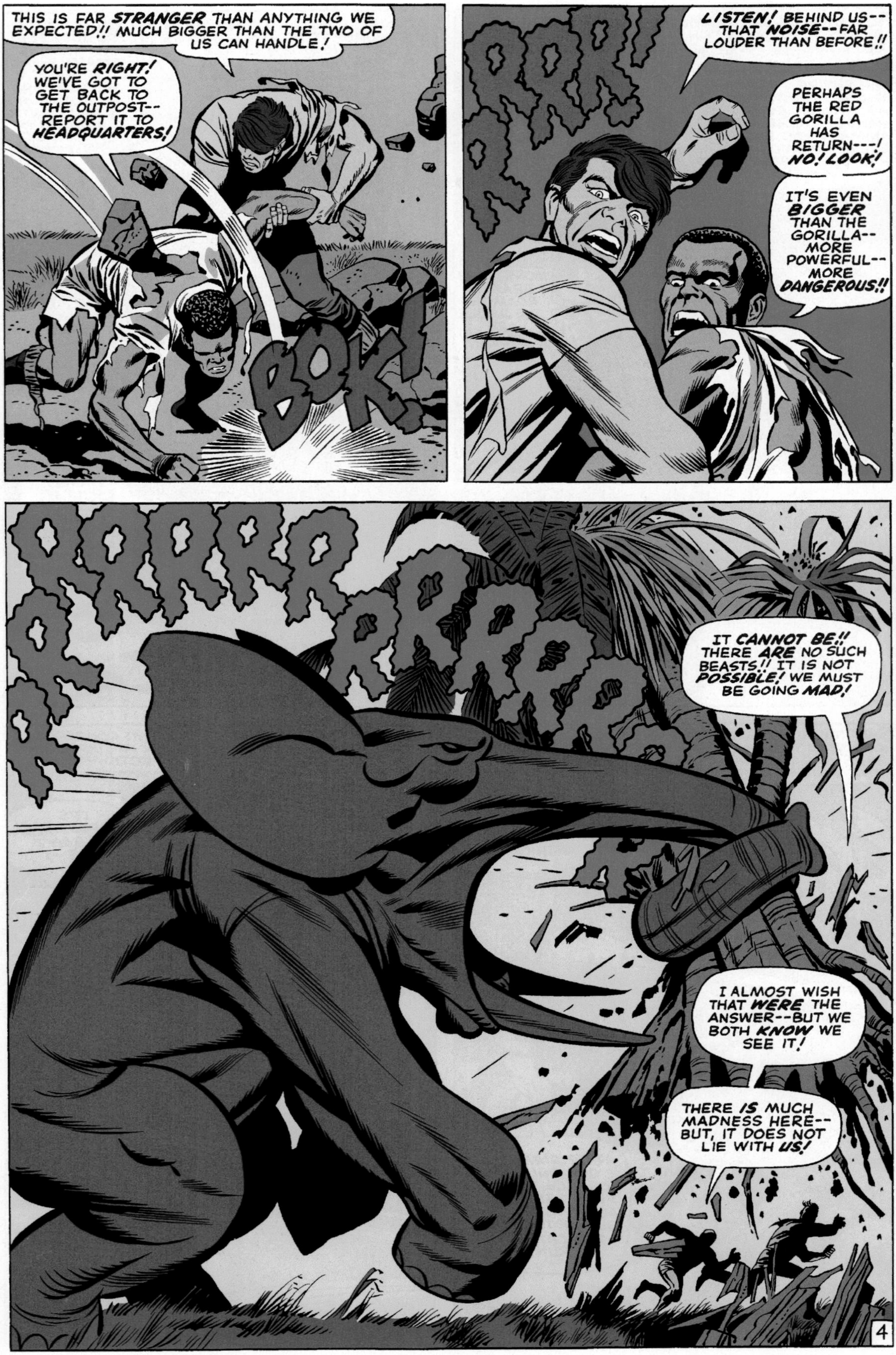

THIS IS FAR STRANGER THAN ANYTHING WE EXPECTED!! MUCH BIGGER THAN THE TWO OF US CAN HANDLE!
YOU'RE RIGHT! WE'VE GOT TO GET BACK TO THE OUTPOST--REPORT IT TO HEADQUARTERS!
BOK!
LISTEN! BEHIND US--THAT NOISE--FAR LOUDER THAN BEFORE!!
PERHAPS THE RED GORILLA HAS RETURN---! NO! LOOK!
IT'S EVEN BIGGER THAN THE GORILLA--MORE POWERFUL--MORE DANGEROUS!!
IT CANNOT BE!! THERE ARE NO SUCH BEASTS!! IT IS NOT POSSIBLE! WE MUST BE GOING MAD!
I ALMOST WISH THAT WERE THE ANSWER--BUT WE BOTH KNOW WE SEE IT!
THERE IS MUCH MADNESS HERE--BUT, IT DOES NOT LIE WITH US!

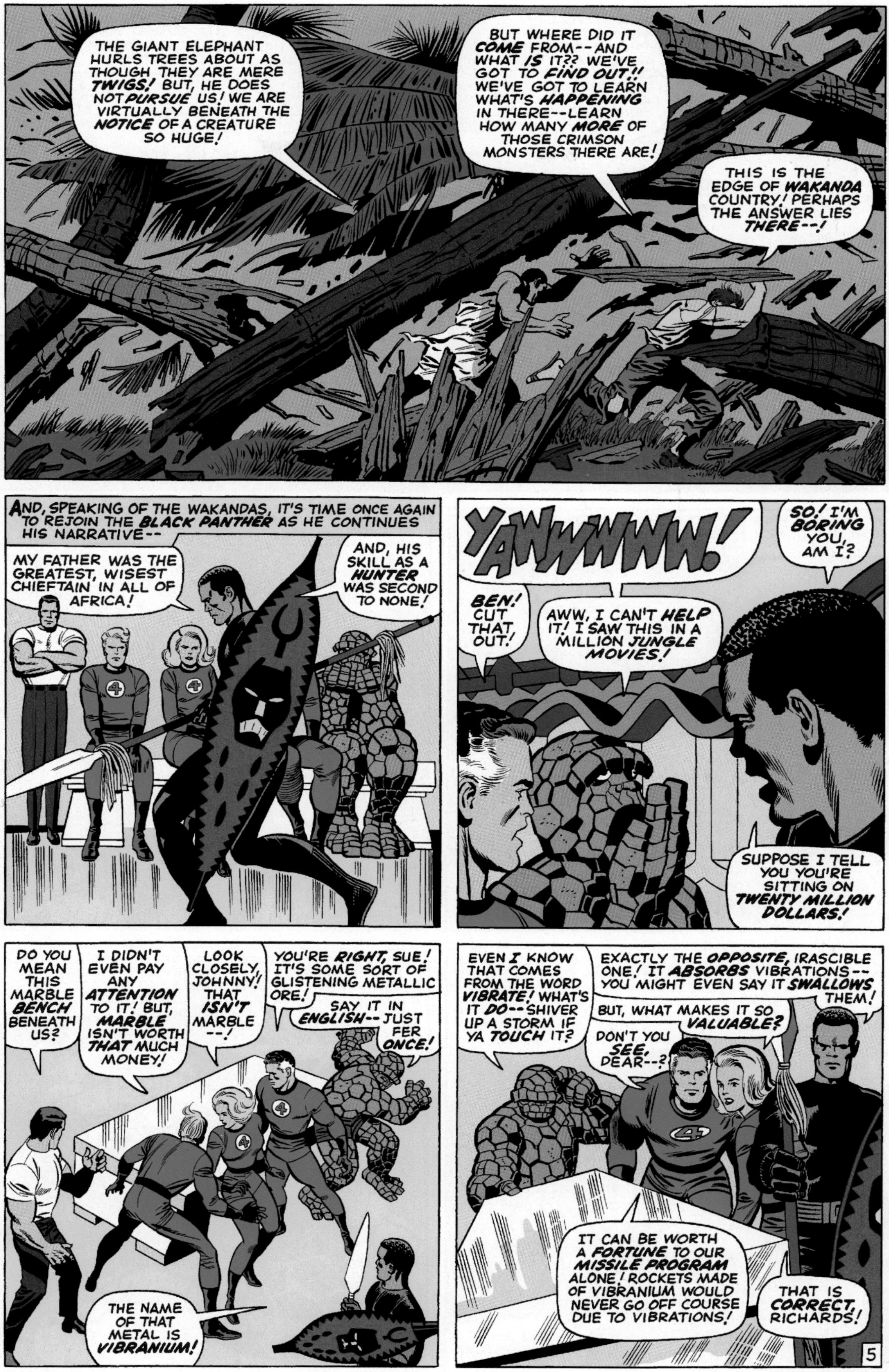

THE GIANT ELEPHANT HURLS TREES ABOUT AS THOUGH THEY ARE MERE TWIGS! BUT, HE DOES NOT PURSUE US! WE ARE VIRTUALLY BENEATH THE NOTICE OF A CREATURE SO HUGE!
BUT WHERE DID IT COME FROM--AND WHAT IS IT?? WE'VE GOT TO FIND OUT!! WE'VE GOT TO LEARN WHAT'S HAPPENING IN THERE--LEARN HOW MANY MORE OF THOSE CRIMSON MONSTERS THERE ARE!
THIS IS THE EDGE OF WAKANDA COUNTRY! PERHAPS THE ANSWER LIES THERE--!
AND, SPEAKING OF THE WAKANDAS, IT'S TIME ONCE AGAIN TO REJOIN THE BLACK PANTHER AS HE CONTINUES HIS NARRATIVE--
MY FATHER WAS THE GREATEST, WISEST CHIEFTAIN IN ALL OF AFRICA!
AND, HIS SKILL AS A HUNTER WAS SECOND TO NONE!
YAWWWWW!
SO! I'M BORING YOU, AM I?
BEN! CUT THAT, OUT!
AWW, I CAN'T HELP IT! I SAW THIS IN A MILLION JUNGLE MOVIES!
SUPPOSE I TELL YOU YOU'RE SITTING ON TWENTY MILLION DOLLARS!
DO YOU MEAN THIS MARBLE BENCH BENEATH US?
I DIDN'T EVEN PAY ANY ATTENTION TO IT! BUT, MARBLE ISN'T WORTH THAT MUCH MONEY!
LOOK CLOSELY, JOHNNY! THAT ISN'T MARBLE--!
YOU'RE RIGHT, SUE! IT'S SOME SORT OF GLISTENING METALLIC ORE!
SAY IT IN ENGLISH--JUST FER ONCE!
THE NAME OF THAT METAL IS VIBRANIUM!
EVEN I KNOW THAT COMES FROM THE WORD VIBRATE! WHAT'S IT DO--SHIVER UP A STORM IF YA TOUCH IT?
EXACTLY THE OPPOSITE, IRASCIBLE ONE! IT ABSORBS VIBRATIONS--YOU MIGHT EVEN SAY IT SWALLOWS THEM!
BUT, WHAT MAKES IT SO VALUABLE?
DON'T YOU SEE, DEAR--?
IT CAN BE WORTH A FORTUNE TO OUR MISSILE PROGRAM ALONE! ROCKETS MADE OF VIBRANIUM WOULD NEVER GO OFF COURSE DUE TO VIBRATIONS!
THAT IS CORRECT, RICHARDS!
5

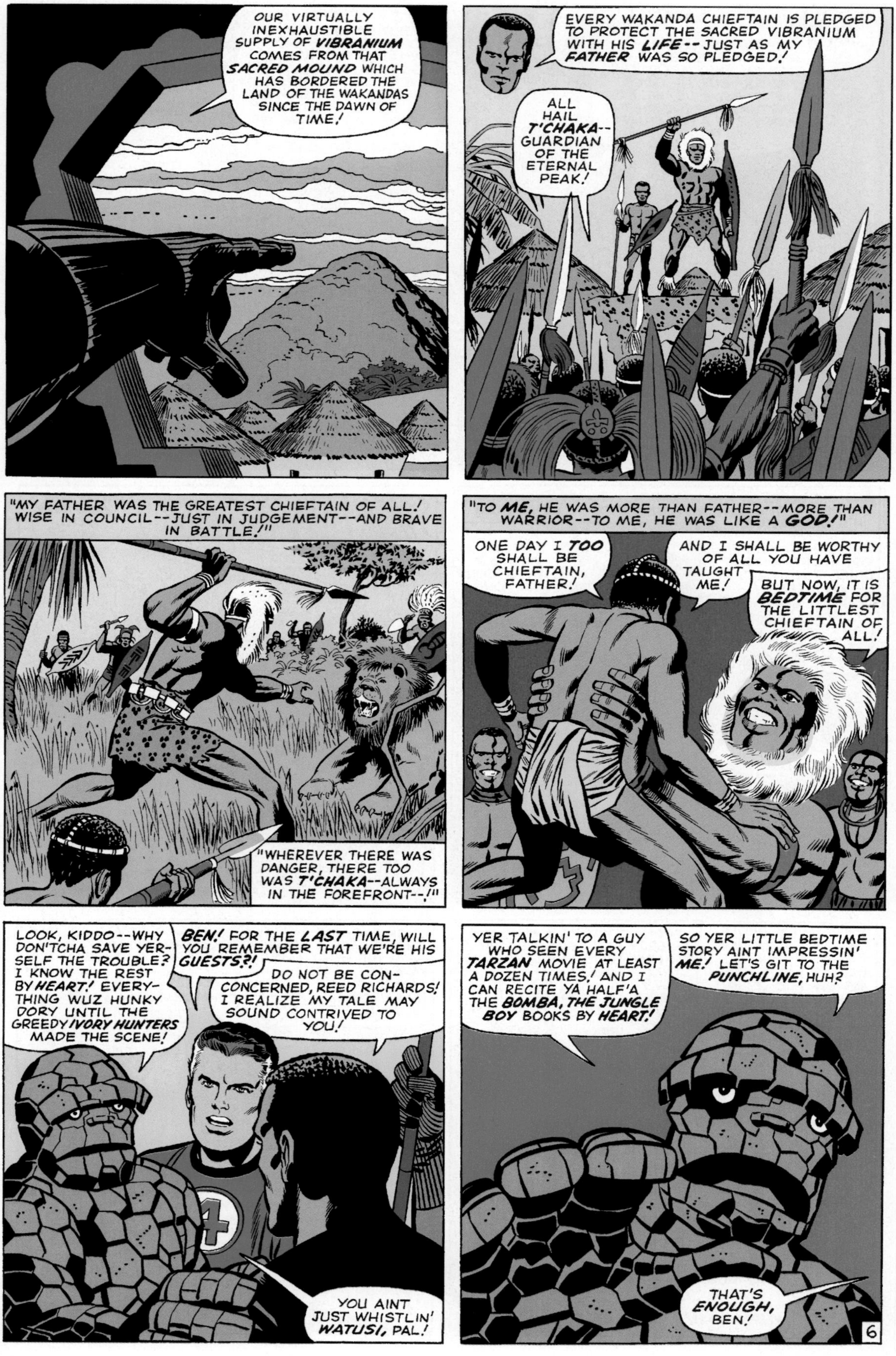

OUR VIRTUALLY INEXHAUSTIBLE SUPPLY OF VIBRANIUM COMES FROM THAT SACRED MOUND WHICH HAS BORDERED THE LAND OF THE WAKANDAS SINCE THE DAWN OF TIME!
EVERY WAKANDA CHIEFTAIN IS PLEDGED TO PROTECT THE SACRED VIBRANIUM WITH HIS LIFE--JUST AS MY FATHER WAS SO PLEDGED!
ALL HAIL T'CHAKA--GUARDIAN OF THE ETERNAL PEAK!
"MY FATHER WAS THE GREATEST CHIEFTAIN OF ALL! WISE IN COUNCIL--JUST IN JUDGEMENT--AND BRAVE IN BATTLE!"
"WHEREVER THERE WAS DANGER, THERE TOO WAS T'CHAKA--ALWAYS IN THE FOREFRONT--!"
"TO ME, HE WAS MORE THAN FATHER--MORE THAN WARRIOR--TO ME, HE WAS LIKE A GOD!"
ONE DAY I TOO SHALL BE CHIEFTAIN, FATHER!
AND I SHALL BE WORTHY OF ALL YOU HAVE TAUGHT ME!
BUT NOW, IT IS BEDTIME FOR THE LITTLEST CHIEFTAIN OF ALL!
LOOK, KIDDO--WHY DON'TCHA SAVE YERSELF THE TROUBLE? I KNOW THE REST BY HEART! EVERYTHING WUZ HUNKY DORY UNTIL THE GREEDY IVORY HUNTERS MADE THE SCENE!
BEN! FOR THE LAST TIME, WILL YOU REMEMBER THAT WE'RE HIS GUESTS?!
DO NOT BE CONCERNED, REED RICHARDS! I REALIZE MY TALE MAY SOUND CONTRIVED TO YOU!
YOU AINT JUST WHISTLIN' WATUSI, PAL!
YER TALKIN' TO A GUY WHO SEEN EVERY TARZAN MOVIE AT LEAST A DOZEN TIMES! AND I CAN RECITE YA HALF'A THE BOMBA, THE JUNGLE BOY BOOKS BY HEART!
SO YER LITTLE BEDTIME STORY AINT IMPRESSIN' ME! LET'S GIT TO THE PUNCHLINE, HUH?
THAT'S ENOUGH, BEN!
6

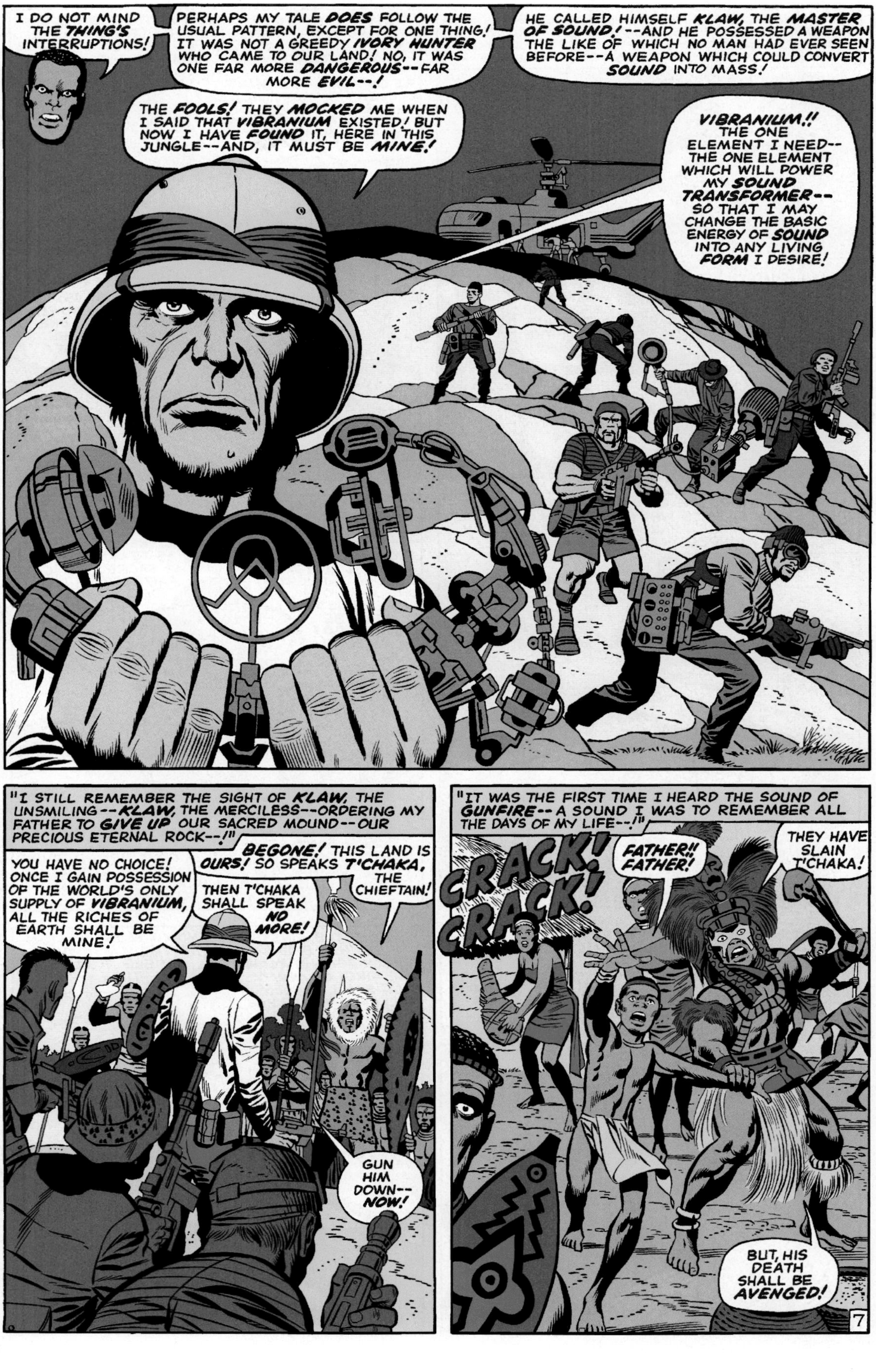
I DO NOT MIND THE THING'S INTERRUPTIONS!
PERHAPS MY TALE DOES FOLLOW THE USUAL PATTERN, EXCEPT FOR ONE THING! IT WAS NOT A GREEDY IVORY HUNTER WHO CAME TO OUR LAND! NO, IT WAS ONE FAR MORE DANGEROUS--FAR MORE EVIL--!
HE CALLED HIMSELF KLAW, THE MASTER OF SOUND! --AND HE POSSESSED A WEAPON THE LIKE OF WHICH NO MAN HAD EVER SEEN BEFORE--A WEAPON WHICH COULD CONVERT SOUND INTO MASS!
THE FOOLS! THEY MOCKED ME WHEN I SAID THAT VIBRANIUM EXISTED! BUT NOW I HAVE FOUND IT, HERE IN THIS JUNGLE--AND, IT MUST BE MINE!
VIBRANIUM!! THE ONE ELEMENT I NEED--THE ONE ELEMENT WHICH WILL POWER MY SOUND TRANSFORMER--SO THAT I MAY CHANGE THE BASIC ENERGY OF SOUND INTO ANY LIVING FORM I DESIRE!
"I STILL REMEMBER THE SIGHT OF KLAW, THE UNSMILING--KLAW, THE MERCILESS--ORDERING MY FATHER TO GIVE UP OUR SACRED MOUND--OUR PRECIOUS ETERNAL ROCK--!"
YOU HAVE NO CHOICE! ONCE I GAIN POSSESSION OF THE WORLD'S ONLY SUPPLY OF VIBRANIUM, ALL THE RICHES OF EARTH SHALL BE MINE!
BEGONE! THIS LAND IS OURS! SO SPEAKS T'CHAKA, THE CHIEFTAIN!
THEN T'CHAKA SHALL SPEAK NO MORE!
GUN HIM DOWN--NOW!
"IT WAS THE FIRST TIME I HEARD THE SOUND OF GUNFIRE--A SOUND I WAS TO REMEMBER ALL THE DAYS OF MY LIFE--!"
CRACK! CRACK!
FATHER!! FATHER!
THEY HAVE SLAIN T'CHAKA!
BUT, HIS DEATH SHALL BE AVENGED!
7

"I, WHO HAD LIVED IN THE JUNGLE SINCE BIRTH, HAD NEVER SEEN SUCH VIOLENCE AS I BEHELD THAT MOMENT--WHILE THE MACHINE-GUN FIRE OF KLAW FELL UPON OUR WARRIORS WITHOUT MERCY--!"

WE ARE HELPLESS BEFORE THE WITHERING FIRE OF THE INVADERS!!

FLEE, MY BRAVE ONES-- FLEE! WE MUST LIVE TO FIGHT ANOTHER DAY!

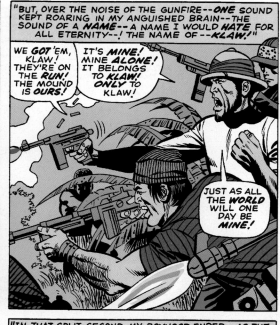

"BUT, OVER THE NOISE OF THE GUNFIRE--ONE SOUND KEPT ROARING IN MY ANGUISHED BRAIN--THE SOUND OF A NAME--A NAME I WOULD HATE FOR ALL ETERNITY--! THE NAME OF--KLAW!"

WE GOT 'EM, KLAW! THEY'RE ON THE RUN! THE MOUND IS OURS!

IT'S MINE! MINE ALONE! IT BELONGS TO KLAW! ONLY TO KLAW!

JUST AS ALL THE WORLD WILL ONE DAY BE MINE!

"SECONDS LATER, THE FIRING HAD CEASED--BUT, THE DEADLY SILENCE WHICH FOLLOWED WAS MORE DEAFENING--MORE FRAUGHT WITH DREAD--THAN ALL THE THUNDER THAT HAD GONE BEFORE!"

FATHER!

MY FATHER--!

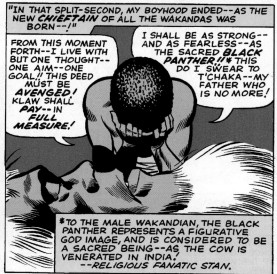

"IN THAT SPLIT-SECOND, MY BOYHOOD ENDED--AS THE NEW CHIEFTAIN OF ALL THE WAKANDAS WAS BORN--!"

FROM THIS MOMENT FORTH--I LIVE WITH BUT ONE THOUGHT-- ONE AIM--ONE GOAL!! THIS DEED MUST BE AVENGED! KLAW SHALL PAY--IN FULL MEASURE!

I SHALL BE AS STRONG-- AND AS FEARLESS--AS THE SACRED BLACK PANTHER!!* THIS DO I SWEAR TO T'CHAKA--MY FATHER WHO IS NO MORE!

*TO THE MALE WAKANDIAN, THE BLACK PANTHER REPRESENTS A FIGURATIVE GOD IMAGE, AND IS CONSIDERED TO BE A SACRED BEING--AS THE COW IS VENERATED IN INDIA! --RELIGIOUS FANATIC STAN.

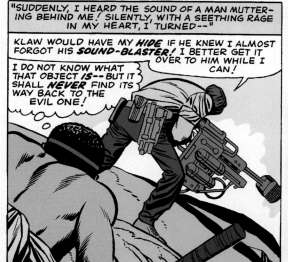

"SUDDENLY, I HEARD THE SOUND OF A MAN MUTTER- ING BEHIND ME! SILENTLY, WITH A SEETHING RAGE IN MY HEART, I TURNED--"

KLAW WOULD HAVE MY HIDE IF HE KNEW I ALMOST FORGOT HIS SOUND-BLASTER! I BETTER GET IT OVER TO HIM WHILE I CAN!

I DO NOT KNOW WHAT THAT OBJECT IS--BUT IT SHALL NEVER FIND ITS WAY BACK TO THE EVIL ONE!

THERE! THE FIRST BLOW HAS BEEN STRUCK AGAINST KLAW! THE FIRST OF MANY THAT SHALL ENDLESSLY FOLLOW, UNTIL HE HAS BEEN COMPLETELY DESTROYED!

NOW I MUST HASTEN AFTER HIM--WHILE THERE STILL IS TIME--!

8

"FINDING THE STRANGE WEAPON SURPRISINGLY LIGHT IN WEIGHT, I LIFTED IT, CARRYING IT WITH ME, UNTIL I REACHED THE GATES OF OUR VILLAGE, WHERE MY EYES BEHELD KLAW'S FINAL ACT OF VILLAINY--!"

MY *PEOPLE*-- FLEEING FOR THEIR *LIVES*!! OUR VILLAGE IN *FLAMES*!!

THIS IS NO *MAN* I SEEK TO BATTLE!! TRULY, HE IS *EVIL INCARNATE*!! HIS VERY PRESENCE BEFOULS THE EARTH UPON WHICH HE STANDS!

*OUT!* DRIVE THEM *OUT!* THE MOUND OF *VIBRANIUM* MUST BELONG TO *KLAW!* ONLY *I* AM DESTINED TO BE SUPREME! ONLY *I* AM *MASTER OF SOUND!*

"WITHOUT CONSCIOUS THOUGHT, I AIMED THE FEARSOME OBJECT IN MY ARMS DIRECTLY AHEAD OF ME --WHILE MY FINGER BEGAN TO TIGHTEN ON THE TRIGGER, AS I CRIED--"

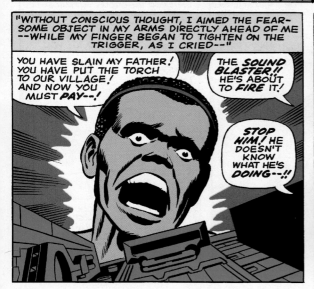

YOU HAVE SLAIN MY FATHER! YOU HAVE PUT THE TORCH TO OUR VILLAGE! AND NOW YOU MUST *PAY*--!

THE *SOUND BLASTER!!* HE'S ABOUT TO *FIRE* IT!

STOP *HIM!* HE DOESN'T KNOW WHAT HE'S *DOING*--!!

TOO *LATE!* HE *DETONATED* IT!

IT WAS AN *ACCIDENT!* HE DOESN'T EVEN KNOW HOW TO *AIM* IT! THE SHOT FELL *SHORT!*

I'LL MAKE SURE HE GETS *NO* SECOND CHANCE!

*ZAK!*

YOU LITTLE *FOOL!* YOU CANNOT REALIZE THE *FORCES* YOU ARE TAMPERING WITH! THE DEVICE YOU HOLD CONVERTS *SOUND* INTO PURE *ENERGY!* IN THE WRONG HANDS, IT CAN WREAK UNMENTION-ABLE *HAVOC!!*

*YOURS* ARE THE HANDS THAT ARE WRONG, EVIL ONE--NOT *MINE!*

LOOK OUT! HE'S GONNA FIRE AGAIN!

THE LITTLE *SAVAGE* WOULDN'T *DARE!*

I *SEE* YOU STARTING TO *SQUEEZE* YOUR TRIGGER! BUT, YOU ARE *TOO LATE*--!

*THIS* IS FOR T'CHAKA-- THE WARRIOR KING!

MY *HAND!*

*ZAK!*

9

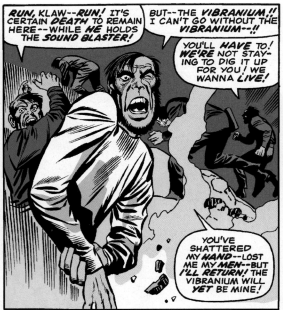

RUN, KLAW--RUN! IT'S CERTAIN DEATH TO REMAIN HERE--WHILE HE HOLDS THE SOUND BLASTER!

BUT--THE VIBRANIUM!! I CAN'T GO WITHOUT THE VIBRANIUM--!!

YOU'LL HAVE TO! WE'RE NOT STAYING TO DIG IT UP FOR YOU! WE WANNA LIVE!

YOU'VE SHATTERED MY HAND--LOST ME MY MEN--BUT I'LL RETURN! THE VIBRANIUM WILL YET BE MINE!

THAT WAS TEN YEARS AGO--TO THE DAY!

I COULD NOT THEN PURSUE HIM, FOR THE SHOCK OF FIRING THOSE TWO MIGHTY BURSTS HAD DRAINED MY YOUTHFUL STRENGTH!

BUT, I KNOW HE WILL RETURN--I CAN SENSE THAT THE TIME HAS COME!

Y'KNOW-- THAT STORY'S JUST PLAIN NUTTY ENUFF TO BE TRUE!

AND THIS TIME--I SHALL BE READY!

IT IS TRUE! I SOLD SMALL PORTIONS OF VIBRANIUM TO VARIOUS SCIENTIFIC FOUNDATIONS, ENABLING ME TO AMASS A FORTUNE--THE EQUAL OF ANY ON EARTH!

SO THAT'S HOW YA COULD AFFORD THAT FAR-OUT MECHANIZED JUNGLE OF YOURS!

THAT? I JUST DID IT FOR A LARK!

IT WAS A SIMPLE EXERCISE, TO TEST MY SKILL--FOR I HAD ATTENDED THE FINE UNIVERSITIES OF BOTH HEMISPHERES!

HOW ABOUT YER PANTHER POWER-- THE WAY YA SEE IN THE DARK, 'N STUFF--!

A SECRET-- HANDED DOWN FROM CHIEFTAIN TO CHIEFTAIN!

WE EAT CERTAIN HERBS--AND UNDERGO RIGOROUS RITUALS--OF WHICH I AM FORBIDDEN TO SPEAK!

BUT, WHY THE HECK DIDJA TRY TO TRAP US?!!

I HAD TO! YOU FOUR WERE THE SUPREME TEST!

IF I COULD FIGHT YOU TO A STANDSTILL, THEN I AM READY FOR-- KLAW!

ALTHOUGH HE HAS KEPT HIDDEN FROM ME ALL THESE YEARS, I KNOW HE IS PLANNING TO--

WAIT!!

IT HAS COME! THE LONG AWAITED, CRITICAL DANGER SIGNAL!!

WHEEE WHEEEEE WHEEEEE WHEEEE

CLICK

NOW WHAT?

WOTTA DEAL! YA MOVE ONE OF THEM CRAZY PANTHER STATUES, AND THE WHOLE BLASTED WALL SLIDES BACK!

QUIET! THIS SENSA-SCOPE IS RECORDING THE APPROACH OF A NAMELESS MENACE --FROM THE DIRECTION OF OUR SACRED MOUND!

KLAW HAS RETURNED!

10

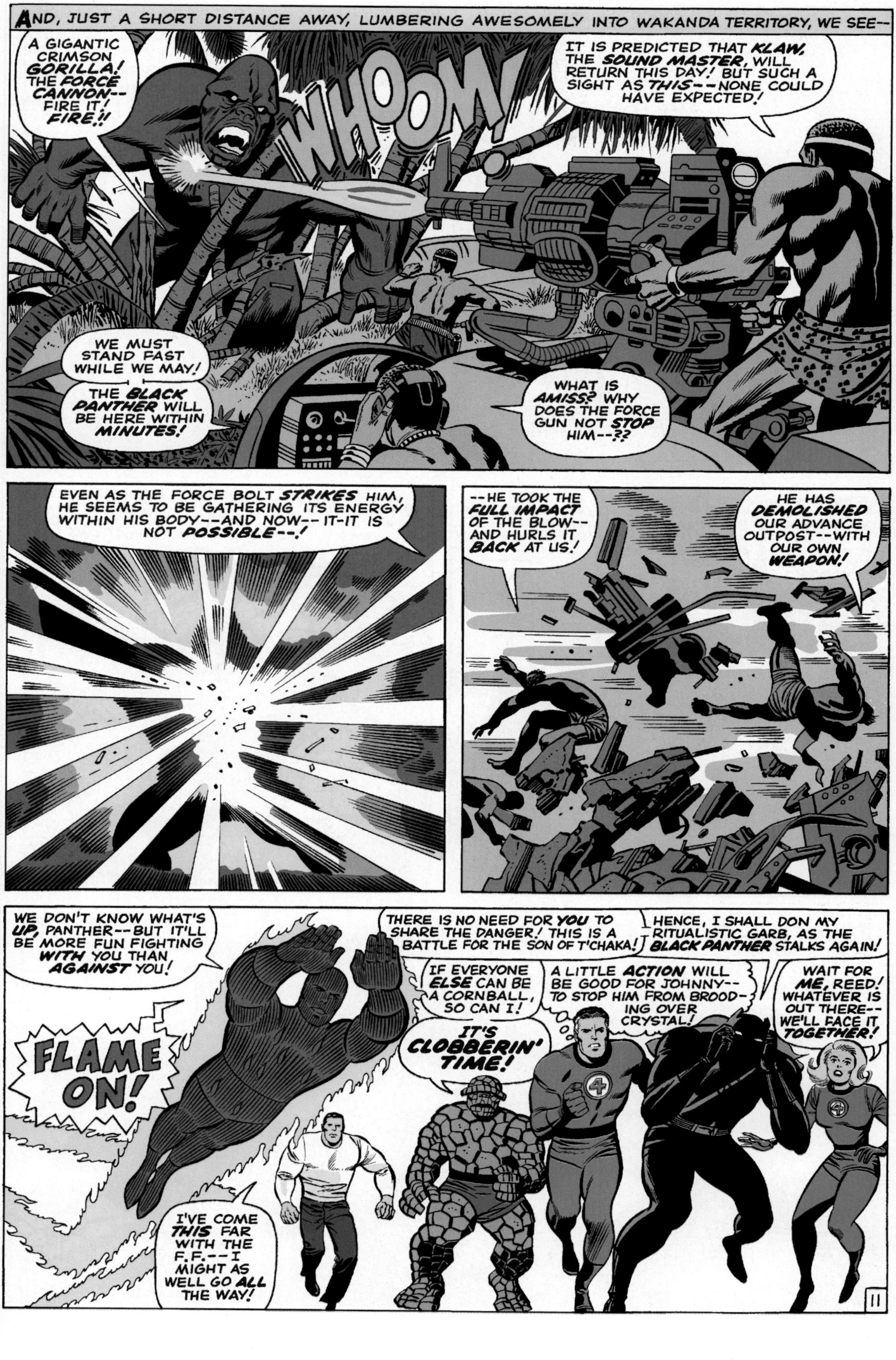
AND, JUST A SHORT DISTANCE AWAY, LUMBERING AWESOMELY INTO WAKANDA TERRITORY, WE SEE--
A GIGANTIC CRIMSON GORILLA! THE FORCE CANNON-- FIRE IT! FIRE!!
WHOOM!
IT IS PREDICTED THAT KLAW, THE SOUND MASTER, WILL RETURN THIS DAY! BUT SUCH A SIGHT AS THIS--NONE COULD HAVE EXPECTED!
WE MUST STAND FAST WHILE WE MAY!
THE BLACK PANTHER WILL BE HERE WITHIN MINUTES!
WHAT IS AMISS? WHY DOES THE FORCE GUN NOT STOP HIM--??
EVEN AS THE FORCE BOLT STRIKES HIM, HE SEEMS TO BE GATHERING ITS ENERGY WITHIN HIS BODY--AND NOW-- IT-IT IS NOT POSSIBLE--!
--HE TOOK THE FULL IMPACT OF THE BLOW-- AND HURLS IT BACK AT US!
HE HAS DEMOLISHED OUR ADVANCE OUTPOST--WITH OUR OWN WEAPON!
WE DON'T KNOW WHAT'S UP, PANTHER--BUT IT'LL BE MORE FUN FIGHTING WITH YOU THAN AGAINST YOU!
THERE IS NO NEED FOR YOU TO SHARE THE DANGER! THIS IS A BATTLE FOR THE SON OF T'CHAKA!
HENCE, I SHALL DON MY RITUALISTIC GARB, AS THE BLACK PANTHER STALKS AGAIN!
IF EVERYONE ELSE CAN BE A CORNBALL, SO CAN I!
A LITTLE ACTION WILL BE GOOD FOR JOHNNY-- TO STOP HIM FROM BROOD-ING OVER CRYSTAL!
WAIT FOR ME, REED! WHATEVER IS OUT THERE-- WE'LL FACE IT TOGETHER!
FLAME ON!
IT'S CLOBBERIN' TIME!
I'VE COME THIS FAR WITH THE F.F.--I MIGHT AS WELL GO ALL THE WAY!
11

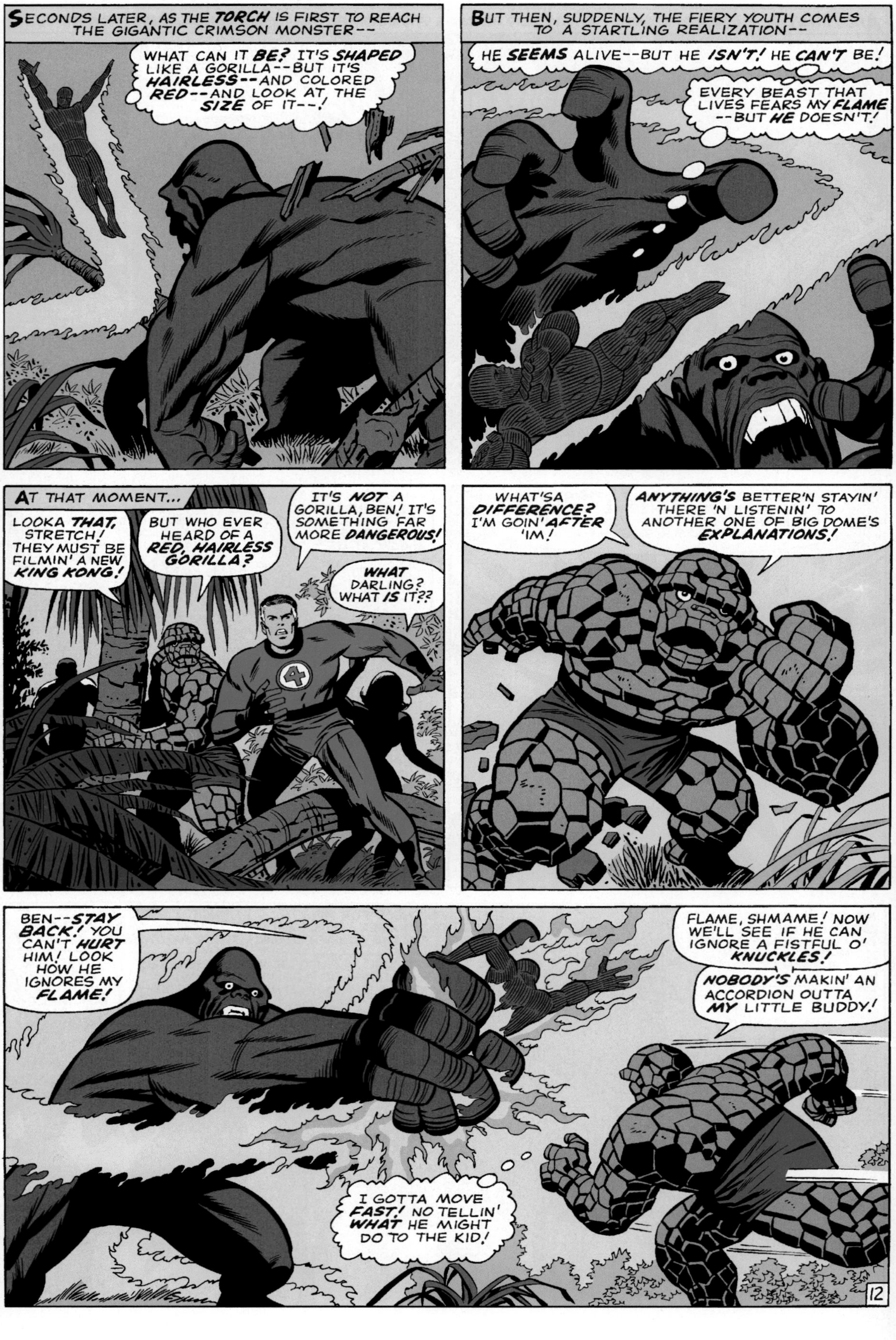
SECONDS LATER, AS THE TORCH IS FIRST TO REACH THE GIGANTIC CRIMSON MONSTER--
WHAT CAN IT BE? IT'S SHAPED LIKE A GORILLA--BUT IT'S HAIRLESS--AND COLORED RED--AND LOOK AT THE SIZE OF IT--!
BUT THEN, SUDDENLY, THE FIERY YOUTH COMES TO A STARTLING REALIZATION--
HE SEEMS ALIVE--BUT HE ISN'T! HE CAN'T BE!
EVERY BEAST THAT LIVES FEARS MY FLAME--BUT HE DOESN'T!
AT THAT MOMENT...
LOOKA THAT, STRETCH! THEY MUST BE FILMIN' A NEW KING KONG!
BUT WHO EVER HEARD OF A RED, HAIRLESS GORILLA?
IT'S NOT A GORILLA, BEN! IT'S SOMETHING FAR MORE DANGEROUS!
WHAT DARLING? WHAT IS IT??
WHAT'SA DIFFERENCE? I'M GOIN' AFTER 'IM!
ANYTHING'S BETTER'N STAYIN' THERE 'N LISTENIN' TO ANOTHER ONE OF BIG DOME'S EXPLANATIONS!
BEN--STAY BACK! YOU CAN'T HURT HIM! LOOK HOW HE IGNORES MY FLAME!
FLAME, SHMAME! NOW WE'LL SEE IF HE CAN IGNORE A FISTFUL O' KNUCKLES!
NOBODY'S MAKIN' AN ACCORDION OUTTA MY LITTLE BUDDY!
I GOTTA MOVE FAST! NO TELLIN' WHAT HE MIGHT DO TO THE KID!
12

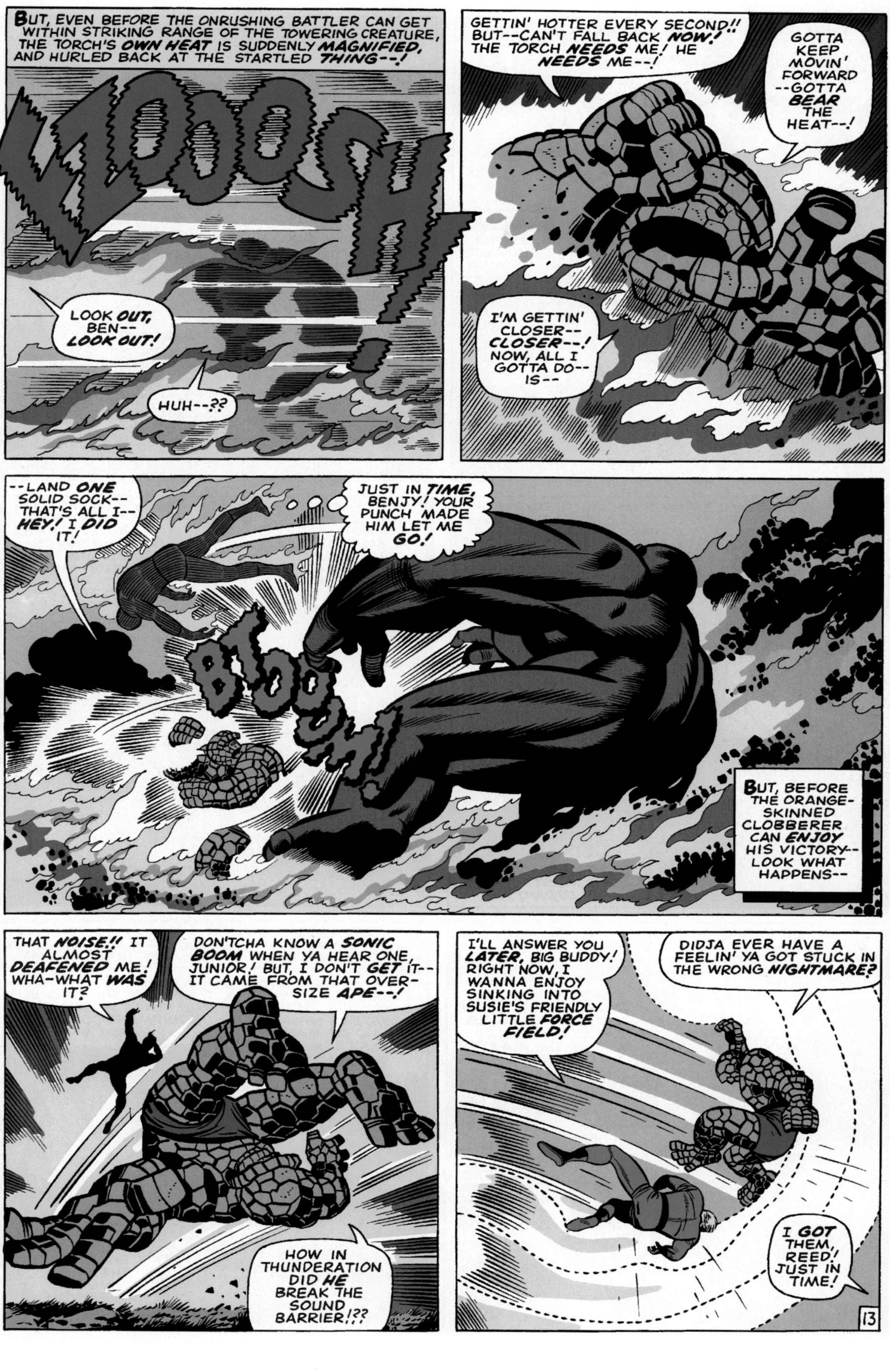
BUT, EVEN BEFORE THE ONRUSHING BATTLER CAN GET WITHIN STRIKING RANGE OF THE TOWERING CREATURE, THE TORCH'S OWN HEAT IS SUDDENLY MAGNIFIED, AND HURLED BACK AT THE STARTLED THING--!
ZZOOOSH!
LOOK OUT, BEN-- LOOK OUT!
HUH--??
GETTIN' HOTTER EVERY SECOND!! BUT--CAN'T FALL BACK NOW! THE TORCH NEEDS ME! HE NEEDS ME--!
GOTTA KEEP MOVIN' FORWARD --GOTTA BEAR THE HEAT--!
I'M GETTIN' CLOSER-- CLOSER--! NOW, ALL I GOTTA DO-- IS--
--LAND ONE SOLID SOCK-- THAT'S ALL I-- HEY! I DID IT!
JUST IN TIME, BENJY! YOUR PUNCH MADE HIM LET ME GO!
BTOOOM!
BUT, BEFORE THE ORANGE-SKINNED CLOBBERER CAN ENJOY HIS VICTORY-- LOOK WHAT HAPPENS--
THAT NOISE!! IT ALMOST DEAFENED ME! WHA-WHAT WAS IT?
DON'TCHA KNOW A SONIC BOOM WHEN YA HEAR ONE, JUNIOR! BUT, I DON'T GET IT-- IT CAME FROM THAT OVER-SIZE APE--!
HOW IN THUNDERATION DID HE BREAK THE SOUND BARRIER!??
I'LL ANSWER YOU LATER, BIG BUDDY! RIGHT NOW, I WANNA ENJOY SINKING INTO SUSIE'S FRIENDLY LITTLE FORCE FIELD!
DIDJA EVER HAVE A FEELIN' YA GOT STUCK IN THE WRONG NIGHTMARE?
I GOT THEM, REED! JUST IN TIME!
13

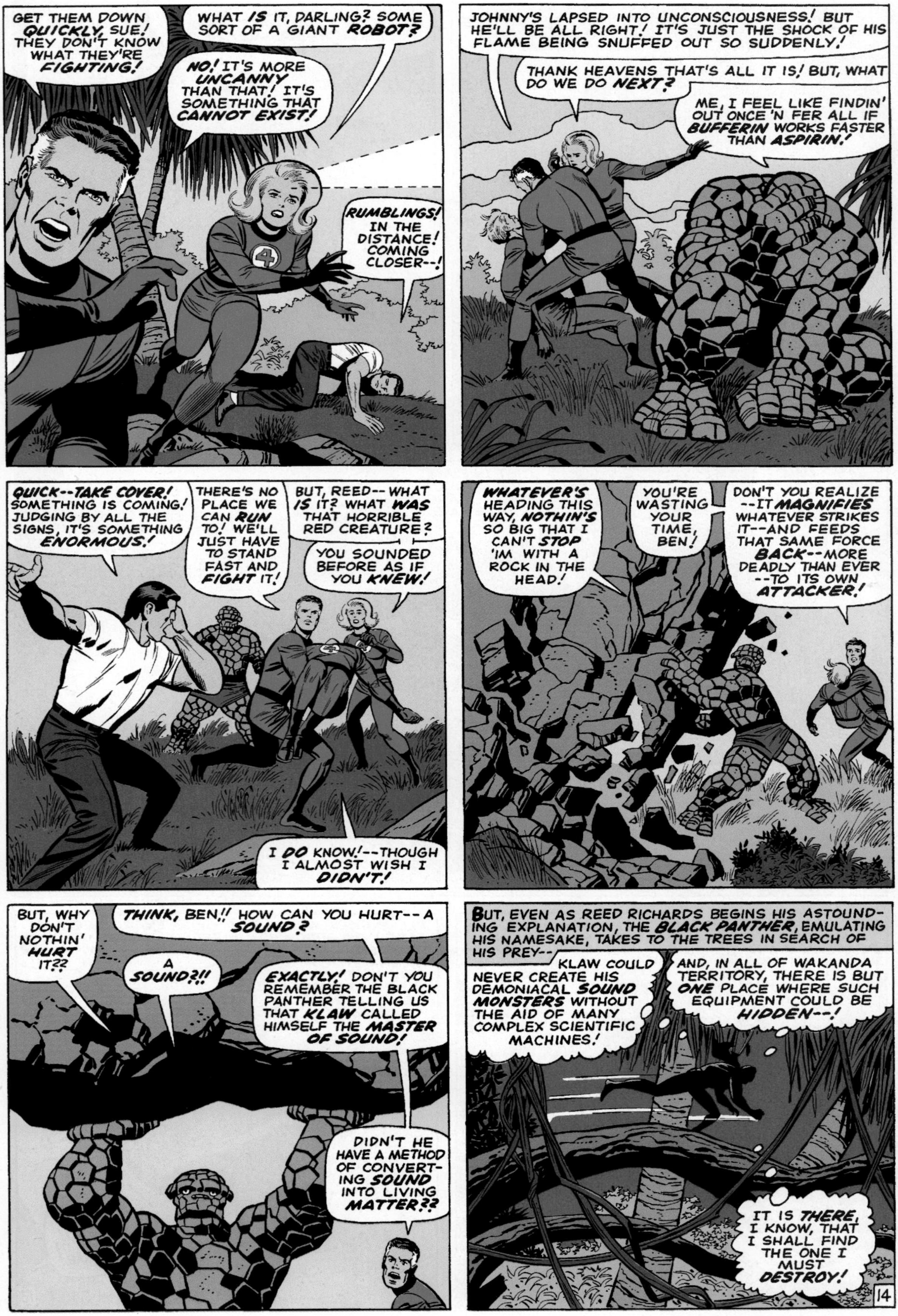

GET THEM DOWN QUICKLY, SUE! THEY DON'T KNOW WHAT THEY'RE FIGHTING!
WHAT IS IT, DARLING? SOME SORT OF A GIANT ROBOT?
NO! IT'S MORE UNCANNY THAN THAT! IT'S SOMETHING THAT CANNOT EXIST!
RUMBLINGS! IN THE DISTANCE! COMING CLOSER--!
JOHNNY'S LAPSED INTO UNCONSCIOUSNESS! BUT HE'LL BE ALL RIGHT! IT'S JUST THE SHOCK OF HIS FLAME BEING SNUFFED OUT SO SUDDENLY!
THANK HEAVENS THAT'S ALL IT IS! BUT, WHAT DO WE DO NEXT?
ME, I FEEL LIKE FINDIN' OUT ONCE 'N FER ALL IF BUFFERIN WORKS FASTER THAN ASPIRIN!
QUICK--TAKE COVER! SOMETHING IS COMING! JUDGING BY ALL THE SIGNS, IT'S SOMETHING ENORMOUS!
THERE'S NO PLACE WE CAN RUN TO! WE'LL JUST HAVE TO STAND FAST AND FIGHT IT!
BUT, REED--WHAT IS IT? WHAT WAS THAT HORRIBLE RED CREATURE?
YOU SOUNDED BEFORE AS IF YOU KNEW!
I DO KNOW!--THOUGH I ALMOST WISH I DIDN'T!
WHATEVER'S HEADING THIS WAY, NOTHIN'S SO BIG THAT I CAN'T STOP 'IM WITH A ROCK IN THE HEAD!
YOU'RE WASTING YOUR TIME, BEN!
DON'T YOU REALIZE --IT MAGNIFIES WHATEVER STRIKES IT--AND FEEDS THAT SAME FORCE BACK--MORE DEADLY THAN EVER --TO ITS OWN ATTACKER!
BUT, WHY DON'T NOTHIN' HURT IT??
THINK, BEN!! HOW CAN YOU HURT-- A SOUND?
A SOUND?!!
EXACTLY! DON'T YOU REMEMBER THE BLACK PANTHER TELLING US THAT KLAW CALLED HIMSELF THE MASTER OF SOUND!
DIDN'T HE HAVE A METHOD OF CONVERTING SOUND INTO LIVING MATTER??
BUT, EVEN AS REED RICHARDS BEGINS HIS ASTOUNDING EXPLANATION, THE BLACK PANTHER, EMULATING HIS NAMESAKE, TAKES TO THE TREES IN SEARCH OF HIS PREY--
KLAW COULD NEVER CREATE HIS DEMONIACAL SOUND MONSTERS WITHOUT THE AID OF MANY COMPLEX SCIENTIFIC MACHINES!
AND, IN ALL OF WAKANDA TERRITORY, THERE IS BUT ONE PLACE WHERE SUCH EQUIPMENT COULD BE HIDDEN--!
IT IS THERE, I KNOW, THAT I SHALL FIND THE ONE I MUST DESTROY!
14

SOFTLY, SILENTLY, THE **BLACK PANTHER** DROPS TO THE GROUND, A FEW MINUTES LATER--LANDING WITH THE GRACE AND EASE OF A TRUE FELINE--!

THIS PORTION OF MY BELOVED JUNGLE--LAID **WASTE** BY THE POWER OF **KLAW,** AND HIS **DEADLY** CREATIONS!

BUT, FROM THIS MOMENT ON --HE WILL DESTROY **NO MORE!**

THIS HIDDEN **CAVE--** THE LARGEST IN WAKANDA--HE COULD SAFELY CONCEAL **ANYTHING** WITHIN ITS DEPTHS!

EVEN IN THE SHADOWS-- EVEN IN THE GLOOM--HE IS UNMISTAKABLE! I HAVE **FOUND** MY QUARRY!

FIRST, I'LL DISPOSE OF THESE TWO UNSUSPECTING **GUARDS!**

AND THEN, THE **REAL** CHALLENGE WILL COME--WHEN I'M FACE-TO-FACE WITH **KLAW,** AT LONG LAST!

I WAS **RIGHT!** IT **IS** HIM!

AND **THAT** MUST BE HIS MASTER CONVERSION SYSTEM FOR CHANGING BASIC **SOUND** INTO **LIVING MATTER!**

AT **LAST** I'M READY TO LAUNCH MY **MAIN** ATTACK!

FOR **YOU,** KLAW, THERE SHALL **BE** NO MORE ATTACKS! FOR **YOU**--THERE IS ONLY **RETRIBUTION!**

THAT **VOICE!** I LAST HEARD ONE LIKE IT **TEN** YEARS AGO-- BUT I CAN NEVER **FORGET** IT!

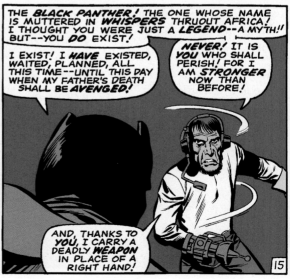

THE **BLACK PANTHER!** THE ONE WHOSE NAME IS MUTTERED IN **WHISPERS** THRUOUT AFRICA! I THOUGHT YOU WERE JUST A **LEGEND**--A MYTH!! BUT--YOU **DO** EXIST!

I EXIST! I **HAVE** EXISTED, WAITED, PLANNED, ALL THIS TIME--UNTIL THIS DAY WHEN MY FATHER'S DEATH SHALL BE **AVENGED!**

**NEVER!** IT IS **YOU** WHO SHALL PERISH! FOR I AM **STRONGER** NOW THAN BEFORE!

AND, THANKS TO **YOU,** I CARRY A DEADLY **WEAPON** IN PLACE OF A RIGHT HAND!

15

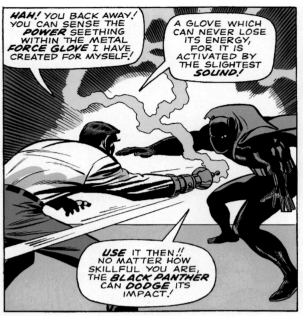

HAH! YOU BACK AWAY! YOU CAN SENSE THE *POWER* SEETHING WITHIN THE METAL *FORCE GLOVE* I HAVE CREATED FOR MYSELF!

A GLOVE WHICH CAN NEVER LOSE ITS ENERGY, FOR IT IS ACTIVATED BY THE SLIGHTEST *SOUND!*

*USE* IT THEN!! NO MATTER HOW SKILLFUL YOU ARE, THE *BLACK PANTHER* CAN *DODGE* ITS IMPACT!

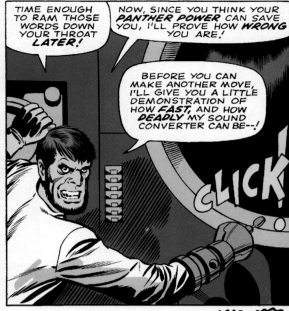

TIME ENOUGH TO RAM THOSE WORDS DOWN YOUR THROAT *LATER!*

NOW, SINCE YOU THINK YOUR *PANTHER POWER* CAN SAVE YOU, I'LL PROVE HOW *WRONG* YOU ARE!

BEFORE YOU CAN MAKE ANOTHER MOVE, I'LL GIVE YOU A LITTLE DEMONSTRATION OF HOW *FAST,* AND HOW *DEADLY* MY SOUND CONVERTER CAN BE--!

CLICK!

ONLY *KLAW* CAN INSTANTANEOUSLY CHANGE THE BASIC ENERGY OF *SOUND*--AND TRANSFORM IT INTO A SIMULATION OF ANY *LIVING CREATURE*--

AND, WHAT CAN BE MORE IRONIC-- MORE *JUST*--THAN HAVING YOU MEET YOUR FATE BENEATH THE TALONS OF *ANOTHER* BLACK PANTHER--A FAR *SUPERIOR* ONE!

*THUS,* DOES THE *MASTER OF SOUND* EXACT HIS FINAL REVENGE!

BUT, JUST IN CASE THE PRECEDING SEQUENCE WAS TOO NERVE-WRACKING IN ITS SHEER, STARK INTENSITY, WE'LL EXERCISE OUR EDITORIAL PEROGATIVE BY BRIEFLY *SWITCHING SCENES* ONCE MORE, AS WE REJOIN THE GIGANTIC RED *ELEPHANT* WHICH IS CHARGING MURDER-OUSLY TOWARDS THE INDOMITABLE *THING*--

YOU DON'T SCARE *ME,* DUMBO! IF YER FEELIN' *HUNGRY*--HERE'S A KING-SIZED *PEANUT* TO CHEW ON!

CRASH!

16

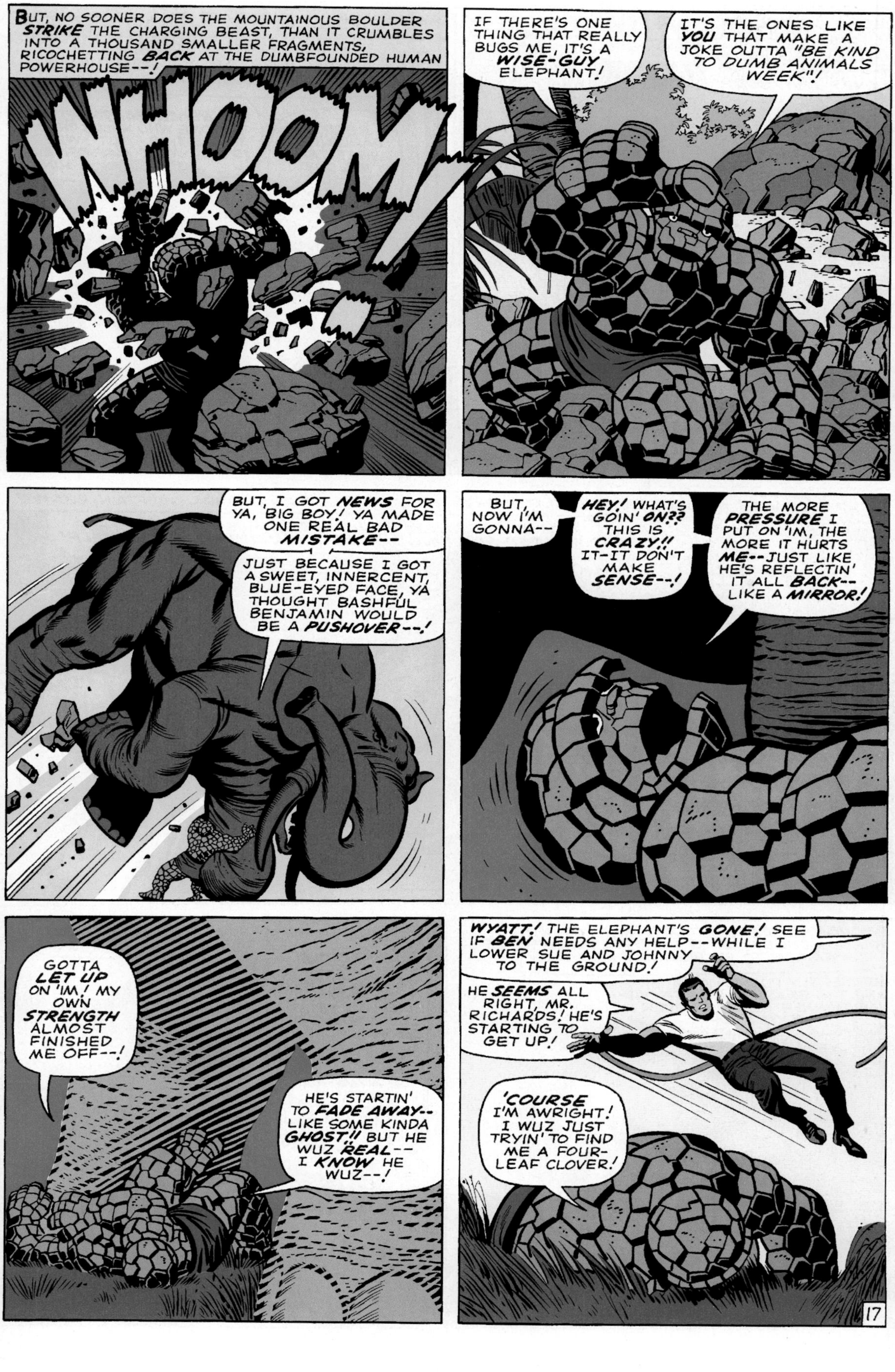
BUT, NO SOONER DOES THE MOUNTAINOUS BOULDER STRIKE THE CHARGING BEAST, THAN IT CRUMBLES INTO A THOUSAND SMALLER FRAGMENTS, RICOCHETTING BACK AT THE DUMBFOUNDED HUMAN POWERHOUSE--!
WHOOM!
IF THERE'S ONE THING THAT REALLY BUGS ME, IT'S A WISE-GUY ELEPHANT!
IT'S THE ONES LIKE YOU THAT MAKE A JOKE OUTTA "BE KIND TO DUMB ANIMALS WEEK"!
BUT, I GOT NEWS FOR YA, BIG BOY! YA MADE ONE REAL BAD MISTAKE--
JUST BECAUSE I GOT A SWEET, INNERCENT, BLUE-EYED FACE, YA THOUGHT BASHFUL BENJAMIN WOULD BE A PUSHOVER--!
BUT, NOW I'M GONNA--
HEY! WHAT'S GOIN' ON?? THIS IS CRAZY!! IT-IT DON'T MAKE SENSE--!
THE MORE PRESSURE I PUT ON 'IM, THE MORE IT HURTS ME--JUST LIKE HE'S REFLECTIN' IT ALL BACK-- LIKE A MIRROR!
GOTTA LET UP ON 'IM! MY OWN STRENGTH ALMOST FINISHED ME OFF--!
HE'S STARTIN' TO FADE AWAY-- LIKE SOME KINDA GHOST!! BUT HE WUZ REAL-- I KNOW HE WUZ--!
WYATT! THE ELEPHANT'S GONE! SEE IF BEN NEEDS ANY HELP--WHILE I LOWER SUE AND JOHNNY TO THE GROUND!
HE SEEMS ALL RIGHT, MR. RICHARDS! HE'S STARTING TO GET UP!
'COURSE I'M AWRIGHT! I WUZ JUST TRYIN' TO FIND ME A FOUR-LEAF CLOVER!
17

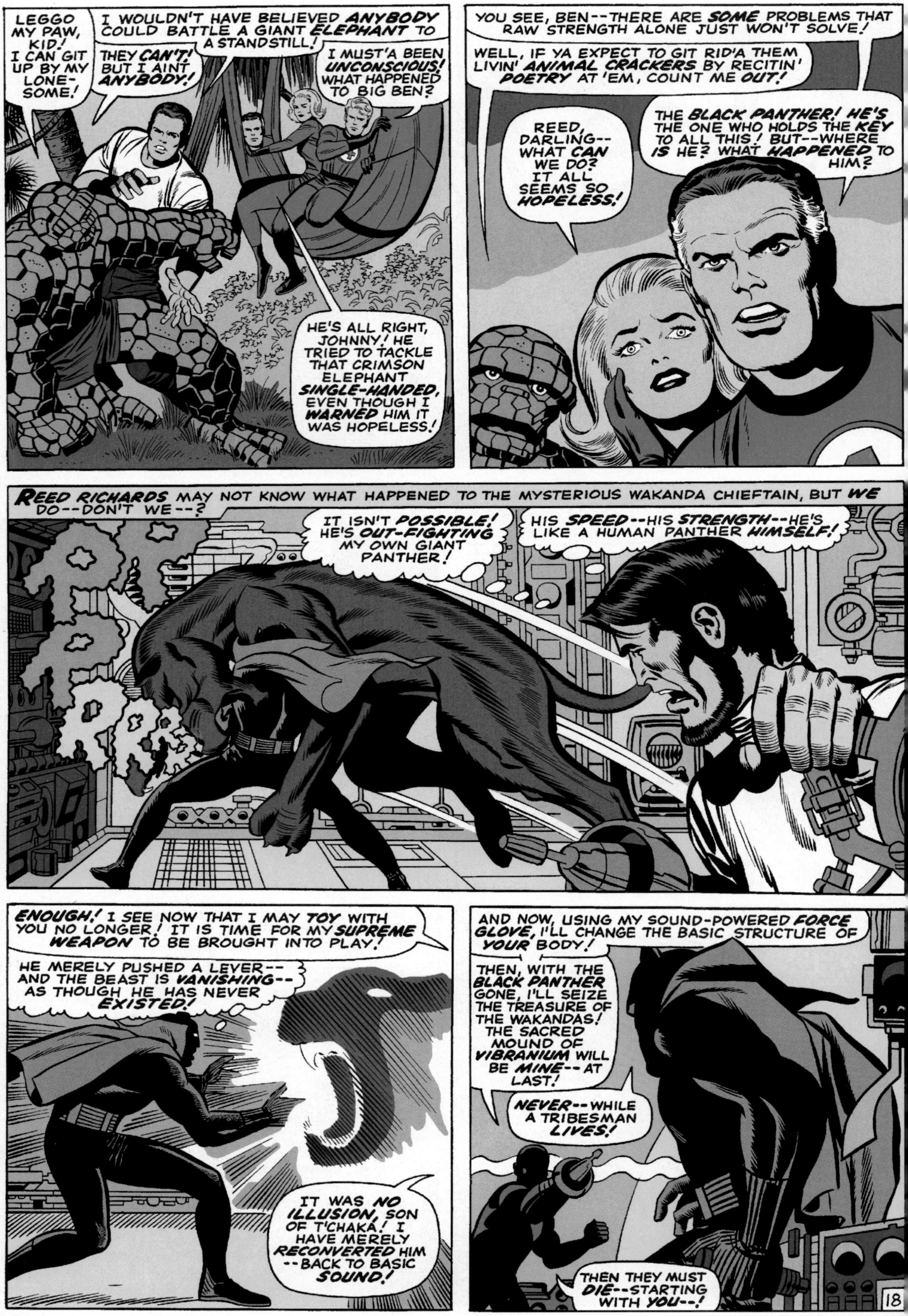

LEGGO MY PAW, KID! I CAN GIT UP BY MY LONESOME!
I WOULDN'T HAVE BELIEVED ANYBODY COULD BATTLE A GIANT ELEPHANT TO A STANDSTILL!
THEY CAN'T! BUT I AINT ANYBODY!
I MUST'A BEEN UNCONSCIOUS! WHAT HAPPENED TO BIG BEN?
HE'S ALL RIGHT, JOHNNY! HE TRIED TO TACKLE THAT CRIMSON ELEPHANT SINGLE-HANDED, EVEN THOUGH I WARNED HIM IT WAS HOPELESS!
YOU SEE, BEN--THERE ARE SOME PROBLEMS THAT RAW STRENGTH ALONE JUST WON'T SOLVE!
WELL, IF YA EXPECT TO GIT RID'A THEM LIVIN' ANIMAL CRACKERS BY RECITIN' POETRY AT 'EM, COUNT ME OUT!
REED, DARLING-- WHAT CAN WE DO? IT ALL SEEMS SO HOPELESS!
THE BLACK PANTHER! HE'S THE ONE WHO HOLDS THE KEY TO ALL THIS! BUT--WHERE IS HE? WHAT HAPPENED TO HIM?
REED RICHARDS MAY NOT KNOW WHAT HAPPENED TO THE MYSTERIOUS WAKANDA CHIEFTAIN, BUT WE DO--DON'T WE--?
IT ISN'T POSSIBLE! HE'S OUT-FIGHTING MY OWN GIANT PANTHER!
HIS SPEED--HIS STRENGTH--HE'S LIKE A HUMAN PANTHER HIMSELF!
RRR
ENOUGH! I SEE NOW THAT I MAY TOY WITH YOU NO LONGER! IT IS TIME FOR MY SUPREME WEAPON TO BE BROUGHT INTO PLAY!
HE MERELY PUSHED A LEVER-- AND THE BEAST IS VANISHING-- AS THOUGH HE HAS NEVER EXISTED!
IT WAS NO ILLUSION, SON OF T'CHAKA! I HAVE MERELY RECONVERTED HIM --BACK TO BASIC SOUND!
AND NOW, USING MY SOUND-POWERED FORCE GLOVE, I'LL CHANGE THE BASIC STRUCTURE OF YOUR BODY!
THEN, WITH THE BLACK PANTHER GONE, I'LL SEIZE THE TREASURE OF THE WAKANDAS! THE SACRED MOUND OF VIBRANIUM WILL BE MINE--AT LAST!
NEVER--WHILE A TRIBESMAN LIVES!
THEN THEY MUST DIE--STARTING WITH YOU--!
18

BUT, BEFORE THE MAD *MASTER OF SOUND* CAN ACTIVATE HIS STRANGE WEAPON, THE *BLACK PANTHER*, MOVING AS SWIFTLY AS HIS NAMESAKE, HURLS THE FATAL *POWER SWITCH* WHICH HIS NIMBLE FINGERS HAD BEEN SILENTLY GROPING FOR--!

MY *CONVERTER!* IT--IT'S BEING *BLOWN APART!!*

IT *HAS* TO END THIS WAY-- IN THE NAME OF *JUSTICE!*

YOU DID *NOT* REALIZE-- I AM A SCIENTIST, TOO--!

THUS, I COULD TELL *WHICH LEVER* TO THROW IN ORDER TO *OVERLOAD* YOUR DELICATE ELECTRONIC CIRCUITS!

AND NOW, ONLY MY PANTHER *SPEED* CAN SAVE ME FROM THE *HOLOCAUST* WHICH IS ABOUT TO *BEFALL*--!

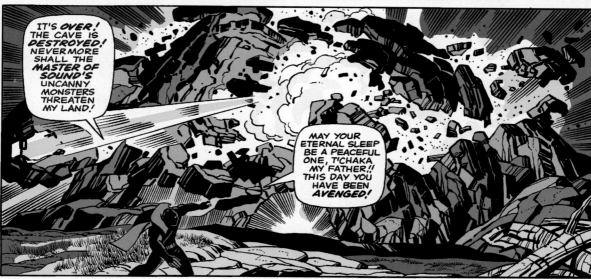

IT'S *OVER!* THE CAVE IS *DESTROYED!* NEVERMORE SHALL THE *MASTER OF SOUND'S* UNCANNY MONSTERS THREATEN MY LAND!

MAY YOUR ETERNAL SLEEP BE A PEACEFUL ONE, T'CHAKA MY FATHER!! THIS DAY YOU HAVE BEEN *AVENGED!*

AT THAT MOMENT, THOUSANDS OF YARDS AWAY, FIVE PAIR OF STARTLED EYES SEE THE ELECTRIFYING UPHEAVAL--

THAT ENTIRE *HILL*--IT'S BEEN *SHATTERED* INTO *NOTHING-NESS!*

WHAT *IS* IT, REED? WHAT DOES IT *MEAN?*

I'M NOT SURE, JOHNNY--BUT I HAVE A FEELING THAT THE *BLACK PANTHER* IS SOMEHOW RESPONSIBLE!

THE SOUND IS *DEAFENING!!* IT'S LIKE THE END OF *THE WORLD!* HOLD ME, MY DARLING--!

HEY! LOOK--OVER *THERE!* A COUPLE MORE OF THEM REFUGEES FROM *GOD-ZILLA!*

BUT--THEY'RE *FADING AWAY!!* THEY MUST SOMEHOW BE *LINKED* TO THE *EXPLOSION!*

WHATEVER IT WAS THAT HAS BEEN *DESTROYED*, MUST HAVE BEEN THE THING THAT *CREATED* THEM!

19

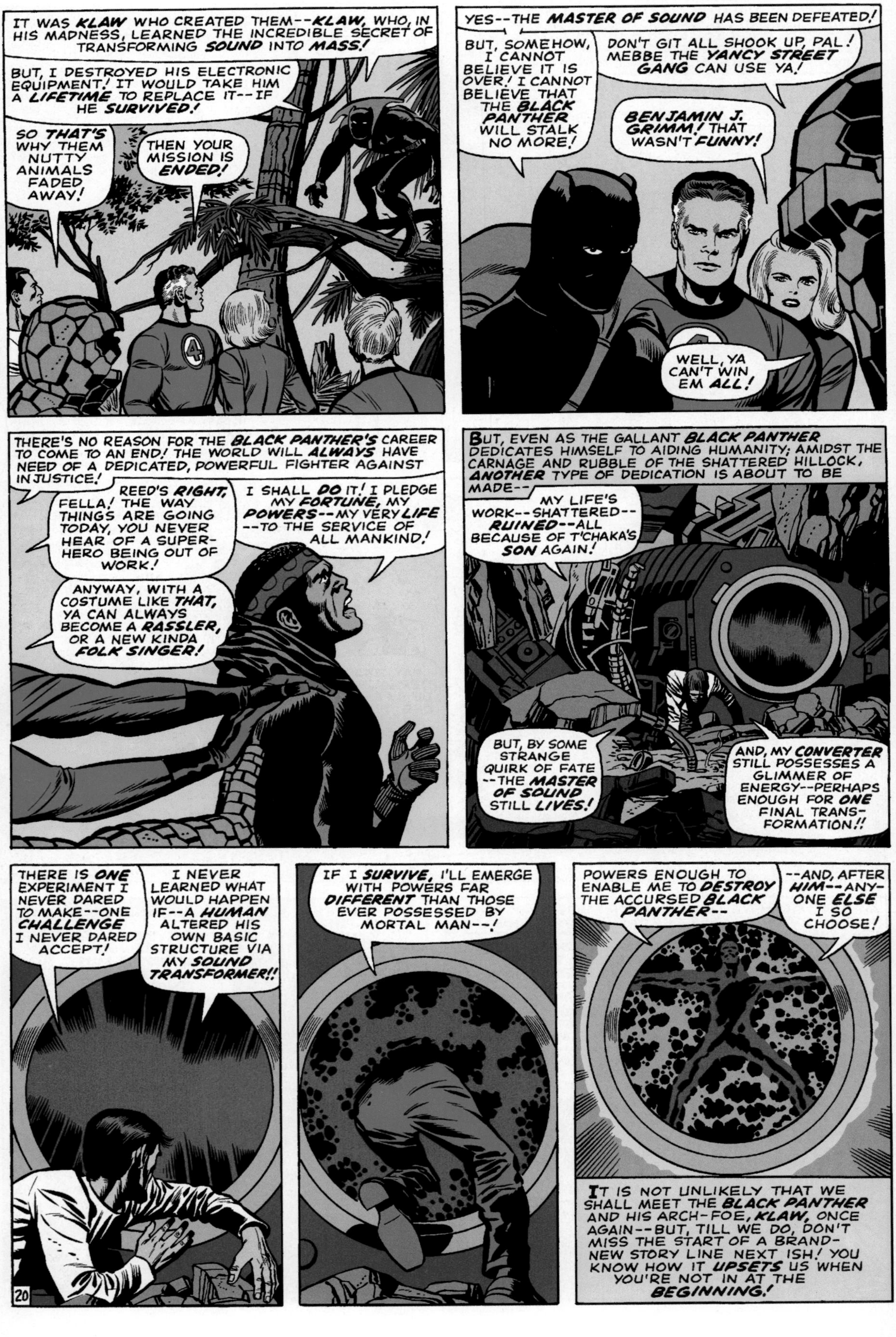
IT WAS KLAW WHO CREATED THEM--KLAW, WHO, IN HIS MADNESS, LEARNED THE INCREDIBLE SECRET OF TRANSFORMING SOUND INTO MASS!
BUT, I DESTROYED HIS ELECTRONIC EQUIPMENT! IT WOULD TAKE HIM A LIFETIME TO REPLACE IT--IF HE SURVIVED!
SO THAT'S WHY THEM NUTTY ANIMALS FADED AWAY!
THEN YOUR MISSION IS ENDED!
YES--THE MASTER OF SOUND HAS BEEN DEFEATED!
BUT, SOMEHOW, I CANNOT BELIEVE IT IS OVER! I CANNOT BELIEVE THAT THE BLACK PANTHER WILL STALK NO MORE!
DON'T GIT ALL SHOOK UP, PAL! MEBBE THE YANCY STREET GANG CAN USE YA!
BENJAMIN J. GRIMM! THAT WASN'T FUNNY!
WELL, YA CAN'T WIN EM ALL!
THERE'S NO REASON FOR THE BLACK PANTHER'S CAREER TO COME TO AN END! THE WORLD WILL ALWAYS HAVE NEED OF A DEDICATED, POWERFUL FIGHTER AGAINST INJUSTICE!
REED'S RIGHT, FELLA! THE WAY THINGS ARE GOING TODAY, YOU NEVER HEAR OF A SUPER-HERO BEING OUT OF WORK!
I SHALL DO IT! I PLEDGE MY FORTUNE, MY POWERS--MY VERY LIFE--TO THE SERVICE OF ALL MANKIND!
ANYWAY, WITH A COSTUME LIKE THAT, YA CAN ALWAYS BECOME A RASSLER, OR A NEW KINDA FOLK SINGER!
BUT, EVEN AS THE GALLANT BLACK PANTHER DEDICATES HIMSELF TO AIDING HUMANITY; AMIDST THE CARNAGE AND RUBBLE OF THE SHATTERED HILLOCK, ANOTHER TYPE OF DEDICATION IS ABOUT TO BE MADE--
MY LIFE'S WORK--SHATTERED--RUINED--ALL BECAUSE OF T'CHAKA'S SON AGAIN!
BUT, BY SOME STRANGE QUIRK OF FATE--THE MASTER OF SOUND STILL LIVES!
AND, MY CONVERTER STILL POSSESSES A GLIMMER OF ENERGY--PERHAPS ENOUGH FOR ONE FINAL TRANSFORMATION!!
THERE IS ONE EXPERIMENT I NEVER DARED TO MAKE--ONE CHALLENGE I NEVER DARED ACCEPT!
I NEVER LEARNED WHAT WOULD HAPPEN IF--A HUMAN ALTERED HIS OWN BASIC STRUCTURE VIA MY SOUND TRANSFORMER!!
IF I SURVIVE, I'LL EMERGE WITH POWERS FAR DIFFERENT THAN THOSE EVER POSSESSED BY MORTAL MAN--!
POWERS ENOUGH TO ENABLE ME TO DESTROY THE ACCURSED BLACK PANTHER--
--AND, AFTER HIM--ANYONE ELSE I SO CHOOSE!
IT IS NOT UNLIKELY THAT WE SHALL MEET THE BLACK PANTHER AND HIS ARCH-FOE, KLAW, ONCE AGAIN--BUT, TILL WE DO, DON'T MISS THE START OF A BRAND-NEW STORY LINE NEXT ISH! YOU KNOW HOW IT UPSETS US WHEN YOU'RE NOT IN AT THE BEGINNING!
20

WHO'S THE WISE-GUY THAT'S HOLDIN' OUT?

**THE M.M.M.S. *STILL* WANTS YOU!**

Make out check or money order for $1.00 to:  **M.M.M.S. MARVEL COMICS GROUP**
625 MADISON AVE., NEW YORK, N.Y. 10022

Hi Gang! Let's face it, I'm a Marvel Mad-man too! Here's my hard earned buck! Rush all your nutty gizmos to . . .

NAME_____

ADDRESS_____

CITY_____STATE_____

ZIP_____AGE_____

School, College or Occupation:

# Fantastic Four ④ Fan Page

Send letters to LEE and KIRBY
THE MARVEL COMICS GROUP
SECOND FLOOR 625 MADISON AV.
NEW YORK 10022 N.Y.

Dear Stan and Jack,

I've just finished F.F. #49 and I must say, it was great!!! But one thing bothers me; if Galactus is really the star conqueror he claims to be, why does he have a big "G" on his chest plate? Is the English alphabet universal?

Dan Madaj, 21046 Cyman
Warren, Michigan

**It is in Marveldom, Daniel! Anyway, with a name like Galactus, think how silly he'd have looked with a big "*W*" on his chest!**

Dear Stan and Jack,

I must take back all I ever said about continuous stories. At first, I was afraid of your becoming too sparse on plot and art, but this has been proven completely false. Then I thought, "What if new readers pick up a copy of F.F. and stop reading it because they have been tossed right into the middle of the plot?" Well, after F.F. #49, I feel if they can't figure it out, it's because F.F. is too good for them. By the way, a very interesting part of your magazine is the letters page. To comment on letters, I myself have felt that Stan's great potential shouldn't be left in the comic book field, even if one of his great creations is "the World's Greatest." When is he going to start writing full-length science fiction novels? If Stan looked back over some of the weird things he has created in a few months, he might even scare himself. Remember: there's only one Stan Lee, but Irving Forbush can always carry on!! If Stan G. stops coloring the F.F., may the Punisher change the "World's Greatest" in your title to "New York's Greatest!" Now to the notice of greatest importance. The Fantastic Four have always fought greater and more evil villains in every issue. Now that you have almost reached the top in greatness, it will be easy to decline. If this climb in the F.F. is to go forward, you will have to face many dangers in the road of imagination. And till my stationery kit arrives I bid farewell and Fantastic Success.

Charles Hutler, 9 Sheridan Ave.
Kearny, New York

**Never farewell, Charlie — merely "see ya around"! Anyway, why should Stan bother writing full-length sci-fix tomes when it's so much more fun paving the road to Marvel madness with our novel-length, full-color spectaculars? We're not gonna be satisfied until the book writers are clamoring to write comic mags — and that day may not be as far off as you think, C. B. — just wait'n see!**

Dear Stan and Jack,

Because I am so kind, modest, supreme, and great, I have decided to save you from Mike Glicksohn's letter in F.F. #49. He says, among other things, that Black Bolt is impossible on three grounds. If any one of his three statements could be disproven, it would mean that Black Bolt is possible . One of those statements is that Black Bolt cannot absorb electrons as a source of power because the absorbed electron could only give him about one-half the power that it took him to absorb it. This is quite correct, except for something that no one thought of. Suppose Black Bolt has another source of power with which to absorb the electrons. Since he only gets back one-half of the

power that he puts in, his power is reduced by half. However, he is willing to make this sacrifice in order to exchange his other power source for a form of energy which he can use. If it seems impossible to use electricity to power a human being(?), we must all be dead! It just so happens that Brooklyn College sent a lecturer to my school. He said that if "eight candy bars could be oxidized at once, they would yield 1,018,000 amps." In other words, we run on electricity! So, if you are ever told that Black Bolt is incredible, you may answer, "Nay, he is supremely credible!" (With apologies to Silver Surfer!) Off with this science jazz. I wanna tell you that your mags are great, fab, gear, and good even. If they weren't I would never have searched, begged, and suffered to get whole collections of all your superhero mags, plus Sgt. Fury. The script of Stan Lee, the cover and art of Kirby and Sinnott, and even the lettering of Sammy Rosen made F.F. #49 a hit! So, as I eagerly await F.F. #50, I say hail Irving Forbush, hail Hydra, and make mine Marvel!

John Bonhomme, 429 Dumont Ave.
Brooklyn, N.Y. 11212

**It's kinda hard to answer a letter when your eyes are filled with tears of gratitude, Johnny! To think that one faithful fan — one dauntless Marvelite, would go to such trouble — take such great pains — to prove that Black Bolt is more than a figment of our bullpen's imagination! The senses reel at such loyalty — such devotion to the cause of super-heroics — But, suffice it to say that King Kirby himself has nominated you to be the recipient of our oak-leaf cluster no-prize — and surely no greater homage can be paid a mere mortal — if such indeed you be! Or, in the immortal words of Honest Irving Forbush — "Wha'd he say? Wha'd?"**

Dear Stan and Jack,

I'm never going to send any child of *mine* to Metro or Empire State Universities, because said institutions obviously accept only those students whose mental capacity does not exceed that of a cretin. Practical jokes, Stan? Petty feuds , infantile jealousies , and those heart-rending misunderstandings—in college, Leader? In a track 5 High School sophomore class, just maybe—but a college? Please, O shining gem of American storytellers, do not further malign Higher Learning! On bended knee, we implore you: have Jack erase the May panels in which the professors are giving each other hotfoots, and the Regents are wearing chicken-inspector badges.

Dennis O'Neil, 162 E. 2nd St.
New York, N. Y.

**Okay, Denny — they're erased, expunged, and irrevocably eradicated! By the way, aren't you the same Denny O'Neil who's now one of Stan's bright young assistants? Did Rollickin' Roy Thomas put you up to that letter? *Boy!* If we don't keep our eyes on you two cut-ups every second — cheee!**

Dear Stan and Jack,

What do the illustrator, the inker, and the colorer do? I thought I knew about the first two, but your answer to Kevin Morgan's letter in FF #49 threw me off. By the way,

I want to congratulate you on your art. That sequence where the Watcher sends Torch to Galactus' home galaxy is great, especially the third frame on page 15, where Torch appears in negative. Keep it up (as if you were going to stop!). Mark Mandel, St. John's College Annapolis, Md. 21444

**Believe it or not, Mark, ol' Stan is answering your letter in a sunny hotel room in Palm Beach, Florida, where he's taking his first vacation in years! (Some vacation! Fabulous Flo and Jolly Solly send him all the mail and assorted mishmash every day!) So, unfortunately, he doesn't have the copy of F.F. #49 which you alluded to — but anyway, it may come as no shock to you to learn that the colorer — now hold onto your hat — the colorer is the pussycat who *colors* the pages! — And we wish *all* our frantic fans' queries were as easy to answer as yours was, tiger!**

Dear Stan and Jack,
Woweee!! That was a pretty good write-up the N. Y. Herald-Tribune gave you in the January 9th Sunday edition. Also, I just finished reading FANTASTIC FOUR #49 . . . It was great, stupendous, superior, startlingly stunning, and as usual, it was good. There's one thing I wanna ask you, Stan . . . Do you *really* fill in the dialogue *after* the picture layout comes in? Hoo boy! But, as always, there must be a method to merry Marvel's madness. F.F. #49 was a cliffhanger, but how are you gonna conclude the whole thing in only one more ish (I hope)? The Silver Surfer is one of the most original characters I've seen. I heard that you have recalled quite a few characters from the bygone era, such as the Human Torch (who was supposed to be a synthetic man and was supposed to have a sidekick named Toro), the Sub-Mariner, who was originally drawn by Bill Everett, Captain America, and a couple of characters invented in 1943 or thereabouts. I read a fan's letter in ish #49 . . . MODEL KITS!!!! Why, that'll be the greatest thing since Stan learned how to type! If you answer this letter seriously, without one smart remark, *I* will send *you* a brand-new, stainless steel tax-deductible chrome-plated one-piece no-prize, super De Luxe model type. (Psst, Stan! It's a no-file for hacking through the bracelets that handcuff you to the typewriter!) Guy Michel, 548 Riverside Drive New York, N. Y.

**Stan's not merely handcuffed to the typewriter, Guy! By now, he *is* the typewriter! Anyway, if you want serious answers (whatever *they* are), here goes — Yep, the dialogue is written after the pix are drawn! It makes it more confusing that way, and wreaks havoc on the artists' nerves — because they never know what their cavortin' characters will end up saying! Sure, we've revived characters from Marvel's golden age — and sure we're gonna soon flood the market with Aurora Model Kits of our hysterical heroes — just be sure you buy your share, fella — 'cause we'll be watchin' you! Remember, the eyes of Marvel are ever upon thee! (See? *Who says* this isn't the Marvel Age of Serious Letter Answers!)**

Dear Stan and Jack,
I am pleased to announce that, with your forthcoming May ishes of F.F. and SPIDEY, I have been reading and collecting these fine mags for one year. Therefore, I shall state all of the MARVELous changes in both mags (of occurrence in both periodicals) that truly set your brand of literature apart from all others: (1) The artwork itself is fantastic! Your soul-shattering titles such as "If This Be Doomsday!" and "The Final Chapter", to name a few. And, if that's not enough, you give us covers to match the titles. But inside the book, you supply us with full-page masterpieces and combination photo-drawings. Just one request, though—puh-lease try to publish more of your fab pin-ups. I'm sure many of your followers, myself included, missed them!! (2) The written content (yer stories!) is more than might be expected of mere mortals, or even people like you! Just about the greatest thing ever to happen to Marveldom is your continued classics!! Why do I call them the greatest? Mainly because, if *you* guys have a continued story, *us* guys receive more of Stan's great plots, more of King Kirby's fantastic artwork, more of some one's BRAAKKS!, WOKS!, and FOOFFS! But, most of all, we receive more nerve-shattering, senses-swimming, eye-catching, mind-wracking suspense! (3) The M.M.M.S.,

of course, speaks for its beautiful self; so I needn't bend your ear about it. So, as you can plainly see . . . it's been a very good year!!!! Paul Kalenak, 3543 Vineland Ave. Astabula 4, Ohio

**And it's been a dandy few minutes for us as we read your liltin' letter, Paul — many thanks.**

Dear Stan and Jack,
What have you done to the Watcher? In FANTASTIC FOUR #48 and 49, if I were to judge by your illustration, he'd better cease watching and start doing and dieting. He is positively pudgy. Actually, my son and I are Marvel maniacs from 'way back. He agrees with Johnny that Crystal is extra special. (I thought she resembled Jean of the X-Men.) And Sub-Mariner is an old favorite of mine from the 40's. Don't know how you dream up the plots, but I enjoy all your stories very much!! Incidentally, please add my name to the skillions who are waiting for Reed to find a way for Ben to switch to the Thing when necessary and back to Ben when danger is over. Although, the way your stories have been going, he still wouldn't be Ben too often. As you no doubt have guessed, I enjoy your endeavors very much! Mrs. Sarah Doll, 539 Silver St. Manchester, N.H.

**And, as you no doubt have guessed, we enjoy the priceless privilege of having fabulous fans like you, Mrs. D.! But, enough small talk. Since you mentioned it, we've got to get busy and put the Watcher on a diet — that is, as soon as we learn to pronounce the names of the extraterrestrial foods he eats!**

Dear Stan and Jack,
F.F. #49 was a great story and the villains were even greater, but don't let Alicia fall for the Silver Surfer. By the way, where did the Surfer learn to surf à la Waikiki Beach? I'd like to see the Thing, Hulk, Sub-Mariner and Spider-Man team up to fight some aliens or some super powered villain. Oh yeah, how come sometimes, the Watcher is about four feet tall, and the other times he's a giant? Is it because he can change his size or are you guys making boo-boos again? Bill Duff, 507 East Main St. Bellevue, Ohio 44811

**Thanks for giving us an out, Billy! Now all we have to say is — sure, he can change his size! (Unless we wanna tell the truth! Then, we've gotta own up to the fact that none of us can ever remember how big that sheet-wearin' swinger is supposed to be!)**

Dear Stan and Jack,
Wah-hoo!! Only seconds ago I was speaking to the editor of *Existential Psychiatry* Magazine and director of the American Ontoanalytic Association; and he said that, if it were possible, he would like to publish the line from F.F. ANNUAL #3 ("The Impossible Man") which reads, "Name? We Poppupians have no names—we know who we are!" Imagine! Marvel quoted in a highly-respected national psychiatry magazine! 25,000 copies distributed nationwide to the elite upper crust of America!! $#"%'&#°! Pardon me, I'm getting so excited that I'm beginning to become incoherent! I told him that he just had to let me write you, so here it is. My one worry is: Do you think his mag is classy enough to have a quote from Marvel? Scott Palmer, *Journal of the American Ontoanalytic Association* 300 No. State St., Suite 5908 Chicago, Ill. 60610

**As far as we're concerned, Scotty boy, *no mag is! But, if we haveta be quoted by somebody, it might as well be an Existential Psychiatry pub — whatever that means! (Actually, although we're trying to sound blasé, we're really kinda thrilled! We just hope that what they wanna do is quote us — and not analyze us!)**

NEXT ISH: By popular demand! (This guy we know, named Sam Popular, demanded it!) The Human Torch heads for the land of the Inhumans, to free the girl named Crystal! But, on the way, he encounters — aww no! It's too good to tell now! But, we can tell you that the F.F. sort-of go it alone for a while, in one of the most pulse-pounding, provocative, pace-setting thrillers of the season! So, if you can spare the time, why not join them? It might just turn out to be one of the most exciting experiences of your life!

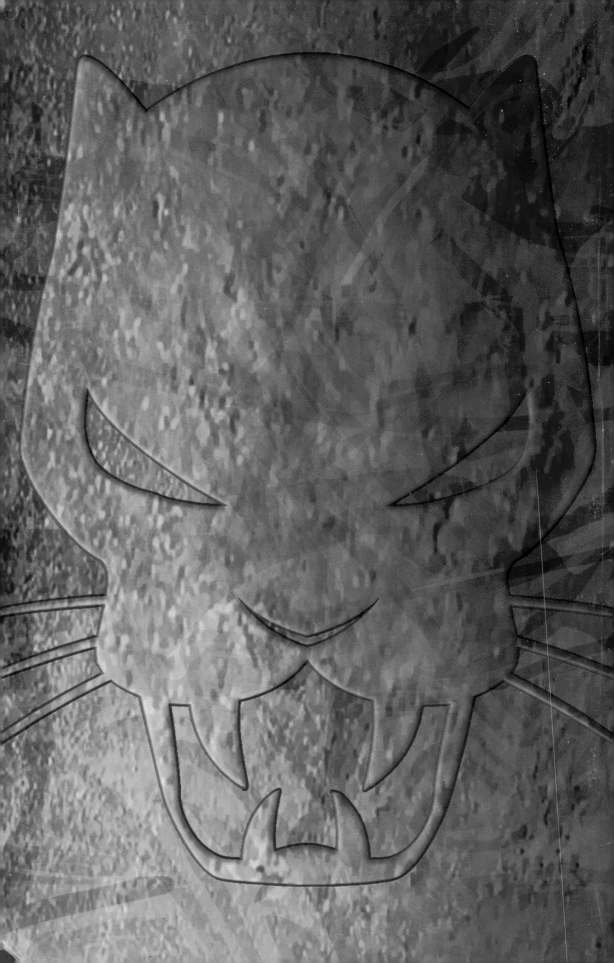